Metternich and Austria

Metternich and Austria

An Evaluation

Alan Sked

First published 2008 by
PALGRAVE MACMILLAN
Houndmills, Basingstoke, Hampshire RG21 6XS and
175 Fifth Avenue, New York, N.Y. 10010
Companies and representatives throughout the world

PALGRAVE MACMILLAN is the global academic imprint of the Palgrave Macmillan division of St. Martin's Press, LLC and of Palgrave Macmillan Ltd. Macmillan® is a registered trademark in the United States, United Kingdom and other countries. Palgrave is a registered trademark in the European Union and other countries.

ISBN-13: 978–1–4039–9114–0 hardback
ISBN-10: 1–4039–9114–6   hardback
ISBN-13: 978–1–4039–9115–7 paperback
ISBN-10: 1–4039–9115–4   paperback

This book is printed on paper suitable for recycling and made from fully managed and sustained forest sources. Logging, pulping and manufacturing processes are expected to conform to the environmental regulations of the country of origin.

A catalogue record for this book is available from the British Library.

A catalog record for this book is available from the Library of Congress.

10	9	8	7	6	5	4	3	2	1
17	16	15	14	13	12	11	10	09	08

Printed and bound in China

For Mum and Laddie
with all my love

Contents

List of Maps

List of Illustrations

Preface

Metternich is undoubtedly one of the key figures in modern European history. It is extremely surprising, therefore, that there has never been any full account in English of the role he played in Habsburg and international affairs between 1809 and 1848. This book now seeks to fill that gap. It is not a biography and still less is it an account of his famous love life. It does not seek to place him on a pedestal or turn his many epigrams into a political philosophy. It recognises the limits to his room for action both as the servant of an absolute dynasty and as foreign minister and state chancellor of by no means the most powerful of the great European states. However, it does aim to put his considerable achievements into perspective and to destroy several of the myths associated with 'the age of Metternich'. It builds on the views I have already developed in the second edition of my *Decline and Fall of the Habsburg Empire, 1815–1918* (2001) and rejects the new view of international relations in the Metternich era put forward by the American scholar Paul Schroeder. All in all, it seeks to provide the reader with a comprehensive understanding of Metternich's role in history – the key part he played in the downfall of Napoleon, how he shaped the European state system between 1815 and 1848, and the role he played in the domestic affairs of the Habsburg Monarchy between the overthrow of Napoleon and the revolutions of 1848. It will not be the last word on the subject – certainly not my last word – but I will be immensely happy if it serves to reawaken interest in a period of history which is now unfashionable and neglected. New monographs are badly needed, not merely on Metternich's diplomacy after the downfall of the Congress System but on most of his colleagues as well as on the fiscal system of the Monarchy between 1815 and 1848. In spite of that I think it imperative to give readers an up-to-date account of what should be known about Metternich already.

One final point. My editor at Palgrave Macmillan, Kate Haines, has been extremely gracious in all her dealings with me but even her generosity with regard to word limits has failed to make it possible to cover every aspect of Metternich's activities. Hence I have stopped at 1848. I hope to be able to cover Metternich's career after that date either in a later edition of this work or in another book or article.

LSE   **Alan Sked**

x

Map 1 The Habsburg Monarchy in the age of Metternich

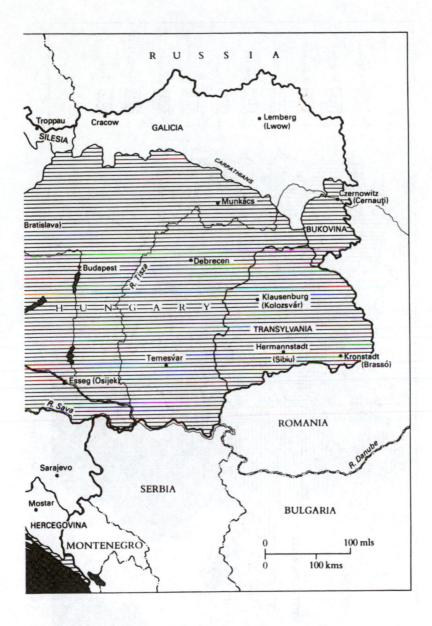

R U S S I A

Troppau   Cracow   • Lemberg
                            (Lwow)
SILESIA   GALICIA

CARPATHIANS

Munkács
Czernowitz
(Cernauţi)

Bratislava)   BUKOVINA

Budapest   R. Tisza   • Debrecen

H   U   N   G   A   R   Y   • Klausenburg
                               (Kolozsvár)

                          TRANSYLVANIA

                          Hermannstadt
Temesvár   (Sibiu)   • Kronstadt
                                        (Brassó)
• Esseg (Osijek)

R. Sava

                          ROMANIA

                                    R. Danube

Sarajevo

                  SERBIA

Mostar   BULGARIA

HERCEGOVINA

MONTENEGRO

0   100 mls

0   100 kms

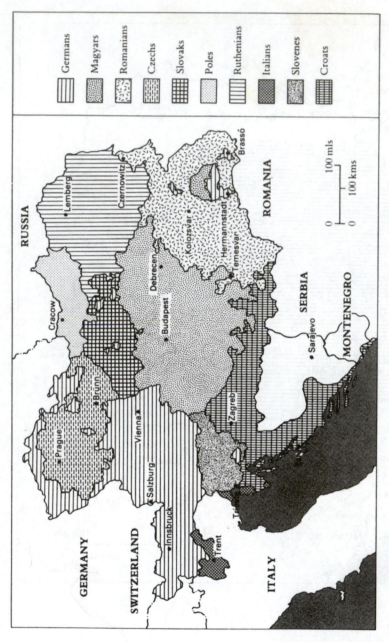

Map 2 The Nationalities in the Monarchy

Figure 1 Francis I, Emperor of Austria

1
Introduction: Has Metternich been Misunderstood?

Metternich and the Habsburg Monarchy

Prince Metternich was the greatest diplomat of his age, conducting the foreign policy of Austria from 1809 to 1848. He was also a, perhaps *the*, leading influence in her domestic affairs between 1815 and 1848. For almost the whole of this period the Habsburg Monarchy was a peaceful and prosperous place, while many other states in Europe were troubled by revolutions, radical republican and reform movements, secret societies, riots and changes of dynasty. Nothing like this happened in Austria. In Galicia in 1846, when exiled Poles attempted to spark off a revolution among the local Polish peasants, the latter slaughtered them spontaneously in the name of their Austrian overlord.[1] Even Lombardy-Venetia, by 1848 the most troublesome part of the Empire, was by common consent the best run part of Italy;[2] indeed, after revolts in Piedmont and the Papal States, Metternich would come under pressure from the local populations there to annex parts of these territories.[3] Finally, after Metternich's fall from power in 1848, which did spark off revolutions within the Monarchy, there was no republican or revolutionary takeover. The Habsburg dynasty remained popular, and the Emperor was cheered by the so-called 'revolutionary' crowds; Metternich's old colleagues – Kolowrat, Ficquelmont, Wessenberg and others – some of them colleagues since the Napoleonic Wars – simply took over the reins of government. True, matters got out of hand when the Hungarians broke their promises with respect to foreign, defence and financial affairs,[4] and when the Lombards and Venetians attempted to exchange rule by the House of Habsburg for rule by the House of Savoy; true, too, Austria had a parliament for a short while, but by the end of 1849 the revolutions were over, parliament ceased to exist and soon afterwards Metternich returned to Vienna to be a force behind the scenes until his death in 1859.

Whether his diplomacy can serve as a useful example today will be examined later on, although this book will not really concentrate on his diplomacy. If most books on his life and career[5] dwell almost exclusively and rather unoriginally on his foreign policy and love life, this one will examine most of the other questions that are usually raised about Metternich although seldom satisfactorily answered – did he run a police state, did he want to federalise the monarchy, was he an implacable opponent of nationalism, did his policies ruin the peoples of the Monarchy and drive them to revolution? Its main perspective will be an unusual one, examining why the Monarchy was at peace for so long, why there were so few domestic disturbances, why there was no republicanism in the Monarchy and very little real liberalism either, whether Metternich was in fact a reactionary. After all, he did not seek to restore the Holy Roman Empire, was happy to give Prussia leeway in North Germany, recommended legal and administrative reforms to the truly reactionary and absolutist sovereigns of Italy, respected the rule of law, refused to bow to the papacy and welcomed economic and industrial growth, while his monarchical masters presided over both quite an extensive state welfare system and a rather progressive legal one.

Still Metternich was no democrat or liberal and made no pretence to be one. So historians, most of whom, quite rightly, are democrats and liberals, have condemned him. They more or less agree with the critic who wrote in 1830:

Never was a man more feared or detested than Metternich. From Belgium to the Pyrenees, from the frontiers of Turkey to the borders of Holland, there is only one opinion of this minister and it is one of execration. For it is he who has principally contributed to giving Europe its present political form, who has been the inventor and main spring of the Holy Alliance, that embryo of great events . . . Liberty has never had as dangerous an enemy as Metternich.[6]

In fact, all sorts of historians have condemned him – from Viktor Bibl, the German nationalist who denounced him as 'the demon of Austria',[7] directly responsible for the downfall of the Monarchy, to the conservative Henry Kissinger, whose admiration for Metternich's diplomacy between 1809 and 1822 nevertheless did not prevent him from also asserting that Metternich's domestic principles left the Monarchy in the last resort a lost cause.[8] Yet this is fantasy. The Monarchy was able to reinvent itself many times in the nineteenth century and to reform itself. In 1914, just as during the 'age of Metternich', almost no one was calling for its demise. It disappeared as a direct result of its defeat in the First World War, which certainly cannot be blamed on Metternich. Was its demise somehow inevitable, stemming from long-term domestic problems? Certainly not. It clearly had problems, but if a man with even severe medical problems is run over by a bus, it seems safe to blame the bus for his death. Likewise, we should blame the end of the Monarchy on the First World War.

Let us return to Metternich. If Metternich can contribute little to the understanding of contemporary political thought or practice – diplomacy is quite a different matter – contemporary affairs should enable us to understand him much better. For Metternich's career was dedicated to waging a war on terror and he did this without resorting to torture, or undermining the rule of law, although he negotiated what would today be seen as international anti-terrorist conventions, employed a mild, if efficient, censorship and used a secret intelligence service (or police). This is what gave him his sinister reputation. Yet by the standards of today, it was all very small-scale, despite the fact that during his lifetime many more people were killed, more atrocities took place and the threat to established governments was much greater than today.

The Terrorist Threat

The terrorist threat came after the outbreak of the French Revolution. At first practically no one in Europe was troubled by events in France – enlightened despots after all had been introducing reforms all over the Continent. The Austrian Emperors, Joseph II and Leopold II, moreover, had a low opinion of the French royal family (including Marie Antoinette) and Leopold even declared: 'I have a sister, the queen of France, but the Holy Roman Empire has no sister, Austria has no sister. I can only act as the welfare of people's demands, not out of family interests.'[9] The Younger Pitt, for example, in his budget speech of 1792 said famously: 'There never was a time in the history of this country when from the situation of Europe we might not reasonably expect fifteen years of peace than at the present moment.'[10] But with the execution of the King and Queen of France, the declarations of war against so many European neighbours, the installation of the terror against domestic enemies on a huge scale, such complacency disappeared. Chateaubriand was to write: 'The Revolution would have carried me away had it not started in crime. I saw the first head carried on the end of a pike, and I drew back.'[11] By 1793, Pitt was complaining of the

French: 'They will not accept, under the name of Liberty, any model of government, but that which is conformable to their own opinions and ideas; and all men must learn from the mouth of their cannon the propagation of their system in every part of the world.'[12] When Fox accused him of making war on opinion, Pitt replied: 'It is not so. We are not in arms against the opinions of the closet, nor the speculation of the school. We are at war with *armed* opinion.'[13] That was always to be Metternich's defence.

Metternich and others saw that something new had happened in France. The Revolution – and the causes of this transformation can be debated[14] – had turned into 'something which went far beyond the normal aggressions of international politics'.[15] The revolutionaries condemned their opponents as the enemies of mankind. They themselves now spoke on behalf of the 'people' and a doctrine of popular sovereignty, soon transformed into one of national sovereignty, became the basis for what has been called 'totalitarian democracy'.[16] The nation – in fact, the French – could now justify the physical elimination of all their enemies, domestic and foreign. As the abbé Sieyes wrote in his famous tract of 1789, *Qu'est-ce que c'est le tiers état?*: 'The Nation exists before all things. It is sufficient that its will is manifested for all positive law to vanish before it. In whatever manner a nation wills, it is sufficient that it does will: all forms are good, and its will is always the supreme law.'[17] It had to obeyed. In the words of St Just: 'You no longer have any reason for restraint against the enemies of the new order . . . You must punish not only traitors but the apathetic as well; you must punish whoever is passive in the Republic . . . We must rule by iron those who cannot be ruled by justice.'[18] Such a view was made real on 10 June 1794 with the law of 22 Prairial. Accused persons now lost the right to a defence lawyer and could be convicted on moral rather than material proof. Jurors could use their consciences to decide on verdicts if evidence was lacking. Political crimes now included criticising patriots or attempts to 'deprave morality'; not just plots against the security of the republic but even attempts to 'dilute the energy and purity of revolutionary principles' were now crimes. In short, mere criticism, or even suspicion of criticism or lack of positive support for the regime, could bring a guilty verdict. And the only punishment was death.[19] In Austria, meanwhile, Francis II insisted that the Austrian Jacobins who were arrested in 1794 were all given a fair trial in accordance with established Austrian jurisprudence.[20]

Another Jacobin was kind enough to explain the implications of the new, revolutionary French doctrine for foreigners:

The citizens of a nation which is ruled by a tyrant [a Metternich or Pitt for example], a disturber of the public peace, should neither endure the vices of their leader, nor hinder him from being defeated, punished and consequently pursued wherever he may be. The citizens ought therefore not to oppose . . . the entry, passage or lodging of the French in towns and countryside which forms the retreat and perhaps the fortifications and ambushes of the leader, their enemy . . . To do so would be to render themselves his accomplice.[21]

Metternich, Gentz, Burke and others all saw through this. Pitt, again, expressed matters succinctly in Parliament:

In what is called the government of the multitude, they are not the many who govern the few, but the few who govern the many. It is a species of tyranny, which adds insult to the wretchedness of its subjects, by styling its own arbitrary decrees the voice of the people, and sanctioning its acts of oppression and cruelty under the pretence of the national will.[22]

And he was right. St Just admitted in 1794: 'A revolution has taken place within the government but it has not yet reached civil society.'[23] Billaud-Varenne told the Convention, again in 1794: 'To put it bluntly, we must re-create the people that we wish to make free, for we need to destroy old prejudices, change outdated customs, restore jaded feelings, restrain excessive wants and annihilate deep-rooted vices.'[24] This was the language of future totalitarians, whether communists, fascists, Nazis or Islamists. Man and society had to be reshaped by a totalitarian elite to carry out, both at home and abroad, the will of the totalitarian party – in this case, the Jacobins. Metternich, for his part, never blamed the people. He had seen the revolutionary mob at work as a student at Strasbourg; he knew the revulsion that the execution of the King and Queen of France had caused in the ranks of the Austrian army; his family's Rhineland estates would later be overrun by the French; he realised his life's work would be devoted to resisting the Revolution in all its forms; but:

Frenchmen of that day did not at all comprehend the Revolution; and, indeed, I do not believe, with a few exceptions, they ever succeeded in doing so. But this weakness is not the exclusive property of the French, for people in general do not even guess the true causes or the purpose of events which take place before their eyes.[25]

Events in revolutionary France, were, of course, extremely gruesome.[26]
The events of 10 August 1792, when a mob brought the royal family back
to Paris from Versailles, left over 1,000 people dead; the September
massacres of the same year cost the lives of another 1,100–1,300 people.
Then came the execution of the king in January 1793 and the arrest in
June of the Girondins, who had voted against it. With their arrest came
the so-called 'federalist revolt' of the provinces – some 49 departments in
all, which repudiated the revolutionary Convention in Paris. Key towns
were involved – Lyons, Marseilles, Caen, Toulon – and counter-revolu-
tionary armies were raised. And all this came over and above the continued resistance in the Vendée. The result was the rise of the Committee of
Public Safety in Paris as the true government of France and the execution
of 3,000 enemies of the Republic a month by guillotine there. In the
provinces either the regular army or 'revolutionary armies' led by 'representatives on mission' crushed the revolt. Thousands were executed by
shooting or by being guillotined. Other methods were also used to speed
things up. Collot d'Herbois at Lyons invented the *mittraillade*, shooting
groups of prisoners at a time with cannons; Carrier at Nantes invented
the *noyades*, herding groups of prisoners onto barges on the River Loire,
taking them out at night and then holing the barges and leaving them to
drown. (St Just, to give him his due, calmed Alsace without a single
execution.) Finally, the revolution turned on itself. The Girondins had
already met their fate; now, in turn the Hébertistes, the Indulgents and
the Jacobins met theirs. According to Louis Blanc,[27] the 'White Terror' of
1795, which lasted more than a year, 'surpassed in horror even the
September massacres, even Collot d'Herbois's wholesale shootings, even
Carrier's drownings.' It was mere personal vengeance or, in Mathiez's
giveaway phrase,[28] 'butchery inspired by no ideal'.

Altogether historians estimate that some 50,000 people died as a
result of executions or imprisonment for political crimes during the
revolution – mainly artisans and peasants, who lacked revolutionary
zeal. (These 'traitors' were hated by the Jacobins even more than reactionary aristocrats and priests.) Yet some 300,000 people were also
condemned to prison; and another 200,000 died in the civil wars in the
Vendée. All in all, therefore, the cost in human lives of Jacobin 'totalitarian democracy' as a domestic experiment was enormous.[29] And,
given that the experiment spread across Europe, which experienced war
and invasion from the armies of the Revolution and Napoleon over a
period of almost quarter of a century (1792–1815),[30] it is little wonder
that 'democracy', French or European-style, was at a discount for much
of the nineteenth century.

Future progressive, liberal, socialist and communist historians – particularly but not exclusively in France – however, tended to overlook all this. With the twentieth century and the Bolshevik Revolution of 1917, with the creation of communist party cells around the world, and with the ideological claim that the Russian Revolution represented the proletarian revolution in world history, succeeding the French bourgeois revolution as predicted by Marxist eschatology, European historians on the whole swallowed the notion that both revolutions were essentially progressive, popular and inevitable. Only with the fall of communism in 1989 did it become fashionable – particularly in France due to the work of François Furet – to see the French Revolution once again as a dismal experiment in totalitarian democracy. Amazingly, a July 1989 poll by *L'Express* magazine found that on the bicentenary of the French Revolution, no less than 42 per cent of French history teachers in secondary schools agreed that between the Terror and Stalinism, 'there are differences, but they are phenomena of the same order'.[31]

In the other part of the revolutionary world of the late eighteenth century, the USA, the French Revolution meanwhile also had a huge impact. More even than Hamilton's financial measures, it was responsible for creating the first political party system there as Federalists and Democratic Republicans split over the significance of events in France. As in Europe, the first reactions were sympathetic, with even George Washington expressing sympathy. But very soon, Washington himself, his vice-president and successor, John Adams, and particularly Hamilton, were expressing their reservations. By 1793, Hamilton was denouncing the revolution in France as repugnant to the true principles of liberty. In 1794, he warned Washington: 'The example of France may be found to have unhinged the orderly principles of the People of this country and . . . a further assimilation of our principles with those of France may prove to be the threshold of disorganisation and anarchy.'[32] Washington's Neutrality Proclamation of 22 April 1793, and especially his Farewell Address of 17 September 1796 which denounced the 'tools and dupes' in America of a 'favourite (foreign) nation' (France), were meant, therefore, to separate the rational and enlightened American republic from its totalitarian sister republic. The dupes that Washington had in mind were people like Jefferson, Madison and Monroe, who all praised events in Paris. Yet by the end of the 1790s, particularly after the XYZ Affair of 1797–8, when Talleyrand as French foreign minister demanded huge bribes to meet with American diplomatic representatives, American opinion turned against France and Europe. In 1799, one federalist could even write: 'Who does not remember when foreign influence, like the golden calf, seduced the multitudes from the worship of true liberty?'[33] And even the French ambassador as early as 1796 was reporting to Paris of Jefferson himself that he 'is American and, for this reason, he cannot sincerely be our friend. An American is the born enemy of all European nations.'[34] The events in France and Europe scared many decent, liberty-loving, progressive Americans by 1800 as much as they scared Metternich and, curiously, it was in his translation of Metternich's future secretary Gentz's *The Origin and Principles of the American Revolution Compared with the Origin and Principles of the French Revolution* that John Quincy Adams, the future president and son of president John Adams, emphasised that Gentz had rescued America from the slur that it shared the same principles as had determined the course of the French Revolution. The two, he said, were completely different: 'A modern philosopher may contend that the sheriff, who executes a criminal, and the highwayman, who murders a traveller, act upon the same principles; the plain sense of mankind will still see the same difference between them, that is here proved between the American and French revolutions. The difference between *right* and *wrong*.'[35] America, therefore, pursued its own course, appalled by what had happened in France. Repudiation of French atheism and deism was even decisive in furthering the Second Great Awakening – the great evangelical revival at the end of the 1790s that also celebrated American pragmatism and condemned European, especially French, intellectualism. The United States, therefore, became self-centred in focus, isolationist and pragmatic in temper and highly suspicious of European revolutionary theories.[36] Even Jefferson himself, after hearing the news of Waterloo in January 1816, and looking back on his own flirtations with the Revolution in France and his quarrels with his old adversary, John Adams, happily confessed, indeed explicitly apologised, to the latter in these words: 'Your prophecies ... proved truer than mine; and yet fell short of the fact, for instead of a million, the destruction of 8 or 10 millions of human beings has probably been the effect of these convulsions. I did not in '89 believe that they would have lasted so long, nor have cost so much blood.'[37] Yet Jefferson, whose foreign policy as president for two terms after 'the revolution of 1800' had also been one of isolation from Europe, knew that Jacobinism or Bonapartism could never again trouble America. Metternich after 1815 was not so lucky. By 1817 a Protestant in France was jailed for proclaiming that within three months Napoleon would return following which 'the aristocrats, the priests, and the Catholics would have their heads cut off'.[38] The millenarian goal which underlay this enthusiasm was explained by a local official as follows:

Bonaparte is no longer the ruthless despot who is returning to claim his leaden sceptre, but the hero who will bring forth the liberation of the people. Upon his return he will be appointed Protector of the Republic, and by a remarkable effect on the faithful, this Platonic dream will replace the cult of the true King. At the moment of this sinister metamorphosis, another great sacrifice will be needed, and just as in 1793 it will be necessary to found public felicity upon the extermination of priests, aristocrats, and royalists of all shades. After this deluge of blood and fire, a new light will appear and the first dawn of the new golden age will arise.[39]

Hence, after almost twenty-five years of war against totalitarian democracy and military despotism, Metternich still had to safeguard Europe from the very real threat that the whole cycle of revolutionary and military violence could start all over again. And that threat never ceased to exist during his whole, long tenure of power. Historians have far too easily forgotten this.

During the whole period 1815–1848, there was the danger that France in particular would attempt to undermine the 1815 settlement. In Roger Bullen's words, 'French condemnation of the Settlement was total; all parties were united in their opposition to it. For decades to come an attack on the Treaty [the second Treaty of Paris between a defeated France and the allies after Waterloo] was a necessary credential for patriotism.'[40] France, it was thought, had been humiliated by the loss of her so-called 'natural frontiers', by the indemnity imposed on her by the allies and by the allied army of occupation. So great was popular hostility to the 1815 settlement that Victor Hugo's ode to Boulogne, composed as late as 1840, had to be turned down by the town council since it implied that the current lack of war in Europe was merely a truce, a 'fragile peace resonating with silent struggles', and hoped that the French would soon avenge Napoleon by recapturing the Rhine; finally, it pledged 'an eternal hatred' for the criminal English nation which had 'mutilated' France.[41] After 1821 there was also the possibility that Russian ambitions to undermine the Ottoman Empire could upset the diplomatic status quo. Indeed, the Eastern Question, as this problem was called, might even allow France the opportunity to start a European war and overthrow the 1815 treaties. This almost happened in 1840, when Louis Philippe, King of the French since 1830, had to dismiss his bellicose prime minister Thiers, who wanted to start a European war over the Eastern Crisis. In Thiers's own words:

I could not bear his [King Louis Philippe's] *paix à tout prix*. My *rêve* was a war by France and England against Austria and Russia. Such a war would have freed Italy and secured the independence of Turkey. *And there were half a dozen occasions when but for him we might have had one* [Author's italics]. The greatest blunder, however, that his *rage pacifique* betrayed him into was the Syrian affair. If he had stood by me for only two months we should have come out of it not merely successfully but gloriously.[42]

We shall return to this issue in Chapter 3 when Metternich's diplomacy will be discussed, but for the meantime, it should be noted that Metternich's fears that a liberal France might recommence the whole cycle of war and revolution during the period 1815–1848 were certainly justified.

Certainly, the period was not to lack in revolutionary developments. In 1817, Serbia revolted against the Turks; in 1820–1 there were revolts and revolutions in Piedmont, Naples, Portugal and Spain; the Greek War of Independence began in 1821 and continued till 1829; 1825 saw the Decembrist revolt in Russia; in 1830, the Belgians revolted against the Dutch, and the Poles against the Russians; France also had a revolution in 1830, as did parts of Germany and Italy; in 1832, after a two-year nationwide campaign, the Great Reform Bill was passed in Britain, whose historical geography by now included Cato Street and Peterloo; the revolutionary secret society 'Young Italy' was formed in 1831 and linked in 1834 to 'Young Europe'; there was a relative relaxation of tension in the late 1830s and the early mid-1840s, but in 1846 Polish exiles attempted in vain to stir up the Poles of Austrian Galicia; the Corn Laws were repealed in Great Britain; and Pius IX was elected Pope; the year 1847 saw civil war in Switzerland and set the stage for the revolutions of 1848. Most of these events had local and particular causes. Yet as far as Metternich was concerned, several factors linked them all: the spread of new ideas, the resentment of unemployed, former bureaucrats and army officers of Napoleonic regimes, the role of the press and universities in spreading new ideas of nationalism, liberalism and democracy. But what concerned him most was the role of secret societies, explicitly dedicated to revolution and insurrection, sects which from time to time attempted to carry out such plans or to assassinate rulers. His main fear was always a return to 1793, something that was shared long after 1815 even by potential democrats. Thus Mazzini himself, the leader of Young Italy and founder of Young Europe, in a famous essay entitled *Thoughts on Democracy in Europe* published as late as 1847, could write:

Even among the friends of democracy there are men who put their hands to the work with hesitation, and who sometimes appear seized with vague terror. One would say that the echo of that wild cry uttered some ten years since by a statesman speaking of the working classes, *'The barbarians are at our gates'*, still rings threateningly in their ears . . . There are men who no sooner hear the name of democracy than the phantom of '93 rises immediately before them. With them democracy means the guillotine surmounted by a red cap.[43]

So Metternich's fears, far from being the paranoid delusions of an unrepresentative, aristocratic Jeremiah, were actually shared by wide sections of society. Historians have never wanted to concede this. Yet we shall return to secret societies and insurrections presently. Before that it is necessary to make another point, to understand why, hitherto, there has been such a reluctance on their part to do so.

Metternich, 'Progressive' Historians and the Role of Social Forces

Traditionally, modern historians have always preferred instead to picture Europe in the first half of the nineteenth century as having been at the mercy of large forces which Metternich could neither understand nor control. For most of them his role was simply that of a latter-day Canute, attempting to hold back the tide of progress. This tide was fundamentally Marxist in nature, composed of a capitalist middle class, with demands for new or reformed constitutions and greater electoral power, and propelled by economic changes brought about by industrialisation.[44] Seen from this perspective, a 'progressive' warmonger like Napoleon or a 'progressive' terrorist like Mazzini deserved far greater praise than a peace-loving, conservative guardian of international law and domestic tranquillity such as Metternich. And today Metternich's reputation still stands lower than theirs.

This picture, however, needs a great deal of modification. In France, for example, it is now known that 1789 did not represent the overthrow of a feudal nobility by a capitalist bourgeoisie. On the contrary, there was a considerable land-owning bourgeoisie in place before the revolution of 1789. Indeed, it owned as much land there as the Church and aristocracy combined. It is also known that the capitalist middle classes played almost no part in the revolution. So it is difficult to see the events of 1789 as the overthrow of the feudal order by emerging capitalists.[45] After 1815, it was the landed bourgeoisie – an untitled aristocracy – that gained most from the Revolution. And it dominated French political life for the whole period 1815–48, not in competition with the aristocracy but in alliance with it.[46] Nor was the latter forced out in 1830 – legitimacy was a political cause, not a social class.[47] The differences between legitimists and Orleanists were political and geographical, not social. The same landed class, therefore, continued to run France after 1830 and this was as true of Paris as the provinces. Indeed, far from representing the commercial middle classes, Parisian politics was also dominated by the landed bourgeoisie. In 1842, no less than 50 per cent of electors there described themselves as 'landowners' who were 'without profession'; only 29 per cent described themselves as belonging to the *professions économiques*.[48] The ruling class was a mixture of the old and the new, the titled and untitled landed elite, with large sections of the commercial bourgeoisie probably without a vote. Even under Louis Philippe, only one man in 170 had the vote and the main qualification was the amount of land tax paid. It might be argued, therefore, that it was the limited franchise that led to revolutions in France (it had an electorate of 90,000 under the Restoration and one of between 200,000 and 240,000 under Louis Philippe), although this is problematical. Belgium, after all, only gave the vote to 1 per cent of the population and was spared revolution in 1848. Charles X's real crime in 1830, rather, had been to annul the election results and to muzzle the press. The political system, insofar as it had demonstrated popular dissatisfaction, had worked. Louis Philippe's government, on the other hand, did not lose the ability to win elections. The trouble was that the king interfered too much and always kept his favourite in power, so that Guizot looked as if he was undefeatable. His opponents therefore started a reform campaign – they were not opposed to limited constitutional monarchy but simply wanted an equal chance to run it.

In Britain, too, there was hardly any social or political transformation between 1815 and 1848. Indeed, the survival of the economic and political power of the British aristocracy was clearly evident well into the twentieth century. After 1815, meanwhile, Lord Liverpool supported laissez-faire, the Duke of Wellington Catholic emancipation, Sir Robert Peel the repeal of the Corn Laws, and Lord Grey the Great Reform Bill, all without undermining the aristocracy's political position. To explain this, it must be remembered that the British aristocracy was well entrenched politically.[49] The House of Lords was part of the legislature and had the right of initiative; as the highest court of appeal, it exercised judicial functions of the highest order. Peers almost always formed a majority of the cabinet and through control of pocket boroughs influenced the political composition of the Commons. As lords lieutenant of the counties they helped organise the militias and advised on appointments of justices of the peace. Through their territorial possessions, control of local councils, popular deference to their political leadership, not to mention their tradition of public service, they were usually respected figures. However, they never constituted a rigid political caste: the entry of Scottish representative peers, the changing episcopal bench, the influx of eminent soldiers, sailors and statesmen, not to mention the rapid extinction of even recent creations, meant that the composition of the upper house was always changing. Besides, the lords found that, along with the gentry, they could readily adapt to political change (what was Whiggery all about if not that?) and absorb rivals from the commercial world, while much of the electoral structure and social deference they profited from remained in place and proposals for land reform faltered. If the rise of the middle classes continued apace, it was not at the expense of the peers.[50]

In Germany, meanwhile, the most that the middle classes achieved was entry into the bureaucracy by part of the educated bourgeoisie, which was then usually absorbed into the ruling system by the device of 'service nobility'.[51] Inside the (by 1848) most troublesome parts of the Habsburg Monarchy, Lombardy-Venetia and Hungary, there is also little evidence that there was a problem from the rise of the middle classes. True, Paul Ginsborg has claimed that the 1848 Revolution in Venice was driven by a new (and apparently very small) class of commercial lawyers (some of whom were nobles), but his evidence is confusing and contradictory.[52] Much more reliable is the conclusion of Greenfield's exhaustive account of economic liberalism in Lombardy-Venetia during the Risorgimento which concludes:

> It would be natural to infer that Italian liberalism reflected a movement by the middle class to gain control of society. The defect of this thesis is that the liberal programme was initiated, expounded, and propagated, not by an aspiring and self-conscious bourgeoisie, with strong economic interests to serve, but by landed proprietors and groups of intellectuals, many of whose leaders were of the aristocracy . . . There is no evidence to colour the view that the liberal publicists were being pushed by a rising capitalistic class or were prompted to act as its mouthpiece.[53]

Certainly, the Austrian authorities in Lombardy-Venetia saw the Italian aristocracy as its main opponents.[54] As for Hungary, even under the communist regime, the Institute of Historical Research of the Hungarian Academy of Sciences could inform us in an official national history:

> It is one of the anomalies of Hungarian social development that the change to bourgeois conditions depended little on the class which should have been responsible for the ideological transformation and for the practical realisation of the actual development, that is to say the bourgeoisie itself. It was the result of grave historical circumstances that when the time came for the actual change to bourgeois conditions, there was no bourgeois force capable of carrying out the task. The bourgeoisie of the royal towns in fact fought on the side of the court, defending feudalism against national independence as represented by the liberal nobility.[55]

It would seem clear, therefore, that 1848 was not the result of the rise of a capitalist middle class which, as a force of history in the Marxist sense, made Metternich pointless. The old 'progressive' Marxist framework for the period 1815 to 1848 must be abandoned, which is not to say, of course, that wider forces were not at work.

Perhaps other classes were to blame for revolutionary disturbances? Louis Chevalier once suggested that the real challenge to the status quo during this period came from the 'labouring and dangerous classes' in Europe's cities. The poorest classes, who had been forced to seek employment in the slums of Paris and other large towns, were so sickened by the crime, prostitution, hunger, begging and disease to be found there that their very humanity drove them to revolt.[56] David Pinkney, the American expert on the French Revolution of 1830, also believed there was some evidence for this.[57] However, research by Charles Tilley has shown that, whereas the greatest periods of migration and urban expansion in France were the late 1850s and 1870s, the periods of greatest political disturbance were 1830–4, 1847–8, 1851 and 1871. The growth of Paris was socially much more explosive after 1851 than before. Moreover, disturbances were just as common in slow-growing cities like Nimes or Grenoble as in quickly expanding ones as Bordeaux or Lyons. Other fast-growing cities such as Toulon, Marseille and St Etienne, however, experienced very few disturbances. Other conclusions can also be drawn from Tilley's work – for example, it was the older rather than the newer cities that experienced both political and social revolts, while it was the older classes of resident, not the new *Lumpenproletariat* which was too busy struggling simply to survive, that participated in these revolts.[58] Tilley's evidence is supported by analyses of lists of those who were killed or wounded fighting on the barricades in Milan, Vienna and Berlin in 1848.[59] They came not from the 'dangerous classes' but from traditional trades, skilled workers or craftsmen who were neither uprooted or poor – the same types in fact as were described in 1789 as 'sans-culottes'. This research in turn is supported by that of George Rudé, whose analysis of the 'crowd in history' between 1789 and 1848 particularly, but not exclusively, in England and France, concluded that riots were of a pre-industrial kind with distinguishing features as follows:

> First, the prevalence of the rural food riot as the typical form of disturbance; second, the resort to direct action and violence to property; third, 'spontaneity' and lack of organisation; fourth, leadership drawn from outside the crowd; fifth, the crowd's mixed composition with the emphasis on small shopkeepers and craftsmen in towns, and weavers, miners and labourers (or peasants) in villages; and sixth, as a prime motive of rebellion, a 'backward looking concern for the restoration of lost "rights"'.[60]

All this seems acceptable. In 1830, for example, there was a spontaneous revolt in Paris when Charles X cancelled the election results; in 1848 in Vienna, crowds gathered after news reached the city of the fall of Louis Philippe in Paris; and in Milan in 1848 a similar crowd gathered after news arose of the fall of Metternich. Two further conclusions need to be drawn, however: the crowds were well-informed and they had political views about what needed to happen next. They also received outside leadership – from journalists and students as it often turned out – so that Metternich kept his eye on the committed revolutionaries (often journalists and students) who, after all, had always promised to provide that leadership. Clearly, there was a connection between these people and the larger forces at work in society even if these forces were not the ones associated with the rise of capitalism.

The growth of political consciousness and awareness in Europe between 1815 and 1848 had been influenced by a number of factors: student movements in the universities; the rise of the press; and a growing fashion for liberal and socialist ideas. Metternich knew and worried about all of these factors, although they were hardly regime-threatening. Still, from his point of view, students finally graduated to be civil servants, professors and men of influence. So they had to be checked. Journalists could spread subversive views. Liberals, by their very nature were a danger, socialists even more so if they could influence the masses. The main student problem was represented by the *Burschenschaften* in the German universities. These examined constitutions, drew up ideal versions of their own and stimulated demands for change. By 1819, therefore, the German monarchs agreed to close most of them down and to restrict student activities. The movement revived between 1827 and 1832 with a body calling itself 'Germania', fêting a Polish revolutionary general (Dombrowsky) at Jena in 1832 and calling at a congress at Stuttgart that year for a revolution to promote German unity, but once again it was repressed.[61] In 1831, the universities of Turin, Modena and Genoa were also closed down by the local authorities as politically unreliable, while Metternich unsuccessfully tried to stop Austrian students visiting German universities and vice versa. (The constitution of the German *Bund* proved too difficult a problem for him.) He worried, too, about the establishment of new universities in the 1820s in London and Madrid.[62] Yet the student problem – insofar as one really existed – was easily dealt with. It was only in 1848 that students got a real chance to play at politics.

A greater political consciousness was fostered by the growth of information about events elsewhere partly through a new travel literature but more particularly by the growth of the press. As far as travel literature was concerned, reports on Austria and Russia tended to be very critical while the French became infected by a Germanophilia, the influence of which among intellectuals meant that it was not unimportant for international relations.[63] It dated back to Madame de Staël's *Allemagne* of 1814 which had praised the Germans as an upright, honest, liberal race.[64] Henrich Heine in 1835, on the other hand, warned the French that: 'You have more to fear from a liberated Germany than the whole of the Holy alliance.'[65] The Germans, for their part took an added interest in Italy, a 'land of ruins' in Goethe's phrase. Yet Arndt, Mittermaier and Raumer, all of whom would later sit in the German National Assembly in 1848, in spite of visiting Italy, refused to believe in Italian unity. Raumer even condemned the idea as 'completely impracticable, unattainable, pernicious'.[66]

As far as the press was concerned, its growth had a huge impact on public opinion. Greenfield, for example, has commented on a 'Risorgimento of journalism' in Lombardy-Venetia before 'the third decade of the Restoration'.[67] M. S. Anderson has pointed out that the Press Association, founded in Denmark in 1835 to counter the censorship in force there, soon had branches throughout the country and was very influential in encouraging liberalism.[68] There were even occasional press wars. For example, as we shall see below, the so-called 'Galician Massacres' of 1846 embroiled Metternich's State Chancellery in press exchanges with newspapers in France and Germany.[69] In Hungary, meanwhile, Metternich's support for the neo-conservatives was expressed through the *Világ* and opposed by Kossuth's *Pesti Hírlap*. It was in Britain and France, however, that newspaper sales expanded most quickly. By 1836, sales of London newspapers were almost three times what they had been in 1801. The pauper press expanded most quickly, however, establishing a new social base for a new type of campaigning journalism.[70] In 1781, only 76 newspapers and periodicals had been printed in England and Wales; by 1825, the number was 250.[71] In France, the rate of increase in press circulation was even greater. In 1814 the *Journal des Débats*, the best-selling newspaper, had a circulation of about 23,000. The total circulation of newspapers in Paris in 1830 amounted to only 60,000. By 1845, on the other hand, the latter figure, thanks to the founding of Girardin's cheap and steamy, *La Presse*, had shot up to 148,000.[72] Censorship, which was severe throughout Europe (Britain was the exception), curtailed further growth, but technological developments worked in the opposite direction. Steam power meant that newspapers by 1848 could print 16,000 copies an hour (compared with 500 an hour in 1815) – more than the entire circulation of *The Times* in 1815. The invention of the railroad and telegraph also meant that information could be collected and disseminated far more quickly by the 1840s; indeed, the first great international news agency was established in Paris in 1832.[73]

Politicians naturally were quick to see the importance of the press – indeed, Kossuth, Thiers and Cavour more or less made their careers out of it. Still others – Canning, Brougham and Palmerston are excellent British examples – took great care to establish good relations with editors. Palmerston indeed often wrote anonymous articles praising his own policies for insertion in friendly newspapers. Maybe this was just as well, since in France the press often acted irresponsibly, accusing the government of all sorts of crimes (complicity in the murder of the Duc de Berri in 1820, for example) while newspapers in Paris and Lyon in 1834 even called for the overthrow of the government.[74] It was no accident that the 1830 revolution in Paris was launched from the offices of the *National* by Thiers in 1830 or that in 1848 the majority of the members of the national government should have been on the editorial staffs of the *National* and the *Réform*.[75] The growth of the press, therefore, was a source of suspicion and fear for most governments between 1815 and 1848. Censorship could do much to restrain irresponsibility, but on the whole the press was seen as instrumental in spreading new ideologies such as liberalism and socialism. (Nationalism will be dealt with in a later chapter.)

As far as liberalism was concerned, this amounted for the most part to a belief in progress and a desire for a constitution. Some constitutions were, of course, in place – the famously unwritten British one pre-eminently, but also the French constitutions of 1814 and 1830, the Belgian and Dutch constitutions after 1830 and the few constitutions granted after 1815 to the Southwest German states, notably Baden, Bavaria, Weimar, Württemberg and Hesse. Yet the franchise everywhere was extremely restricted – the Hungarian Diet allowed more men to vote for it before 1848 than the French Chamber[76] – and it is not at all clear that in themselves these constitutions aided either social peace or economic progress. Certainly states like Prussia, Piedmont and even Austria could make progress without them. Metternich worried that they would encourage discontent and false hopes, although it was not until the 1840s, even the late 1840s, that liberalism began to cause him real concern – and then on account of a spectacularly unexpected liberal pope and modest indications that local diets in Austria were showing unprecedented, if still small, signs of life. In fact, foreign parliaments had a mixed record. Arguably, British liberal and reform movements – factory reform, parliamentary reform, abolition of the slave trade, poor law reform, etc. – prevented revolution in Britain in 1848 but arguably, too, it was the 180,000 special constables, the 50,000 troops, the sand-bagging of London, the armed ships on the Thames and other military measures that saved the capital from the Chartists in April 1848.[77] The French parliament failed to demonstrate the same reforming zeal – *enrichissez-vous!* was Guizot's notorious advice, but it was the refusal of the French national guard to save the king amidst the chaotic scenes in Paris at the end of February that put an end to a previously stable regime. And revolution in Paris brought not liberal progress but the June Days and then Napoleon III. So international liberalism proved no great threat to Metternich; Guizot, in any case, had been cooperating with him diplomatically between 1846 and 1848.

Socialism, of course, was even less of a threat, primarily since its development required the process of industrialisation to expand before it could become influential.[78] Still, the term had been coined, suppos-edly by the Frenchman Pierre Leroux in 1832. The idea went back at least to Babeuf's conspiracy and Buonarotti's account of Babeuf, published in France in 1828, revived interest in such ideas. Certainly by 1848 there were many socialist schemes to choose from in France: the industrial plans of the Saint-Simonians; Fourier's blueprints for self-governing communities; Proudhon's anarchism; Blanqui's theory of class struggle and dictatorship; Louis Blanc's state-financed 'social workshops', not to mention Cabet's plan for *Icarie* – a communist island utopia. In England, too, there were socialist ideas around – Robert Owen might even have invented the term before Leroux. But thinkers such as Thomas Hodgskin and William Thompson were not much more advanced than Ricardo in their ideas and Owen's ideas were almost non-political – he advocated 'harmony communities' and 'cooperatives'. It is also difficult to see Chartism as having had any socialist input. Its most famous leader, Feargus O'Connor, was described as 'a radical tory anti-socialist', who himself described his Land Scheme of 1845 as about as socialist as the Comet. If O'Brien and Jones were more Marxist in outlook, they had little influence on the movement, for in the words of G. D. H. Cole, it produced 'no Socialist theories of its own – only echoes of Owen, of Louis Blanc and of Karl Marx, to which the workers for the most part refused to listen'.[79] Germany at this stage had not yet undergone much industrialisation, so socialist ideas were mostly imported there from France by people like Wilhelm Weitling and Ludwig von Stein. Indeed, the latter's best-known book, published in 1842, was entitled *Socialism and Communism in France Today*.[80] In Austria, there had been outbreaks of machine-breaking in Bohemian factories in 1844 and printing workers had organised self-help against the economic consequences of illness between 1834 and 1836, but no socialist movement had been allowed to develop. In 1844, two brothers, Charles and Joseph Schestag, spent two months in the Spielberg for having joined Weitling's League of the Just.[81] Marx and Engels had only begun their careers as revolutionaries (mostly spent in England, of course). But in 1844 they had published *The Holy Family* and in the winter of 1847–8 wrote *The Communist Manifesto*. Curiously, this may have been a reply to Mazzini's 1847 essay, already referred to, entitled *Thoughts upon Democracy in Europe*. For in that, Mazzini had demolished the case for utilitarianism, moderate liberalism and all kinds of socialism, utopian and scientific. Already in 1847, he had predicted the consequences of communism – totalitarian dictatorship. To make socialism work, he wrote:

> You must have an arbitrary hierarchy of chiefs, having the entire disposition of the common property: masters of the mind by an exclusive education; of the body by the power of deciding upon the work, the capacity, the wants of each. And these imposed or elected

chiefs – it matters little which – will be, during the exercise of their power, in the position of the masters of slaves in olden times; and influenced themselves by the theory of interest which they represent, seduced by the immense power concentrated in their hands, they will endeavour to perpetuate it; they will strive by corruption to re-assume the hereditary dictatorship of the ancient castes.[82]

Thus Mazzini had made an absolutely correct diagnosis of the origins of communist dictatorship, even before Marx and Engels had written their manifesto.

Terrorism Again

With Mazzini, however, we must return to the problem of Metternich and terrorism. So far, the argument has been that Metternich was right to be concerned – as many contemporaries, even democrats and liberals in Europe and America were – lest the totalitarian democracy and violence associated with the period 1792–1815 should revive. This might occur if the European settlement of 1815 were overturned either by the diplomacy of France or by the conspiracies of revolutionaries. If historians have dismissed his fears, preferring instead to interpret him as a simple-minded reactionary unable to see the progressive forces of history at work with the rise of a new capitalist middle class, it has been demonstrated that this is their illusion, and that Metternich was more astute in looking out for other dangers. He was, of course, well aware of the rise of public opinion and the fashion for liberalism, but organised controls of the press and universities through international action made it possible to contain these factors. Yet he was also well aware – as modern research seems to confirm – that revolts in most of Europe seemed to be led by disaffected outsiders – often journalists, students, former employees of Napoleon's many bureaucracies or armies, political dreamers and fanatics, men who often formed or joined secret societies, and he was determined to pursue and crush them.

Metternich certainly never underrated the secret societies – particularly in Italy. He told his agent in Lombardy, the Chevalier de Menz in 1833:

> For many years all those who had pointed to the existence of a *comité directeur* working secretly for universal revolution were met everywhere only by incredulity; today it has been shown that this infernal propaganda exists, that it has its centre in Paris, and that it is divided

into as many sections as there are nations to regenerate . . .
Everything that refers to this great and dangerous plot cannot, therefore, be observed and surveyed with too much attention.[83]

Historians, again, however, have been traditionally suspicious of
Metternich's obsession with terrorists. True, plots existed. Alexander I
of Russia, for example, blamed the revolt of his Semenovsky guards on
the sects and it is known that the Decembrists in 1825, just like the
Hungarian Jacobins of 1794, were organised into two groups, one with
a fairly liberal, another, which directed the first, with an outright revolutionary programme. But was there ever a European-wide conspiracy?
In the aftermath of the Napoleonic wars the greatest revolutionary sect
was undoubtedly the Carbonari. This is estimated to have had between
400,000 and 600,000 members and was known to have taken a leading
part in the 1820 revolution in Naples. But that revolt was crushed and,
since research seems to demonstrate that the organisation had confused
aims and ideals save for Italian unity (i.e. it had radical and conservative, republican and monarchist, clerical and anti-clerical members), its
influence has been rather written off.[84] Perhaps the true conclusion to
draw, on the other hand, is that an organisation that could recruit up
to 600,000 members, stage a revolution and unite all sorts of disparate
elements should be treated very seriously. The Charbonnerie, the
French version of the Carbonari, had 'only' 40,000–80,000 members
according to historical research and 'only' succeeded in subverting a
few French troops during mutinies in the 1820s.[85] Might not a similar
conclusion be drawn? The mutinies were crushed but an organisation
of that size that could help instigate mutinies in France is, again, one
that needs to be treated seriously. The truth is that with just a bit more
luck these organisations could well have changed the course of history.
One surely need not dwell on contemporary parallels to make the
point.

Yet it was from the 1830s that Metternich's worst nightmare seemed
to emerge, personified by Mazzini. The latter was the mirror image of
Metternich – drawn from the ordinary people, a proponent of international republicanism, a believer in the rights of man and a terrorist.
Today, he is chiefly remembered as a writer – his collected works fill no
fewer than 106 volumes and took almost ninety years to edit – yet in his
time he planned and led revolutions and plotted assassinations. When
he founded Young Italy in 1831 – having been expelled to France from
Piedmont for Carbonari activities after an eminently fair trial – the
statutes of the new organisation included the following:

The means by which Young Italy proposes to reach its aims are education [propaganda] and insurrection, to be adopted simultaneously and made to harmonise with each other . . . Education, though of necessity secret in Italy, will be public out of Italy . . . Insurrection – by means of guerrilla bands – is the true method of warfare for all nations desirous of emancipating themselves from the foreign yoke.[86]

The result was that almost immediately the existence of Young Italy was known. And very soon it recruited thousands of members in Italy. Accounts normally credit it with 50–60,000 members by 1833, but some estimates reach 140,000.[87] Mazzini also ran its newspaper – also called Young Italy (*La Giovine Italia*), of which there were six issues, all with more than 200 pages, three in 1832, two in 1833 and one in 1834, which were smuggled in by sailors to Italian ports. Metternich had his agents send him a couple of copies. But Mazzini's real concern was action and Young Italy was soon busy attempting invasions of Piedmont, while other agents went, Che Guevara-like, on ill-fated expeditions by ship against various parts of the Italian coast. Mazzini also agreed in 1833 to give a dagger – a stiletto he had on his desk – to Antonio Gallenga, whose aim was to assassinate King Charles Albert of Piedmont-Sardinia. Previously, in 1831, Mazzini had written the first of his 'open letters' to the king, beseeching him to take the lead in freeing Italy. Now he was plotting his death. Converted by Carlo Bianco's work of 1830, entitled *Of National Insurrectionary Warfare by Bands Applied to Italy*, Mazzini wanted action on the widest scale: insurrections, assassinations, propaganda and also an expanded organisation.[88] Hence in 1834 he organised Young Europe to promote revolution all over the Continent. Like some mad Brussels commissioner, he proclaimed: 'Europe is the lever of the world. Europe is the land of liberty; Europe controls the universe. Here is the mission of progressive development that encompasses humanity.'[89] The Pact of Young Europe was signed at Berne on 15 April 1834 by 17 founding members representing Young Italy, Young Germany and Young Poland. One potential version of Metternich's 'great and dangerous plot', therefore, had come into existence. Mazzini, like most terrorists, could talk in visionary and emancipatory language, often in deeply religious language:

What is the present movement but an attempt at the practical realisation of [the Lord's] prayer. We are labouring that the development of human society may be, as far as possible, in the likeness of this divine society; in the likeness of the heavenly country, where all are equal; where there exists but one love, but one happiness for all. We seek the paths of heaven upon earth; for we know that this earth was given to us for our workshop; that through it we can rise to heaven; that by our earthly works we shall be judged; by the number of poor we have assisted, by the number of the unhappy we have consoled.[90]

However, Metternich was more concerned by the thought of how much violence such language would bring about, about how many would die as a result of insurrectionary warfare and revolution. Revolutionary goodness, he well knew, did not spare the innocent. So Radetzky's troops in Italy, many of them Italian, were informed about Mazzini's new organisation in 1833 as follows:

When twelve years ago the sect called the Carbonari threatened civil order in the Italian states with its complete overthrow, His Majesty warned you, his subjects, of the harmful and seditious teachings of this sect and of their criminal and treasonous aims in order 324 of March 1821. This was made known to everybody in order to ensure that even the most inexperienced and careless men, from whom the leaders of this sect took care to conceal their aims, would know of them and hence would abstain from joining the Carbonari.

The monarch's same fatherly care now compels him in view of recent events to issue the same order with regard to a no less dangerous sect, indeed, one which represents a higher form of Carbonari, called Young Italy. The aim of this organisation is the overthrow of existing governments and of the complete social order; the means which it employs are subversion and outright murder through secret agents.[91]

Troops who joined it or refused to inform on it were therefore guilty of high treason, but those who did provide information would be dealt with confidentially.

Throughout his period in office, therefore, Metternich's main concern was to protect Europe from revolutionary violence, which might once again engulf the Continent either if France were allowed to start a European war, as Thiers and others wanted, or if revolutionary sects like Young Italy succeeded in provoking revolutionary insurrections, as they regularly tried to do. (NB: It was a failed assassination attempt on Napoleon III in 1858 by Young Italy member Felice Orsini, with Mazzini's approval, that pushed the Emperor of the French, himself a former member of the Carbonari, into conspiring with Cavour to start a war with Austria in Italy. Metternich's fears were not delusions). Metternich was only too well aware that political change between 1815 and 1848 usually came about violently as a result of revolutions and insurrections by people claiming to be democrats. Indeed, there was nowhere in the world at this stage where democracy seemed able to exist without violence. (Britain and the USA were not yet democracies and in any case still had very turbulent political episodes.) So seriously did Metternich fear a rerun of 1793 that according to one memoirist he used to warn his colleagues that if revolution did engulf Austria they themselves would all be executed by the revolutionaries.[92] The Archduke John and the King of Prussia certainly believed the same.

In 1846, however, revolution did strike the Habsburg Monarchy. Polish conspirators, organised from Paris, plotted to restore the Kingdom of Poland by seizing Krakow (technically a free state under the 1815 treaties) and from there stir up Austria's Polish province of Galicia.[93] The local Polish peasants, however, resisted the conspirators, whose supporters were found among the Polish lesser nobility or gentry, and slaughtered them and their allies – including some noble ladies – before loading the dead and dying onto carts which they then took to the Austrian authorities. Opponents of Metternich claimed falsely that the Austrian authorities had organised and paid for these 'Gallician horrors' which cost the lives of over 1000 people. Colonel Benedek was sent to put down the revolutionaries, which he did, but he also complained that the peasants were possessed of a bloodlust, which he saw at first hand when peasant auxiliaries, against his orders, slaughtered rebel prisoners he had taken. News that the peasants had sided with the Emperor (there was even a rumour that he had suspended the Ten Commandments) was spread around the Monarchy by a grateful government, but Metternich was once again made aware, as he had been throughout his long period in office, that the normal route for political change was bloody violence. This was why he had always taken what preventive measures he could – diplomatic conventions and alliances, exhortations to sovereigns and foreign ministers to abide by the 1815 treaties, censorship of newspapers, control of student bodies, not to mention sensible economic and welfare measures, and only very rarely military interventions, to keep the spectre of revolution at bay. Yet it could never be completely exorcised. The French wanted to revise the 1815 settlement, revolutionaries wanted to redraw the map of Europe and abolish, if not execute, kings and emperors, so that revolutionary war, totalitarian democracy along the lines of 1793, was always on the cards. When news came of the fall of Louis Philippe in France, Metternich told his special envoy in Milan, Count Ficquelmont: 'You know what I have always thought about the solidity of the throne of July; I am not surprised by his fall . . . Europe finds itself again in 1791 and 1792! Will there be no 1793?'[94]

History never repeats itself and in 1848 the French were wise enough not to export their revolution across their frontiers. Which is not to say that revolution did not break out there anyway. Metternich was forced to resign, but this time, without French aid, the revolutions were quickly defeated. In exile in London, Metternich told everybody that he had been right all along, he had made no mistakes. This book will show that for most of the time, from his own point of view, he was probably correct.

2
What Part Did Metternich Play in the Downfall of Napoleon?

Diplomatic commentators, even his critics among them, found it difficult to deny that Metternich was Europe's leading statesman. For example, the Frenchman Capefigue, who at the height of the Napoleonic revival in France in 1843 published a series of portraits, translated into English in 1845 as *The Diplomatists of Europe*, introduced Metternich (who had allowed himself to be interviewed, perhaps several times, beforehand) as a 'statesman who must be placed in a superior rank to all others'.[1] After asserting that Metternich also ran domestic policy in Austria, he continued:

> The political life of a statesman is bound up in the work he has undertaken. It is not my habit as a historian to adopt the narrow views inspired by party spirit or worn-out declamation: when a minister has achieved the greatness of an empire, resisted vassalage under Napoleon, and furnished the most extensive field for the page of history, I will not, from a weak patriotism, raise my voice against this master-mind. We may meet with enough men who destroy; we ought to feel respect for those capable of creating, and then maintaining their work.[2]

Capefigue had obviously been charmed by Metternich when he had interviewed him: 'He (Metternich) said to me wittily one day: "I am to a certain degree, the confessor of all the European cabinets; I give absolution to those who have committed the fewest sins, and I thus maintain the peace of their souls."'[3]

Another writer who must also have met Metternich several times was the American *chargé d'affaires* at the court of Vienna, William H. Stiles, who in his very critical and democratic, two-volume account of *Austria in 1848–49*,[4] had much to say about Metternich and his foreign policy. According to Stiles:

> Prince Metternich has long held, by common consent, the rank of the most distinguished statesman of Europe. Two conditions are essential to the highest renown in public life, the possession of great qualities and great opportunities for their exercise; and with both he was sufficiently provided. The career of the prince has been the longest, the most difficult, and (for his own principles) the most triumphant in the annals of modern diplomacy . . . The fortunes and policy of the imperial house of Austria have been more than once identified with the characters of those supreme servants of state, whose ministerial functions have been extended to the utmost limit of absolute power, and protracted beyond the ordinary duration of human life. But of these illustrious ministers, who have lived in the long and secure administration of one of the greatest empires of the earth, none ever retained that high and responsible position amid events of such infinite magnitude and variety, or with so unlimited control, as Clement, prince of Metternich.[5]

Stiles singled out one achievement of Metternich's in particular: 'The art with which Metternich passed from the alliance with Napoleon to neutrality, from neutrality to mediation, and from mediation to the coalition against him, will in every age be considered a masterpiece of diplomacy.'[6] Later on, according to Stiles, Metternich's principles were, first, to preserve legitimacy throughout all governments and, second, to maintain peace and to secure the balance of power in Europe.[7] Indeed, Metternich, more so than Louis Philippe who arrogantly claimed the title, deserved to be known as 'the Napoleon of peace'![8] All this, it should be stressed, was written by an American democrat who abominated Metternich's domestic principles and whose secretary of state, Daniel Webster, dismissed Austria as 'but a patch on the earth's surface',[9] but who, none the less, strove to be objective. Thus if he attributed the usual qualities to Metternich – 'His whole person, countenance, and demeanour, are indicative of high station, superior intellect, and finished elegance. He was not remarkable for his native genius or subsequent acquirements, but his distinguishing traits were his knowledge and perception of character, and the arts by which he bent them to his own purpose'[10] – he also knew that democratic Europe was wrong in describing him as some sort of bloodthirsty ogre:

Metternich was never the sanguinary tyrant that some have supposed; he was averse to all extreme measures and particularly opposed to shedding human blood. No political executions ever took place at his instance. Those which occurred upon the tumults in the empire, which followed the French revolution of 1830, occurred on the express orders of the Emperor Francis. Metternich's disposition is more truly exemplified by the general amnesty for all political offenders throughout the Empire, with which commenced the reign of the imbecile Ferdinand, and during whose term Metternich was 'indeed the state'.[11]

Stiles also quoted Francis I who was heard to say, 'In forgiving and pardoning I am a bad Christian; it is too difficult for me; Metternich is much more compassionate.'[12] Yet it should not be forgotten that all the Austrian and Hungarian Jacobins who had been imprisoned in 1794 were pardoned by Francis in 1801–2 and released and that Confalonieri, Pellico, Andryane and other conspirators all had their death sentences commuted by Francis (perhaps on Metternich's advice). The issue of political prisoners, however, will be addressed in a later chapter; the point to be stressed here is that even Stiles, the American democrat, felt it absolutely necessary to give Metternich his due as far as diplomacy was concerned: in his view, despite all his criticisms, Metternich *was* the greatest diplomat and statesman of his day.

Metternich and Napoleon

There is, of course, no room, in a book of this size to give a year-by-year account of Metternich's diplomacy. Instead, what I intend to do is look at the major issues connected with his career and explain why Capefigue and Stiles reached the conclusions they did. I also want to examine how the European state system worked during 'the age of Metternich'.

When Metternich became foreign minister in 1809, Austria had been defeated by France for a fourth time and stood on the brink of extinction. The Peace of Campo Formio of 1797 had forced Austria to recognise the French conquest of the Austrian Netherlands (Belgium) and to accept the Rhine as the French frontier, to cede Lombardy to the Cisalpine Republic (under French control) and to accept the already plundered and ruined Republic of Venice (without the Ionian Islands) in return. The Treaty of Lunéville of 1801 further diminished the Austrian position by expelling the junior members of the House of

Habsburg, the Duke of Modena and the Archduke of Tuscany, from Italy and forcing Austria to compensate them with Alpine territories (Breisgau and Salzburg). It also forced Austria to recognise the French republics set up in Switzerland, Holland and Italy and to promise to compensate the German sovereigns who had lost territory on the left bank of the Rhine with territories from within the Holy Roman Empire. The end of that ancient body was now therefore also on the cards. Napoleon's harsh Peace of Pressburg of 1805 then deprived Austria of Venetia and Tyrol (which went to Bavaria along with Vorarlberg), while the rulers of Bavaria and Württemberg were made kings and freed from any obligations to Francis II. (Francis had taken the title Austrian Emperor in 1804 although he remained the duly elected Holy Roman Emperor – he could not be inferior to the new hereditary Emperor of the French; in 1806 he dissolved the Holy Roman Empire altogether rather than risk Napoleon being elected Holy Roman Emperor by his German allies, in which position Napoleon would then have become sovereign over part of the Austrian Empire.) Austria had also to accept a war indemnity of 40 million francs. After the war of 1809, Austria was further humiliated by the Peace of Schönbrunn. Salzburg, Berchtesgaden and the Innviertel went to Bavaria; Görz, Istria, Trieste, Croatia, Dalmatia, as well as parts of Carinthia and Carniola, went to France to form her 'Illyrian Provinces'; Austria had to join the Continental System to guarantee an amnesty for the Tyrolese and Vorarlberger who had revolted against the Bavarians; in Poland she lost East Galicia to the Grand Duchy of Warsaw and West Galicia to Russia; while she had to accept an indemnity of 85 million francs (to be paid for in hard currency, not Austria's now notorious paper money) and a reduction of her armed forces to 150,000 men. Altogether she lost 3.5 million people and was deprived of access to the sea. Given Napoleon's alliance with Russia forged at Tilsit (1807) and Erfurt (1808), and Russian activity in Turkey and the Balkans, there was every reason to suspect that Napoleon would one day simply wipe Austria off the map and divide up her territories between various marshals and relatives, say as King of Bohemia, King of Hungary, with himself perhaps as Emperor of Germany. In exile, after all, he was to confess that his ultimate aim had been 'to re-establish the kingdom of Poland as a barrier against the Muscovite barbarians, divide Austria, declare Hungary independent, break up Prussia, form independent republics in England and Ireland, control Egypt, drive the Turks out of Europe, and liberate the Balkan nations'.[13]

It was under these extremely inauspicious circumstances that

Metternich became foreign minister. At the time neither he nor anybody else could have expected Austria to recover, far less defeat Napoleon. Yet that is what in fact occurred. In the first volume of his memoirs, he tells the story of how that came about and how, with logic and persistence, he made it happen. But did he? Helmut Rumpler has called his account the 'retrospective justification of a successful politician', adding, 'In 1809 the position was completely different.'[14] Felix Markham wrote:

> In his Memoirs Metternich presents himself as the arbiter of Europe who lured Napoleon to destruction by a subtle and far-sighted diplomacy. According to this version his peace negotiations were never genuine but only intended to brand Napoleon as the warmonger and to gain time to complete the Austrian mobilization and bring her over to the side of the allies. The great French diplomatic historian, Sorel, accepted and developed this theme, which justified Napoleon's intransigence.'[15]

Elsewhere Markham wrote that Metternich's motive had been 'to deceive posterity by posing as the conqueror of Napoleon and the statesman who deliberately engineered his downfall', whereas he would really have preferred a negotiated peace with the Emperor.[16] Most recently, Paul Schroeder has concluded: 'Metternich is sometimes seen as an implacable enemy of the revolution and Napoleon, forced for the moment to lie low and feign friendship with Napoleon to survive, but always looking for the chance to restore the European balance and regain Austria's independence. This is Metternich's propaganda . . .'.[17] Historians then have different views on Metternich's policy during the contest with Napoleon. Some see his aim as having always been, simply and consistently, the overthrow of the tyrant;[18] others believe he really wanted to keep Napoleon in power in a France reduced to her 'natural', if still extended, frontiers to balance the growing influence of Russia and Prussia;[19] while still others see his real aim as having been above all else the frustration of German nationalist ambitions to create a united German state out of the chaos of war in Europe.[20] Pan-Germans and German nationalists were later to condemn Metternich bitterly for this fault as they saw it.[21] Some historians, like Paul Schroeder, however, have found it difficult to find any consistent thread in Metternich's policies, save the need for Austria to survive: 'Metternich's tactics were certainly subtle and deceptive. He never told anyone the full truth, even his Emperor or Austria's representatives abroad; he always tried to lure others into commitments while remaining ready himself to change course and cover his tracks in retreat'[22] – although Schroeder adds immediately: 'Much of this is normal in diplomacy.'[23]

So where does this get us? For a start, it should be remembered that Metternich could only play the cards he had been dealt. That meant, on the positive side, a better economic situation inside Austria despite the huge amount of paper money in circulation.[24] The wars with France had led to an economic, albeit inflationary, boom so that from 1800 loans could be negotiated inside Austria from a large number of Viennese banking houses as well as from various provincial diets and individuals. And over and above came subsidies from Britain. The national debt rose horrendously but the fact remains that Austria was able to cover her costs and to raise and equip an army of some 250,000 men at a time (1813) when Napoleon calculated that she would be lucky to raise only 75,000 at most.[25] Secondly, the nature of warfare had changed by 1809 and 'moved beyond Napoleon's comprehension or adaptation'.[26] The wars fought between 1809 and 1815 were different from those of 1805–7. By 1805 Napoleon had essentially created a new type of army which would fight a new type of war – a very large force (the *Grande Armée* consisted of 210,000 men with 396 guns by 1805) which, although it contained many veterans, depended for its existence on conscription and on the full mobilisation of the French state. It also had an executive general staff headed by Marshal Alexandre Berthier and by now had adopted and fully integrated a system of army corps (seven army corps, a cavalry reserve corps and the Imperial Guard, to be precise). Each corps was an army in itself with its own staff and component divisions. A corps consisted of 20,000–40,000 men and was difficult to destroy. The French estimated that a corps could fight by itself for a day or so. This new type of army, therefore, was able to defeat the essentially *ancien régime* forces of Austria, Prussia and Russia in 1805–7. Yet by 1809 these powers had reformed their armies along French lines. Austria mobilised 400,000 men and 742 guns in 1809 and now also used an army corps system. Napoleon, as a result, was defeated for the first time in his life by the Archduke Charles at Aspern-Essling. The Prussians and Russians reformed too. At Borodino, 130,000 French and allied troops with 587 guns faced 120,000 Russians with 640 guns. By now artillery fire was crucial (as it had been at Aspern where Napoleon was outgunned) and the Russians fired 90,000 rounds in a single day. These trends – increased sizes, corps, artillery duels – continued. In 1813, the allies assembled a coalition of 800,000 men, with front-line forces consisting of 500,000 men and 1,380 guns. Napoleon amazingly had raised 700,000 men, of whom 400,000 were in the field with 1,284 guns. By now army corps themselves were being consolidated into field armies with huge numbers of guns and great resiliency. After his defeat at Leipzig in 1813, however, Napoleon could no longer assemble much more than half the allied troops. So the allies were able to march on Paris. Metternich, Francis and most of the allied leaders, however, did not really absorb all this and consequently the allied armies under Field Marshal Prince Schwarzenberg moved very slowly into France. On the negative side, therefore, Metternich wisely still felt obliged to keep in mind Napoleon's military genius and the military threat that he personally never really ceased to pose to his opponents. (Moreau, the brilliant French general who later deserted to the allies, advised: 'Expect a defeat whenever the Emperor attacks in person. Attack and fight his lieutenants wherever you can. Once they are beaten, assemble all your forces against Napoleon and give him no respite.')[27] Again, on the negative side, Metternich always had his critics at court in Vienna who had the ear of Francis I.[28] Some of these wished to restore the old German Empire, while others took a blatantly 'stock-Austrian' rather than European view of events. But since both these camps found so much to criticise in Metternich's diplomacy, the prince (promoted from count after Leipzig) had always to ensure that Francis stood by him.[29] Finally, by 1809, Austria was all too well aware that she could not rely on either Russia or Prussia – never mind the lesser German states – to back her in any challenge to Napoleon; nor could she trust them not to make separate deals with him. Metternich, very wisely, therefore, in 1812–13 chose to let Russia and Prussia worry about Austrian good faith. Yet the challenge from Napoleon could not be ducked and it became very personal. It was Napoleon for a start who demanded that Metternich should be appointed Austrian ambassador to France in 1806[30] and it was Napoleon who kept discussing plans with him about future wars. It was Napoleon, too, who unexpectedly decided to marry into the Austrian imperial family, bringing Metternich back to Paris for most of 1810 and linking the Bonapartes and Habsburgs dynastically thereafter. It was Napoleon who accepted Metternich's changes in foreign policy towards France, first from alliance to armed neutrality and later from armed neutrality to armed mediation. It was also Napoleon who consistently refused to negotiate with Metternich, thus forcing Austria to pursue the war against him, whether Metternich really wanted this or not.[31] So Napoleon himself put Metternich centre stage. None the less, Metternich's diplomatic strategy still needs to be unravelled. The key to it is that in the welter of constantly changing military and diplomatic circumstances, Metternich's desires and expectations with regard to Napoleon rarely coincided. In the end as Metternich put it, 'he would not allow himself to be saved';[32] or as Srbik stated: 'Napoleon destroyed himself.'[33] Yet Metternich certainly played his part.

Metternich's Background

Perhaps a brief review of Metternich's career is in order here.[34] Clemens Lothar Wenzel von Metternich-Winneburg-Beilstein was born in 1773 in the Rhineland and did not see Vienna until he was twenty-one years old. His family was part of the *Standesherren*, about 400 German princes who formed the highest rank of the German nobility. These princes were the immediate vassals of the Emperor and were represented at the Diet or Reichstag at Regensburg. Metternich's father was a *Reichsgraf* or imperial count, whose estates, midway between Coblenz and Trier on the Mosel River (Winneburg on the right bank and Beilstein on the left), formed a property of some 75 square miles and 6,200 inhabitants with an annual revenue of 2,000 guilders, which enabled the family to live in comfort if not great elegance at Coblenz. The Metternichs were not among the highest ranking of the nobility; above them were princes, margraves, dukes and electors. About forty of these since 1648 enjoyed the privilege of *Landeshoheit*, which meant that they were removed from the jurisdiction of the Imperial Treasury, could recruit their own armed forces and could make alliances with other princes, even those outside the Empire. Many of these acted as sovereigns in their own right and indeed some were – the King of England (Elector of Hanover), the King of Denmark (Duke of Holstein) and the King of Prussia (Elector of Brandenburg). If for these people the Reich was rather a nuisance, the lower nobility, the *Reichsritterschaft*, made up of about 350 barons (*Freiherrn*) and some 1,500 imperial knights, who held their fiefs directly from the Emperor but who were not represented in the Reichstag, valued the Empire, which provided them with certain privileges – exemption from imperial taxation, for example – as well as social status and job opportunities. For the Habsburgs, the Empire was something of a waning asset. It took up a lot of time and brought foreign policy involvements and complications, although it also helped provide the dynasty with better educated civil servants, army recruits and officers than were available in its alpine and other provinces. This background is necessary because after 1773 Metternich's father, Count Franz Georg von Metternich, became imperial minister to the courts of Trier and Cologne and later to the electoral court of Mainz and to the *Kreis* of

Lower-Rhine-Westphalia, all the time residing in the *Metternicher Hof,* his home at Coblenz. Still, Franz Georg, despite a reputation for being dull and conventional, ensured that Clemens got a good education (excellent private tutors followed by university enrolment at Strasbourg and Mainz between 1788 and 1792, allowing Clemens as a student to witness the French Revolution at first hand); he also ensured that Clemens was able to officially attend the imperial coronations of Joseph II and Leopold II at Frankfurt in 1790 and 1792. It helped that in 1791 Franz Georg had been appointed resident minister in the Austrian Netherlands (Belgium), although he was to be unfairly blamed for the loss of the province in 1794 when the post was abolished. (Metternich wrote a pamphlet in support of his father and against his enemies in Vienna but it was also an appeal against the revolutionaries.)[35] Metternich had himself been in Belgium in 1793–4, when the opportunity arose to visit England. His 1794 visit there included meetings with the Prince of Wales and all the leading politicians, attendance at the trial of Warren Hastings and visits to parliament to hear debates. Most spectacularly, he was allowed to be the guest of Admiral Howe just before the British fleet set out to win its famous victory of the First of June over the French off Ushant. He described the departure of four hundred ships from Portsmouth as 'the most beautiful sight I have ever seen, I might say, indeed, the most beautiful that human eyes have ever beheld.'[36] Yet if the French lost at Ushant, they were winning in the Rhineland, so that lost too at this time were the Metternich estates. The result was that by November 1794, Metternich and his family found themselves refugees in Vienna. His father was out of favour and out of a job, but Clemens beat off distinguished rivals to win the heart of Princess Eleanor Kaunitz, granddaughter of Maria Theresa's famous chancellor. He became engaged in 1794 aged twenty-one and married in 1795. He was now a young man of greater social importance than his father who, at last, in 1798, was given a minor part to play at the negotiations between the Empire and the French at Rastatt. Here the smaller imperial nobility were betrayed in order to compensate the German princes who had lost territory on the left bank of the Rhine, as agreed by the Treaty of Campo Formio of 1797. Clemens made the best of affairs by seeking compensation for himself and quarrelled with Franz Georg over his father's continued opposition in principle to the mediatisation of estates within the Empire. The younger Metternich hereafter took the view that all states should be centralised and diets pretty much ignored; his father, on the other hand, always supported the traditional rights of diets everywhere.[37] (In 1803, the Metternichs received the Abbey of Ochsenhausen, south of Ulm, as compensation for their much smaller estates on the Mosel; the Emperor also made it a principality, so that Franz Georg now became a prince.)[38]

After the Treaty of Lunéville of 1801, the Emperor Francis invited an apparently reluctant Metternich to enter the diplomatic service and become an ambassador. Metternich chose Dresden for his first position (where he first met the publicist and his future secretary, Gentz) but by 1803 had been transferred to Berlin as ambassador there, where he witnessed the war of 1805–6. Thereafter he was told that he would replace Count Stadion in St Petersburg, as Stadion was being made foreign minister. Napoleon, however, objected to Cobenzl as the new ambassador to France, so Metternich was instructed by Stadion to go to Paris instead, apparently at the request of the French Emperor himself. The greatest chapter in Metternich's career – the contest with Napoleon – had now begun. So let us return to it.

Metternich and Napoleon Again

Metternich was later to describe Napoleon as 'the most marvellous man the world has ever seen',[39] but would also boast: 'I conquered the conqueror of the world.'[40] His duel with Napoleon, as he saw it, was the most significant part of his life's work: everything beforehand was mere preparation; everything afterwards ordinary history.[41] Yet, when he took up his post in Paris in 1806, he had not the faintest idea how Napoleon would be defeated. His speculations over future policy would range from (1806) a conservative alliance of Russia, Austria and Prussia, leaving the entire rest of Western Europe including Spain, Portugal and Italy[42] to the conqueror, to (1807–9) an alliance of France, Austria and Russia aimed at a partition of the Turkish Empire.[43] His greatest fear was that an isolated Austria would be swallowed up into Napoleon's own Empire. Meanwhile, he believed that it would be 'madness' to contemplate another war with Napoleon without the help of Russia, although that is exactly what happened in 1809 with almost all historians believing he approved of it.[44]

In all of these speculations, Metternich moved from certain fixed principles. First, that Napoleon might one day destroy Austria completely; second, that Napoleon's Empire was, however powerful, still something essentially temporary and unnatural and could not outlast his death; third, that if Austrian diplomacy could only appease Napoleon – or even better – ally with him, Austria could survive until the great day of Napoleon's death or defeat, when a true European balance of power could at last be established. Nor was he alone in these thoughts. Many in France who wanted peace to enjoy the gains that war had brought them, he discovered, felt the same. In particular Prince Talleyrand, Napoleon's erstwhile foreign minister, thought so. In fact, the French as a whole were extremely war-weary. But so what? Everything still depended on the will of the French Emperor. All these problems, therefore, the new Austrian ambassador to Paris had to deal with. 'I carry the world on my shoulders,' he wrote to his father as early as 16 September 1806.[45]

As has been indicated, Metternich soon convinced himself that the French were weary of Napoleon. In a report of 15 October 1806, he expressed a view that he would repeat regularly thereafter: 'The whole of France has only one wish, it displays only one demand: to see the plans of its ruler frustrated. News of defeats are greeted as happily here as reports of victories are elsewhere. People believe that defeats are a guarantee for future peace, a counterweight to the ambition of the Emperor.'[46] Indeed: 'Only the extreme use of force by the sovereign could suppress so much repugnance and make possible what a weak government would scarcely dared to have conceived.'[47] So much for the French. The trouble was, as Metternich also felt obliged to report, however:

The insidious activity of the Cabinet of St Cloud no longer recognises any other rival in Europe than Austria . . . [Napoleon] fears our political principles . . . We are assuredly the first of the victims who he believes have to be sacrificed to his insatiable ambition, to his ridiculous system of universal domination; we alone still disturb him in the execution of this plan.[48]

And Talleyrand himself would confess in his memoirs that Napoleon wanted to be Emperor of the French, King of Italy '*as well as head of the House of Austria*' (author's emphasis).[49] As has already been hinted, Metternich had to play a waiting game. Napoleon's Europe was 'contrary to nature and civilisation'.[50] Yet if he could overthrow thrones, Napoleon could not undermine principles, 'which, like reason, are eternal'.[51] The correct policy therefore was to wait for 'the great day'[52] when Austria would play 'the first part in Europe', 'when three hundred thousand men united, ruled by one will and directed towards one end', would efface the traces of the conqueror.[53] Or as he put it slightly later to Stadion:[54] 'We will have won everything if we maintain our independence and territorial integrity, we will have lost nothing if we retain the possibility, one day to throw into the balance the incredible means which foresight has placed in the hands of His Majesty. This day will come! A power like ours must survive the life of a single man.' He had no illusions about the Emperor of the French: 'Napoleon meditates our destruction; he meditates it because our existence is incompatible, as to principles, and as to the extent of our territory, with a universal supremacy . . .'[55]

In the meantime, Metternich was convinced that Austria had to appease, indeed ally with, Napoleon. As early as 21 December 1806 he had warned Stadion: 'we are simply not in the position to risk the integrity of the Monarchy under completely unknown chances of success.'[56] Thus he listened carefully to the advice of Talleyrand who by now believed that Napoleon's ambition was a threat to France and who feared that the Emperor's death would usher in a European war that would reverse all his achievements. Talleyrand had urged a 'pro-Austrian' policy on Napoleon in 1805, telling him:

> Your Majesty can now either break up the Austrian monarchy or set it on its feet again; once it is broken up, however, it will no longer even be in Your Majesty's power to reassemble its broken fragments. The existence of this collectivity of states is essential, nay indispensable, from the point of view of the future of civilisation . . . If the Austrian monarchy were unduly enfeebled in the West, it would no longer be able to maintain its sway over its remaining dominions and the Hungarians . . . might well desert . . . and hand themselves over to the Russians . . . and if the Russians were masters of Hungary, they would be too powerful for the rest of Europe . . .[57]

At the negotiations at Pressburg that year he had reduced the Austrian war indemnity by 10 million francs.[58] Later at Erfurt in 1808, he persuaded Alexander I in secret to ignore Napoleon's demands that he (Napoleon) should have the right to decide when Russia should attack Austria and that only on his decision should the Russians immediately send troops across the Austrian border.[59] Metternich quoted Talleyrand's policy as presented to Alexander I of Russia at Erfurt: 'The Rhine, the Alps and the Pyrenees are the conquests of France. The rest are the conquests of the Emperor of France and we shall not hold them.'[60] But by now, Talleyrand had resigned and was in disgrace, although he still cherished the hope that Napoleon would listen to him.

Metternich, therefore, still tried to please a Napoleon who was always making it known that one day he would choose between Austria and

Russia. One attempt to please the Emperor of the French, for example, involved Austrian mediation between Britain and France to broker a new peace; however, the negotiations fell through.[61] Metternich's favourite scheme was to create an alliance of France, Russia and Austria, so that one day he might win over Russia to a joint attack on France. He believed that in isolation, Napoleon would never allow Austria to survive. He also believed Prussia was finished[62] and that Britain 'was outside this world like the moon'.[63] Nor did he care about a partition of Turkey, if that was the price that had to be paid for a *Dreibund*: 'We cannot save Turkey; therefore we must help in the partition and endeavour to get as good a share of it as possible. We cannot resist the destructive and invasive principles of the Emperor of the French; we must therefore turn them away from ourselves.'[64] So a Russian alliance was vital, especially once Napoleon allied himself to Russia at Tilsit (1807) and Erfurt (1808), when it seemed as if Alexander I and Napoleon would divide the world between them. Vienna, meantime, was wary. It preferred to uphold the integrity of the Ottoman Empire; it insisted on the independence of the Austrian army if a campaign against Turkey actually took place; and likewise it wanted no rectifications of the Austrian border in the aftermath of one. It also became reluctant to make other concessions to Napoleon (e.g. give him the Golden Fleece or recognise the thrones now occupied by his family – especially those of Spain and Naples after 1808). It also did not trust Talleyrand, despite his flattery of Austria and Metternich. Perhaps Talleyrand was simply being used by Napoleon to lure Austria into a sense of false security.[65]

This was important since Stadion in Vienna was planning a war. The French invasion of Spain and Portugal in 1808 not merely diverted Napoleon's attentions from Turkey, but gave rise to all sorts of hopes in Vienna that Napoleon might now be vulnerable to defeat. Perhaps 'the great day of judgement' had arrived. Metternich himself did not foresee the significance of events in Spain. Talleyrand had deliberately misled him and, in any case, Metternich assumed that Napoleon would secure a quick victory.[66] After Spain, Metternich believed Napoleon would fix his attention once more on Turkey, before attacking Russia and then Austria. He would certainly leave no independent dynasties in Europe. This being the case, he reported to Stadion that Austria had to use the time she had until then to reform herself financially and militarily.[67] In the meantime, though, Metternich still hoped that it would be possible to control Napoleon through an alliance with France and Russia. Spain did not *immediately* change anything at all.

In Vienna, however, Metternich's reports were misinterpreted.[68] Stadion and Francis believed that, after Spain, Austria was next on Napoleon's list of conquests. Any invasion of Turkey, therefore, would see Austria treated as Portugal had been – a territory to be picked up on the way to somewhere else. No French troops, therefore, would be allowed to enter Austrian territory on their way east. The very idea of a *Dreibund* was out. Metternich could only counsel peace as he always had done: 'To provoke a war with France would be madness; it must therefore be avoided, but can only be avoided by strong measures.' (1 July 1808);[69] 'I want peace with France because we unconditionally require it' (27 April, 1808);[70] Postponing war would be 'an enormous victory' (25 July 1808)).[71] Paris meanwhile was full of rumours of war and Metternich had to explain to Champagny, the new French foreign minister, that Austria was rearming simply because she could no longer recruit soldiers in Germany and Italy and because other states had gone over to the French system of conscription. She was merely using her first breathing space in almost fifteen years to introduce necessary, but peaceful, military reforms. Amazingly, the French accepted his assurances, since Napoleon did not believe that Austria could go to war without Russia.[72] Meanwhile Stadion warned Metternich: 'We will do everything possible to avoid war, but if it is not to be avoided, it would be better to start it ourselves than to wait for it.'[73]

The position became complicated by French demands that the order of the Golden Fleece be bestowed on Napoleon and that Joseph Bonaparte be recognised as King of Spain. Alexander I of Russia also demanded that Austria should stop rearming and at Erfurt said that if Austria attacked France, Russia would support France. Metternich argued that it was silly to recognise Napoleon himself as Emperor in France but to refuse to recognise his siblings; he simply avoided the issue of the Golden Fleece, telling Talleyrand that it required aristocratic ancestry.[74]

Still, Metternich believed he had prevented war, boasting to his father on 3 September 1808: 'I am completely absorbed by the notion that I alone am the whole of Austria . . . that I have taken all the decisions upon myself . . . Thus we have peace and hopefully we shall have it for a long time. Austria is emerging stronger than ever before from a struggle in which so many other powers have gone under . . .'[75] But he was in for a surprise because, when he returned to Vienna for political consultations between November 1808 and January 1809 during Napoleon's absence in Spain, he discovered that the war party was in control of the court and that preparations for a war in the spring of 1809 were already far advanced in the capital.

Curiously all the leading historians of Metternich, with the exception of Schroeder who believes that Metternich's position was 'not clear' (although he concedes he had been a 'long-time advocate of passive resistance'),[76] portray Metternich as an enthusiastic supporter of war.[77] Kraehe even makes him out to be a supporter of the German mediatised princes who wanted to stir up German national resistance in order to restore the Holy Roman Empire.[78] In fact, Metternich was never a German nationalist, saw Germany, like Italy, as a 'geographical expression' and thought in European terms. It is not even clear whether he approved the plans for war once back in Vienna.[79] However, he did draw up three memoranda, one on the domestic position of France,[80] one on the chances of an Austrian–Russian rapprochement[81] and one on the effects of the Spanish war on Napoleon's military position,[82] all of them including reservations, but showing that he had none the less fallen into line; these memoranda have confused historians.

Metternich argued that Austria was twice as strong as in 1806 and Napoleon half as strong and lacking the support of his people, so that the two sides would be evenly matched in any war, although the French would fight back. A lot of his thinking had clearly been influenced by Talleyrand who, Metternich believed, had to be judged as a 'man of systems'[83] who thought in terms of fixed principles, despite his well-known lack of morals. Stadion, for his part, clearly accepted Metternich's view that Napoleon no longer represented the French people, writing in April 1809: '. . . we must ensure that the will of the nation does not unite with that of the ruler. A war against France will bring this unity, a war against Napoleon, against his external power, will keep his people separate from him as well as several of his own state councillors.'[84] This was to be the strategy of 1813–14. Metternich, however, did not expect that Austria would be backed by Russia, who would probably remain neutral. As for the war in Spain, this, Metternich reckoned, would leave Napoleon with only 200,000 troops for use against Austria, half of which would come from Germany. His reserves would be made up of young, inexperienced recruits, so at first the two sides would be equal. Metternich, however, stressed his incompetence to judge in military matters. He merely assumed the case for war; he did not argue it. In fact, military events more or less confirmed Metternich's predictions – although men and strategy would lose the war. There can be no doubt that while in Vienna, therefore, Metternich submitted to the war party; there was little else he could do. Yet his memoranda merely rationalised this position. They may have misled many into seeing him as a positive proponent of war, but this he was not.

On his return to Paris, Metternich was instructed not to provoke Napoleon, not to talk of war and not to trust Talleyrand. Stadion was worried that Talleyrand was using Metternich; that his position was becoming 'more ambiguous each day'; and that he was 'still far from deserting his master' whom he still wanted to save, although he would no doubt desert him at what he judged to be the right time.[85] Stadion, however, need not have worried. Although Talleyrand was now successfully demanding hundreds of thousands of francs for his help, in return he was sending the Austrians the details of Napoleon's military plans.[86] On 23 March 1809, therefore, Metternich could boast in his report to Vienna that the Archduke Charles must know the French army as well as his own. The figures were sent to Vienna on 27 February 1809 in code through a Russian courier via Dresden. One table listed the details of the Army of the Rhine, another those of the Army of Spain – the first for 3 February, the second for 20 January. At the start of February, there were 90,000 French troops across the Rhine with 160,000 men in reserve in France. On 17 March 1809, Metternich sent Vienna through another Russian courier the positions of all the regiments of the French Empire with their strengths and locations, including those of auxiliary troops from the Confederation of the Rhine.[87] On 23 March he reported: 'I am now making arrangements for keeping in touch with Talleyrand *during the war*';[88] Frankfurt was chosen as the best halfway house.

It is not clear for how long Talleyrand remained a paid agent of Vienna. Certainly after 1809 both he and Metternich worked in concert and in 1810, when war was brewing between France and Russia, he wrote to the Tsar: 'I stand in need of a million and a half francs and it is essential that I should have them by November . . .'[89] He also begged Alexander I 'to burn this letter'. But the Tsar replied that secrecy could not be assured and Talleyrand 'would become the object of universal suspicion' if he paid up. In any case, he would not break his own rules of doing business with foreign powers. He ended: 'It is with regret therefore that I am denying myself the pleasure it will always give me to serve you.'[90] Alexander, of course, kept the letter. Talleyrand, with the approval of Nesselrode, his contact with the Russian court, then asked for a licence for trade between Russia and England, something allowed only exceptionally under the Continental System. It is not known whether it was granted.[91] Napoleon never did discover Talleyrand's high treason. He told the Governor of St Helena: 'I defy anyone to catch me out. Humanity would have to be very corrupt to be as evil as I assume it to be.'[92] But he had underestimated Talleyrand.

As has been seen, the war of 1809 found Austria isolated, deserted by

Germany (save for Hofer's uprising in the Tyrol) despite an appeal for German national solidarity issued in manifestos by Stadion and the Archduke Charles, proclaiming that Austria's cause was Germany's. Russia, however, had promised neutrality in advance. True, the Archduke Charles beat Napoleon at Aspern, but his strategy both before and after the battle was defective and he retired from the army, which was defeated at Wagram. Then came the Treaty of Schönbrunn, the loss of three and a half million subjects and access to the sea. The new Napoleonic kingdoms had to be recognised and Metternich, although now promoted foreign minister, was in an even worse situation regarding Napoleon than in 1806 when he had arrived in Paris. Austria had also been saddled with a war indemnity of 85 million francs and a reduction of her armed forces to 150,000 men. The outlook was bleak.

We have now come full circle and are back to the controversy regarding Metternich's final defeat of Napoleon. From his period as ambassador, however, it should be noted that he had learned not to trust in military success, not to move against Napoleon without Russian aid and to work for a Europe in which there would be a balance of power against Russia and France and in which the powers would have to work together. He knew that Russia could start and withdraw from campaigns at will merely by retreating within her vast frontiers; he knew of Russian ambitions in the east; and he was all too well aware of the vulnerability of the middle powers. A balance of power, therefore, would mean reducing France at least to her natural frontiers and creating an alliance of the German states, although he had no plan to restore the Holy Roman (i.e. German) Empire. The middle states would have to be strengthened – particularly Austria and Prussia – but problems still remained. How could Russia be kept out of Europe? And should Austria retain any geographical contact with France? He certainly thought that Austria should dominate both Italy and the Adriatic, but Austria might be best positioned without common frontiers with either France or Russia.

Metternich's position was saved, his problems solved by the breach between France and Russia and by Napoleon's decision to marry into the Austrian imperial house when the Russian one seemed to reject him. This meant not merely that there would be no joint campaign against Turkey but that the possibility opened up for an alliance against Napoleon. The latter meanwhile deceived himself that Austria would never make war on its Emperor's son-in-law and that in any case it was too weak to risk another military confrontation. He was certainly right to believe that Emperor Francis would now only very reluctantly agree to military measures. However, that made it all the easier for Napoleon to contemplate war against Russia: he would always risk everything on winning his next battle; the French, he believed, would never accept him as their ruler in peacetime; his very legitimacy in his own eyes derived from his military genius. (Metternich ironically believed the opposite. In his view the French valued Napoleon for maintaining law and order at home and were tired of his battles.)

So the contest with Napoleon was renewed, albeit on different terms. This time, Russia and Prussia had to do the fighting first and beg for Austrian support; this time peace terms were defined by Austria before the fighting started; and this time the peace terms were drawn up from a European perspective. And as the war progressed, the basic terms were made public; time and time again Napoleon was given an opportunity to accept them. In fact, the whole debate about Metternich attempting to deceive either Napoleon or his own coalition allies or both appears artificial. No one knew what the fortune of war would bring at any time; no one underestimated Napoleon's military genius; all the powers agreed terms before offering Napoleon any deal; all the powers had their private hopes and fears concerning the final outcome; all subscribed to the manifesto of 1813 which told the French that Napoleon alone was preventing peace on generous terms; while by 1814 all had more or less agreed to the terms of the final settlement in France and Europe. The diplomacy of 1813–14 was so multilateral and public that it simply does not make sense to accuse Metternich – or any other statesman or ruler – of attempting to deceive anyone.

The story therefore is a very straightforward one. The marriage in 1810 between Napoleon and Marie Louise – a proposition that had to come from Napoleon himself – meant that Austria had a breathing space. She also knew that Napoleon was moving away from his alliance with Russia. Even in 1808 at Erfurt, the Tsar had rejected Napoleon's plans regarding Austria and in 1809 had failed to aid his ally. Meanwhile it had become clear that Napoleon was not wanted by Alexander as a brother-in-law. An older sister had been quickly married off to the Duke of Oldenburg, while the hand of a younger sister was declined. Napoleon had then suggested the marriage to Marie Louise of Austria. Other differences also served to undermine relations between the two rulers: in Germany, the Russians disapproved of Napoleon stationing French troops in Prussia and limiting the size of the army there after Prussia's defeat in 1806; in Poland they resented the grant of the Duchy of Warsaw to the King of Saxony and its enlargement in 1809 after the Austrian war – they rightly feared it would be used as a springboard for an attack upon themselves; then in 1810 Napoleon occupied Oldenburg despite the marriage of its duke to the Tsar's sister; finally, there were differences over Turkey and over the Continental System when Alexander I in 1810 relaxed its enforcement in the Baltic ports. In 1810, too, Napoleon had an unofficial conversation with Metternich in which he discussed what might happen if war broke out between France and Russia.[93] What would Austria do? If she allied herself to France, she could regain the Illyrian provinces but lose all of Galicia. If she backed Russia, then she would of course remain neutral and hope for gains afterwards – which would be small.[94] Metternich rejected Napoleon's terms but also rejected an offer from Russia of an alliance. He wanted Austria to have a free hand. He advised Francis to reform and rearm on the assumption that Napoleon would attack Russia in 1812. Austria's policy would be one of 'armed neutrality', which would allow her to make a decisive impact on the final outcome. Count Bellegarde was given the vital task of supervising a necessarily covert rearmament.[95]

Events then turned out as Metternich foresaw. War broke out in 1812 and Napoleon demanded military aid from Austria, in Metternich's words, not as a material reinforcement but 'as a military guarantee of the restraint of the other part of the Austrian army'. Francis agreed to an auxiliary corps of 30,000 men so long as both sides respected Austria's neutrality and territorial inviolability. Both did. Russia wanted Austrian territory closed off as a theatre of war. Hence Metternich could exult in what had happened – all due to the 'strange' and 'fantastic' and 'abnormal' circumstances of 1812.[96] Better still, the abnormal continued. Napoleon was defeated in Russia and out of 600,000 men returned with an army of merely 35,000. The Austrian corps had not been used – it had been made up of the cadres of twenty different regiments and Napoleon had despised it. Metternich explained that since Austria's last defeat she had not been allowed or able to raise proper regiments.[97] In fact, it was now withdrawing to Galicia and would later withdraw to Bohemia to meet and organise the 200,000 men that Bellegarde would send there. The Russians, in turn, moved forward to give the appearance that Austria's frontiers were threatened so that Austria's troops could legitimately remain there out of Napoleon's reach.

With Napoleon's retreat from Moscow, the Prussian army had gone over to the Russians; Prussia in February 1813 had then signed the Treaty of Kalisch with Russia, by which she was promised, in return for her military support, as much territory as she had in 1806 as well as compensation for her Polish territories which would go to Russia.[98] Prussian patriots (who had done nothing in 1805 or 1809 to aid Austria) meanwhile called for Austria, too, to enter the war against France, but Metternich refused. His policy now became one of 'armed mediation'. Austria would offer both sides a just peace on the basis of a balance of power. This was Metternich's greatest contribution to history. At a time when the major powers were all looking to their own interests and territorial expansion, he insisted on forcing them to work within a European framework for the greater good. In Germany this would mean restoring Prussia to her boundaries of 1803 or 1805 and establishing a German Confederation. A restoration of the Holy Roman Empire was ruled out – the German rulers had experienced too much independence – as was a united Germany (Metternich saw Germany as merely a geographical entity, not a national one). France would retain its natural frontiers. If one side did not accept, then Austria would join the other. Bohemia, meanwhile, was turned into an armed camp. The plan was put into action after Napoleon's victories at Lützen and Bautzen in May 1813. At Wurschen on 16 May, the Russians and Prussians had given Austria the terms on which they would negotiate: the restoration of Austria and Prussia to the extent of their territory and population in 1805; the dissolution of the Duchy of Warsaw; the freedom of Holland; the restoration of the Bourbons in Spain; the exclusion of France from Italy; and the dissolution of the Confederation of the Rhine and the cession by France of the annexed North German states. After Napoleon's victory at Bautzen (20 May) and the armistice of Pläswitz (4 June), however, Metternich got them to moderate their terms at Gitsin. The four demands that now became conditions sine qua non were: the dissolution and partition among the allies of the Duchy of Warsaw; the enlargement of Prussia; the return of the Illyrian provinces to Austria; and the freedom of those parts of North Germany annexed by France in 1810. At subsequent negotiations for the Treaty of Reichenbach of 27 June, it was agreed that if Napoleon did not accept the four points by 20 July, then the Wurschen proposals would apply. But would Napoleon agree to armed mediation by Austria? Metternich was summoned to meet him at Dresden on 26 June 1813 when Napoleon harangued him for almost nine hours. Metternich told him that the world needed peace and that he must consent to 'reduce [his] power within bounds compatible with the general tranquillity'.[99] This meant for a start the dissolution of the Duchy of Warsaw, the restoration of Prussia and the Hanseatic towns and the return of the Illyrian provinces to Austria, but all else was negotiable. Napoleon's famous reply was: 'Never. I shall know how to die, but I shall not yield a handbreadth of soil. Your sovereigns, born to the throne, may be beaten twenty times and still go back to their palaces; that I cannot – the child of fortune, my reign will not outlast the day when I have ceased to be strong and therefore to be feared.'[100] He further argued that he had rebuilt his army, that the Emperor Francis would never make war on his own daughter, and that, in any case, Austria could raise no more than 75,000 troops. The French, he insisted, would support him – he had lost only 30,000 Frenchmen in Russia – and he was already winning more battles. Metternich pointed out that his troops were now juveniles – 'mere children' – but Napoleon would not budge. Metternich left telling him 'You are lost, Sire',[101] but was summoned once again and Napoleon now agreed to armed mediation at a conference at Prague from 10 July to 10 August. He even agreed to the Austrian military build-up in Bohemia, to an extension of armistices and to the provisioning of Russian and Prussian troops from Bohemia.

It cannot be stressed strongly enough that Austria at this point definitely preferred peace. Francis I wrote to Metternich:

I have to thank you, chiefly, for the present glorious state of my kingdom. I depend on you in my endeavours to maintain it. Peace, lasting peace, is certainly that which is most longed for by every sensible man, still more by me as the miseries entailed by war fall so heavily on the faithful dependencies and beautiful countries to which I am attached heart and soul.[102]

He continued:

We must strive to attain this end; we have hitherto been in treaty for this; we must now go further. We must not be deceived by momentary advantages or by increase of territory. To avoid, as much as possible, everything which can be derogatory to the honour of the Emperor Napoleon, has already been so much considered that he can hardly have one sensible reason for not accepting.[103]

Capefigue, who before writing his book had several interviews with both Metternich and Pozzo di Borgo, asked them both: 'Was there really a sincere desire for peace at Prague?'[104] The response?

They both answered in the affirmative. Pozzo di Borgo, in his hatred for Napoleon, described to me the anxiety he felt at witnessing the hesitation of Austria; and Metternich justified himself to Europe for the indecision of his conduct by his desire to bring his diplomatic mediation to a happy issue, for the interests of Napoleon, Austria and the general peace.[105]

This is important because the French later believed, in the words of Prince Napoleon on the negotiations of 1813: 'Everything might still have been set right, Austria alone ruined everything – [and] with how much duplicity.'[106]

As it was, Napoleon's credentials for his envoys at Prague never arrived in time. He was the one who had been bluffing, so the war continued, Metternich convincing himself that Napoleon would never agree to negotiations until he had been driven across the Rhine. Thereafter the allies agreed at Teplitz to the restoration of Austria and Prussia to their 1805 strength, the restoration of Hanover, the dissolution of the Confederation of the Rhine leaving a Germany of independent states, the restoration of German territory annexed to France and an amicable dissolution of the Duchy of Warsaw. Nothing specific was said of the freeing of Italy, Holland and Spain from Napoleonic rule, but these were British war aims and, given the Wurschen proposals, clearly there would be no objections to them. One difficulty was that the restoration of Austria to her 1805 strength would mean that she would have to regain territory – Tyrol, Vorarlberg, the Inn District, Brixen, Trent, Salzburg – from Bavaria, the leading member of the Confederation of the Rhine, which was to be dissolved. Yet the allies needed to win over the German states. With the help of the Tsar, who promised to compensate Bavaria, Metternich succeeded, however, in negotiating the generous Treaty of Ried on 8 October, by which Bavaria was promised adequate reconstruction on a suitable scale as a compact state enjoying 'full and entire' sovereignty. In return, Bavaria left the Confederation and promised to accept allied war aims and undertook not to sign a separate peace. She also allowed Austrian armies to enter the Tyrol and to furnish 36,000 troops against Napoleon. Other German states then followed Bavaria's lead. Meanwhile the allies had agreed to contribute 150,000 troops each and not to conclude a separate peace. The supreme command was given to the Austrian Prince Scharzenberg and it was decided that the war should proceed in clear stages with fixed objectives. The first was to reach the Rhine and, with their great victory over Napoleon at Leipzig, (16–19 October) this was soon accomplished. Napoleon was forced across the Rhine and Germany could be mostly cleared of French troops. Perhaps the Emperor of the French would now agree to negotiate?

Metternich arranged to send him the so-called 'Frankfurt proposals' through the captured brother-in-law of the French foreign minister. France could keep her 'natural frontiers' but the German states would be independent, the Bourbons would be restored in Spain and Holland would become independent. There would also be absolutely independent states between France and Austria towards the Italian frontier. No armistice was promised but if Napoleon accepted these bases for negotiation a peace conference could be held on the right bank of the Rhine. Castlereagh was rather critical of these proposals (he would have made further demands and wanted a swifter prosecution of the war) but he was not yet on the Continent. The French reply simply ignored the bases, although it offered a conference. Metternich dismissed it and on 1 December 1813 issued a proclamation to the French people telling them that Napoleon, not the allies, was preventing a generous peace. Meanwhile, happy to hear that Castlereagh wished for post-war guarantees and on being told that Napoleon would only negotiate with the British present, Metternich, with the agreement of the Tsar, sent Pozzo di Borgo (Napoleon's Corsican nemesis) to England to bring Castlereagh to Europe (the British cabinet agreed on 20 December). He also stirred up agitation in Saxony for the restoration of the king there (he had gone over to Napoleon after Bautzen) and made a treaty with Murat, recognising him as King of Naples in return for a contribution of 30,000 troops against Napoleon.

At the start of 1814, some squabbling occurred. Alexander, who had in vain opposed Austrian troops entering Switzerland and who before that had himself wanted to be supreme commander of the allied armies, now made it clear that he preferred Bernadotte, the former French marshal who was now crown prince of Sweden, as candidate for the French throne after Napoleon. This the Austrians would simply never permit. There were also behind-the-scenes negotiations over Poland with Metternich promising Prussia the whole of Saxony, if Prussia promised to oppose Alexander's designs on that country. Then, on 18 January, Castlereagh arrived at allied headquarters. He, like Metternich, agreed that only the Bourbons could replace Napoleon. Yet Castlereagh, on his way to Switzerland, had agreed that Holland should be combined with Belgium in an independent state as well as having made agreements with the House of Orange regarding maritime rights and the Cape of Good Hope. A conference at Langres then brought all the powers together. France would be offered her ancient frontiers with a few adjustments but she would play no part in the wider European settlement. The question of her head of state was left unsettled. As for the rest of Europe, Germany was to be composed of independent, sovereign states linked by 'a federal bond', whatever that meant. A congress to discuss terms with France then opened at Châtillon on 5 February 1814. The Tsar almost scuppered this by announcing that he would prefer to march on Paris instead of negotiating an armistice. But another victory by Napoleon plus Metternich's diplomacy restrained him. Napoleon, it was agreed, could keep his crown (if the French agreed); Britain would restore most of the French colonies; and France would be allowed her ancient frontiers. Napoleon, however, encouraged by military success, withdrew from negotiations, so that the allies were faced with deposing him. Metternich twice got the time limit for negotiations extended (till 18 March) but finally they were broken off. Castlereagh now negotiated the Treaty of Chaumont (19 March 1814), whereby the four powers agreed to contribute 150,000 men each till Napoleon accepted their terms; Britain promised subsidies amounting to £5 million; while, after the war, all four powers would keep armies of 60,000 men in the colours for twenty years to jointly resist any future French attack on their possessions. Secret articles confirmed decisions already made on Germany, Switzerland, Spain, Holland and Italy, while Spain, Portugal, Holland and Sweden were invited to accede to the treaty. There would be no going back on this agreement; a captured letter, dictated by Napoleon on 19 March to Coulaincourt, who had been conducting negotiations with the allies, read: 'The Emperor wants you to remain vague concerning everything respecting the handing over of Anvers, Mayence and Alexandria, if you have been obliged to consent to these cessions, it being his intention, *even if he should have ratified the treaty* [author's italics], to take into consideration the military position of things.'[107] Napoleon's good faith could therefore no longer be accepted, with the result that events moved swiftly on until by 10 May he had abdicated.

Metternich had played the key role (latterly aided by Castlereagh) in holding the allies together and setting the precedents that had enabled them to negotiate as a whole. Indeed, he had acted as the prime minister of the coalition. Yet if he had recognised the need to negotiate with Napoleon right up to the end, so too had all the others. In any case, who else was there to negotiate with? The war went well in the end, but no one beforehand had taken that to be inevitable. Napoleon was still capable of inflicting defeats right up to February 1814. That it was unlikely he would ever compromise to make peace was something everybody knew, not merely Metternich. Hence I repeat the point I made before: the whole argument about Metternich deceiving his allies – or his enemy – is an artificial one. Napoleon himself, quite consciously, openly and consistently, risked total defeat and lost everything. He acted till the end exactly as he had predicted he would in his conversation with Metternich at Dresden in 1813.

By the Treaty of Fontainebleau of 10 April, he was given the island of Elba in full sovereignty, granted an annual income of 2 million francs, while his Empress was given the Parma Duchies, and the rest of his family was provided for. He himself had opposed a regency for his son, as had Francis I of Austria and Metternich. (Only Talleyrand had cherished this hope – gambling that he himself would be de facto regent!)[108] Francis thought the burden would be too great for his grandson; Metternich saw it as a source of instability; besides, only Napoleon had the genius to rule as a Bonaparte; his charisma was not transferable to a child.[109] In the end, therefore, there was simply no alternative to the Bourbons. Metternich was not disposed, as Alexander was, to allowing some convention to be set up to allow the French to choose a ruler. The return of the Bourbons had been agreed.[110]

Hence it was with Louis XVIII that the first Peace of Paris was signed on 30 May. By this France secured her 1792 frontiers. But she had to agree to the free navigation of the Rhine, the independence of Switzerland, a confederated Germany, an augmented Holland, the cession of Italian territories to Austria and the acquisition by Great Britain of Malta, St Lucia and Tobago. Secret articles stated that most of the Austrian Netherlands should go to Holland, that free navigation should be established on the Scheldt and that the left bank of the Rhine should be partitioned between Holland, Prussia and the other German states. But no indemnity was imposed on France, there was to be no army of occupation, and she was allowed to keep Napoleon's looted art treasures. In negotiations in London that followed, it was also agreed that Britain would pay Sweden for Guadeloupe which, although earlier promised to Sweden, had been returned to France. Britain also paid Holland £2 million for the Cape of Good Hope, which sum Holland agreed to spend on barrier forts. By Secret Article 32, the French agreed that a congress would be held within two months at Vienna to complete the work of the treaty and that the French would agree to accept the allied decisions there. Yet given allied diplomacy in wartime plus the agreements reached under the first Peace of Paris, there would really be little to quarrel over at Vienna, save the future of Poland and Germany and the anomaly of Murat's survival in Naples.

And so it turned out. Metternich's agreement that Prussia should get the whole of Saxony was rendered null and void when the King of Prussia agreed to Alexander I's plan for Russia to take the whole of

Poland. The Tsar made it plain that he would fight over this and he did occupy Poland. So the key question for the powers regarding the balance of power in Central Europe then focused on Saxony. Fortunately, Alexander became less interested in it after his success over Poland, but Prussia was determined to take the whole of Saxony and this posed a problem. If this were allowed to happen, then Prussia would dominate Germany and in alliance with Russia would destroy any balance of power in Europe. When Hardenburg then threatened war, Metternich and Castlereagh brought Talleyrand into the negotiations and signed the draft of an alliance against Prussia and Russia on 3 January 1815.[111] Soon after this the Russian–Prussian joint front collapsed and Castlereagh, after rejecting a Russian proposal that the Saxon dynasty be transferred to the Rhineland somewhere, negotiated a compromise settlement. Under this, Prussia received about two-fifths of Saxony's population and about three-fifths of its soil (Leipzig was not included). She also got Thorn in Poland, along with Danzig and Posen. Austria received Galicia and Krakow was made a free city. The rest of Poland went to Russia and Alexander became its king. Inside Germany, Bavaria was rewarded with Wurzburg, Frankfurt and the Palatinate, although Mainz was made a federal fort of the Germanic Confederation and placed under the sovereignty of Hesse. Hanover became a kingdom and was enlarged when she obtained East Frisia from Prussia in return for Lauenberg, which Prussia ceded to Denmark in return for Pomerania and the island of Rügen, which Sweden had given to Denmark in return for Norway. Sweden, having received Norway, could then cede Finland to Russia. The King of Holland received the Duchy of Luxemburg, which was part of the German Confederation and whose fortress was garrisoned by Prussia. Germany was organised into a Confederation of thirty-four sovereign states and four free towns, all enjoying independence and equal rights. Austria was to be president of the Confederation but would run it along with Prussia. Yet it was in Italy that Austria received her main compensation. Already by the Peace of Paris Francis had acquired Lombardy-Venetia, although the details concerning the rest of Italy (save for Genoa/Liguria which was earmarked for Piedmont-Sardinia) had to wait for further negotiations. Murat was a problem because the French demanded the restoration of the Bourbons in Naples. Talleyrand made such a nuisance of himself over this that finally Metternich dealt with Louis XVIII in Paris on the subject behind Talleyrand's back. Fortunately, Murat made things easier by backing Napoleon during the Hundred Days, so that once he had been defeated by the Austrians and fled to Switzerland, Ferdinand of

Naples could be restored. (By a treaty of 12 June 1815, however, Metternich got his agreement not to grant a constitution.) Tuscany and Modena reverted to Habsburg rule, Marie Louise got the Parma Duchies (the reversion being left open for the moment), while the Pope got back the Legations of Ravenna, Bologna and Ferrara, in which Austria retained the right of garrison. Indeed, save for Piedmont-Sardinia and Lucca (which went to Maria Louisa of the Parma branch of the Bourbons), almost all of Italy came under Austrian control. To reinforce the *cordon sanitaire* around France, Nice and Savoy (as well as Genoa) were given to Piedmont-Sardinia, and Switzerland was given new boundaries as well as a guarantee of neutrality from the allied powers plus France. Finally, the Ionian islands were placed under British protection with Austrian and Russian agreement. This showed how little Alexander of Russia really cared about the Greeks.

As a result of Napoleon's escape from Elba and his warm reception by the French, a second Peace of Paris had to be signed with France after Waterloo. This was done on 20 November 1815 and as a result her frontiers were reduced to those of 1790, she had to pay an indemnity of 700,000,000 francs, restore Europe's looted art treasures and suffer an army of occupation in certain areas for five (in fact only three) years. Metternich, Castlereagh and Wellington (even the Tsar) banked on moderation to keep the balance of power. But they also wanted to renew the Treaty of Chaumont. Holland, Prussia and the German states wanted much tougher terms. Talleyrand, for his part, resigned as foreign minister rather than accept the new treaty – to Louis XVIII's relief. The Bourbons were again restored, once again being the only possible choice. On the same day as the Second Treaty of Paris was signed, the four great powers also signed a Treaty of Defensive Alliance. It bound the allies to defend the Treaty of Paris, to repel any return to power in France of Napoleon or his family, and to repel by force any attack on the allied occupation forces. However, Article VI provided for periodical conferences in the future to facilitate the execution of the treaty or to further the peace, prosperity or repose of Europe. The wording was vague, however, and did not prescribe either when or why or how often such conferences should occur. Yet clearly the aim was to continue the kind of diplomatic intimacy that had developed during the latter part of the Napoleonic wars. Entirely missing from this new 'quadruple alliance' too was any general guarantee. People such as Castlereagh and Gentz had previously given thought to this matter, but it was allowed to drop. (Castelreagh probably knew no British government could ever agree to it.)[112] Alexander I's Holy Alliance of 1815, which preached justice, charity and peace and bound its signatories to act as brothers under Christ to bring about the happiness of nations, is sometimes thought of as a general guarantee. But to the rulers of Europe in 1815 it was an embarrassment. Metternich dismissed it as a 'loud-sounding nothing' and Castlereagh as 'a piece of sublime mysticism and nonsense'. It was eventually signed by all the sovereigns of Europe out of politeness, save for the Pope, who could not associate with heretics, the Sultan, who was not a Christian, and the Prince Regent, who had to defer to Parliament.[113] It was referred to later only by radicals who wanted to attack Metternich and other opponents of revolution.

Given Napoleon's return and the subsequent dissatisfaction in France with the peace settlement, Metternich could only hope that enough had been achieved to sustain a balance of power in Europe. France had been given a legitimate dynasty, surrounded by states which had been strengthened by increased territory (Holland and Piedmont) or a guarantee of neutrality (Switzerland), while Germany had been reconstituted as a confederation of independent states which, since it contained both Austria and Prussia, might be thought strong enough to defend Central Europe against France or Russia. (Three-fifths of Saxony survived to balance Prussia.) The trouble was that although the Confederal constitution would provide for federal military contingents and federal fortresses, no federal army was to come into being until war was declared. Austria herself completely dominated Italy, while both Britain and Russia had signed up to a twenty year defensive alliance against any French breach of the treaties. Under these circumstances, Metternich could surely have believed that he had succeeded. Moreover, he had removed Austria from direct geographical contact with France and given her a potentially far easier task of coexisting with the German states than had been the case with the Holy Roman Empire. Some conservative critics, of course, believed that he had potentially allowed Prussia to take the lead in standing up for Germany against France by placing her on the Rhine; liberal critics everywhere, on the other hand, accused him of selling out the small powers to strengthen the great ones – all in the name of the balance of power. Sir James Mackintosh, for example, a critic of Castlereagh, noting that Genoa had not been restored (other critics deplored the fate of Norway, Finland and Belgium, not to mention various German and Italian states), declared:

To destroy independent nations in order to strengthen the balance of power, is the most extravagant sacrifice of the end to the means . . .

In the new system small states are annihilated by a combination of
the great . . . The Congress of Vienna seems indeed to have adopted
every part of the French system, except that they have transferred the
dictatorship of Europe from an individual to a triumvirate.[114]

In like fashion, the young Marquess of Salisbury would condemn 'the
vicious system adopted at Vienna of parcelling out the populations of
Europe like herds of cattle among the various royal litigants who
claimed to own them.'[115] Gentz agreed: 'the real purpopse of the
Congress was to divide amongst the conquerors the spoils taken from
the vanquished,' he wrote, adding that all other phrases were 'uttered
to tranquillise the people and give an air of dignity and grandeur to this
solemn assembly.'[116] Indeed, most people at the time regarded the
results of the congress as a cynical carve-up of Europe by, and in the
interests of, the great powers. As a leading French historian later wrote:
'. . . the Treaties of Vienna were regarded by contemporaries as products
of the Ancien Régime . . . they took account only of the facts of power,
and divided peoples into lots, like an inheritance. The 1815 treaties
ignored the moral forces which first the French Revolution and then
Romanticism had unleashed in Europe.'[117] Historians today, however,
seem interested in different aspects of the settlement. Paul Schroeder in
particular has recently argued that the Congress represented a revolution in international relations in that it saw the powers more interested
in principles than in power.[118] This is a view that would have aston-
ished contemporaries, but will have to be discussed to determine
Metternich's role in international affairs. Hence before discussing
Metternich's policies between 1815 and 1848 and looking at how the
international state system really operated during this period,
Schroeder's new paradigm will have to be examined.

Paul Schroeder's Revisionist Paradigm of International Relations during the Metternich Period

The idea that the nineteenth century diplomatic system rested on generally accepted notions of a balance of power has been challenged by the
American historian Paul Schroeder who, in a series of articles on the
nineteenth century state system and in his latest magnum opus, *The
Transformation of European Politics, 1763–1848*, has put forward an alternative view.[119] This asserts first, that there was no balance of power
established in 1815 but a hegemony of Britain and Russia. Of the Vienna
Settlement he writes: 'Its essential power relations were hegemonic not

balanced and a hegemonic distribution of power, along with other factors, made the *system*[120] work.'[121] A true balance, in Schroeder's mind, would have involved French control over West Germany, Italy and Spain. But Napoleon threw away the chance of establishing this. He continues: 'Thus Britain and Russia were so powerful and invulnerable that even a (highly unlikely) alliance of the three powers against them would not seriously threaten the basic security of either, while such a (hypothetical) alliance would likewise not give France, Austria or Prussia security comparable to that which Britain and Russia enjoyed on their own.'[122] And for good measure he adds: 'Even when Russia and Britain were not in alliance, no combination of other states could coerce or control them.'[123]

Schroeder's argument is more complicated still. As opposed to historians like myself who do talk in terms of a balance of power in 1815, he insists that what was established was an 'equilibrium'[124]. This he defines more as a 'moral and legal term'[125] rather than a political one. In his words, the European equilibrium established in 1815 refers to 'a condition of international stability, peace, respect for rights and law, the preservation of order, the suspension of international affairs and legitimisation of change through the Concert of Europe.'[126] The whole system was now based on a mutual recognition of norms, rules, respect for law, rights and duties, status, securities, claims and satisfactions, rather than on power. There was also a system of sub-hegemonies, but like the hegemonies of Britain and Russia these were benign, not predatory. In fact, power relations, according to Schroeder, seem to have disappeared. He writes: 'the statesmen of Vienna were remarkably sensitive to the problem of small-power independence and security'[127]; Talleyrand's concern for legitimacy was sincere and widely shared;[128] while 'France after 1815, though still an object of suspicion, was Britain's normal partner in European affairs, to be restrained through watchful partnership'.[129] In Schroeder's view, therefore, 1815 brought about '*systemic* change',[130] so that power relations in Europe became determined by two hegemonic states working within a new, more moral equilibrium based on a concern for rights and working through a system of sub-hegemonies or 'intermediate bodies'.[131] He doubts whether there was an agrarian or industrial revolution at the turn of the eighteenth and nineteenth centuries, but he is sure that there was one in international relations.

Before examining Schroeder's work, let me stress one point. Schroeder is at great pains to insist that his arguments are not merely about semantics. Quote: 'I am not here twisting the language and meaning of the time to fit a particular theory, as some may think. It is rather the proponents of the balance of power view, especially British and American ones, who do this, undoubtedly unwittingly, when they routinely render such terms as *équilibre européen* or *politisches Gleichgewicht* into English as "balance of power".'[132] Or again:

> One should not expect too much precision and consistency in the use of political terminology, of course, especially with a term like 'balance of power'. None the less, to describe an international system like that of 1815, in which such great disparities existed between the major actors (to say nothing of the many lesser ones) in terms of raw power, alliance capability, security, influence and opportunities and freedom of action as one of a 'balance of power' is to block understanding and scholarly progress rather than advance it.[133]

How then are we to judge Professor Schroeder's new contributions to diplomatic history? My own view is that, like many of his past contributions, they are highly interesting, but deeply flawed. There are many objections to be considered, but first of all allow me to mention those raised by eighteenth-century specialists, who argue that that century was not nearly as awful or anarchical as Schroeder would imply. Hamish Scott, for example, has pointed out that there was little difference diplomatically between carving up the Empire of Charles XII in the eighteenth century and that of Napoleon in the nineteenth. He adds that if the eighteenth century saw the partitions of Poland, so too did the Congress of Vienna.[134] Both Scott and Charles Ingrao,[135] the American historian, stress the overriding importance of dynasticism in eighteenth-century Europe and question whether wars of succession can therefore really be seen as frivolous or arbitrary. Poland, by the way, should be seen as a special case; it had an elective monarchy and a weak internal system of government. This unique combination of circumstances – not the European state system – invited trouble. Both historians point out that wars in any case were very limited in scope as eighteenth-century rulers were loath to risk their troops in battle – a point which Schroeder has now accepted. Finally, Ingrao rejects the overall charge that the eighteenth-century balance was less in equilibrium than that of the nineteenth century. Schroeder, he argues, fails to allow for the rise and fall of powers within the system and the need of the eighteenth-century diplomacy to accommodate the rise of Prussia and Russia as great powers simultaneously. After all, one might add, the nineteenth century had to accommodate the unification of Germany

and the twentieth century the intrusion of the USA, both accommoda-
tions arising out of wars. Yet Ingrao also believes that Schroeder ignores
much of what actually characterised the eighteenth century:

> We should not let Schroeder's understandable focus on eastern
> Europe divert us from appreciating the stability that obtained in the
> western half of the continent. The book treats most of Europe – the
> Iberian, Italian, and Scandinavian peninsulas, the Low Countries, as
> well as the territorial masses of all the great powers except Austria –
> with benign neglect, because in all of those regions the great powers
> readily accepted the *status quo* that was supported by indisputably
> legitimate borders and effective means of deterrence . . . Schroeder's
> negative assessment of the Habsburg–Bourbon alliance, which
> 'worked to sustain the European system while doing nothing for the
> power or security of the two partners' (p. 42) minimizes its tremen-
> dous achievement in stabilizing the entire western half of the conti-
> nent, while freeing both parties to pursue goals elsewhere. While the
> alliance permitted Austria to focus on its threatened eastern buffers,
> it ended any chance that France could be invaded by Britain's long-
> term Austrian surrogate.[136]

So much then for the eighteenth century. Let me now turn my attention to the long nineteenth, that is the period 1815–1914. Here there
are many objections to Schroeder's latest contributions. For a start,
there was nothing really different about nineteenth-century diplomacy.
The period 1814–15, which Schroeder characterises as the birth of the
new, moral equilibrium, was dominated by the Polish–Saxon dispute
which, as Enno Kraehe has pointed out, was resolved by a classical
resort to balance of power politics.[137] Both Russia and Prussia, one will
recall, were preparing to deprive the King of Saxony of his throne
during a repartition of Poland, when the joint opposition of Britain,
France and Austria prevented this. The King of Saxony, of course, still
lost much of his territories, showing just how *insensitive* the great
powers were to the claims of small powers, legitimacy, law, custom or
anything else. The Congress of Vienna, after all, paid scant attention to
the claims of many small states: the German imperial knights and
princes were ignored, the Pope's rights were hardly fully restored,
Norway was transferred to Sweden and Belgium to Holland. Everyone at
the time regarded – and rightly regarded – the settlement as a carve-up
of Europe in the interests of the great powers. If Talleyrand invoked the
principle of legitimacy, it was merely to strengthen the case for the

Bourbons, whose own rights and claim to be restored could not even be taken for granted. Schroeder is one of the few historians to take Tallyrand's propaganda seriously.

His treatment of the Metternich period as a whole is also unacceptable. What are we to make of statements like the following?

> Deterrence under the Vienna system took the form of moral and legal pressure, the threat that reckless or unlawful behaviour would cost the offending state its status and voice within the system leading to its isolation from it and the attendant loss of systemic rewards and benefits. This kind of deterrence was highly effective. It helped keep Russia from going to war with the Ottoman Empire in 1821–3, France from trying to exploit the Belgian revolution of 1830–2, Austria and Italy [*sic* – I presume he means France] from clashing over Italy, France from sabre-rattling its way into war in 1840 and everyone from generally upsetting the peace.[138]

This is nonsense. Schroeder totally overlooks the fact that the real reason why Russia held back in 1821–3 was opposition to revolution, that Britain threatened war with France over Belgium, that France sent an army to Ancona in Italy in 1832, that Thiers had to be sacked as prime minister in 1840 for threatening European war and that Britain almost went to war with France on several occasions between 1830 and 1848. Far from there being a 'benign partnership' between the two nations during this period, there was a very real possibility of war over Belgium, Spain, Morocco and even Tahiti. Lord Aberdeen believed that only his close friendship with Guizot actually prevented one between 1841 and 1846, while Palmerston was hardly worried by the thought. In 1838 he wrote:

> My doctrine is that we should reckon upon ourselves; pursue a policy of our own; aim at objects of our own, and act upon principles of our own; use other governments as we can, when we want them and finding them willing to serve us; but never place ourselves in the wake of any of them. Lead when and where we can; but never follow.[139]

In 1843 he wrote:

> If you teach them (i.e. foreign governments) that war induces you to cession there is no doubt they will go to war. The true policy therefore is to teach them that you will not gratify passion so pursued; that you know there is no economy in cession and that it is wiser and

more to your interest to continue even expensive wars than by unwise and foolish concessions to purchase a temporary peace neither safe nor honourable.[140]

Under his instruction the *Chronicle* wrote: 'We shall not be deterred from insisting on the necessity of showing spirit in foreign affairs by the common outcry that an independent tone leads to war or that we are a war party.'[141] Even Peel was declaring in 1845: 'Let us prepare for war . . . They [the French] are much more likely to presume upon our weakness than to take offence at our strength.'[142]

Occasionally, Schroeder writes as if he were Alexander I promoting the Holy Alliance. But that was ridiculed by everyone as a loud-sounding nothing. Statesmen did not want a general guarantee. They wanted a balance of power and said so quite clearly – and that is what they got. Far from cooperating in the way Schroeder claims, even the so-called Congress System broke down under the pressure of divergent national interests. Britain – even under Castlereagh – objected to jointly supervising the affairs of Europe. His famous State Paper of 1820 now reads like a rebuke to Schroeder as much as to the Tsar or Metternich. The Quadruple Alliance, he stressed, had been established to liberate Europe from the French. 'It never was, however, intended as a Union for the Government of the World or for the Superintendence of the internal affairs of other states.'[143] Nobody at the time – and nobody since save for the recent exception of Schroeder – has ever believed that cooperation between the powers after 1815 was aimed at justice, peace or anything else but the suppression of revolution, which they seriously believed was directed centrally in Europe by an executive committee of professional revolutionaries based in Paris, plus the protection of their own positions. Thus Austria ensured that her armies alone suppressed the Italian revolts, kept German policy strictly within the confines of the *Bund*, and opposed unilateral French or Russian action in Spain; Russia ignored Austria with regard to the Near East; and France ignored all the others – including the British – when she invaded Spain in 1823. There is little evidence here of any new spirit of cooperation.

Schroeder, I fear, gets almost everything wrong. This is true both of his hegemonic balance and his 'sub-hegemonies' or 'intermediary bodies'. I cannot accept his protestations about semantics either. He is really only playing around – and not very usefully – with words. What in the end he is talking about is simply old-fashioned balance of power politics and spheres of influence. His new vocabulary is merely confusing since it does not fit the facts. Sub-hegemonies were not benign to those involved, nor did they create cooperation between the powers. On the contrary, they very often created serious risks of wars. This was true of Belgium throughout the 1830s and early 1840s, of Spain right up to 1846, of Switzerland in 1847 and of the Near East between 1830 and 1841. Spheres of influence were where the powers clashed, not where they cooperated. Previously, Schroeder had suggested that Austria herself should be regarded as some sort of intermediary body. But since my book on *The Decline and Fall of the Habsburg Empire, 1815–1848*,[144] in which I pointed out that Austria had threatened war in 1830, 1854, 1878, 1887 and 1912–13, he has recanted and now apparently agrees with my point of view.[145]

With regard to the hegemonic balance Schroeder describes, once again I think he is confused. The two hegemons were perhaps invulnerable in their own spheres – the high seas or Asia – but that is hardly the point. Inside Europe, they were vulnerable and felt vulnerable. Britain may have acquired a world empire, but in the words of M. S. Anderson:

> Yet Britain had neither the desire nor the ability to dominate the states of continental Europe. Her army was small and not very efficient. Dislike of European entanglements was strong among her people and became if anything stronger during much of the following century. Except in one or two strategically important areas – the Low Countries, the Straits, the Iberian peninsula – her interest in European complications was often tepid.[146]

Fear of 'Asiatic' Russia, may have been more rational, but Russian technological and administrative backwardness, in fact, offset many of the advantages – including military ones – that she was supposed to possess.[147] Thus she was to be humiliated by the Crimean War, when she was defeated mainly by the French. Nor could Palmerston get his way over continuing the war in Europe. Britain, in fact, was unable to control events in Europe. She could not prevent France from overrunning Spain in 1823 – a considerable humiliation in fact for the power which had won the Peninsular War and insisted that the Quadruple Alliance had been specifically designed to counter French aggression. Nor could Britain prevent the annexation of Krakow in 1846 (when even Metternich agreed to break the 1815 Treaties) or could have prevented the triumph of the *Sonderbund* in 1847 had Austria and France been able jointly to intervene in the Swiss civil war as both Metternich and Guizot desired. France, again, was able to humiliate

Britain over the affair of the Spanish Marriages and obviously did not feel very cowed by the thought of war in the 1840s. It was only the thought of war against all the powers combined that brought Thiers's dismissal as prime minister. And although France was re-admitted into the so-called Concert, nobody at the time acted as if there were a benign hegemonic equilibrium instead of a balance of power at work.

Schroeder's model, finally, is undermined by the emergence of Napoleon III and Bismarck as key players in the diplomatic game. If his hypothesis were to hold good, Napoleon III's France should never have emerged and certainly the unification of Germany should never have taken place. Despite the breakdown in Austrian–Russian relations, Schroeder's two hegemons should have protected their interests and prevented such outcomes. Likewise, his claim that these two powers were invulnerable to the combined attack of all the others seems a little lame. Germany, after all, was able to fend off Britain, Russia and France in combination aided by other states for four years between 1914 and 1918. I realise that Schroeder would like to limit the debate to the period 1815–1848, but his description of this dual hegemony in no way explains why it should collapse simply because Austria became isolated after 1856. His belief, after all, is that the 1848 Revolutions merely confirmed the dual hegemony. The truth seems to be that Russia and Britain were simply ordinary members of the European balance.

Schroeder's view of the nineteenth century omits many things – the growing force of public opinion, the relationship between domestic and foreign policy, cabinet government and economic factors. It also deliberately ignores the fact that 'the balance of power' had no objective meaning.[148] Every state had a different assessment of what its own best interests were and how these interests related to other states. Moreover, politicians and rulers within each state found it impossible to agree on how to interpret the national interests of their own state, far less find agreement on what constituted a reasonable balance of interests for Europe as a whole. Nor did they differentiate between equilibrium and balance. Frederick the Great of Prussia, for example, wrote of the need 'to put the balance back in its correct equilibrium'.[149] All he meant was there was a need to get the balance right as he saw it. Schroeder's fine distinction would have been incomprehensible to him. However, the point which I would like to stress is the persistent efforts by historians like Schroeder to over-systematise the past. States in Europe had to co-exist. They could not do so anarchically, but very rarely did they do so systematically. The word 'system' in the phrase 'European state system' should therefore not be taken too literally.

Metternich himself denied that there was anything such as a 'Metternich System' and he was right to do so. Professional diplomats have always been well aware how easily policies can change. In the words of one eighteenth-century practitioner:

> Algiers being an arbitrary state, is apt like all others of that kind to change its views and politics with new princes . . . no peace made with an arbitrary prince can be depended on in the reign of his successor unless that successor ratify and renew it, because the peace depending on a single will and faith of the prince who entered into it cannot bind the arbitrary will of his successor.[150]

New rulers, particularly absolute ones, were always unpredictable. Napoleon III is a good example. Having won his throne, he set about starting a war with Russia over an issue where there were no French *national* interests involved; he then set about creating a united Italy on France's doorstep, again in contravention of French national interests; finally, he encouraged Bismarck to go to war with Austria, once again undermining French national interests, before allowing a war with Prussia for which he knew France to be unprepared. Henry Kissinger recounts all this with growing disbelief. He concludes: 'Napoleon never had a single line of policy to guide him. Instead, he was driven by a web of objectives, some of them quite contradictory. When he confronted the crucial test of his career, the various impulses cancelled each other out.'[151] My question is simply this: how can such developments be accounted for by reference to any system?

Nor is the problem limited to absolute monarchs. British parliaments cannot bind their successors either. So how did Britain fit into the European state system in the nineteenth century? This is not an easy question to answer, as the previous quote from M. S. Anderson indicates. According to the British historian, Keith Wilson, for example, 'there was no consensus as to what different British foreign policy should be and that if different governments and different ministers had been responsible for it, it would have been quite other than it was.'[152] He adds: 'Resignations of Ministers or threats of resignations on matters of foreign policy were not uncommon . . . They were not simply over means but ends as well. *What* British interests actually were, never mind what they required, was a matter of opinion.'[153] It was difficult to forecast therefore at any given moment of the nineteenth century what British foreign policy was likely to be. Other factors, however, meant that it was unlikely to be very active, especially as far as Europe was concerned. Britain, as I shall now attempt to demonstrate, seemed hardly part of the European state system at all.

One reason for this was her military and naval weakness. This elicited statements from ministers such as 'I am not prepared to be responsible for sending an expedition abroad'[154] (Cardwell, minister of war, in 1870). Palmerston in 1846 said: 'Ships sailing on the sea cannot stop armies on land.'[155] Salisbury in 1871 told the House of Lords that Britain had only 100,000 men at most and that although her navy *might* prevent an invasion, it was 'almost valueless for any other purpose'.[156] In 1887 he had no idea why Bismarck 'even thinks us worth conciliating' and, as for Austria, he asked: 'What use should we be of, in repelling any army who came across the Carpathians?'[157]

Two other factors made British intervention in the affairs of continental Europe improbable. First, she had other priorities across the globe; secondly, constitutional considerations often made this impossible. In the first instance, Disraeli explained in 1866: 'England is no longer a mere European power but the centre of a great maritime Empire . . . she really is more an Asiatic power than a European.'[158] It was North American difficulties, in fact, in the 1860s that restrained her from continental commitments, but Disraeli's general point held true. Britain had a world empire and did not concern herself exclusively or often even primarily with European affairs. With regard to domestic, often constitutional, objections to European involvements, the main problem was the belief that Britain should refrain from any commitments – especially alliances – which threatened to restrict her freedom of action. A number of grounds were given for this: government reliance on a small parliamentary majority or a coalition for support; internal divisions on domestic affairs; the inability of one parliament to bind a successor. Over and above all these was the belief of the Manchester School that intervention in foreign affairs was in principle almost always wrong. Other people should be left to determine their own affairs and Britain's role should be restricted to negotiating free trade treaties, disarmament or arbitrations. Cobden's most famous toast, after all, was 'no foreign politics.'[159] Most British governments were not so modest; however, if they eschewed quite so clean hands, they did prefer free ones.

So, to conclude this discussion of Schroeder's reinterpretation of the framework of European diplomacy between 1815 and 1848, we can assert fairly confidently that he is comprehensively mistaken.

3
Was Metternich Europe's Leading Statesman in the Period 1815–48?

The discussion of Schroeder's views has taken us past Metternich's period in power. Yet this was necessary in order to demonstrate their weaknesses. Let us now return, however, to Metternich and the period 1815–48. Here it is often argued that Metternich's domination of European diplomacy, while brilliant up till 1823, thereafter suffered setbacks until he was eventually sidelined altogether.[1] Indeed, even Austria's geopolitical position as negotiated at Vienna, it has been suggested, left much to be desired.[2] Should she not have worked for a Bonapartist regency for Francis's grandson? Why did she allow Prussia to have her Rhineland provinces? Why did she agree to take back Lombardy and the Illyrian territories? Why did she not demand Alsace? Yet these criticisms are not difficult to refute. A Bonapartist regency would have meant continuous instability in France and regular international crises, especially as long as Napoleon was alive. The alternative to putting Prussia in the Rhineland was to give it to Saxony or Bavaria, either of which might have become a French satellite; besides, where then was Prussia to be compensated? Why not take Alsace rather than Lombardy or the Illyrian provinces? The explanation is, of course, that Metternich – unlike his later critics – was not a German nationalist. Besides he did not want Austria to have territories contiguous with France. Hence his relinquishment of Belgium. He thought that the peace of Europe would be safer if the two powers were geographically separated. Besides, he hoped that the German Confederation would be strong enough to hold the balance in central Europe. (Castlereagh agreed with him, boasting 'A better defence has been provided for Germany than has existed at any former period of her history.')[3] As for Lombardy, it meant that Austria would dominate Italy and keep

Jacobinism out of the peninsula. He was happy to strengthen Piedmont with Nice and Savoy, but more territory for her would only have encouraged Italian nationalism there; besides it would have cut off Austria from the Habsburg Duchies in Italy and weakened her influence in the rest of the peninsula. As for Illyria, its return meant the return of traditionally loyal Habsburg subjects, not to mention further access to the sea. There was one real problem, however, that rarely gets mentioned – the fact that with Russia in possession of most of Poland, Austria's northern border (Galicia, Hungary and Transylvania) lay wide open to attack.[4] Yet the Tsar had made it perfectly clear that he would go to war rather than negotiate over Poland. And, after all, he had 200,000 men there. So Austria and Prussia were lucky to receive parts of Poland at all. To the Russians, Poland was non-negotiable. As the Russian diplomat Meyendorff explained it:

> Poland as understood by the Poles extends to the mouth of the Vistula and Duna, as well as to the Dnieper at Kiev and Smolensk. Such a Poland enters Russia like a wedge, destroys her political and geographical unity, throws her back into Asia, puts her back two hundred years. To prevent the establishment of such a Poland, every Russian will take up arms as in 1812 and fight without counting the number of his foes.[5]

Metternich's only policy, therefore, was to ensure that he maintained good relations with Russia. So much then for the Vienna Settlement as it affected Austria.

With respect to the period 1815–48, Metternich can also be defended. Clearly he did not always control events as well as he did between 1815 and 1823 but, once again, neither did the other powers. If Austria was dismayed by the French invasion of Spain in 1823, Britain was much more affronted. Her liberal principles as well as her whole record in the Peninsular War appeared to have been overthrown. Again, if Austria was humiliated by Russian policy during the Greek War of Independence, it was only very late in the day that Russia gave any real support to the Greeks and in the end Austria was happy to sign up to Greek independence as part of a European deal that did not leave Greece as a protectorate of the Tsar. Finally, if she was unable to provide the most troops against France in either the war scare of 1830 or that of 1840, she was not the only power during this period to find herself over-stretched or under-resourced during an emergency. Russia had to deal with Poland, just as Austria had to deal with Italy in 1830. In 1823,

Britain had no army to send to Spain. In 1833, Britain had no ships to send to Turkey. Russia found herself in military difficulties in 1828 against Turkey and in financial ones when faced with war in the near East in 1840. Thiers, for all his military bluster in 1840, kept having to argue with Louis Philippe that he only needed another six months or so before he would have sufficient troops to take on Europe. Nor indeed in 1836 had he been able to convince the king that France had sufficient resources to invade Spain again, just as de Broglie had concluded in 1835 that France could not risk a new military intervention in Spain which might possibly lead to a simultaneous war with the Eastern powers. Finally, when after the war scare of 1840 a federal military commission was eventually established to inspect the troops available to the German Confederation, it was the Prussian ones which were criticised (whereas it had been the Prussians in 1830 who had been rude about the Austrian army).[6] Taking the period as a whole, Austria remained at peace with the powers, none of whom threatened her existence, two of whom were allied with her for the whole period, and one of whom (Russia) after 1833 even promised to protect her mentally-retarded future Emperor. During the whole period every power in Europe backed the views of the Russian, Nesselrode, who wrote in 1848 of the Monarchy: 'The void which its disappearance would create would be so enormous and the difficulty of filling it so great, that it ought to continue for a long time yet, given the lack of anything which could be put in its place.'[7]

There were, it is true, two so-called 'liberal powers' in Europe after 1830, but they, too, wished to keep the Habsburg Empire as an essential part of the European balance of power as was shown in 1848. (Indeed, the 1829 Polignac Memorandum (see below) offered Austria new territory.) Moreover, if Canning prevented Spain from re-conquering her Spanish American colonies, did Metternich really have to care very much? (He was happy enough to recognise monarchist Brazil.) And if Palmerston triumphed in London in 1831 over Belgium and in 1841 over the Straits, the results on neither occasion undermined the European peace or aided France. In fact, if we look at the diplomatic system that operated between 1815 and 1848, it may become clear that it operated along lines which Metternich for the most part approved of. So while, he at times despaired – 'Nobody wants to listen to me. I am in the midst of chaos, like a man who at the approach of the flood finds himself alone on a desert island'[8] – as late as 1847 he could boast that the whole of Europe was on his side and against Palmerston's England:

Abandoned by France and defeated on every diplomatic field, England now finds herself alone and paralysed in face of the continental Powers. All her resources are inadequate for the purposes of her government, since she cannot make war for any of the ends which she pursues. She did not dare do it when she had France on her side and could count upon allies in every European country. Today if she threw down the gauntlet to anyone, she would force France to take sides; and there is no doubt as to which side France would take.[9]

Was this really the voice of someone who had been sidelined? Had Palmerston really taken over the diplomatic leadership of Europe? How great were the differences between the two men in any case? Perhaps the confusion in the secondary literature should be dispelled.

The powers which Metternich had to deal with after 1815 were Russia, Prussia, Britain and France. Two of these – Russia and France – were thought potentially to pose enormous threats to Europe's balance of power. France, of course, had been at war with her European neighbours for almost quarter of a century and had proved extremely difficult to defeat. She would show enormous powers of recovery, would soon pay off her war indemnity, and soon became the only great power with both a large army and a large navy. Britain – easily the world's greatest naval power – would worry about French naval strategists (the so-called *jeune école*) who saw the coming of steam power as a way in which to catch up with perfidious Albion on the oceans. As well as an efficient system of raising troops, France also had an effective one of raising taxes, although industrially she remained some way behind Great Britain.[10] (By 1850 she had only half the mileage of railway track of the German states and a quarter of Great Britain's; by 1842 only 41 of her blast furnaces were using coke.)[11] She was also regarded as an unstable power. The assassination of the Duke of Berri in 1820, the revolution in 1830, the domestic unrest for much of the 1830s, the assassination attempts on Louis Phillipe, not to mention the alleged existence in Paris of a revolutionary committee directing all of Europe's terrorists, all served to confirm this. Nicholas I of Russia, for example, in the words of one of his ambassadors, believed that France was simply 'not a regular power on which one can rely'[12] – this in 1839, 'even before the European war scare of 1840'. Instead, he agreed with Metternich that 'all the efforts of the French government are persistently directed at weakening foreign governments.'[13] The main problem was that France bitterly resented the terms of the Vienna Settlement, thought that the powers wanted to discriminate against her perpetually, was jealous of the increases in territory that they had all acquired in 1815, and wanted to regain her 'natural frontiers' – Belgium, Nice and Savoy, and the left bank of the Rhine. Talleyrand, it will be remembered, had refused to accept the second Treaty of Paris and the restored Bourbons had agreed to it merely out of impotence. In fact, Louis XVIII had been dethroned in 1814 by the French, who even after all of Napoleon's wars and millions of dead, still preferred to fight for national honour and to regain the natural frontiers rather than support the Bourbons. The latter, therefore, would always be willing to go to war in order to win domestic popularity – hence the 1823 invasion of Spain, the sending of French troops to the Morea after Navarino to clear out Ibrahim Pasha's Egyptian troops, and the expedition to Algiers in 1830. War, it was agreed, would bring prestige and therefore domestic popularity and tranquillity. In 1821, Richelieu and his advisers in the French foreign office contemplated launching a European war in alliance with Russia over Turkey in order to gain the natural frontiers.[14] Charles X speculated in 1829 that 'perhaps a war against the court of Vienna would be useful to me, in that it would put an end to internal wrangling and bring the nation to act together as it desires.'[15] That was the year that the French foreign office, now under General Baron de Richemont, again began drawing up plans for a re-division of Europe with the aid of the Tsar after his defeat of Turkey. Two plans were conceived, according to which Britain could get Holland, Austria the Balkans, Russia the Straits, Prussia Hanover and Saxony, while France could get either Belgium or the Rhineland. A so-called 'Polignac memorandum' was even transmitted to Nicholas I – but he simply ignored it. However, as, Bullen comments, 'war was the logical outcome of [the] plan.'[16] In 1830, Louis Philippe made himself unpopular by refusing to make his son King of Belgium and rejecting aid to Poland. His eldest son, the Duke of Orleans told him that the more unpopular he was in Europe, the more popular he would be in France. For his own part, the Duke said that he 'would rather be killed on the Rhine than in the Paris gutter'.[17] So Louis Philippe knew all about the pressures for war. The main reason why he refused to extend the franchise, it has been well argued, was that he knew this would only lead to more pressure for wars.[18] Louis Philippe was not stupid. He also knew that war was the rallying cry of the left. Thiers, after all, had written in 1830: 'If peace prevails, the moderate system may prevail . . . If war prevails, we shall go over to the extreme Left.'[19] The main point to note, however, is that France remained under both her monarchies between 1815 and 1848 a menacingly revisionist and potentially revolutionary state which wanted to overthrow the European balance of power. Even the pacifistic Louis Philippe in 1840 could shout at foreign ambassadors: 'This time, do not believe that I shall go against my government and my country; you want war, you shall have it, and if necessary I shall unleash the tiger. [i.e. revolution]'[20] He had complained to Thiers of the other European powers: 'They owe the peace of Europe and the security of their thrones to me, and this is their gratitude!'[21]

The other power that deeply worried European statesmen in the first half of the nineteenth century was Russia. Her victory over Napoleon in 1812, her march on Paris and her occupation of Poland all seemed to prove that she was invincible. Events, moreover, seemed to confirm this as Russia chalked up the Convention of Akkerman (1826), the Treaty of Adrianople (1829), the Treaty of Unkiar Skelessi (1833) and the Straits Convention of 1841. Gentz himself had written in 1818 of the Tsar: 'He is the head of the one standing army really capable of action in Europe today. Nothing could resist the first assault of that army . . . none of the obstacles that restrain and thwart the other sovereigns . . . exist for the Emperor of Russia. What he dreams of at night he can carry out in the morning.'[22] Lord Aberdeen in 1829 told Princess Lieven: 'Russia dominates the world today; notwithstanding the modesty of your language, you are omnipotent everywhere.'[23] One American commentator, writing in 1822, wrote of the Russian eagle extending its wings and unfurling its charts over the Tower of London itself,[24] while Nicholas I declared: 'the geographical position of Russia is so advantageous that it . . . makes her independent of what occurs in Europe; she has nothing to fear.'[25]

In fact, western fears of 'this monster of an empire'[26] were greatly exaggerated. Alexander and Nicholas were not very interested in expansion in Europe or the Balkans, while under them Russia fell even further behind the rest of Europe both economically and socially. British consumption of iron was more than fourteen times that of Russia, British cotton consumption, nine times as great. Russian railways until the late 1860s were overwhelmingly dependent on foreign technology in terms of rails, locomotives, and freight cars.[27] According to E. L. Woodward, 'the military strength of Russia was never the danger imagined by European statesmen from Metternich to Disraeli.'[28] Russian army officers were 'idle, ill-instructed, hated or feared by their men' (the real cause of the Semenovsky regiment's revolt in 1820 – yet the 'liberal' Alexander had the troops involved run six gauntlets as a punishment, while their sadistic commander was promoted.[29] See below.) The industrial resources of the country were 'undeveloped'. The administration was 'crude, dishonest, ignorant and inefficient'. Thus 'it was almost as difficult for a Russian army to leave Russia as for a foreign army to invade the country.'[30] Every generation during this period saw Russia fall further behind the West. Lord Salisbury would write by 1877:

> I cannot go very far with those who dread the Russians. Except the size of the patch they occupy on the map, there is nothing about their history or their actual condition to explain the abject terror, which deprives so many Anglo-Indians and so many of our military party here of their natural sleep. Except in conflict with barbarous Orientals – or Poles who were little better – their military history has been one long record of defeat. Their only trophies . . . Moscow and Poltowa. Their naval history simply does not exist. Their finances, never good, are now desperate; their social condition is a prolonged crisis threatening at any moment of weakness, socialist revolution. Their people are unwarlike – their officials corrupt – their rulers only competent when borrowed from Germany. And yet we are asked to believe . . .

Fortunately, whatever assessment people arrived at between 1815 and 1848, Russia's tsars were not much interested in gaining territory. Nicholas told the French: 'I do not plan to add a single inch of territory to the holdings of Russia which is already large enough as it is.'[31] To the British he said: 'I do not claim one inch of Turkish soil.'[32] On the subject of the Greeks, he told the Austrian ambassador:

> I abhor the Greeks, although they are my co-religionists; they have behaved in a shocking, blameable, even criminal manner; I look upon them as subjects in open revolt against their legitimate sovereign. I do not desire their enfranchisement; they do not deserve it, and it would be a very bad example for all other countries, if they succeeded in establishing it.[33]

Alexander had told Capodistrias in 1821: 'If we reply to the Turks with war the Paris directing committee will triumph and no government will be left standing. I do not intend to leave a free field to the enemies of order. At all costs means must be found to avoid war with Turkey.'[34] When war did come eventually in 1828, the Russian army was found to be in a poor condition. The soldiers had to carry far too much on their backs and the commanding general (Wittgenstein) had to be replaced.

General Kiselev wrote: 'the state is without funds and industry . . . a colossus with feet of clay.'[35] The Prussian diplomat, Küster, reported to his king: 'Europe can at least derive the consolation . . . of knowing that Nicholas will never be a conqueror.'[36] At the end of the war, the Tsar sent General Krasinsky to Vienna to explain Russia's poor military position to Metternich who, in a memorandum to Francis, described it as 'almost approaching genuine disintegration'. 'The Russian army', he wrote, was 'in a pitiable condition' and had lost 150,000 men in the war with Turkey. But the aim of Krasinsky's mission had not been to inform Austria of Russian military weakness; its real aim had been to prove that Russia had no designs on European Turkey and in particular to end rumours that Austria was secretly arming Turkey and even preparing to undertake a diversionary war against Russia. These rumours the Tsar took very seriously indeed and, given the state of his army, he obviously had to. Indeed, his brother, the Grand Duke Constantine, before fleeing Warsaw in 1830, would leave behind him detailed plans worked out by the Russians for a possible campaign in Hungary. Nor was the Tsar altogether mistaken in his fears. Documents in the Vienna archives show that Metternich was indeed allowing the Turks to import arms secretly from Austria, although he had no plan, of course, to declare war on Russia. Once the war with Turkey was over, the Polish revolution of 1830–1 confirmed Russia's weak military position. In the spring of 1831 its strength stood at merely 210,467 men, and it could only afford to send 110,000 against the Poles, who themselves by then had managed to call up 91,000 men. Still, they thought they were facing a Russian foe of potentially one million men. The truth, rather, was that the Russians now felt compelled to make special arrangements with Austria for their forces to withdraw into Galicia should they be defeated, and for the Austrians to prepare food stores for them in case they were needed (which they were in July 1831). By May 1831, the Tsar was discussing a new partition plan with Prussia, which even foresaw France getting Belgium as compensation, while he and the Russian court appeared to have reached the conclusion that ruling the ungrateful Poles since 1815 had been a mistake. His adjutant general told the Austrian ambassador to St Petersburg:

The Polish revolt has put Russia back thirty years in her development. Tsar Alexander, a man of such high and excellent spirit, made a bad mistake in creating the Kingdom of Poland. We should never have crossed the Weichsel. Since we thereby occupied a great space in the middle of Europe, we frightened it and turned the whole world against us . . . Russia was too aware of its own strength, it became too arrogant. We all needed a lesson.[37]

Hence Metternich was much more aware of a reciprocity of obligations as far as Russia was concerned than of his dependency on her, which has been the old chestnut of diplomatic historians now for a century and a half.[37] Still, Russia could hardly be ignored.

The other powers were all satiated ones. Britain wanted peace to trade with the world; Prussia needed time to incorporate her Catholic Rhineland provinces; while Austria wanted no more territory than she already had. Metternich's ideal was to keep the powers united in support of the 1815 status quo and against the forces of nationalism and liberalism. With the suicide of Castlereagh in 1822 and the emergence of first Canning and then Palmerston as the voice of England, and with the 1830 revolution in France, however, he was often hard pressed to achieve this. The decade after Waterloo had seen the powers arrange congresses and conferences to keep the peace of Europe but he told Ficquelmont in 1832: 'from the time that Liberalism gained the upper hand in France and England, this kind of meeting began to degenerate . . . for it is an attempted compromise between the temper of the Right and the temper of the Left, and these two powers are mutually destructive of one another.'[38] None the less, his eye never moved from the ball: 'There exists in Europe only one issue of any moment and that is Revolution.'[39] It is now time to look briefly at the history of international relations during the period and then to consider how best to analyse them to discover how exactly Metternich's policies fitted in.

Basically, the history of the period is one of the 'congress system' followed by the Greek War of Independence, followed by the 1830 revolutions, followed by the two Mehemet Ali crises followed by the breakdown of the *entente cordiale* between Britain and France. The Greek war and the Mehemet Ali crises constituted 'the Eastern Question' – the diplomacy revolving around the future (if any) of the Ottoman Empire. The other crises were largely about revolutions or counter-revolutions, although both streams of events converged spectacularly in the 1840 war crisis when France, alone among the great powers, backed Mehemet Ali against the Sultan and for a short period threatened to go to war with the rest of Europe to get better terms for the Pasha of Egypt. Metternich is usually credited as dominating the diplomacy of the congress period, while Palmerston is given the laurels for solving both the Belgian crisis of 1830–1 and the Eastern

Question-cum-war scare of 1840–1. Sir Charles Webster and others have spent a great deal of ink congratulating Palmerston for holding the conferences involved in London rather than in Vienna, but this rather misses the point that, despite a small gain for the conservative powers in Krakow in 1846, counterbalanced by a small gain for Palmerston in Switzerland in 1847, Europe in 1848, just as in 1815, was still basically organised around an agreement to contain a potentially revolutionary France.[40] Any hope of a liberal alliance between France and England was dead, so that in 1848, the year of revolutions, France felt constrained to do nothing to aid the Poles, the Italians, the Hungarians, the Germans or anyone else, relinquished the opportunity to gain her natural frontiers and watched idly by while the Eastern powers put down revolutions everywhere and, at least geographically, re-established the status quo. England, too, gave no help to the revolutionaries and liberals; indeed, even Palmerston hoped that the Hungarians (though not the Italians) would be quickly crushed.[41] Palmerston himself told the House of Commons in 1849:

> Austria is a most important element in the balance of European power. Austria stands in the centre of Europe, a barrier against encroachment on the one side, and against invasion on the other. The political independence and liberties of Europe are bound up, in my opinion, with the maintenance and integrity of Austria as a great European power; and therefore anything which tends by direct or even remote contingency to weaken and to cripple Austria, but still more to reduce her from the position of a first-rate power to that of a secondary state, must be a great calamity to Europe, and one which every Englishman, ought to deprecate and try to avoid.[42]

The Metternich System, therefore, did not come to an end in 1848 – it triumphed in 1848. It died in the 1850s.

In 1815 under Article VI of the Quadruple Alliance, the allies had agreed to meet from time to time to discuss affairs of common interest.[43] The first such meeting – or congress, since heads of state were present – was held in 1818 at Aix-la-Chapelle. It was clear that the allied army of occupation and the allied conference of ambassadors under Pozzo di Borgo in France were causing irritation. The Duc de Richelieu, the French premier, was demanding that France be treated as an equal ('France may be called upon to suppress a revolution in Prussia, just as much as Prussia to suppress trouble in France'[44]) and was ready to strike a deal to pay off the French war indemnity.

Metternich was susceptible to reaching an agreement since Russia at this stage seemed to want to exploit French (and Spanish) grievances to form some sort of maritime alliance against Great Britain, Alexander was still in his 'liberal' phase, and Capodistrias, the Russian diplomat, was again suggesting the formation of some sort of general guarantee. In the end, the allies agreed to settle the debt, signed a collective note agreeing the conclusion of peace and invited Louis XVIII to unite his counsels with theirs in future in the interests of mankind. If secretly they renewed the Quadruple Alliance against him, the fact was that France was now part of the European concert. Richelieu praised the part played by Alexander in all this, but was soon sacked by Louis, which the Tsar took as a personal slight. Castlereagh and Metternich between them, meanwhile, had established Article VI alone as the basis for future congresses and had thus prevented the emergence of any general guarantee, so that both were pleased with the outcome at Aix. Indeed, Metternich boasted that he had 'never seen a prettier little congress'.[45] His diplomatic prowess was on full display soon afterwards because at Carlsbad in 1819 he managed to persuade the German states (in fact, they needed little or no persuasion after the assassination of the right-wing journalist and Russian agent, Kotzebue) to pass the Carlsbad Decrees, which closed down student societies, obliged universities to sack radical professors, instituted press censorship and set up an investigating commission at Mainz into German radicalism. In 1820, by the Final Act of the Congress of Vienna, the German states also agreed to alter Article 13 of the Confederation so as to invest German sovereigns with full sovereignty and make any of their constitutions merely advisory. However, all this was done without the interference of the other great powers and Metternich boasted with respect to Carlsbad: 'It is the first time that such a group of correct, peremptory, anti-revolutionary measures have appeared. I did what I have wished to do since 1813 and I have done it because that terrible Emperor Alexander, who always spoils things, was not there . . . If the Emperor of Germany doubts that he is Emperor of Germany, he is mistaken.'[46] The collected diplomats of Germany, indeed, had voted Metternich their thanks: 'If this task . . . for which you have assembled us, has been concluded in a manner not unacceptable to you, then we owe it to your . . . wise leadership . . . you recognised the real cause of the evil and that which we have accomplished here is no more than what you already conceived then.'[47] Kissinger comments: 'Metternich had succeeded in a *tour de force* . . . the power which had most to gain from the Carlsbad decrees emerged as the most disinterested party.'[48]

The Russians (and French) were highly displeased with the Carlsbad decrees and Metternich's influence over Germany. Yet matters would change. After the congresses of Troppau and Laibach in 1820–1, Alexander's views would become more conservative.

In 1820, the King of Spain was forced by a military revolt and revolution to adopt the radical Spanish constitution of 1812. The French wanted to intervene to impose their Charter as a solution; the Russians also called for intervention and soon offered to intervene themselves, something which the French could not allow (Russian troops would have had to march through France!). French efforts over their Charter got nowhere, so for the moment nothing happened, save that Castlereagh denounced the idea that the powers had any collective right to suppress revolution. In his famous State Paper of 5 May 1820[49] he wrote that the alliance 'never was . . . intended as a Union for the Government of the World or for the superintendence of the Affairs of other States'. Yet when in July 1820 the revolution spread to Naples and yet another Bourbon monarch – indeed another Ferdinand – was forced to adopt the Spanish constitution of 1812, both Castlereagh and Wellington in London gave their support to Austria to intervene to suppress the revolution under her 1815 treaty with Naples. This was too much for France and Russia. Richelieu (again in office in France) and Pozzo were unwilling to 'grant to Austria the right to dispose of Italy uncontrolled' and so called for another congress to be convened.[50] The Tsar agreed and one was held in Troppau. Castlereagh duly protested and Britain sent only an observer (an expedient followed by France which did not want to appear too reactionary). Metternich, however, managed to escape humiliation by agreeing to intervene on behalf of the alliance while getting Alexander to agree to make the aim of intervention purely restorational. This was no mean achievement since Capodistrias, Alexander's chief adviser on foreign affairs, and a lover of constitutions,[51] had proposed intervention on the basis of 'the establishment of an order of things which would guarantee the realisation of an authentically national desire'.[52] But after a series of private talks and the sending of many memos on the threat of European revolution, Metternich succeeded in getting the aims of intervention in Naples changed simply to freeing the king in order to 'consolidate his power' and to 'offer guarantees of stability to Naples and to Europe'.[53] An effort at mediation on the basis of the French Charter was conceded but the Eastern Powers signed the notorious Troppau Protocol which gave them the right to intervene against revolutions in other countries, even if they were not invited:

States which have undergone a change of government due to revolution, the results of which threaten other states, *ipso facto*, cease to be members of the European Alliance and remain excluded from it until their situation gives guarantees for legal order and stability. If owing to such alterations immediate danger threatens other states, the powers bind themselves by peaceful means or if need be by arms, to bring back the guilty state into the bosom of the Great Alliance.[54]

The congress then adjourned to Laibach to meet the King of Naples himself and Capodistrias had a chance to check Metternich again, but it became clear that mediation had failed, the rebels had rejected the Charter, allowing Metternich to scoff at the French and to denounce the Neapolitans as 'half-African' and 'barbarians'.[55] The French, Russians and Prussians, it is true, sent commissioners to accompany the Austrian army of intervention but they had no influence. Austria meanwhile also found herself intervening to put down revolution in Piedmont and leaving military garrisons in Tuscany and the Papal States. Alexander gave Metternich his full support. The mutiny of his Semonovsky guards, the news that the French had been issuing passports to Neapolitan rebels and the outbreak of revolution in Greece now convinced him that a great revolutionary conspiracy directed from Paris actually existed. Metternich had been right along. 'I deplore', the Tsar confessed,[56] 'all that I said and did between the years 1815 and 1818. I regret the time lost; we must study to retrieve it. You have correctly judged the condition of things. Tell me what you want of me and I will do it.' Little wonder Metternich was described by one diplomat as exulting 'in the full pride of his triumph.'[57] Paul Schroeder, on the other hand, once suggested that the price of Metternich's triumph had been the permanent estrangement of Great Britain and the breakdown of European solidarity;[58] from Metternich's viewpoint, however, the main task of Europe was to resist revolution and 'with such a France and such an England how is it to be withstood?'[59] In any case, Schroeder is mistaken. The British were happy to allow Austria to dominate Italy, so that in Roy Bridge's words:

> In terms of the practical issues of the day, the fundamental community of interests between Britain and Austria had not been affected at all . . . British observers had after all gone to Laibach; Castlereagh had done nothing to hinder Austria's progress in Naples; and over Piedmont he had coldly rebuffed French criticism of Metternich. As the Greek Question arose to the fore in the summer, so too did the Anglo–Austrian community of interests.[60]

Castlereagh wrote to Alexander I arguing that the Greeks were just another bunch of rebels, while he and Metternich met in Hanover in 1821 to discuss how to prevent a Russo–Turkish war. Yet Alexander, fearful lest war should allow the Paris Directing Committee to unleash revolution all over Europe, agreed to leave matters to a European congress which Metternich was trying to arrange in Vienna; Capodistrias was sacked; and the French agreed to follow Metternich's lead. The congress had to be postponed and rearranged in Verona (Castlereagh had committed suicide) but there the Tsar agreed to condemn the Greek revolt as a rash and criminal enterprise and as yet another instance of the spirit of revolution. The trouble was that he now demanded action over Spain, where the French were determined to keep a free hand, but where neither Austria nor Britain was disposed to see a reassertion of French power. Metternich tried to arrange a compromise between the powers by getting agreement from everyone save Britain, that diplomatic notes should be delivered in Madrid simultaneously condemning the progress of the revolution there. This gesture of moral solidarity, he hoped, might just bring the Spanish to their senses. Alas, the new French foreign minister, Chateaubriand (who himself had been present at Verona) refused to act simultaneously, and then, with Russian backing, organised a French invasion of Spain, which proved a military triumph. Ferdinand VII was restored to his throne and the 1812 constitution overthrown, although the French Charter did not replace it. As a result, the Congress System came to an end.[61]

French intervention is often seen as a great setback for Metternich who had thereby clearly lost his ability to control the French who, in turn, were certainly boosted by their victory in Spain. Yet the crushing of the Spanish Revolution was clearly something Metternich could live with, while the power which was really humiliated was Britain. Castlereagh's more popular successor, George Canning, admitted as much but his diplomacy was now directed to frustrating Spain's attempts to regain control of her Latin American colonies which had already declared or were in the process of declaring their independence. He attempted to work with the United States to do this, although President Monroe in 1823 preferred, in the light of Anglo–US commercial rivalry, to act unilaterally, by warning all European countries from intervening in or colonising South America in what became known as the Monroe Doctrine. The enforcement of this doctrine, however, depended on the willingness of Britain's royal navy to stop Spanish, French or Russian warships from crossing the Atlantic. And, in any case, Britain easily won the commercial race with the USA in Latin America.

The restored Spanish monarchy soon discovered, therefore, that French backing was of little use in helping it to achieve its goals. Moreover, there was little enthusiasm in Spain to make French Bourbon princes kings of new Spanish American monarchies. The outcome was that in October 1823, in the first so-called Polignac memorandum, France informed England that she would not use force to overthrow the new republics which would be independent of Spain. Eventually on 31 December 1824, Canning extended British recognition to all the new republics, while in a famous speech, having admitted that the French invasion of Spain had been 'in a certain sense a disparagement – an affront to the pride – a blow to the feelings of England', he asked, 'was it necessary, in order to avoid the consequences of that occupation, that we should blockade Cadiz?' To this, his own question, he gave a most famous answer: 'No. I looked another way: I sought materials for compensation in another hemisphere. Contemplating Spain, such as our ancestors had known her, I resolved that if France had Spain, it should be Spain without the Indies. I called the New World into existence to redress the balance of the Old.'[62]

What about Metternich? Did he worry very much? He obviously had no objections in principle to absolute monarchy being restored in Madrid and ideally he would have liked monarchy to survive in Latin America as well. But even he soon became bored with Spain's dithering about what to do to enforce her rights south of the equator. He wrote in 1824 to his embassy in London: 'No one has contested these rights, but has Spain the means to make them prevail with a hope of success? If she possesses these means, what is the most useful way in which she can employ them? If she does not . . . how will she be able to retain the colonies?'[63] At about the same time he was writing to his embassy in France: 'From another viewpoint, the powers have a political interest in seeing the colonial problems of Spain decided.'[64] Much as the King of Spain's interests should be protected, 'the powers should nevertheless try to reach an understanding with this monarch concerning the means of reconciling his rights and interests with the great issue of a general pacification.'[65] Metternich had no wish to create new republics in Latin America or to strengthen the influence of the USA there; occasionally, even he (not to mention Chateaubriand and even Canning, who also disliked republics) dallied with the expedient of new French Bourbon monarchies in South America. However, he was content to wait until the Iberian monarchs themselves took a sovereign lead which he could follow. Hence he opposed Canning's policy of recognising the new republics (and even French recognition in 1825 of the black republic of

Haiti). On the other hand, he was clearly rather frustrated by Spanish dithering and was quite prepared in the case of Portugal (where the Brazilian Empress was a Habsburg Archduchess) to work with Canning for a reconciliation between the Emperor of Brazil (which had declared its independence in December 1822) and his father, the King of Portugal. Clearly, the whole issue of Latin America was a rather tedious one. As Metternich put it in a letter to the London embassy: 'The more we wish to not to violate the principle of legitimacy, the more we desire that His Catholic Majesty and His Faithful Majesty should both take the measures most apt to ensure a result which would directly secure their interests and the maintenance of tranquillity in Europe.'[66] Canning's policy in Latin America can scarcely, therefore, be seen as a body blow to either him or Austria.[67] Moreover, despite frequent false assertions that Canning wished to isolate Britain from both Europe and Metternich, he was in fact quite willing to seek European solutions to European problems. As far as Latin America was concerned, his main objective was to keep a free hand for Britain there, in order to prevent this one issue from complicating good relations with the European powers in general. Hence, to Metternich's disgust he kept refusing suggestions of a European conference on the issue. In April 1824, for example, he told the British ambassador in St Petersburg: 'in [refusing to attend a conference] the British Cabinet flatters itself that it took the best chance of avoiding contest and of avoiding complications which might have put to hazard on one separate question that general harmony and confidence, which happily prevail between His Majesty and his Allies on so many subjects of vital interest, and which it is His Majesty's earnest desire to cultivate and maintain.'[68] In any case, if anyone in the British Cabinet was an isolationist it was Liverpool, not Canning. Wellington, of course, given his record as a colleague of Castlereagh, was much more European, whilst Canning found himself manoeuvring between the two in the formulation of British policy.[69]

The whole issue of the monarchies of Spain and Portugal became a very complex one during the 1820s, 1830s and 1840s.[70] Britain had diplomatic ties with Portugal going back to the fourteenth century which included a treaty of alliance. Hence Canning had demanded of the French in 1823 that not only would their occupation of Spain be temporary but that it would not be used to interfere in Portuguese affairs. Guarantees were duly received on both accounts. These guarantees were vital since there had been a coup in Lisbon in 1820 and the British squadron in the Tagus was needed to protect the new constitutional regime. In fact, Canning had to dispatch more marines in 1824 and 4,000 more troops in 1826. In 1827, however, he had secured agreement from the French to recognise each other's predominant position in each other's client state. By now Portuguese affairs had been made even more complicated by the death of King John VI since his successor, Dom Pedro, Emperor of Brazil, had abdicated in favour of his young daughter, Dona Maria, leaving her to reign under a council of regency and a new constitutional charter, now seen, however, as a threat to absolutism in Spain. It was the threat of Spain arming Portuguese deserters and sending them home to subvert the constitution that had caused Canning to act in 1826. Even in 1827, matters refused to settle down. Dom Miguel, the uncle of the Queen of Portugal, seized the throne and began to persecute the country's liberals once the British had withdrawn their forces. In this he was aided by Ferdinand VII of Spain and, in British minds, by the Eastern Powers. The Iberian Question, however, became even more complicated when first, in 1830, Louis Philippe became King of the French and, secondly, Ferdinand VII of Spain died to be succeeded by his young daughter, Isabella. It was now the turn of her uncle, Don Carlos, to stage a coup, armed by Portuguese absolutists, leading the Queen Regent of Spain to throw her support behind the constitutionalists. This offered Palmerston, now British foreign secretary, the opportunity to cooperate with France to drive absolutism out of the Iberian peninsula. Since Orleanist France now lacked the support of the Eastern Powers, Palmerston believed she would have to play second fiddle to England. Talleyrand, in London as French ambassador since the Belgian crisis (see below), hoped that he could conclude a treaty of alliance, but found that he had to settle instead for a Quadruple Alliance in 1834 along with Spain and Portugal. Under this, Britain was allowed to use her naval power along with Spanish military forces to expel the two pretenders from Portugal, something that was achieved very quickly without any help from France. ('Additonal Articles' were soon required to clarify roles when more action was needed.) Palmerston hoped that military success, based on the treaty, would consolidate constitutional regimes in Spain and Portugal, identify France and Britain with the liberal cause, build a liberal bloc in Western Europe to balance the absolutist one in the East, and last but not least give Britain a base from which to resist Russian threats to Turkey. Yet it was not to be. The governments of Spain and Portugal saw the 1834 treaty as a means of using their protecting powers to solve their domestic political problems and would play them off against each other. Thus between 1834 and 1847, they asked for military or naval intervention on no less than six occasions. The treaty consequently caused increased tension between Britain and France. Britain saw it as a means to assert equal influence with France in Spain, so France in turn demanded equal influence with Britain in Portugal. In the end cooperation failed. Britain achieved a dominant position in Spain after France failed to aid Madrid in 1836 but then in 1844 the pro-French Moderado party ousted its rival pro-British Progressistas leaving France predominant, leading in turn to the Anglo-French crisis over the 'Spanish Marriages' (see below). In 1847, finally, the Portuguese government, backed by those of France and Spain, asked Britain to intervene in Portugal under the terms of the Quadruple Alliance to crush radical rebels. An exasperated Palmerston replied that the treaty was by now 'worked out', but real fear that Spain might intervene if Britain did not forced another British intervention anyway, this time assisted by French naval and Spanish land forces. By now Palmerston deeply regretted the 1834 treaty, although he argued that intervention was 'a very unusual measure for the British government to take' and was 'much more after the fashions of Austria and Russia'.[71] We shall have to ponder that assertion later.

Meanwhile, another power was being called upon to intervene in yet another part of Europe. In 1821, the Greeks rose up against their Turkish masters and expected support from their co-religionist, the Tsar of Russia. The ensuing war of independence, which ended with the establishment of an independent Greece in 1832, although the Turks had conceded defeat in 1829, has led even distinguished historians to talk of Metternich's isolation in the 1820s. (The excellent Roy Bridge, for example, writes of 'a catastrophic decline in Austria's position among the Powers in the 1820s' and of 'the fatuity of Austria's claim to be taken seriously as a Great Power'.)[72] True, Austria had financial problems at this time ('We are armed for perpetual peace,' wrote Kolowrat, hoping that Austria would not be dragged into the Greek war.)[73] Yet the power that was really isolated was Russia, whose tsars, as we have already seen, did indeed see the Greeks as rebels and who were sincere in their opposition to Greek independence. Nor did they have any desire to increase Russian territory in Europe or to destroy the Ottoman Empire. At the most they wanted to see Greece divided into a number of autonomous protectorates under Turkish suzerainty along the lines of Moldavia and Wallachia, a policy which they stuck to consistently. As Alexander told the British ambassador in November 1822: 'the idea of Greek independence was an absolute chimera, and that the utmost extent of His wishes was that the Greeks should be placed in the same relation to the Porte as the Inhabitants of Servia, or if it could be affected, as those of Wallachia and Moldavia.'[74] However, he would wait for Britain 'to take the state of Greece into consideration' and to 'make some efforts' for its 'improvement'.[75] The British were split but everyone concerned with British policy-making feared a war between Russia and Turkey. As Liverpool put it in April 1824:

> The Power and even the Existence of the Turks in Europe may not be of long Duration but after all Europe has suffered in the course of the last Thirty Years, Repose must be our first Object & it is impossible not to look with apprehension to the Consequences which must arise from the dismemberment of an Empire so Vast in its extent and containing within it many of the finest and most fertile Provinces of the World.[76]

Metternich was more blunt. Turkey, he wrote, 'is scrupulously true to her word [and] we regard contact with her as equivalent to contact with a natural frontier which never claims our attention or dissipates our energies'.[77] Europe, therefore, should not meddle in her affairs. If the Balkans were to fall into Russian hands and Russian ships allowed into the Adriatic, Austria, he knew, would become a Russian satellite, encircled north and south by Russian territory. Hence 'the complications which may ensue in the east defy all calculations', he concluded.[78] As for the Greeks, he remained indifferent: 'Over there, beyond our frontiers, three or four hundred thousand individuals hanged, impaled or with their throats cut, hardly count.'[79] He was exaggerating, one hopes, in order to make his point. Yet it is difficult to escape the conclusion that, if only the Turks had managed to suppress the uprising quickly, Europe's great powers would not have stopped them.

Russia meanwhile showed remarkable restraint. In the words of a leading scholar, both Alexander I and Nicholas I, who made foreign policy themselves, displayed in their attitude to the Eastern Question 'a width of view and freedom from merely national and selfish considerations that could be matched by no other European ruler of the period. To them, and particularly to Alexander, ideological loyalties were more important than material advantage'.[80] And insofar as material advantages were concerned in the 1820s, these, it must be stressed, concerned territory on the Black Sea and in the Caucuses. The fertile steppe around the Black Sea was fuelling the spectacular growth of Odessa as a grain-exporting port. In comparison, Russian attempts to win the sympathies of Balkan Christians had as yet provided meagre results. The real issues at stake between Russia and the Porte in 1821 were those concerning the proper interpretation of the Treaty of Bucharest of 1812, particularly 120 miles of disputed Black Sea coast.

Still, Russia could hardly ignore Greek affairs, if for no other reason than the war between the Greeks and Turks was fought with unusual savagery on both sides. There was also the growth of philhellenic societies around Europe and these, Alexander warned the British, would soon have the same emotional reach in Britain as the movement to abolish the foreign slave trade. Yet all Russian efforts (including a variety of proposals for diplomatic cooperation with Britain and Austria in 1822–3) got nowhere. Neither did a conference in St Petersburg on the subject in June 1824 when both Greeks and Turks rejected Russian compromise proposals. In 1825, a Protocol signed by Russia, Austria, Prussia and France called for an end to the fighting but this again produced no results. By the end of the year, Nesselrode was accusing the other powers of stalling.

By now, moreover, matters were deteriorating. The Turks had prevailed on the Pasha of Egypt, Mehemet Ali, to send his son, the general Ibrahim Pasha, with an army and the Egyptian fleet to Greece to crush the rebels. This he did with great brutality and rumours spread that he intended to expel if not exterminate the whole Greek population of the Morea. Alexander I also died in 1825 to be succeeded by Nicholas I. Things now began to move, although Nicholas's views on Greece were the same as those of his late brother. In any case, in March 1826 he sent envoys to the Porte with a long list of grievances to settle. Then on 4 April the Duke of Wellington agreed to sign a Protocol in St Petersburg (he had gone for Alexander's funeral and to pay his respects to the new Tsar), allowing for 'joint or separate' Anglo–Russian mediation in the Greek war. (He missed the vital significance of the phrase.) Under British pressure to preserve the peace, the Turks then agreed to all Nicholas's demands and in the Convention of Akkerman of October 1826 conceded all the lands claimed by Russia, granted more autonomy to Serbia, restored the privileges of the Danubian principalities and allowed ships under the Russian flag to navigate all seas and waterways of the Ottoman Empire. Finally, in 1827 by the Treaty of London, France adhered to the St Petersburg Protocol, although Metternich was firmly opposed. Nevertheless, nothing was really being done to help the Greeks. Ibrahim was still in military command of the situation, while Russia from June 1826 had to divert her attention to a war with Persia. Russian diplomacy was still achieving little – the Sultan even took care to implement his concessions very slowly. However, Canning in 1825 had come to the conclusion that cooperation with Russia was needed to keep her under control, so great were the pressures on her to aid the Greeks. Still, his aim had been to control Russia, not to allow her a free hand in the Balkans. Then an accident happened. When the combined British, Russian and French fleets entered Navarino Bay to negotiate with Ibrahim Pasha, a shot from a Turkish ship began an unplanned battle which ended in the destruction of the joint Egyptian–Turkish fleet. This ended any Turkish hopes of defeating the Greeks. Metternich agreed with Nicholas it was 'a deplorable catastrophe';[81] a shocked Wellington (now prime minister after Canning's death) called it an 'untoward event'.[82] A naturally furious Sultan, however, renounced the Convention of Akkerman and declared a holy war on Russia.

When the Russians took up the fight in 1828, 'there was a good deal of uneasiness in St Petersburg over the possibility of Austrian military intervention . . . It was at least partly through fear of Austrian hostility that Nicholas steadily resisted any suggestion that the Balkan peoples, under Turkish rule or suzerainty, and particularly the Serbs, should be brought into the struggle as auxiliaries of Russia.'[83] Austrian claims to great power status were by no means fatuous. The Russians also feared British intervention, and Aberdeen did state in July 1828 that 'the existence of Turkey as a European power was essential to the preservation of [the] balance of power.'[84] Yet Peel declared for the Wellington government: 'When Turkey gave Russia a fair justification for hostilities, on what account could we interfere?'[85] And even Palmerston in opposition had to agree – the Turks should have made timely concessions.[86] The point is, however, that Russia was still basically isolated, despite the Treaty of London. Fortunately, her own military performance was poor, as has already been noted, although she won the war in the end and by the Treaty of Adrianople of 1829 reaffirmed her gains of the Convention of Akkerman. Apart from that she took only a tiny slice of territory at the mouth of the Danube. It was in the Caucuses that she made her mark, forcing the Turks to recognise Georgia and eastern Armenia as Russian, while Russia began to claim suzerainty over Circassia. Nesselrode had already proclaimed at the start of 1828 that Russia 'in Europe wishes for no territorial gains at the expense of the Ottoman Empire.'[87] Austria could not to be ignored, even though Metternich was not consulted on the Adrianople negotiations.

The Russians in any case had been examining their policy towards Turkey in a committee chaired by Count Kochubey whose conclusions in 1829 would determine Russian policy for the next two decades.[88] The main one was that the advantages of the preservation of the Ottoman Empire to Russia outweighed all the disadvantages. If Turkey did collapse, however, its partition should be agreed upon peacefully by the powers. Any attempt by Russia to seize Constantinople and the Straits before then would merely lead to a competition by the powers for territories, which would bring them into too close proximity with Russia herself. Kochubey had formulated similar ideas as far back as 1802, while the most active member of the committee, Dashkov, argued in 1828 that if Turkey lost her European territories she might become a reformed Asian power, capable of causing trouble for Russia in the Caucuses. In December 1832, therefore, Russia's envoy to the Porte was told that Russian policy was 'to maintain Turkey in the stagnant state in which she finds herself'.[89]

Between 1829 and 1832, the powers decided that they still mistrusted Russia. So instead of leaving Greece under Turkish suzerainty (and dependent on Russia), they awarded her more restricted borders but gave her full independence under a new king, the seventeen-year-old, Prince Otto of Bavaria. Metternich had to reconcile himself to this. He had deplored the diplomacy of 1826–9 (Petersburg, London, Akkerman, the lot) as corrupting the aims of the European alliance; he himself had had no objections to mediation but he did not agree that the powers had the right to impose their terms on a ruler at war with rebels. Russia, he pointed out, would never accept such forced mediation with respect to Finland, nor Britain with respect to Ireland (Schwarzenberg would make the same riposte to Palmerston over Italy in 1848). As usual, then, he took his stand on general principles. He therefore welcomed Russia's military difficulties during the 1828 campaign and was so unsparing in his comments that the Russians officially protested.[90] In the end, however, he accepted an independent Greece as a *pis aller*. Greece, he quipped 'had been condemned to life'.[91] But although the powers were soon quarrelling over the new state – Prokesch-Osten, the Austrian ambassador, advising the new king that the Greeks were not fit for a constitution and had not been for centuries; Palmerston, telling him that he would have no peace till he introduced one; Lord Lyons, the British ambassador, proclaiming that Greece must be either British or Russian and that Greek independence was a 'nonsense'[92] – Metternich by 1839 came round to the view that perhaps the best thing that might happen would be for Greece to be enlarged by all the Greek-speaking territory between Athens and Constantinople, indeed for Greece itself to acquire Constantinople, with the greater Greece thus created acting as Austria's buffer against Russia. He told all this to Prokesch when the latter visited Vienna. But it was only a speculation, a daydream: he had no idea how or when such a 'plan' could ever be realised.[93]

The Greek war had been followed in Europe by the revolutions of 1830. These had been sparked off by the foolish decision of Charles X of France to cancel the 1830 election results and muzzle the press. Even Nicholas of Russia condemned his actions, but he also condemned Louis Philippe as 'a vile usurper' of the French throne and the product of revolution.[94] The result was that he moved towards Austria once again to enhance the solidarity of the three eastern powers. Indeed, when the French revolution spilled over into Belgium, which declared its independence from Holland, the opportunity arose to confront France head on. The King of Holland was a member of the German Confederation as Grand Duke of Luxembourg but, in any case, he was a sovereign whose territory as defined by the Vienna settlement was now threatened by revolution from France. Still, there were reasons for caution. Metternich preferred to take military action, yet the Archduke Charles in Vienna was loudly opposed on both military and financial grounds, while the Prussians ridiculed the state of the Austrian army. Indeed, Austria's plan in the case of a French advance across the Rhine was to retreat towards the Danube.[95] The Russians for their part were soon caught out by a revolution in Poland which had to be bloodily suppressed, while Austria and Prussia were confronted with revolutions that had broken out in Germany and Italy. The main reason for caution, however, was that Britain had given immediate recognition to the Orleanist monarchy in France and had sent a squadron to the Scheldt to protect Belgian independence (more menacingly, the French army would invade Belgium temporarily to do the same). Palmerston, although he twice threatened France with war to get her out of Belgium, managed to stop a son of Louis Phillipe's from acquiring the Belgian throne (which went to Leopold of Saxe-Coburg, the widower of England's Princess Charlotte, who had just turned down the Greek one) and chaired a conference in London which drew up frontiers for Belgium that the powers all found acceptable in 1831 – although William I of Holland did not agree to them till 1838. The French were fobbed off by acquiring a few of the barrier fortresses on the Belgian border. Metternich believed that the failure to aid the Dutch was a stain on Austria's and Europe's honour,[96] but, as with Greece, he was prepared to bend to circumstances. In any case, Austria and Prussia were able to put down revolution in Germany with ease. The Diet passed the Six Acts of 1832 which confirmed the provisions of 1820 and a commission was established to see which diets had already encroached on sovereign powers. As a result, several diets and universities were in fact closed down. A stricter police and censorship system was also introduced. All this, however imperfectly executed in the individual German states,[97] was, as far as Metternich was concerned, far more important than the development of the various customs unions in Germany in the late 1820s, all of which were absorbed in the Prussian *Zollverein* by 1834. The economic, far less the political, importance of these have been greatly exaggerated by most historians. In any case, Prussia was deserted by most *Zollverein* member states in its hours of need in 1850 and 1866. And by a commercial treaty of 1853, Austria negotiated more or less free trade with that body in any case.[98] There was remarkably little friction between Austria and Prussia at this time. As Engel-Janosi has put it:

> Metternich strove during the period of cooperation between Austria and Prussia to smooth over all possible sources of irritation between the two states with intelligence and tact. He took into consideration the sensitivities of the Prussians regarding German policy and avoided pressuring them by means of the votes of the smaller of the German kingdoms or states in the Federal Diet at Frankfurt. He always took care that Berlin and Vienna had reached agreement over important issues before they came before the Diet. Since his interest was more concerned with the European problem as a whole than with the German one, since his fears lay with the social question (in 1849 he called himself more of a socialist than a politician), Metternich was satisfied that during this period Prussia assumed the predominant position in North Germany.[99]

In Italy, too, Austria found little difficulty in suppressing revolution in the Papal States and the Duchies. The French prime minister, Casimir Périer, sent a French squadron to the papal port of Ancona in 1832 to dispute Austria's hegemony in Italy, but the measure was counterproductive.[100] The Pope was incensed and the powers were made even more suspicious of Louis Phillipe. It made no difference in any case to Austria's position in Italy. Metternich, on the other hand, soon realised that interventions there were both expensive and tiresome. He had already in the 1820s spent much time and effort trying to get the Neapolitans to reform their administration and now he attempted to do the same with the Pope – with no success. His advice, which was actually incorporated in the proceedings of the Laibach congress, was always the same: that Italy's sovereigns should create a centralised administration run by a professional bureaucracy recruited from men of talent; a legal system purged of the confusion, inequity and inhumanity of the old regime and incorporating the principle of equality before the law and some guarantee of equal rights against arbitrary procedures; a financial system capable of producing an adequate revenue without overburdening taxpayers; and an efficient police and military capable of maintaining internal order. Yet unlike in Germany, Metternich had few means of enforcing policy. There was, despite all his best efforts over the years to create one, no Italian League equivalent to the *Bund*; there was no investigating commission on police matters; and no customs union. In fact, Austria in the mid-1830s had a tariff war with Naples and another in 1847 with Piedmont. The latter state had also to be stopped from creating a customs union or league which did not include Austria.[101] In short, the Italian sovereigns believed that Austria would always pull their chestnuts out of the fire for them, however ungrateful they were. By 1847, therefore, Austria was completing new defensive alliances with the Duchies, determined that, should revolution break out in Italy again, she would simply await it in Lombardy-Venetia.

In 1832, the Eastern Question flared up again. Thanks in part to the 1830 revolutions, the diplomacy of the crisis would now be very different. Just as the Turkish war of 1828–9 had shown Russia's grave military weaknesses, the Polish revolution of 1830 had not only confirmed them but once again had demonstrated Russia's need for Austrian support.[102] Metternich, for his part, had been quick to provide it; he had very clearly told the Poles to submit to their legitimate sovereign, Nicholas, and had refused to mediate in any way between the Poles and the Russians – just as he had warned Alexander and Nicholas not to interfere between the Greeks and the Sultan. All this must have had a rather delicious irony for him, all the more so as he is supposed to have told the French ambassador in Vienna that: 'Do you think, as a minister, I would not prefer as a neighbour a Poland, ever friendly, ever benevolent, to a Russia, ever jealous, ever intruding?'[103] Austria had had to turn down offers from Warsaw of the crown of Poland, made officially or unofficially, to the Duc de Reichstadt, the Archduke Charles and even Francis himself. In the words of Metternich's wife, the Princess Melanie, quoting her husband:

We are once again playing an excellent role, since, instead of doing what so many others have done and seizing the favourable opportunity offered to us to enlarge ourselves, we pursue the correct path, give matters the right direction and uphold the peace. We prevent great shedding of blood at this moment and stop the Russians from having to run the danger of losing a decisive battle for the whole of Europe.[104]

Not that the Russians were immediately grateful. When Metternich proposed that all the great powers should meet together as in 1815 to outlaw revolution and recreate a grand alliance, Russia would have none of it. This had been the case in August 1830 when all Metternich could get out of Nesselrode had been the famous 'Chiffon de Carlsbad' – a pledge on mutual cooperation against the revolution.[105] Now, especially after events in Poland, Nicholas did not want to be too grateful to Metternich and would not even agree to a joint meeting between the three northern powers: 'There is Metternich's great desire, to be at the head of affairs, clearly and precisely on display; now, from what we know about him from previous meetings, I would only consent to it if Prussia desired it and the proposal were made to us from her side.'[106] Instead, Nicholas wanted to meet alone with Francis: 'We have to talk about the future . . . I have much to say to him that can be said only to him, and that can only be done verbally.'[107] But this indicated Metternich's strength, not his weakness. Nicholas was only too conscious of how weak his own position had been in 1828–31 and how keenly Metternich had been aware of this. Indeed, Metternich's reply to the rebellious Poles, who argued that Austria had to back Poland out of fear of Russia, was simply that since the Russo–Turkish war, Austria had no fear of Russia.[108] After the Polish revolt, she could feel even more secure about her northern neighbour.

To return to the Eastern Question: the Sultan, once more, was being attacked by a rebel, yet Mehemet Ali, the Muslim Pasha of Egypt, had no call on the Christian Nicholas who, in any case, had just crushed the rebellious Poles. Nicholas was determined that the Turkish Empire should remain weak; the last thing he wanted was it to be reformed, strengthened and modernised under a new ruler who had close links with France. Russia and Austria could, therefore, work together. And if Britain was at first suspicious, she too had no interest in helping a pasha whose dominions, if extended to include Syria, Anatolia and Arabia, as he seemed to desire, would block the land route to India. Mehemet Ali sent his son Ibrahim to make war on the Sultan in 1831. By February 1833, he had overrun Syria and was about 150 miles from Constantinople. He called on Britain to assist him, yet Britain was in no position to help. Her ships were being used to blockade the Dutch coast and to aid Queen Maria of Portugal against Dom Miguel. This at least was Palmerston's excuse to the House of Commons on 28 August 1833.[109] It was, in fact, only part of the reason; the other part was that the Cabinet, fearing that public opinion was apathetic, refused to commit itself. Metternich, who had supplied the Turkish envoy with arguments on his way to London, later said that at this stage a mere promise of armed support from England would have deterred the Egyptian ruler. Palmerston, in 1838, agreed: 'What Metternich says of our shirking from helping the Sultan when Mehemet was at Acre and when a word might have stopped the Pasha without a blow is perfectly true, and there is nothing that has happened since I have been in this office which I regret so much as that tremendous blunder of the English government.'[110] The Sultan, however, had been forced to turn to Russia, which in March began disembarking the first of 14,000 troops in the Turkish capital. Fortunately the Sultan agreed to grant the aged Mehemet Ali the pashaliks of Syria, Tarsus and Adana during his lifetime, so that the invading army could retreat in peace, but he now agreed to sign a defensive alliance with Russia whereby the latter maintained the integrity of Turkey and in return Turkey promised to close the Straits to foreign warships if Russia were at war. Not long before the conclusion of the treaty, Nicholas had a long conversation with the Austrian ambassador, Ficquelmont, in which he expressed grave doubts about the future viability of Turkey. He even suggested that Turkey might be replaced by a Greek empire under King Otto. (Was Ficquelmont's report perhaps the source of Metternich's later speculations to Prokesch?) However, he confirmed that 'If [Turkey] falls, I do not desire its *débris*. I need nothing.'[111] In the meantime, however, Nesselrode was explaining to Lieven in London and Orlov in Constantinople the meaning of the defensive treaty of Unkiar Skelessi of 8 July 1833 as he saw it. It would take Turkey out of the French and British spheres of influence and give Russia a legal basis for intervention in Turkey. Crucially, it would 'justify if the circumstances arise, the presence and use of our forces and will permit us again to be on the ground the first and the strongest in the theatre of events, so as always to remain masters of the question, either admitting the preservation of the Ottoman Empire as possible, or finally admitting its dissolution as inevitable.'[112] Yet 1833 would be the only time in history that Russian troops would ever camp in the Turkish capital.

Metternich had no objections to the treaty. He had been the first to suggest the use of force against Mehemet Ali and had even recommended that England and France should send naval squadrons to the Levant in the autumn of 1832. This suggestion had, very unwisely, been refused. Metternich's aim was to preserve Turkey, if possible by the concerted agreement of the powers, but Ficquelmont had reported the Tsar's intentions. He had nothing against Unkiar Skelessi and had arranged to meet Nicholas (for the first time) at Münchengraetz in

September. One reason for his confidence was military in origin. Russia could not hope to remain in Constantinople in 1833 – or at a later date hope to seize it and keep it should the Ottoman Empire suddenly face collapse – without establishing land communications through Bulgaria and the Danubian Principalities. In 1833, these communications were still maintained through the occupation of the Turkish fortress of Silistria on the right bank of the Danube. However, by mobilising in Transylvania, Austria could threaten these long and tenuous lines of communication and force the Russians to retreat to the Pruth.

> Military necessity therefore forced the Russian government to aban-
> don its attempt to carry on a completely independent policy in
> regard to Turkey. No sooner had Russia signed the Unkiar Skelessi
> Treaty with Turkey than she began to prepare the ground for a new
> agreement with Austria. This agreement, signed in the autumn of
> 1833 at Münchengraetz, greatly limited Russian freedom of action in
> the Eastern Question.[113]

Austria did indeed count as a great power. One other factor also greatly increased her military or strategic importance for Russia, should war break out over Turkey. Given that France might seize the opportunity to turn it into a European war to recover her natural frontiers, Russia had to be sure of the support of Austria, Prussia and the German Confederation in such an eventuality. The opposition of Austria in the Balkans and Europe could prove disastrous. Russia had to bear all this in mind in 1840 and again, much to her distress, in 1854–6.

Cooperation between Austria and Russia had begun again after 1830 when the two powers signed the so-called 'chiffon of Carlsbad', later adhered to by Prussia, by which these powers committed themselves not to intervene in the domestic disputes of France but not to allow France to disrupt the material interests of Europe as established by general transactions or to disrupt the internal affairs of European states. Metternich saw this as the least the conservative powers could do to assert their principles. It was at Münchengraetz, however, that true conservative principles and Austro–Russian friendship were restored. Here Nicholas told Metternich: 'I am come to put myself under the command of my chief. I look to you to give me a hint when I make a mistake.'[114] In any case, his meeting en route at Schwedt with his father-in-law, Friedrich Wilhelm III of Prussia, had not gone well. The Prussian King's lack of grasp of international affairs made Nicholas suffer a bilious attack. Metternich, on the other hand, was a past master of diplomacy. Everything went extremely smoothly. The Emperors of Austria and Russia on 6 September agreed to do everything to maintain the Turkish Empire, to defend it against Mehemet Ali, and to consult on a mutual course of action should the Turkish Empire collapse despite their best efforts. They also agreed to mutually guarantee the security of their Polish possessions, to aid each other should disorders break out there and to extradite political criminals to each other's territory. Less than a month later the agreements became binding on Prussia when on 13 October the three powers signed the Berlin Convention which expressed conservative solidarity and support for non-intervention in the affairs of other states save by direct invitation from the legitimate sovereign. They would also jointly oppose the efforts of any other powers designed to resist such intervention. Metternich and Nicholas were extremely pleased with these developments. The alliance against revolution had been restored. In 1834, moreover, Russian garrisons were withdrawn from the Danubian Principalities where they had been maintained since 1829 despite the fact that the Turks had not yet fully paid off their war indemnity. 'This too was a gesture, and quite a substantial one, towards cooperation with Austria even at the cost of some sacrifice to Russia.'[115]

Metternich was so happy with the outcome at Münchengraetz that he wanted to extend the alliance to include Britain and France. He offered Palmerston a Four-Power Pact, which was rejected. Palmerston and especially his new ambassador in Constantinople, Lord Ponsonby, were violently Russophobic. They thought the Unkiar Skelessi treaty had secret clauses which would allow Russian warships to pass through the Straits at will and that Münchengraetz was a secret agreement to carve up Turkey. Nothing that the Russian ambassador or even the Tsar himself said could change their minds. Nicholas was accused of wanting to dominate Europe and Asia and for eight months in 1834 Palmerston even gave Ponsonby a 'discretionary order' allowing him to use British ships to force the Straits if necessary.[116] France was also hostile and both countries in the years after 1833 held naval demonstrations off the Turkish coast to prove their zeal to save Turkey. Metternich, who deplored the division of Europe into two ideological camps, attempted yet again to act as umpire and gave lurid assurances to both Britain and France that he, too, would resist any Russian encroachments on Turkey; the Tsar, he added, could be trusted.[117] It was all in vain. Russia, against Metternich's advice, would not make public the secret clauses of her agreements with Austria or Turkey and loathed and distrusted France, particularly Louis Philippe. Palmerston, on the other hand, took an egregiously aggressive stance towards Russia. Yet the Eastern Question would have been far less threatening had Metternich been listened to in 1832 or 1834. As it was, relations between Russia and Britain deteriorated: the Russian navy in 1836 humiliated Palmerston by seizing a British ship, the *Vixen*, which had been caught trying to run the Russian blockade of Circassia; then fear of growing Russian influence in Afghanistan led the British to an unnecessary war there in early 1839. Meanwhile, the signing of a commercial treaty between Turkey and Britain in 1838 (which Nicholas feared contained secret clauses) and (albeit vain) Turkish attempts to raise loans in London meant that Russia's preponderant position in Turkey looked insecure.

As it was the dispute between the Sultan and Mehemet Ali flared up again in 1838, although it was not until 1839 that fighting broke out. The Sultan sent his army into Syria and was again defeated by Ibrahim Pasha. His fleet, which was sent out of the Straits, simply sailed to Egypt to surrender. The Sultan then died just before news of these catastrophes reached his capital. By 1838 the great powers had already been making contingency plans. Palmerston was determined that there should be no repeat of 1833. But if Russia was not to fight the Egyptians, who would? Palmerston suggested that the five powers should hold a conference at which it should be agreed that the three maritime powers should give assistance by sea and that Austria should give military assistance by land. Russian action should be excluded because of the 'great jealousy' it would excite in the West. So, he wrote: 'we propose the military action of Austria, which, from the intimate union existing between Austria and Russia, would be perfectly compatible with the honour of Russia; while on the other hand, from the geographical position of Austria, it would not be the source of the same jealousy to England and France.'[118] Metternich denounced this 'monstrous idea', which he saw aimed at dividing Austria from Russia, and ridiculed Palmerston. He wrote to Nesselrode: 'If Lord Palmerston believes that Syria is a province adjacent to Austria, he still has, doubtless, as an excuse the well-known ignorance of the statesmen who sometimes are found in charge of affairs of state in England.'[119] Austria would contribute naval forces to overthrow Mehemet Ali in 1840 and the Archduke Friedrich would become 'the hero of Acre', but Austria had no desire to usurp Russia in defending Turkey militarily against Egypt.[120] Britain, however, was in no position to use military force herself. Her own troops were scattered in Canada, Persia and Afghanistan, while a war with China was in the offing. The French were not militarily prepared either. So if the Russians were to be blocked, Austria had seemed the best bet. Yet Metternich in 1838 met with Nicholas again at Teplitz, where the monarchs of the Eastern Powers had met regularly since 1833. Here Nicholas and he agreed that, should it be necessary, Russia would repeat her actions of 1833 and save the Sultan in accordance to her 1833 treaty rights. When Palmerston was read the despatch from Teplitz, he commented that the Tsar was his own master and could act on his own, but 'if circumstances arose, England would not fail to intervene even at the risk of bringing on war.'[121]

In the end the Russians decided to avoid unilateral action, while Anglo–French relations went into decline. There were differences over Spain, over Greece, over the final settlement with Belgium and Holland in 1838–9, while the French were wary of British naval superiority in the Mediterranean. Palmerston, in any case, never seemed to accept them as equals. Nicholas, of course, loathed the French government, so he took the initiative to approach Britain by sending a special envoy, Baron Brunnov, to London. The eventual outcome was the first London Convention by which Britain, Prussia, Russia and Turkey all agreed that the new Sultan would offer Mehemet Ali hereditary title to Egypt along with a lifelong title to Acre and Syria. If he did not accept within ten days, then Russia, Prussia, Austria and Britain would force the offer upon him, retract the offer of the lifetime pashaliks, cut sea communi- cations between Syria and Egypt, defend Constantinople and maintain the integrity of the Ottoman Empire. The Treaty of Unkiar Skelessi, which was due to expire in 1841, would not be renewed. Indeed, in 1841 the powers would sign the Straits Convention which would make the closure of the Straits in wartime a matter of international law. Mehemet Ali in fact refused the terms he had been offered but a joint British–Austrian squadron forced him out of Syria, leaving him as hereditary Pasha of Egypt. This outcome has traditionally been viewed as a triumph for Palmerston who both defeated the threat to Turkey and got rid of the Treaty of Unkiar Skelessi. But that had never been a threat to anyone in any case. Nicholas of Russia had always intended to preserve Turkey and the agreement on the Straits changed nothing since it merely upheld traditional Turkish and international practice. Traditional British historiography has been too ready to inflate Palmerston's triumph. Nicholas, on the other hand, certainly deserves credit for initiating the accommodation with Britain and thereby possi- bly avoiding the European war that Palmerston might have been silly enough to cause had Russia acted alone. As for Metternich, he had been right all along. Palmerston may have managed to secure four-power agreement in 1840 in London, but if Metternich had been listened to in 1834, this could have happened six years earlier. His European viewpoint, however, had belatedly become reality, his contribution overshadowed as much by the obtuseness of Palmerston as by his success.

One power, however, experienced neither triumph, success nor satisfaction of any kind in 1840 and that power was France. France had ties with Egypt going back to Napoleon's expedition and like Napoleon – whose remains were returned to France in 1840, raising the nationalist temperature there – Mehemet Ali was seen as a modernising force. Moreover, his army had been and was being trained by French officers and French trade with Egypt had grown rapidly. French public opinion in 1840, therefore, was violently on the side of the Egyptian Pasha. During the negotiations in London, the French played for time. Palmerston was known to be isolated in cabinet, and Ibrahim Pasha was thought invincible. The powers, it was reckoned, would give in. The news of the Treaty of London, therefore, came as a thunderbolt. The Paris press denounced it, the public called for war and the new government of Thiers seemed ready to oblige. The fortification of Paris went ahead and Thiers warned all the powers of war. Perhaps he was bluffing, perhaps not. He certainly hoped that Mehemet Ali would prove successful, although the revolt of the Syrians and the unexpected Anglo–Austrian capture of Acre and Beirut left him few cards to play. Palmerston, however, was given to understand by Guizot, now French ambassador in London, that the most trifling concession would be welcomed by the French. He therefore told the British ambassador in Paris: 'to convey to [Thiers] in the most friendly and inoffensive manner possible, that if France begins a war, she will to a certainty lose her ships, colonies and commerce . . . that her army of Algiers will cease to give her anxiety, and that Mehemet Ali will just be chucked into the Nile.'[122] Thiers for his part told Louis Philippe:

> wise and patriotic people desire peace, have little hope of it, yet prefer war to dishonour . . . in fact we are not ready. We shall soon have 489,000 men; thanks to our determined efforts we shall have 639,000 by next April or May . . . Our navy is excellent but not sufficiently numerous; it would win the first battle and lose the last . . .[123]

A speech from the throne drafted by the government for Louis Philippe in mid-October, therefore, announced new measures of rearmament and promised that France would act 'the day she believes the European balance seriously menaced'. It ended with the flourish: 'No sacrifice would be too great to keep her position in the world . . . she will not buy [peace] at a price unworthy of her, and your King . . . wishes to leave intact to his son that sacred heritage of independence and national honour which the French Revolution has placed in his hands.'[124] When Louis Philippe declined to accept the draft, the government resigned.

The possibility that Thiers had just been bluffing over war is contradicted by his conversation in 1852 with Nassau Senior. In that conversation Thiers spelled out the details of his thinking in 1840.[125] Mehemet Ali had 130,000 men, the British 2,000 in Syria. Their ships would have been driven from the coasts in winter. Austria had promised not to send troops to Syria if France did not attack her. France had 500,000 men and a fleet that could have fought one great naval battle with the English. 'All the coalition was trembling.' But Thiers continued: 'The King's great fault was his timidity. He was personally a hero but politically a coward. He never could forget the disasters of 1813, 1814 and 1815 and I could not make him feel that, though inferior to the Continental powers united, we are more than a match for any of them separately.' As the historian of Napoleon, who obviously believed that he had mastered the secrets of Napoleon's military success, Thiers then explained how Prussia even allied with Belgium and Holland could have been destroyed in a 'fortnight'; how 'Austria would not [have been] an affair of more than one campaign' [but still more formidable than Prussia]; and, as for Russia, the most powerful of all military opponents, if France had been fairly pitted against her with no allies on either side, 'we should crush her.' There would have been no march on Moscow. The Russians would have had to march on Paris and extend their lines of communication. They would then have been defeated in Germany and France would have slowly followed their retreat through Poland, 'gradually to eat into the monster'.

Yet Louis Philippe would have none of it and Thiers, apart from accusing the king of political cowardice, could not understand why. Perhaps Metternich had something to do with it. According to Thiers: 'Metternich said, "I have staked all on one card – the chance of a quarrel between the King and Thiers". And it turned up in his favour. But you cannot wonder at my disgust.'[126] Thiers mentioned no other foreign statesman in his discussion of Louis Philippe's climb down in 1840. Did he believe, therefore, that Metternich might have exerted influence of some kind on the king? If so he did not say what. Yet it is entirely possible that Metternich did change the course of history in 1840 in a manner entirely unknown to Thiers.

On 13 December 1842, Sir Robert Gordon, brother of the British foreign secretary and British ambassador in Vienna, wrote to his brother that reports that Metternich had become pro-French were untrue:

> He could not do so as an Austrian and a German and in this matter we should not mistake appearances for reality. His coquetry [*sic*] towards Louis Philippe and his government proceeds from the same impulse which marks his conduct towards Turkey – it is grateful [i.e. gratifying] to him to be counted and consulted by the French Govt., to be appealed to as arbiter and constantly told that through his influence and intervention France refrains from disturbing the peace of Europe.[127]

If so, this was not mere flattery, for Sir Robert then related a rather extraordinary story to his brother, the foreign secretary:

> Metternich has often told me that he holds Louis Philippe in his hands and it is his business to turn this to account. He holds on the following grounds. In 1808, Louis Philippe was most urgent in his desire to enter the Austrian service and wrote sundry letters to P. Metternich entreating him to use his influence with the Emperor of Austria to carry this point; these letters contained most immeasured [*sic*] abuse of his own country, most compromising for him as a French subject and how much more so for him as a king! And these letters are still in Metternich's possession.[128]

If that were not enough, Gordon related yet another story:

> At a subsequent period Louis Philippe opened his whole soul to Metternich when wishing through an intrigue to supplant the elder Bourbons and possess himself of the throne of Louis XVIII – Metternich lent his ear to the whole plot and it was only after Louis Philippe had been enticed into developing all the details of it that Metternich said to him: '*Pour qui me prenez-vous, traitre?*' ('Who do you take me for, traitor?')[129]

The upshot was that Metternich could persuade Louis Philippe to moderate French policy whenever he wanted. In Gordon's words:

> Judge then if a footing of confidence is not established between them at the present day and of this Metternich would avail himself for the benefit of the peace of Europe. With this object in view he would

prefer to address France rather as the 'friend Metternich' than as the Chancellor of Austria and thus in the Franco-Belgian question [an attempt by France in 1842 to establish a Franco-Belgian customs union] he expects more from Louis Philippe's being persuaded by his 'friend Metternich' than from the joint official remonstrances of all the cabinets in Europe.[130] [France dropped the plan for the customs union].

Could it be that in 1840 Metternich 'staked all on one card – the chance of a quarrel between the King and Thiers', as Thiers himself put it, because he knew that Louis Philippe could not survive the publication of his letters of 1808?[131] After all, in 1830 the poster Thiers and others had produced in favour of him had included the following sentences: 'The Duc d'Orléans was at Jemappes. The Duc d'Orléans is a Citizen King. The Duc d'Orléans has carried the tricolour under the enemy's fire.'[132] The knowledge that he had subsequently wanted to desert Napoleon for the Austrians would hardly have allowed him to survive in France in the very year when Napoleon's statue had been replaced on its column in the Place Vendôme (to Louis Philippe's salute) and Napoleon's remains had been brought home to Les Invalides. What more opportune time could there possibly have been for 'friend Metternich' to blackmail the king in order to prevent a war and save the peace of Europe? It is an enticing speculation. Metternich, according to Sir Robert Gordon, had no respect for Louis Philippe, whom he accused of avarice and an inordinate desire to promote the interests of his family rather than those of France. His attempted treason against Louis XVIII would not have helped either. Gordon's revelations might also explain therefore why in the mid-thirties Austria, after playing along for a while to separate France and Britain, would have nothing to do with the proposals of marriage, touted by France, between a son of Louis Philippe and an Austrian archduchess. They certainly go a long way, if true, to explain what Thiers denounced as Louis Philippe's '*rage pacifique*' and '*paix à tout prix*'.[133] Thiers wanted a European war: 'My *rêve* was a war by France and England against Austria and Russia. Such a war could have freed Italy and secured the independence of Turkey. And there were half a dozen occasions *but for him* [author's emphasis] we might have had one.'[134] Was Metternich the blackmailer as significant as Metternich the statesman? In the absence of further proof, one can only guess.

Between 1840 and 1848, the Anglo-French *entente cordiale*, a phrase first used by Lord Aberdeen in English ('a cordial understanding') but taken up by Louis Philippe and Guizot, continually broke down.[135] As has been seen already, tensions in Greece, Spain and over the final details of the Belgian settlement had done much to undermine good relations between the two powers in the 1830s, while the 1840 crisis had undermined them completely. (Russia even offered Britain her Baltic fleet to help ward off a possible French invasion!) Then in 1842, Britain and the other powers threatened war if the proposed Franco–Belgian customs union was effected, which it was not. Still, with the Tories coming to power between 1841 and 1846, Aberdeen tried hard to use his good relations with Guizot to improve relations.

This was not to happen. In the discussion on Schroeder, it has already been demonstrated how often war between Britain and France seemed to be in the offing. The press on both sides of the Channel seemed to want one at different times and clashes over French policy in North Africa (when the bombardment of Tangier in 1844 by the Prince de Joinville, third son of Louis Philippe, and a threatened march on Fez, seemed to portend the French conquest of Morocco) and even Tahiti (where the French imprisoned a British protestant missionary after they annexed the territory) seemed quite capable of providing the occasion. The end of the *entente* was brought about by the affair of the Spanish marriages.[136] Aberdeen, apparently, had agreed with Guizot that the Infanta of Spain could marry the Duke of Montpensier, Louis Philippe's youngest son, but only once her sister, the queen of Spain, had married a Spanish grandee (the Duke of Cadiz) and had already borne a child. Palmerston, however, on his return to the Foreign Office in 1846, heard that Cadiz was impotent and raised (again) the possibility of a pro-British, Coburg candidate to marry the queen. Guizot was furious and the end result was the simultaneous marriages of the queen and her sister. Palmerston protested and the British ambassador to Spain was sent home but, fortunately, the queen produced an heir and a male one at that. After this quarrel, Guizot turned to Austria for diplomatic support and, with Britain isolated, Metternich in 1846 succumbed to Russian pressure to annex the free city of Krakow where a revolution had broken out. (In fact, the Austrians had been running it more or less for a decade after previous trouble there.) Palmerston made little fuss,[137] but when a joint Franco–Austrian intervention in Switzerland appeared on the cards in 1847, and French public opinion prevented these two powers from acting alone, his delaying tactics meant that the radicals had won the civil war there before anything could be done.[138] The breach between France and Britain was confirmed and, as Metternich boasted, the whole of Europe seemed united against England.[139]

Alternative Paradigms to Schroeder's

How then can we assess Metternich's place in international relations between 1815 and 1848? It is useful first of all to examine how diplomacy worked during this period. Paul Schroeder's paradigm of two hegemonic flanking powers (Britain and Russia) controlling a system of benign sub-hegemonies within a European 'equilibrium' that paid due attention to principles of morality and justice has already been rejected as both fanciful and in opposition to the facts. However, there are at least two other possible paradigms which can be examined. The first is one put forward by the late Roger Bullen who argued that Europe's state system functioned as one in which the great powers controlled client states in their particular, if unofficial, spheres of influence, intervening to ensure that their own interests prevailed.[140] Thus Russia controlled Poland and wanted to control Turkey, Britain controlled Portugal and Belgium and used her navy to protect Greece and the Latin American republics, Austria controlled Italy and Germany (with help from Prussia), while France, at first denied any spheres of influence at all, attempted to control Spain after 1823. Peace, according to this paradigm, depended on the powers recognising one another's spheres of influence and refraining from challenging the predominant power in each. At the start of the second Mehemet Ali crisis, for example, the French foreign minister, Count Molé, told the Russian chargé d'affaires:

> You have Turkey, as we have Belgium and Spain. They could not be touched without bringing all our interests into play. Instead of thinking merely of prolonging the present state of things, Lord Palmerston is concerned only with the means of diminishing your preponderance in the Orient. The result is that he comes up with the most inconceivable proposals; sometimes it is an Austrian army which he would like to see placed at the disposal of the Porte; again it is a conference through which he wishes to paralyse your action.[141]

Molé's statement is interesting for another reason – he assumes quite wrongly that the other powers in 1838 saw Belgium and Spain as client states of France. Britain certainly did not. Perhaps that is why he was showing sympathy towards the Russians.

In elaborating his analysis, Bullen made several key points. First, interventions were not acts of war and needed no declarations of war; rather, they were acts of assistance in support of beleaguered, friendly governments. Secondly, interventions were legal and legitimate; they were based on the 1815 treaties and the international order established by them – France indeed, maintained, once she had been admitted to the concert at Aix-la-Chapelle, that she also had a legitimate right to intervene internationally to support that order. The assumption was that international order and domestic tranquillity went hand in hand. Revolution caused war and war caused revolution. However, after 1820 the powers split over the legitimacy of intervention. By the protocol of Troppau, the eastern powers asserted not only was intervention a police action in aid of a government under threat, but that intervention should always take place in the name of the European alliance. This meant that no invitation from the government of the beleaguered state was needed. Neither Britain nor France could accept this and Castlereagh in his State Paper of May 1820 insisted that the alliance was one directed only at France if she again came under the rule of a Napoleon or otherwise threatened the rest of Europe. In any case, there had to be an invitation by a government under threat before one or more of the powers could intervene. In practice the eastern powers conceded this by the 1833 Convention of Berlin which laid down the need to be invited by the government concerned before an intervention could take place. The 1834 Quadruple Alliance and its Additional Articles confirmed this for the western powers. This right to intervene, however, was only debated in Britain and France, particularly in Britain, where radicals and liberals gave loud and principled support to a doctrine of 'non-intervention'. Britain's liberals could never forget that her constitution was based on the 'glorious Revolution' of 1688 (the self-conscious political precedent and model for the Orleanists in 1830 in France), when a legitimate king had been overthrown and replaced. They wanted therefore to allow radicals and reformers elsewhere in Europe the opportunity to introduce reforms and undermine legitimists, without the fear of foreign intervention. In the end, of course, despite supposed British and French support for 'non-intervention', British and French governments became used to intervening regularly in Spain and Portugal, not to mention Greece, Turkey and Latin America. Nor was there much difference between intervention in the Iberian peninsula, for example, and intervention in Italy. Palmerston was no more successful in getting Portuguese or Spanish governments to reform than Metternich was in getting Italian ones to put their houses in order. Moreover, the client states involved in both cases were well aware that, in spite of this, the protecting power would probably intervene in the last resort if asked, in order to maintain prestige and its predominance in its own sphere. Thus, although Palmerston once complained that friendly states could simply not be allowed to 'go to the dogs',[142] the tail of these states could often wag his own dog or that of Austria. The powers, therefore, became reluctant to intervene and instead spent much time lecturing their clients on the need for good, stable government. After all, the costs of intervention could be enormous and there was never any way of knowing what the consequences would be. Hence France's refusal, for example, to intervene in Spain in 1835. Intervention was always, therefore, a policy 'of last resort'.[143]

Two other points should be noted. The Convention of Berlin laid down that the eastern powers were 'the most appropriate powers to render aid' in eastern and central Europe and that no other power could interfere 'with the aid that had been requested and offered'.[144] In other words, France should stay out. But often it was not clear which power was the 'appropriate' one to render aid and so spheres of influence became areas of Europe where the powers clashed and war became possible. This was true of Belgium, Greece, Spain and Turkey. Nor were the acts of the powers involved 'benign'. Usually, they involved military confrontation or conquest or at least the threat or risk of war. Palmerston certainly threatened war over Belgium and Turkey. The Greek crisis and the affairs of Spain and Portugal often carried the risk of war. And, of course, intervention rarely brought justice, enlightenment or reform. Schroeder's vision of benign sub-hegemonies is pure fantasy. The balance of power simply dictated that one great power felt compelled to control lesser states or to prevent other great powers from dominating a particular area strategically or ideologically. Morality had nothing to do with it. Bullen's paradigm is a helpful one, therefore, in explaining much that happened between 1815 and 1848.

It does not explain everything, however, and in particular it does not explain what happened when crises arose outside the client states or between the European great powers in general. Why did some powers insist for example that the influence of others should be excluded from certain areas? Why were there not more general agreements among the powers? Clearly, factors such as geography and military strategies played a role, but often it is suggested, particularly after 1830, that ideology was the key. Europe was divided into two ideological camps: the liberal West and the conservative East. It was the tension between these two camps and the competition between their two spokesmen (Palmerston and Metternich) that determined how the balance of power operated.

How true was this? Palmerston certainly hoped that Britain and France could form a liberal camp in Europe. After the fall of Charles X he declared: 'This event is decisive of the ascendancy of Liberal

Principles all throughout Europe; the evil spirit has been put down and will be trodden underfoot. The reign of Metternich is over.'[145] Fundamentally, he did believe in constitutionalism and the power of public opinion: 'Constitutional states I consider to be the natural allies of this country and . . . no English ministry will perform its duty if it be inattentive to the interests of such states.'[146] There were two great parties in Europe, he said, one of which rested on physical force and the other on public opinion. But the latter would be the winner and would 'subdue the fleshly arm of physical strength'.[147] Melbourne, the British prime minister, was more sceptical and did not see logically why constitutional states should be more Anglophile than others. But Palmerston told him in a private letter of 1836:

> Every day brings fresh proofs of the complete union of the three powers [Austria, Russia and Prussia] on every question of European policy, and affords additional evidence that they are for the present what they told us three years ago they must be considered – namely, a unity . . . The division of Europe into two camps . . . to which you much object, is the result of events beyond our control and is the consequence of the French Revolution of July. The three powers fancy their interests lie in a direction opposite to that in which we and France conceive ours to be placed. The separation is not one of words but of things; not the effect of caprice or will but produced by the force of occurrences. The three and the two think differently, and therefore they act differently, whether it be as to Belgium or Portugal or to Spain.[148]

On the other hand, even Palmerston himself never really trusted the French. He had had to threaten them with war over Belgium, soon became disillusioned with them over events in Spain and Portugal, was challenged by them in Greece and from 1840 not only found himself facing war with them over Mehemet Ali but returned to office in 1846 to find that they had cheated him over the Spanish marriages. Indeed, even between 1841 and 1846 during the period of Aberdeen and Guizot's supposed *entente cordiale*, war had always been on the cards. And between 1846 and 1848, Guizot had turned to Metternich for support. So another side to Palmerston lay not far under the surface – his need to control France. In 1830 he had told Lord Holland: 'the Treaty of Vienna which, however objectionable in some of the details of its arrangements, is yet with its accessories of Paris and Aix-la-Chapelle, the great security of Europe against the inveterately enervating spirit of

France.'[149] When he sent Lord Minto to Italy in the autumn of 1847 to encourage reform there, he made his views clear on where the danger to Europe still lay, despite Guizot's newly found friendship with Vienna:

> Leave things as they are, and you leave France the power of disturbing the peace of Europe wherever she chooses. Two or three million francs, properly applied, will organize an insurrection at any time, and the ascendancy of the Liberal party at Paris, whenever it may happen . . . will soon be followed by an outbreak in Italy. That is the point to which the French Liberals look; they know that if they tried to get back to the Rhine they would have against them all Germany united, Russia and more or less England.[150]

French intervention in Italy, moreover, would lead to war with Austria. This would probably spread to Germany but, stressed Palmerston, 'we can have no wish to see Austria broken down and France aggrandized.'[151] With the declaration of a republic in France at the end of February 1848, he expressed his fear that 'large republics seem to be essentially and inherently aggressive'[152] and believed that France might now be 'despotically governed by eight or nine men who are the mere subordinates of 40,000 or 50,000 of the scum of the faubourgs of Paris.'[153] Perhaps he might even have been tempted to endorse the view expressed by Castlereagh in his last speech to Parliament on 21 February 1821: 'I deprecate the doctrine that subjects of governments which do not enjoy a representative system are justified in throwing off their allegiance and resorting to arms in order to obtain one.'[154]

The Orleanists in France, of course, had always hoped for better things from England, for they were all Anglophiles and believed that Britain and France shared political liberties unknown in Austria, Prussia and Russia. As Thiers, the dominant spirit of the July Monarchy, put it as early as 1822: 'Remember that before '89 we had no annual representation, no freedom of the press, no individual liberty, no voting of taxes, no equality before the law, no eligibility for offices . . . it needed the Revolution to make them legal realities.'[155] And he, like Guizot, believed that after 1688 Britain's liberties also rested on a revolutionary basis. Yet this proved no basis for cooperation between France and England. Palmerston talked of constitutionalism and liberty all the time, but as has been seen, he wanted to control France. He knew that Thiers, Guizot, Louis Philippe and all patriotic Frenchmen resented the 1815 settlement and wanted the natural frontiers. He knew France wanted to run Spain by herself. He had seen her support for Mehemet

Ali which threatened not only the peace of Europe but the balance of power in Asia. And he himself had been tricked by France's own sponsor of the *entente cordiale* over the Spanish marriages. By 1848 he thought the French were itching to start another war in Europe and in 1848 itself feared a return to 1793. 1688 seemed much less relevant.

In the end, therefore, was there much difference between him and Metternich, save that he occasionally had a public opinion and elections to win? Probably not. Both believed in restraining France and Russia, both believed in the 1815 settlement, both wanted Turkey to survive independently in the Near East. Palmerston even believed in 1830 that the continued union of Belgium and Holland 'would have been more advantageous to the general interests of Europe.'[156] Gavin Henderson, therefore, many years ago now in a famous review of Palmerston's foreign policy, approvingly quoted the view of Sir Charles Webster, Palmerston's famous defender, that Palmerston had 'exactly the same plan of making a European centre as Metternich himself.'[157] Only Palmerston wanted it to be in London. He, not Metternich, was to be the arbiter of European affairs, holding the ring between France and the rest of Europe.

Metternich Wins

Metternich's views in 1832 and 1834 would indubitably have served Europe better, although in 1840 Palmerston got the credit for peace. Perhaps then too, as we have hinted, it was Metternich who really deserved the laurels. In any case, it seems inescapable that the real paradigm for European diplomacy between 1815 and 1848 was simply the Metternich system. Basically this consisted of the union of the powers against revolution and this is surely the real dynamic that operated between 1815 and 1848. At times it did seem threatened, but it never really broke down. At all times, however, through one challenge after another, Metternich kept preaching the same message of its fundamental importance. There were spheres of influence and they were important for the rivalries they caused and crises they produced. There were ideological differences between east and west. But fear of revolution was always the bottom line in international affairs even for the British and – ironically – the French. If Metternich passed the Six Acts for Germany in 1832, Britain had already passed her own notorious Six Acts against seditious libels, incendiary political journals, seditious meetings and the acquisition of arms for seditious purposes as early as 1819. Thiers was famous for his 1834 laws which muzzled the French press and political associations (trade unions had been illegal since 1791) and, unlike

Metternich, he became known after 1834 as the leader of 'the massacre of the Rue Transnonain' after personally leading a column of troops to clear rebels out of the Hôtel de Ville that year. Nothing remotely like that happened in Vienna while Metternich was in office. Again, Metternich never had to fear that anyone would attempt to butcher him and his colleagues, as almost happened to the British Cabinet as a result of the Cato Street conspiracy of 1820. (The Emperor of Austria regularly walked about Vienna and other parts of his Empire, often with his Empress, without protection!) Castlereagh had reported the conspiracy to his brother, then ambassador to Vienna, who no doubt passed on all the lurid details to Metternich: 'Had our information not been such as to enable us to watch all their movements, and to interfere when we deemed fit, the fifteen cabinet ministers would have been murdered yesterday in Harroby's dining parlour.'[158] Fourteen men had been picked to slaughter the ministers but the authorities (Britain's secret police!) moved in to arrest them. Since cabinet members were aware for months that they were being shadowed by would-be assassins, Castlereagh felt able to boast: 'you will allow that we are tolerably cool troops.'[159] Little wonder then that Metternich felt unconvinced by the claims of democracy. In any case, 97 per cent of the British population and 99 per cent of the French population had no vote. Thiers, the great voice of French constitutionalism, was elected in Aix-en-Provence in 1830 by 177 votes out of 220 cast; in 1846 he won by 222 out of 238.[160] Did he have much greater claim than Metternich, therefore, to be the voice of the people? Not that it was a claim that it would ever have occurred to Metternich to make. His job was not to speak for the people but to protect them, by keeping France in check and the revolution at bay, by reminding all the powers of their duty to respect the 1815 settlement, to avoid making concessions to domestic radicals and to avoid a European war. More than any other statesman he did this successfully for thirty years.

His so-called principles have been much debated, but at their core was a conservative belief that the powers should work together to preserve peace and to reject any alternative order that promised heaven on earth through violent change or terror. If revolution did break out, then it was to be immediately crushed or at least contained, depending on the consequences. The international legal order had to be preserved, but that order had also to contain the means for its own protection and survival. It is surely little wonder, therefore, that Capefigue and Stiles saw him as Europe's outstanding statesman. His principles still rule the civilised world today.

4
Did Metternich Plan to Federalise the Empire?

At the height of the Cold War, conservative defenders of Metternich in America produced the argument that, far from being a reactionary, Metternich after 1815 had actually wanted to decentralise the Habsburg Monarchy and encourage representative government and states' rights; his federalist vision, however, had been frustrated by the Emperor Francis. Was there any truth in these unlikely assertions? If not, how had they come about? At the bottom of the argument was a series of documents dating from 1817. Here, for example, is the view of US conservative Peter Viereck:

> Metternich in 1817 also urged freer institutions for the rest of the empire, with an embryonic parliament which, once started, would inevitably have assumed an ever greater governing power. Possibly central Europe might even have followed England's evolutionary road of 1832 towards a freer society instead of the revolutionary road of 1848 and 1918. His plans (to summarize from two different memoranda of 1817) included a 'deliberative body of notables', partly elected by provincial diets and partly appointed to represent the country in 'scrutiny of the budget and every law'. Far-sighted, in view of the Slav and Italian revolts that were to wreck the monarchy, is his plan of separate constitutions and separate chancellors for the chief national minorities, protecting them from the oppression of Germanization.[1]

In 1963 this line of defence was powerfully reinforced by the publication of American historian Arthur G. Haas's book *Metternich: Reorganization and Nationality, 1813–1818*[2] which, based as it was on

thorough archival research, appeared to confirm the revisionist interpretation of the 1817 memoranda referred to by Viereck. Haas based
most of his conclusions on documents referring to Lombardy-Venetia
although the book dealt also with Illyria, a subject which he treated
elsewhere.[3] According to Haas,[4] Metternich in 1817 had attempted 'to
form the so badly shaken Monarchy into an inwardly balanced and
stable union of constituent states with equal rights', something that
constituted 'a notable example of statesmanlike foresight and intelligence'. Haas's work was well received by a number of experts.[5] Professor
Bertier de Sauvigny in France, for instance, agreeing that Metternich
had wanted to remould the Empire, wrote in a review[6] that it had been
Metternich's aim 'to bring the turbulent Hungarian nation back into
line by balancing and surrounding it with other entities endowed with
the same privileges and competences'. In Austria, it obviously influenced Professor Heinrich Benedikt's conception of Metternich as he
appears in *Kaiseradler über dem Appenin: Die Österreicher in Italien, 1700
bis 1866*,[7] for there Benedikt wrote of him: 'he was in favour of a federal
state, provincial diets and pointed to the dangers of centralization in
the Emperor's patriarchal rule.' Paul Schroeder expressed some doubts
about Haas's general thesis in a very short but generally commendatory
review in the *American Historical Review*[8] but nowhere was the thesis
subjected to a thoroughgoing critique until I challenged it in an article
I contributed to a Festschrift for A. J. P. Taylor's seventieth birthday.[9]
Since then the few scholars who have examined the subject appear to
have accepted my arguments,[10] namely that Metternich merely wanted
to establish an expanded, more efficient, but still purely consultative,
State Council in Vienna, with a very few representatives added from the
emasculated provincial diets which, unlike Francis I, he wanted to
retain to mask Vienna's central control.

Although this particular debate centred around Metternich's 1817
memoranda, Metternich himself first took up the subject of the machinery of government in the Habsburg Monarchy in 1811. Document 183
of volume two of his memoirs is headed 'On the Organisation of An
Imperial Council of the Empire in Austria', a document drawn up for
Francis I.[11] This long document begins with Metternich's observations
on Kaunitz's council of 1760 in Austria, the Napoleonic Senate and
Russia's Imperial State Council established by Tsar Alexander I. The first
he dismissed as 'nothing more than a ministry with several heads
instead of one premier'. It 'clogged the very wheels of government itself.
It had assigned to it a very important sphere of action, of which the
advising of the monarch on prepared agenda formed only a small

portion'. Kaunitz himself felt that his role as de facto premier demeaned the position of the monarch, but the cooption of other members merely led to jealousy and confusion, which got worse as members died off. (Kaunitz had been Metternich's father-in-law.) The Napoleonic Senate was dismissed by Metternich as 'better organised' but 'suited for a constitutional government'. The Russian Imperial Council he dismissed as 'suited for a new country' and resembling either a high court of justice or a court of exchequer. Much the worst of the three variants, however, had been the Kaunitz council and the reasons for that, Metternich stressed, lay not with its members but with its methods. Here Metternich laid out his fundamental objection to how Austria was governed and how, despite his best efforts at centralisation and ratio- nalisation, it would continue to be governed until 1848. It is very important to understand his position, so here it is in full:

> Without deliberation, without oral debates, no council is possible. Instead of unity a mere circulation of writings took place, the written notes showing differences of opinion without number. What a strong position have the later councillors, who comment not only on the subject itself but also on the preceding counsel; how timidly must councillors go to work. How often would they (as is the case in all oral deliberations) not have modified their ideas if they had known the remarks of subsequent councillors. Lastly, and these are the most important considerations, how little would questions be defined, how little would the monarch be placed in a position to obtain a thoroughly considered, correct, and well-argued opinion. Shall the monarch accept the judgement of one of his ministers or of the whole court, or that of the first, second or third councillor? The subject has circulated and yet everything is in uncertainty. The monarch will be compelled to examine it all himself, which is impos- sible – or to lay it before one of the councillors, or some confidant. What frightful power thus falls into the hands of one man, who unknown, without responsibility, may throw out the well-considered work of the whole council, simply by his single opinion! And if this does not happen and the monarch gives only a partial confidence, it is but a separate, useless vote, which only increases the uncertainty. And if the monarch devotes his life to the work, and endeavours to oversee the whole range of affairs, will he not soon be convinced that time and human strength are quite inadequate? The public censures one or other of the individuals, from whom the censure soon spreads to the whole council.

What Metternich was saying was that reliance on written reports meant that the Emperor always got a series of memoranda that contradicted one another, with those written at the start being criticised by later ones but with no overall conclusion being reached. The Emperor could then rely on one or several for a decision or ask for yet another piece of written advice or even try to do everything by himself, for which he did not have the time. In any case, the end result was confusion and delay with the public criticising one councillor or another or the whole government. Metternich instead wanted all proposals thrashed out orally and a clear decision arrived at. This would speed up business, make it much more efficient and accountable and save on reams of files and paperwork.

Commenting on recent developments, Metternich argued that a reorganisation of the State Council (*Staatsrat*) in 1807 had been the work of subaltern officials who wanted to take control of the executive power themselves. However, since the State Council had been abolished in December 1809, Metternich now felt able to recommend a new arrangement to Francis regarding the machinery of government. He wanted the Emperor to summon a new State Council which would be a deliberative one (i.e. take decisions after full discussions), which would be greater in size, which would 'give the central power more central feeling' and would lighten the monarch's load. The model would be the French Senate 'modified to suit the locality and the present situation'.

Metternich told Francis that he should summon a *Reichsrat* or Imperial Council which should represent all his lands, including all German and Hungarian provinces. He himself should preside over it, but when this was impossible this duty should be assigned to a minister of state (for no longer than a year at a time). The Imperial Council should only be able to deliberate on matters assigned to it by the monarch. It was to consist of imperial councillors, ministers of state and a director. Neither councillors nor ministers should normally preside. It should be divided into separate sections for legal and judicial affairs, internal affairs, financial affairs and military affairs. The number of ministers of state appointed need not be fixed. They would have a vote like any other councillor and would preside over a specific section of the council if so appointed. There should be no more than twenty members of the council in all and three at least should be appointed to each section, one of whom would preside. The Emperor would appoint members to each section every six months. The Emperor's agenda (deliberanda) for each section would be communicated (if necessary through the presiding minister) to the president of each section, who would report back the results of deliberations. These would begin with one council member making a report on the matter to be discussed. If, subsequently, that matter needed to be discussed before the whole Imperial Council, the same councillor would speak to it. A legal copyist from the personnel department of the Council would be appointed to each section to take minutes; while in the Council as a whole, the director would be responsible for the protocols. Clearly, then these proposals of 1811 foreshadowed those of 1817. That they did not foresee any federalist reorganisation was clear from the following remarks: 'Such an Imperial Council will bring about the amalgamation of the different provinces of the empire. German and Hungarian councillors sit in the different sections. Purely Hungarian matters would naturally be given *ad referendum* by the president of the sections to Hungarian members, or to those members entrusted with the affairs of that kingdom' (i.e. they did not have to be Hungarians).

Crucially, Metternich proposed that foreign affairs be kept separate from the deliberations of the Imperial Council. He drew attention to a separate council on foreign affairs that Kaunitz had established alongside his State Council of 1760 but dismissed it as equally useless:

Foreign relations include the whole, and can only be conducted by one mind and one spirit, which must have the control of the whole, the open as well as the secret relations of the powers, and keeps both foreign countries and the Fatherland constantly in view. The organisation of the conference, with its *circulandis* despatches, extracts etc., cannot, and does not, still exist because it was something formed out of nothing. Secret matters cannot be circulated, and the little light that newspapers can give – and such only were the extracts of despatches – on the true relations of the powers is known from the nature of things. This organisation fell, like the Council of State, because the foundations of both made their existence quite impossible.'

In short, Metternich should be allowed to run foreign affairs by himself in the interests of efficiency and state secrecy.

Still, Metternich had not yet finished with his reform proposals. He noted that since the State Council had been abolished, Francis had had a ministerial one. This he regarded as 'of essential use' and wanted to keep it even once an Imperial Council was up and running. For there were many occasions when the heads of all ministries wanted to address the Emperor together, while on other occasions the Emperor might wish to address the ministry as a whole 'on some matter of a more secret kind'. So Metternich proposed a ministerial conference composed of a few select ministers, to be appointed by the Emperor, presumably to expedite the despatch of the most important imperial business. These ministers would remain members of the Imperial Council. The Emperor himself would decide which business would go to the Council and which to the Conference. He would be advised by both but the ministerial conference would presumably have the duty to execute both the policies recommended by the Council and those which were too urgent or secret to be submitted to it.

The memorandum drawn up by Metternich ended with four sections on the principal advantages he saw in his proposals. Two were fairly straightforward: that the council sections would form a good training ground for future statesmen and that provision for well-researched and impartial advice would bring strength and repose to government. His second advantage was meant to flatter the Emperor; such a system as the one he proposed would enable the monarch to become 'the sole true central point of the state, the one point from which everything proceeds and to which everything returns'. His spirit would therefore animate the whole new system which would serve as a 'school of government' even to the heir to the throne – 'there the monarch learns to know his servants, the successor to the throne, his duties, the statesman surveys the whole.' Yet Metternich's real purpose was revealed in his second listed advantage: 'The Council of State [or Imperial Council], according to its proper notion, cannot be an executive body. It advises the monarch, in whom all powers are united in his functions of making and guarding laws.' Metternich then argued that only 'the power which is exercised by ministers' was 'delegated'. There could be no going back to the days of Kaunitz when the State Council interfered with the duties of ministers:

If the monarch deposits a part of his executive power in the hands of a minister, chief of a department, that minister must be free indeed. The security of the state with regard to him lies in his responsibility. How should this be possible if a committee, or what is worse, a single individual to whose talents the monarch has ventured to commit the management of a department in rare cases, can daily interfere with the management of the minister, suffer him only half to act where he ought to do it wholly? The Council of State must not interfere with the course of business; the principles for which the office exists the monarch must establish with an ultimate reference to himself, and must examine all measures proposed.

That was really the nub of his proposed reforms.

The context of the 1811 memorandum was the coming war between France and Russia and Metternich's desire that the Monarchy should be as strong as possible – militarily, economically and constitutionally – once war broke out. Napoleon had forecast that armed neutrality would gain Austria nothing,[12] but Metternich was determined that it should be decisive. Hence the need to strengthen Austria as much as possible beforehand. When it came to the constitution, Metternich explained the context in his memoirs:

> what forced itself upon me was the *strengthening of the central power* [author's emphasis]. The Austrian monarchy is a composite whole, formed of separate districts which are historically or legally, from reasons of necessity or considerations of prudence, held together by having a common head. In a state like this, the idea of unity inseparable from the existence of an Empire requires to be matured and rightly defined, if it is not to become a mere personal union with all the attendant weaknesses. The existence of a moral body convoked to defend supreme sovereign power in the head of the Empire, without at the same time restricting the separate rights of the provinces, seemed to be the most appropriate means by which to assert the conception of imperial unity.[13]

This meant a 'well-organized Council of State', organised as 'one common deliberative body; *to give the central power a more central spirit* [author's emphasis], so as to procure for the monarch, by a higher degree of tranquillity and security, greater facility for carrying out his own work'.[14]

Metternich, therefore, if one takes both the 1811 and 1817 memoranda into consideration, wanted the Habsburg Monarchy to be run by the Emperor as a chief executive who took advice from a State or Imperial Council in Vienna on which were represented delegates from all over the Monarchy. This Council was to reach clear decisions after oral deliberations either in sections or in the Council sitting as a whole. Foreign policy, however, for reasons of state, was not to be part of the area under review by the Council; domestic policy alone would be under its remit. Decisions reached regarding domestic policy were then to be put into effect by ministers who, like the foreign minister, were responsible only to the Emperor who had delegated his authority to them. However, they were collectively to form part of a ministerial conference presided over once again by the Emperor who in this way could review government policy as a whole. The State Council was really a sort of ersatz legislature. Metternich in his memoirs noted Napoleon's conversation of 1812 in which the Corsican had boasted of gagging the *Corps Législatif* and replacing it with the *Conseil d'État*.[15] In the former everyone had run after applause – 'they want to be noticed and applauded . . . they did nothing but make revolution so I put them in order – I dissolved them.' His planned Council of State, on the other hand, would constitute a 'real representation' since it would contain men who were 'well accustomed to business' – 'no mere tattlers, no *idéologues*, no false tinsel'. Metternich hoped that the Imperial or State Council he was proposing would be just as realistic in its approach to Habsburg affairs.

Despite the self-serving nature of Metternich's proposals, given that foreign affairs were not meant to be reviewed by the Council, there was indeed much to be said for his plans. They did indeed provide for rational, strong and coherent government. Yet they unfortunately depended on the Habsburgs providing emperors capable of chairing ministerial and council discussions. And neither Francis I nor his mentally retarded successor Ferdinand I would or could do this. So Metternich was left to complain for decades that the Monarchy was merely 'administered' rather than 'governed'.

Francis had succeeded to the throne in 1792 at the age of twenty-four and was none too sure of himself. So between 1792 and 1805 his former tutor, Count Franz Collerado-Walsee, became his Cabinet Minister and de facto head of government. Collerado lacked the intellectual capacity for the job and, especially after the outbreak of the French Revolution, always counselled caution and conservatism. Francis himself was probably more open-minded at first, trying to keep a balance between the Josephinists and anti-Josephinists at court and welcoming 'frankness' from family members and officials. However, after the discovery of the Jacobin conspiracies of 1794, when previously high-ranking officials were found to have plotted the murder of the imperial family and the establishment of a French-style republic, Francis's conservatism became much more rigid.[16] None of this was a worry to Metternich, but by the time he wrote his memorandum of 1811, Francis had been on the throne for nineteen years and was set in his ways. In particular, according to Friedrich Walter,[17] 'he had a great dislike of communicating through conferences of any size' and had developed a marked preference for working through written memoranda at his desk, a form of government that became associated with him. His deep sense of mistrust in people made him take advice from different experts whose views interested him and who might receive the title of 'cabinet adviser'. Often such people had free access to him and their views might hold more weight than those of state councillors. In this way, Francis could get a pretty good insight into a variety of matters, although it left the system of government disorganised and demoralised. No one knew whose advice would be sought or taken, even if the State Council had made a recommendation. Still, the latter functioned as the main coordinating body of the domestic imperial bureaucracy, although each part of that bureaucracy (commonly known as the *Hofstellen* or 'court offices') was run on collegiate lines (Metternich's *Haus-Hof-und-Staatskanzlei* was not), with votes on policy decisions being taken within each office to finalise policy recommendations, another factor which impeded strong government. (The collegiate system was supposed to encourage individual thought and initiative among officials, but since the president of each court office usually held the upper hand, few dared cast their votes against him, the end result being, in Walter's estimation,[18] 'lost time, increased paperwork, a tedious working method and indecisive half-measures'.) Nor was any ministerial conference put in place by Francis; he did consult with Metternich as foreign minister or state chancellor and with other ministers after 1815 although the post of interior minister fell into disuse almost as soon as it was created in 1818 and that of finance minister was abolished in 1829. Meanwhile, the 'ministerial conference' which met infrequently was attended by Metternich, the chief of police and the heads of the political and financial sections of the State Council. In short, Francis ruled from his desk, consulting whom he liked when he liked. This was called the *Kabinettsweg*.

Why did Metternich not push his proposals harder or more often? Why did he not threaten to resign? In 1811, of course, he was a relatively new foreign minister, still without any major foreign policy success and with relatively little experience of Vienna, so could not have expected to dictate domestic administrative arrangements. In 1817, however, he was in a vastly stronger position. Indeed, with respect to the period 1815–48 as a whole, Constantin de Grunwald claimed that he stamped 'every branch of the administration with his own personality' and 'enjoyed the privileges of a prime minister without being called upon to bear official responsibility'.[19] Viktor Bibl, too, believed that Metternich, albeit unfortunately, controlled internal as well as foreign affairs: 'he was in fact the all-powerful minister, who had the decisive say in the great questions of domestic policy, such as the Hungarian question, and was above all the very soul of the generally detested secret police which destroyed the finances of the state.'[20]

Kolowrat in 1831 lamented to Kübeck: 'Metternich exploits the emperor's anxieties. He awakes and sustains with all means at his disposal the emperor's fear of the spectre of revolution. *Hence he is the indispensable man*'[21] (author's emphasis). Yet the same Russian ambassador who said that 'Austrian politics were based on Francis's character and guided by Metternich's spirit' also said that were Metternich to 'diverge' from Francis's will, he 'would not remain foreign minister for twenty-four hours'.[22] It is difficult to know exactly, therefore, how strong Metternich's position really was. He himself said: 'I may have governed Europe occasionally but Austria never', although he conceded that 'Heaven has placed me next to a man who might have been created for me, as I for him. The Emperor Francis knows what he wants and that never differs in any way from what I most want.'[23] Metternich probably believed that Francis was simply incapable of changing his ways; he also knew that in an absolute monarchy not much could or even should be done about this. He himself, despite his reputation as a ruthless, arch-reactionary, disliked personal confrontations and lacked the determination to force his case. Yet threats of resignation would probably not have meant dismissal. His arch-rival in government, Count Kolowrat, was always threatening to resign. Besides, Francis had far too high an opinion of his chancellor to let him go.

Kolowrat[24] had been brought to Vienna from Prague in 1826 as a state and conference minister to lead the political section of the State Council. A few months later he had been entrusted with the financial section also. In 1829 he was made head of a budget commission, which for the first time managed to balance the imperial books, so that thereafter he ruled the roost as far as Habsburg finances were concerned. His office became known as the 'ministerial department' and he was regarded by many as a sort of de facto prime minister. By all accounts he was not easy to work with. Senior civil servants who were not of noble origin – like Kübeck, head of the Court Accounts Office, for example – complained that he gave preference in promotions to his aristocratic Bohemian relatives. Walter quotes Francis as saying that it would have been impossible to keep the Monarchy together if all his servants had been like Kolowrat.[25] Metternich also came into conflict with him and was bound to. He always needed more money for the police, the army or the diplomatic corps. Meanwhile, Kolowrat disdained his foreign policy:

You are completely wrong about me and the people with whom I mix. You think that my principles are different from yours. That is wrong. I am an aristocrat by birth and by convictions and completely agree with you that people must strive for conservatism and do everything to achieve it. Yet we differ about means. Your means consist of a forest of bayonets and a fixed adherence to things as they are; to my mind, by following these lines we are playing into the hands of the revolutionaries ... Your ways will lead us ... not tomorrow or next year – but soon enough – to our ruin.[26]

Yet we know of no alternative policies put forward by Kolowrat who, none the less, on account of such statements, acquired a false reputation as a liberal.

In March 1835, Francis died and was succeeded by his mentally retarded son, Ferdinand I, whom Metternich had tried in vain in 1826 to persuade to renounce his claims to the throne. Unable to follow an argument or read official documents, there should have been no question of him succeeding. To protect him, his father had persuaded Nicholas I, Tsar of Russia, to agree in 1833 to shield him and his interests. (When he first met the then crown prince in 1835, Nicholas told his wife: 'Good God! But the reality surpassed all description!'[27]) Francis had also on his deathbed signed two documents drawn up by Metternich, one concerning church, the other concerning political affairs. Taken together, these are regarded as his political testament.[28] The first advised Ferdinand to continue the work that had been started in altering the Josephinist settlement of church affairs in accordance with the wishes of the Pope; the second offered advice and rules of behaviour. These included: 'disturb nothing in the foundations of the state structure; rule and change nothing'; 'invest your complete trust in my brother the Archduke Louis'; 'maintain the friendliest relations with your brother' (the Archduke Francis Charles); and finally 'place in Prince Metternich my most loyal servant and friend the confidence which I have invested in him over such a long course of years'; 'make no decisions on personnel or public affairs without having heard him first'. Metternich seemed to have triumphed. Kolowrat was not mentioned; only the Archduke Louis would have any real part in affairs, although Francis Charles would be kept abreast of them. Metternich intended therefore to preside over a ministerial conference as a sort of council of regency. But two days after Francis's death, Kolowrat confronted Metternich and threatened to withdraw to his estates if he were excluded. Metternich, who in personal affairs never had a stomach for a fight, gave in and there was a gentleman's agreement to split power between them and to bring in the Archduke Louis, who was rather dim (so too was Francis Charles), as a shield against the imperial family. Yet there were still differences and a year later Kolowrat did indeed retire to his estates. Metternich now took the opportunity to set up a strong ministerial conference which was separated from the State Council. Kolowrat was to be given the choice of joining the ministerial conference over which Metternich would preside or remaining the head of the financial section of the State Council. Metternich's reasons were perhaps not totally self-serving. He told Ficquelmont on 14 December 1836:

> Count Kolowrat is full of good qualities; he has profound knowledge of the administration . . . however he also makes great mistakes. Troubled by very bad health, his mentality is very noticeably afflicted by his physical condition. He suffers from piles, which easily affect his mental organs; during such attacks he is more or less unfit for business . . . in light of this disadvantage he has a great weakness of character and like all weak men becomes a tool in the hands of subordinate flatterers . . . His principles are blamelessly correct, yet he is taken for a liberal; he is a dyed-in-the-wool aristocrat, but is held to be a moderniser. Although an excellent man of business, he lacks those qualities which mark one out as a statesman. He is incapable of seeing a question as a whole, to understand it, to determine its development, and not to be misled by accidents. He wants what I want. It has never happened that he has refused to accept my views and we have never separated without honestly agreeing with each other. For me he is an inexhaustible source of administrative knowledge. I for my part give him that knowledge of a higher sphere, which he lacks.

None the less, a now very alarmed Kolowrat returned from his estates and got the Archdukes John and Charles (the two intelligent Habsburgs whom Francis had excluded from power for decades) to return to Vienna and upset Metternich's plans. The upshot was that by an imperial decision of 12 December 1836, a new State Conference was established presided over by the Archduke Louis in the name of the Emperor, which would have Metternich, Kolowrat, the Archdukes Louis and Francis Charles as permanent members, while temporary ones might include the heads of court offices, heads of sections of the State Council, and various 'state and conference counsellors' if the need arose. The State Conference was supposed to deliberate orally on all subjects referred to it by the Emperor. Its remit included all state business, especially matters requiring secrecy and those about which the State Council had expressed substantial misgivings or objections. In theory, therefore, Metternich's ideas regarding the machinery of government had not been altogether neglected. But in practice things did not work out quite like that. Louis lacked the talent to preside over discussions about the Monarchy. He played Kolowrat and Metternich off against each other and was soon demanding written reports. The *Kabinettsweg*, in short, soon revived.[29] Kübeck, for one, interpreted all this as 'the complete defeat of Prince Metternich'; Kolowrat controlled the money power, had the imperial family and the State Council behind him and was therefore 'the deciding spokesman in the [State] Conference'.[30] One historian has concluded therefore that Kolowrat 'essentially fulfilled the functions of a prime minister'.[31] Yet Metternich still ran foreign and defence policy and had a large share in policy formulation with regard to the police, Hungary and Lombardy-Venetia. The idea that he was overshadowed by Kolowrat is far-fetched. Imperial affairs at this time largely consisted of debt management, police affairs, foreign affairs and defence. Kolowrat was responsible mainly for the first; he did not run the others. It remains highly uncertain, however, to what degree, if any, the rivalry between Metternich and Kolowrat interfered with the affairs of government.[32] The Archduke Louis, by all accounts, tended to favour Kolowrat, but lacked the courage in any way to move against the state chancellor. Metternich for his part received powerful support both from Count Hartig, the former governor of Lombardy who in 1840 became head of the political section of the State Council, and Baron Kübeck, who in the same year became head of the *Hofkammer* or Exchequer. Both were centralisers who backed Metternich's reform plans for central government and both loathed Kolowrat who used his influence with the high Bohemian aristocracy to back the diets against the centre. They also resented Kolowrat's attempts to keep in with Metternich's critics amongst the intellectuals for they were quite aware that Kolowrat was at least as opposed to liberalism as Metternich. Still, Hartig accused him of wishing to oust Metternich and rule the State Conference himself. He even believed (with a little circumstantial evidence) that in March 1848 Kolowrat was behind a conspiracy to allow a riot to develop in Vienna that would at last allow Louis to demand Metternich's resignation – not that Kolowrat was in any way promoting revolution. The Archduke Francis Charles, meanwhile, resented the fact that he was kept out of real decision-making. And in this he had the support of his formidable wife, the Archduchess Sophie. But neither of them wanted to get rid of 'good old Metternich', despite a legend to that effect.[33]

It was Kolowrat's determination to keep state expenditure under control that caused Metternich most problems, particularly during the Near Eastern Crisis of 1839–41. Kolowrat described military costs as 'a shield that weighed down the rider'.[34] He knew that in 1811 as a result of the Napoleonic Wars the state had had to declare itself bankrupt. He also knew that in the period 1813–15, enormous debts had been incurred. Some order had been restored to the imperial finances after 1815 but in the period 1815–48 as a whole the annual interest paid on the state debt amounted on average to 30 per cent of state revenues. Foreign observers none the less were quite impressed by Austrian finances. The British free trade expert John McGregor MP, in Volume One of his *Commercial Statistics*, published in London in 1843, wrote that 'the public securities of Austria are as safe as any in the world',[35] while a French observer writing three years later found Austrian finances 'in a truly remarkable state of prosperity' (taking the figures for 1840, he calculated that the public debt amounted to not much more than one year's revenue if the sinking fund were subtracted.)[36] Yet Kolowrat regarded all this as complacency. As he perceived matters, for most of the period before 1848 the military budget accounted for some 40 per cent of state revenue and was the largest item of state expenditure. In years of crisis –or intervention – it rose enormously with the result that any active foreign policy threatened the state's reputation for credit-worthiness. Treasury opposition to policies which raised the military budget from 55 million florins in 1819 to 80 million in 1821 and from 46 million in 1830 to 77 million in 1831 had been expressed with vigour. Stadion, Kolowrat's predecessor, had wrung his hands in 1824 on discovering that the costs of the Naples expedition had brought about a deficit of 35 million gulden which had necessitated a loan of 30 million. He had been even more distraught when he heard that Metternich had agreed to the part repayment of an English loan of 40 million, which the British government was now demanding in a show of disapproval. During the Greek War of Independence, when the 1827 military budget had again been reduced to 48 million, Kolowrat told the future field marshal, Prince Windischgraetz, that Austria was 'armed for eternal peace'.[37] He continued: 'We must do everything possible to prevent hostilities: and can only pray that people do not believe our threats. Our hopes rest on the divergence of interest of the three powers who are at present so unnaturally coalesced.'[38] In other words, armed force could only be used in the last resort. Thus when Metternich asked for more resources, Kolowrat wondered how, given that there had only been two short military campaigns against Naples and Piedmont since

1815, the army actually squandered its money: 'It is difficult, therefore, to answer the question how the annual 38–46 million gulden, which sum it is now recognised is insufficient for defence purposes and for protection against internal threat, could have been spent.'[39]

Yet the army had certainly not squandered resources. Officers and men alike were paid miserable wages and endured harsh terms of service.[40] Nor did it stockpile, since it often ran out of supplies. Indeed, according to one statistician, the army only survived by sending one third of its troops home during peaceful periods. In the years 1825, 1826 and 1829, 'almost half of the men were on leave'.[41] The fact was that the army was so run-down, demoralised and ill-led that it could scarcely be described as battleworthy. Thus when Metternich in 1830 suggested that the Archduke Charles might lead the army against France, the Archduke replied that neither the state's finances nor the condition of the army would allow it. When Radetzky asked the Emperor why there had been no war, Francis I told him: 'I held a camp this year near Münchendorf where my troops displayed themselves so badly and apathetically that the Prussians voiced their dissatisfaction. We, therefore, recognised Louis Philippe as King of France at the same time as England. *Isolated, I could not undertake war.*'[42] Radetzky as a result was sent to Italy to reform the army there, but despite a number of reforms and considerable mythology, there were few tangible results. In any case his efforts to consolidate his position against the looming threat from Piedmont before 1848 were also undermined by treasury control. The president of the Court War Council was told by the Emperor in February 1848: 'In future no proposition which entails additional financial expenditure is to be presented to me before a preliminary agreement has been reached with the treasury praesidium.'[43] Radetzky at the same time was told that he would only receive reinforcements if a 'significant rebellion' had already broken out in Lombardy or if the French or Sardinians had attacked – this despite the fact that the field marshal's strategy was based on attacking the enemy first. Austria was nearing bankruptcy again.[44] The fault, though, belonged to Kolowrat. As will be seen (in Chapter 6) it was he who, as head of the imperial finances for years, had been unable to reform them sufficiently to produce the revenue the Empire needed.

Metternich, therefore, despite his attempted coup of 1835–6 and despite all his plans and proposals of 1811 and 1817 to reshape the machinery of government – albeit around efficient central institutions rather than by federalising the Monarchy – ended up both having to live with Francis's and the Archduke Louis' *Kabinettsweg* and having to fend off attacks from Kolowrat and his accountants. That is not to say, however, that his foreign policy lacked success or that the Monarchy suffered from more domestic discontent than the liberal states of western Europe, which criticised him. Metternich's Austria was an oasis of calm. The turbulence took place around its borders.

5
Was Metternich's Austria a Police State?

The greatest criticism of Metternich's Austria was that it was a police state, one, moreover, that deliberately sought to cut itself off from the rest of Europe through a system of censorship, spies, political prisoners and *cabinets noirs*: 'By the nineteenth century it was not unusual for commentators like Ludwig Börne to characterise Austria as the "China of Europe".'[1] Indeed, Goethe described Austria as *'geistiges Ausland'* or 'intellectually a foreign country', while Friedrich Schlegel wrote to his wife in 1819: 'How can you make the strange error of believing that Vienna is located in Germany or that it has the least to do with Germany? They are separated by entire continents, and one could hardly think of more polar opposites.'[2] Many scholars have supported this view, with Viktor Bibl quoting favourably the verdict of Ignatz Beidtel that, under Francis I, Austria had a *Polizeicharakter* 'such as had never been the case in any large state'. Bibl added that a prominent feature of this state had been the suspicion with which both Emperor and police regarded foreigners and he pointed out that the cost of spying on foreign diplomats had risen from an average of 10,000 gulden a year under Joseph II to 50,000 a year by 1814.[3] Even Georg Franz, whose views on the Metternich era were much more sympathetic than those of Bibl, agreed that after the formation of the Zollverein, 'Austria became not only intellectually but economically a foreign country'.[4] Yet it would be unwise to overemphasise the differences between Austria and other German and European states during this period with regard to civil rights, although differences certainly existed. Democracy was then considered a malign political system throughout Europe and democrats – thanks to the French Revolution – were considered little better than terrorists. Friedrich Wilhelm IV of Prussia, for example, wrote to Queen Victoria on 25 November 1847 that the triumph in Germany of democrats and radicals would bring 'torrents of blood' since: 'The murder of kings, priests and aristocrats is no empty sound with them and civil war, in song, writing, word and deed, is their watch-word.'[5] Metternich's views were thus fairly commonplace among European conservatives and the policies pursued by the Austrian government with regard to censorship and political criticism not at all out of place in the Europe of his day. In any case, the best-informed student of the censorship under Francis I and Metternich has written that there was no intention at all of cutting off Austria from other coun-tries – particularly German-speaking ones – to create a 'European China', nor did this happen unintentionally.[6] The charge was just a liberal jibe, albeit one that stuck. Yet his views have also been chal-lenged.[7] Today, therefore, the cliché that Metternich's Austria was a police state deserves a thorough re-examination.

The Austrian Police during the Metternich Era

Liberals in Austria tended to praise Joseph II the more they criticised Prince Metternich,[8] yet it was the reforming Emperor himself who had been responsible for establishing the Court Police Office or *Polizeihofstelle* in 1789 under the urbane Count Pergen.[9] The latter, impressed by developments in France, Prussia and Russia, had lobbied Joseph on the subject since 1784; his views on the role of a modern police force were unambiguous: 'The inner peace, security and welfare of the state can only be established through well-arranged police insti-tutions. The vaster a monarchy is, the more important it is to intro-duce such police institutions as are uniform and coherent and therefore fit constantly to maintain supervision in general and in all parts.'[10] Gains were to be made by the state from proper police arrangements:

1.   If from time to time it learns reliably the true opinions of subjects, because thereafter it is in a position to take measures accordingly;
2.   If it finds out the hindrances which secretly lie in the way of its agencies;
3.   If, finally it can discover and eradicate (*ausrotten*) the dangerous enemies of internal security which undermine it.[11]

Yet the Court Police Office was abolished by Leopold II who showed more interest in the rights of his subjects than the powers of his police. The latter were instructed to treat prisoners with 'all possible respect and kindness' and nobody was to be 'detained for more than three days without the notification of the authority concerned'.[12] Pergen soon resigned, complaining that 'at my age I am no longer able to endure insults without completely destroying my health'.[13] However, Francis II brought Pergen back at the very end of 1792 and on 3 January 1793 the *Polizeihofstelle* was re-established under him. The censorship, on the other hand, was still administered separately and Francis reaffirmed Leopold's proper treatment of prisoners. Indeed, in December 1793, at the height of the Terror in France, Francis refused to permit subjects to 'be punished with the loss of that liberty which they have abused to the detriment of the security of the State' or to allow them to 'remain in detention for as long as the present circumstances last'.[14] He also stuck to the letter of the law over the Jacobin trials of 1794, despite pressure from the justice minister for special arrangements, and allowed no enlargement of police powers thereafter. Meanwhile, advisers like Sonnenfels and Zinzendorf promoted the rule of law rather than that of the police, with Zinzendorf declaring: 'The shortest, clearest, and most infallible political rule, which is based on religion, morality, good policy and common sense is that justice is the Strongest Pillar of the Throne.'[15] Eventually, Francis agreed to subordinate the censorship to the police on 1 September 1801 but in 1798 the so-called 'police ministry' had only eight officials (including Pergen himself) in charge of Vienna's police directorate with its staff of forty-eight men plus a 'military police-watch' of three hundred and fifty-four. This was hardly a huge estab-lishment at the height of the French Revolution. Of course, it could rely on the cooperation of all other (very small) police forces throughout the lands of the Empire. On the other hand, Pergen, before his final retire-ment in 1802, expressed his own view on the final parameters of Habsburg police activity: 'if the police is to fulfil its task during the present era, it must watch over not merely the Habsburg lands, but the spirit that prevails throughout Europe.'[16] Pergen was particularly worried about the secret societies or sects which were spreading throughout the Continent.

Given two French invasions and the rise and fall of the Napoleonic Empire, Francis I soon persuaded himself to believe the same. He would tell his leading financial official, Kübeck, in 1833 that 'Austria ought really to be the police force of Europe' [*Österreich eigentlich die Polizei von Europa machen müsse*],[17] a sentiment with which Metternich, of course, agreed.

The resources of the Habsburg police, however, remained very limited:

About the end of the Napoleonic wars, the Police Ministry at Herrengasse 38 in Vienna had twelve members, four of whom had served since Pergen's day. In addition, there were some thirteen regular censors. As Pergen had struggled so hard to assure, the Minister had at his immediate disposal the police of Vienna, headed by a Directorate [*Polizei-Oberdirektion*] made up of ten leading officials with a staff of about twenty-five. The Directorate included offices for passes and the registration of residence, employment of servants, and regulations about Jews. The inner city had four districts [*Bezirk* or *Viertel*], each with a bureau; the suburbs nine. In addition to the police guard of seven officers, 78 noncommissioned officers and 490 men, there was a mounted guard of one officer and 56 men and also a civilian guard of 64 in the districts. Such was the regular police of the capital.[18]

By 1848, moreover, things had not changed very much. In a famous article,[19] the American historian William L. Langer pointed out that when revolution erupted, Louis Philippe in Paris had 3,000 municipal guards, 84,000 national guards and 30,000 troops to protect him; Queen Victoria in London had 3,000 well-trained 'bobbies', between 150,000 and 180,000 'special constables' and up to 50,000 British troops to protect her; while in Vienna, Metternich and the imperial family had only 1,000 police, a municipal guard of 14,000 (in theory anyway, since it mostly consisted of brass bands) plus 14,000 troops to protect them. In its hour of need, therefore, Metternich's police state seemed fairly puny. (Berlin – another 'reactionary' autocratic capital – was even less well defended by the forces of law and order.) Finally and very ironically, Metternich's old colleague Count Hartig was to record 'that there were no laws against riots was a defect in the legislative system, which was not recognised before the events of March, when the necessity of supplying such a defect became evident.'[20]

Was this defect due to the 'fear and intimidation' caused by the political police with its 'host of spies, informers and *agents provocateurs* attached to the police director's office – whose task it was to ferret out the innermost thoughts of the Emperor's subjects and to check the development of any revolutionary spirit'?[21] Or was it nearer the truth that the 'role of spies was powerfully overestimated'?[22] Why had there been no riots in Vienna and no apparent need to outlaw them? Because the (secret) police there had been so efficient? Or because there had been no real need for them? Certainly Francis saw the police as indispensable: 'In his defensive war against the constantly feared attempts at revolution, the police and censorship played an overwhelmingly (*über-aus*) important role'[23] Metternich likewise relied on constant police reports, ordering his officials before setting out for Italy in May 1817: 'I wish to be kept directly and uninterruptedly informed about matters which relate to higher state police and therefore are important to me.'[24] The policy of both these men was summed up well by Metternich's colleague Gentz in a letter of 10 August 1820 as 'first, freedom [that is, security] for the life of the state, then freedom for the Church, then freedom for all who can make use of it.'[25] But what difference had their reliance on the police actually made?

The police certainly impinged on the daily lives of everyone living in Austria: all subjects – not merely foreigners or paroled prisoners – had to register with them details of where they lived; changes in address, of course, had also to be registered. Innkeepers and hoteliers and even householders had to register their guests and lodgers. The aim was that the Habsburg authorities could easily and rapidly locate anyone resident within the Emperor's dominions. This system pre-dated the Metternich era as did the system whereby Jews had to obey particular regulations by registering with the police. Foreigners required visas from Austrian embassies to visit the Monarchy. The police would advise the *Staatskanzlei* as to who was dangerous. Habsburg subjects, for their part, required permission to travel abroad and, once again, the police would advise on their suitability. Border guards and customs officers had to ensure that those who entered or left the Monarchy had the necessary papers and permissions and were not in possession of letters or other forbidden objects (such as banned publications).

Given that Article XVII of the German Confederation proclaimed freedom of movement to be a right belonging to all subjects of its member states, there was the danger, as Metternich pointed out, that Austria, as its most powerful state, would set a bad example, if it prohibited emigration altogether as was proposed in 1824. The interior ministry had opposed this and Metternich, who himself, of course, had been a founder of the German Confederation, added his weight to the opposition:

In the Austrian Monarchy, under the sceptre of the most just monarch, with a government honoured even by foreigners for its mildness and humanity, in a state, finally, with no lack of work for all hands and no lack of gain for industry, it should be least dangerous to proclaim this principle [of free emigration] . . . though in such a fashion as to provide opportunity to consider each case.[26]

Emerson suggests that in arguing for powers to judge individual cases on their merits, Metternich 'as in so much else' was attempting to assure the government 'as much arbitrary power as possible'.[27] He adds: 'His scorn for the Confederation and for the principles which Austria professed could not have been more evident.'[28] But this seems naive. Emerson has to admit that during the uprising in the Danubian Principalities in 1821–2, Metternich 'insisted that according to the humanitarian principles of the Austrian government Jews fleeing mistreatment should be admitted'.[29] And this happened despite Metternich's prejudice that Jews were prominently involved with the sects as part of Europe's revolutionary conspiracy.[30] Revolutionaries from Greece (or anywhere else for that matter) and their philhellene supporters, on the other hand, were not welcome. Indeed, Prince Alexander Ypsilanti, the leader of a revolt in the Principalities which took place on the eve of the Greek War of Independence, was held prisoner by the Austrians for years after he fled to Hungary in 1821.[31] And when Pope Leo XII declared that the year 1825 would be a Jubilee, during which anyone visiting Rome as a pilgrim would receive a plenary indulgence – a practice adhered to by the Church every twenty-five years since 1450, save for 1800 – travel was still permitted only with police approval. The authorities feared that the sects might use the Jubilee year as an excuse to extend their networks throughout Italy.[32]

The most difficult question regarding free movement arose from the desire of the Austrian authorities to prevent students from the Habsburg lands studying abroad, particularly in Germany, where the student societies or *Burschenschaften*[33] were considered to be as dangerous as the sects, especially after the murder of the well-known poet and playwright, Kotzebue, in 1819 by the German student, Sand. Kotzebue was known to be of reactionary opinions and in the pay of the Russians; Sand was a German nationalist extremist. Thus Gentz in 1818 had written: 'We are completely convinced that of all the evils afflicting Germany today, even including the licentiousness of the press, this student nuisance is the greatest, the most urgent and the most threatening.'[34] Metternich and Sedlnitzky did not quite agree, the former writing in 1819 declaring that 'the greatest and accordingly the most urgent evil today is the press',[35] while the latter in 1817 was already proposing working diplomatically through 'an association of ruling princes' to censor the German press.[36] That did not mean, however, that German student life was seen as less threatening to governments. Students graduated and became bureaucrats; if they held subversive ideas, they might become subversive bureaucrats. In 1819, the Carlsbad

Decrees were passed by the German (Con)Federal Diet, therefore, in an attempt to muzzle both the universities and the press; they would later be renewed in even tougher forms. A Central Investigating Commission was also established at Mainz to look into the whole problem of student unrest.

In the meantime, Metternich cooperated with the Prussians, Russians and others in spying on various student bodies and in attempting to sever the links between them and Habsburg students. A few agents were employed and a variety of students arrested from time to time. The Prussians seemed most concerned about the problem; indeed, one Prussian police minister in 1818 sent Metternich reports on plans to form an all-German union of *Burschenschaften*,[37] while another in 1824 wrote to him outlining the fears behind Prussian policy:

> It is not sufficient to limit surveillance to high traitors. One does not reach this crime in a single step. Regicides and *sans-culottes* do not suddenly appear. In France there were first Encyclopaedists, then Constitutionalists, next Republicans, and finally regicides and high traitors. In order not to have the last types one must prevent Encyclopaedists and Constitutionalists from appearing and becoming established.[38]

Metternich no doubt agreed but there remained the difficult questions both of how to infiltrate student movements in general and how to prevent Habsburg students studying abroad or being politically subverted by foreign students studying in Prague, Vienna or in other universities inside the Monarchy. His task, moreover, was made no easier by the fact that Austria's legal authorities refused to make life easier for the police. Thus when the police arrested a group of liberal Swiss students who in 1817 had formed a 'Swiss Society in Vienna' that met in a pub, *The Burgundian Cross* in the Bräunerstrasse, to discuss literary and political matters in French – they were too poor to hire a separate room – they discovered to their chagrin that the students could not be punished, first, because they had not attempted to overthrow the Habsburg government, secondly, because their reforms were meant for Switzerland, and thirdly, because they had met publicly, not secretly. The students were expelled for criticising conditions in Austria and advocating reforms there too, but even Emerson has to agree that

> In insisting upon the legal distinction between the expression of opinion or intent, on the one hand, and deed on the other, the

Hapsburg judges showed a confidence in the strength of their own government and an unwillingness to curb the expression of opinion which judges in communities that boast of their freedom and justice have not always equaled [*sic*].[39]

Austrian students, on the other hand, were often treated much worse. Schubert's friend Johann Senn, for example, was arrested in Vienna for participating in a group of suspected student radicals, held for thirteen months by the police pending investigations, and then sent back to the Tyrol whence he originated.[40] Senn had been a friend of the son of Count Colleredo-Mansfeld, a suspected student radical. Another of his friends, the Prussian Ernst Förster, was also arrested, put in irons and expelled to Bavaria, having been falsely denounced to the police by a servant who had been sacked by the young aristocrat's father.[41] None of this type of behaviour, however, could restrict the allure of the *Burschenschaften*.

Nor, as it turned out, could Metternich or Francis I achieve their aim of stopping Austrian students studying abroad or preventing German ones from studying inside the Monarchy. This would have occasioned too much criticism inside Germany as a breach – as we have seen – of the freedom of movement enshrined in the constitution of the German Confederation. Indeed, requests were made from influential people on behalf of Frankfurt, Prussia and Saxony to allow their students in, despite the supposedly poor reputation of Austrian universities, while in 1830 Francis I himself felt obliged even after the outbreak of the 1830 revolutions to allow a congress of foreign scientists – the Society of Scientists and Physicians – to meet in Vienna.[42] Thus, although for the most part the Austrian authorities could stop the free movement of students, they never actually succeeded in doing so absolutely, something that worried Metternich, who linked the *Burschenschaften* to the sects. Metternich certainly believed that the sects existed and were centrally organised. He told one of his agents in 1833:

For many years all those who pointed to the existence of a *comité directeur* working secretly for universal revolution were met everywhere only by incredulity; today it has been shown that this infernal propaganda exists, that it has its centre in Paris and that it is divided into as many sections as there are nations to regenerate ... Everything that refers to this great and dangerous plot cannot, therefore, be observed and surveyed with too much attention.[43]

His policy therefore was to use the police to seek out these revolutionaries both at home and abroad. This meant using spies and secret agents
and cooperating with foreign governments. In the end the Austrian
police therefore did indeed become – to a degree – the police force of
Europe. However, only few agents were involved and they were often
unreliable.[44] And although Metternich, as in the case of the
Burschenschaften, could often get cooperation in police matters from
Russian, Prussian, French, Papal and other (particularly German and
Italian) police ministers, and occasionally did them favours in return,
the fruits of this limited cooperation were rather meagre.[45] In cases like
England, there was no cooperation at all:

> Even for the mere surveillance of a person in that country one comes
> up against insuperable difficulties which have their origins in the
> constitution . . . The difficulties of carrying on police activities there
> border on the impossible . . . There are no police there in the real
> sense of the word . . . The English government has neither the means
> nor even the will [he wrote in 1827] to encourage enquiries into the
> nature, the activities, and the plans of the clubs of foreign refugees.[46]

Often he thought the advice and reports he received from abroad were
unreliable. For example, the reports of Cardinal Consalvi, the Papal
Secretary of State, in 1816 that the Turks were about to declare war and
land in Italy, while the Austrian army there and in Hungary would
revolt and the Bourbons be driven out of France, he described as 'the
spectres of a madman';[47] in 1817, when the Roman secret police sent
an agent to Lombardy-Venetia to discover the associates of the sects in
the Papal States, he was arrested at the border by Habsburg officials who
recognised him as a suspected member of one of these sects himself;[48]
the plans of the Austrian minister in Rome, Pacca, to have all the heads
of the secret societies arrested in all Italian states on the same day and
tried by martial law and have amnesties granted subsequently to all
repentant sect members, he considered fantastic.[49] (The proposed
arrests would merely be used as propaganda to aid the sects and perhaps
provoke uprisings. Besides, as Metternich significantly asked, 'What
court would convict without adequate proofs?'[50]) The Minister of Police
in Naples seemed so incompetent that he was suspected of being a
member of the sects himself.[51] The truth was that Count Sedlnitzky, the
head of the *Polizeihofstelle* between 1816 and 1848, like Metternich
himself, had no idea how the sects actually operated or whether they all
existed. What were the connections between the *Carbonari* and the

Guelfi, the *Adelfi*, the *Filadelfi*, the *Société de Grand Arnaud de Nimes*, the *Concistorialii* and the *Congregazione Cattolica Apostolica Romana*?[52] Who were their leaders? Were they supported by foreign powers? Did they have members in the armed forces of any state? Could they act by themselves? Were they supported by the officials of any state? All this was unknown.[53] And not all foreign states wanted to cooperate anyway. The Piedmontese government in 1817 saw no reason to continue to hold Count Maghella, formerly Murat's chief of police, simply because the Austrians considered him dangerous.[54] When in 1822 at the Congress of Verona Metternich revived his proposals of 1817 and 1818 for the establishment of a central investigating commission similar to the one set up in Germany in 1819, Italian governments, especially Rome, turned down the initiative.[55] It was little wonder, therefore, that in Italy Austrian police activity gave sparse warning of the revolutions that broke out in 1820, 1821 and 1830, despite Metternich's belief that the membership of the sects in Italy could be counted in hundreds of thousands.

He consoled himself with the thought that, in any case, these subversives were to be found outside the Habsburg territories themselves and at times was prepared to be quite mild in his reactions to them. Emerson, who is no admirer of Metternich, writes:

He was a master of deviousness and of subtle tactics. In mid-1824 and early 1825 he recommended the political advantages of mild treatment of former political opponents in Italy. Proposing leniency for a Milan lawyer who had fled to Spain, he was confident that such persons would be harmless in Lombardy. Clemency would reinforce their feeling of having erred. On the other hand, continued severity would make them prefer exile, and then poverty might easily lead them into the arms of revolutionaries. It was politically disadvantageous to provide such recruits for the subverters of European order. A policy of well-calculated pardons befitted 'the Austrian Monarchy under the scepter of the most just Monarch with a government honored even by foreigners for its mildness and humanity.' No firm, orderly, and just government such as Austria's, he boasted, could stimulate dissatisfaction as arbitrary administration and injustices did in other Italian states. Here was smugness such as Sedlnitzky had shown in October 1817 in trusting that the superiorities of Habsburg administration removed dissatisfaction more effectively than did any Italian state. The Police Minister had frankly pointed to police watchfulness and Hapsburg military might as well. In 1826 Metternich

believed that the 'sects' grew from the misconduct of the government in Italy and did not themselves cause the troubles of these
governments.[56]

Emerson is loath to allow Metternich the benefit of any doubt.
Whenever he appears reasonable or moderate, he is condemned for
being devious. In fact, the state chancellor was willing to press reform
on other Italian governments and to rely on the strength of the
Austrian administration in Lombardy-Venetia – clearly recognised as
the best in Italy – to be able to defeat the revolutionaries. It was therefore vital to be able to rely, if necessary, on the Austrian army there.
Thus all Marshal Radetzky's soldiers in 1833 were given the following
order:

When twelve years ago the sect called the Carbonari threatened civil
order in the Italian states with its complete overthrow, His Majesty
warned you, his subjects, of the harmful and seditious teachings of
this sect and of their criminal and treasonous aims in order 324 of
March 1821. This was made known to everybody in order to ensure
that even the most inexperienced and careless men, from whom the
leaders of this sect took care to conceal their aims, would know of
them and hence would abstain from joining the Carbonari.

The monarch's same fatherly care now compels him in view of
recent events to issue the same order with regard to a no less dangerous sect, indeed one which represents a higher form of Carbonari,
called Young Italy. The aim of this society is the overthrow of existing governments and of the complete social order; the means which
it employs are subversion and outright murder through secret
agents.

It goes without saying that anyone who knows of these aims, but
who none the less, joins Young Italy, is guilty of high treason. He is
also guilty even if, given that he knows its aims, he merely fails to
prevent its progress or to point out its members and, as guilty, he is
liable to punishment under Article 5 of the Articles of War. Likewise
from the date of publication of this order, no one will be able to
excuse himself by saying that he was a member of Young Italy and
yet was ignorant of its objectives. On the other hand, anyone, who
out of remorse, reveals the members of the same, its statutes, the
aims and undertakings of its leaders, if these are still secret or if their
work can still be prevented, is assured complete immunity from
punishment and his actions will remain secret.[57]

Once again, a policy of incentives was employed, rather than one of mere repression. Once again, it is clear, that Austrian knowledge of the sects in Italy was very limited.

In Germany, as has been seen, the story was much the same, save that, although nothing much had come of police attempts to infiltrate the student societies, an all-German Central Investigating Commission had been established by the Diet to discover the causes of student unrest and the links between the student movement and the sects. This, too, however, turned out to be a very damp squib from Metternich's point of view. Despite inviting its members to dine with him on his Rhineland estate at Johannisberg, by 1828, he was denouncing it as an obstruction to his cause. 'I cannot understand why this torment is not removed,' he complained, adding, 'I shall limit its troublesome effects as much as possible, for only that way can I hope for results.'[58]

The Central Investigating Commission, set up by the Diet on 20 September 1819, consisted of representatives of seven out of the 39 member states, who sat as a body in Mainz. Although they were to consider in detail several hundred political cases of the previous ten years – including the assassination of Kotzebue by Sand – they were to leave all judicial action to the appropriate authorities of the individual German states. Their main task was to analyse the various acts of subversion that had taken place in Germany since 1815. In this, according to one modern historian, the Commission 'acquitted itself surprisingly well' by demonstrating 'remarkable perspicacity and open-mindedness'.[59] The terms of employment of the Commissioners remain unclear, but the clerks employed by it had to take no oath of allegiance to the Confederation or to the ruling houses of the individual states and even those who had themselves previously belonged to 'clandestine political clubs' were treated with 'great tolerance'.[60] The Commission, in fact, turned out to be a rather objective and academic body, perhaps even a liberal one. Its working definition of revolution was: 'efforts . . . whose intention it is to produce from below and in violation of existing laws, changes in the established constitution contrary to the will of governments or at least without their participation.'[61] It also seemed to admire Fichte and feel sorry for Sand. The latter was described as 'brought up under the influence of a pampering enthusiasm . . . and used from childhood to belittle the first authority he encountered in life, his father, as incapable of understanding him or his feelings'.[62] If such anachronistic pop psychiatry were not enough, Fichte was praised for his impressive and courageous lectures 'under the eye of the foreign conqueror' in Berlin in 1808.[63]

When it came to explaining the student movement in Germany, the Commission reported in 1828[64] that first, the revolutionary pressures were almost exclusively intellectual in content ('scant mention' was made of economic or social causes); secondly, it predicted that revolution would only succeed as a result of some foreign crisis beyond any German authority's power to control; while, thirdly, nothing definite could be determined with regard to the new order sought by the movement. Most revolutionaries lamented the lack of German unity, but most also believed that unity and liberty were unachievable in contemporary Europe – hence the great emigration to the USA. Great attention was paid to nationalist movements founded after the Napoleonic invasions – particularly Vater Jahn's gymnastic movement and Julius Gruner's *Tugenbund*. Jahn's movement in 1828 was estimated, however, as having a total membership of only 140, 30 of whom were known to the police. It was potentially dangerous, none the less, since Jahn had been made leader by popular acclamation, since its membership included state officials, army officers and university professors, and since it had links with Gruner, formerly head of the higher police for the whole of Prussia and hence someone with a wide range of contacts. The *Tugenbund* also claimed the right in a national emergency to take action in defence of the state even without official permission; many German nationalists also seemed to want to establish a popular dictatorship should any national crisis occur, perhaps along the lines of Arndt's *Phantasien für ein zukünftiges Deutschland*. However, Gruner had died in 1820.

The Commission concluded:

What has caused the changes in the European spirit during approximately the last fifty years and the disposition to search for political innovation must be answered with reference to the discoveries made over the past three centuries in regard to the nature of politics and the means of wielding political power – also discoveries in the art of war, in the communication of ideas and their dissemination, and in the volume of metal used as monetary currency.[65]

The full text, according to Liang,[66] took up 15 pages and was a complete survey of western civilization since the fifteenth century. Its political implications were, first, that no police forces could be expected to control such forces but, secondly, that international police cooperation provided the only plausible means of containment. It was little wonder, therefore, that Metternich described the Commission as a 'torment'.

If the government struggled to suppress the sects and the student movement within and without the Monarchy, what of the lives of ordinary people? Were they the oppressed inhabitants of a police state? Views on this varied. Charles Sealsfield (the pseudonym for the Austrian Karl Postl) wrote that order was kept remarkably strictly in Vienna: 'When the clock strikes eleven the whole city including the suburbs sinks into the deepest silence as if by magic. Everybody is, or should be at home. Shouting, singing or the least noise in the streets would be something quite unusual. The police curfew is strictly imposed.'[67]

The American chargé d'affaires in Vienna in 1848, Stiles, wrote in his account of the revolution in Austria:

> The secret police consists of a body of people of all classes, needy men and women of rank, mistresses etc., down to the waiters in coffee houses, and the lowest visitors of taverns and brothels, who report whatever they hear against the government . . . these spies are the most worthless part of the community and . . . may even invent stories to make themselves important or serve some diabolical end. On the reports of such miscreants men's lives, liberty and property depend; and the charges being kept secret, no means are afforded of refuting them. . . .
>
> In no country of Europe – without, perhaps, it be Russia – is the secret police more thoroughly organised, and its inquisition more vexatious and oppressive, than in the Austrian empire. Besides the regular corps of spies, who have no other occupation or means of subsistence, almost every other man you meet with is under the pay of the police – the man with whom you transact business in the city, the servants who attend upon your wants at home, and often even the companion who enjoys your hospitality, and to whom you confide your inmost thoughts, leaves you, and repairs to the police office to report your unguarded expressions . . . The great object, however, of the system of espionage is not so much the information the spies are enabled to collect, which is generally not worth the cost of the collection, but it is to keep down public opinion – to exercise a terrorism over the people, and thus effectually stifle the utterances of any liberal, and consequently deemed injurious sentiments . . . To avoid the dungeons of the Spielberg for life, there existed no other safeguard than either the maintenance of the most profound silence on all political and social questions, or the exercise of subserviency to the hypocritical extent of acquiescing in or extolling whatever was permitted to be seen, said, and believed by

the community, or ordered to be received with demonstrations of satisfaction.[68]

This was palpable nonsense. Not even those convicted in the courts of high treason – and the courts, as has been seen, were independent – rotted in the Spielberg for life – but the charges made by Stiles occasionally resurface, albeit in a diluted form, in works of modern scholarship. Robert Justin Goldstein, for example, writes in his recent survey of *Political Repression in 19th Century Europe*:

> The Austrian secret police were the most notorious during the 1815–1860 period . . . Huge numbers of informants – especially in such occupations as servants, prostitutes, waiters and doormen – were hired to report to the police on the activities and conversations of Austrians and an extremely effective shroud of intimidation was lowered over the Austrian public that was not significantly lifted until after 1860.[69]

The truth is probably very different. The British traveller Peter Evan Turnbull, for example, whose two volumes on *Austria*, published in 1840 are among the very best sources for the Monarchy in the Metternich era, recorded:

> Were it not for the order and security everywhere prevailing, a stranger might hardly suppose, beyond the walls of the cities, that any police existed except only at frontiers. In no continental country have I ever travelled, in which, except in the provincial capitals, is so little of it either seen or felt . . . those persons are in my mind greatly to be pitied, whose credulous imagination takes the alarm at the fancy of agents in disguise ever haunting their footsteps and watching their conduct. As regards the natives themselves (I confine myself as usual to the German provinces) no country in Europe probably stands so little in need of secret paid police as Austria . . . That the whole police establishment of the empire is not considerable may be inferred from the fact, that its entire expense is only 1,643,500 fl. or 164,350l. sterling per annum; although in this sum is included all charge for equipments and support of the two Italian regiments; of the armed forces in the German states; all salaries from the 15,000 fls. paid to its chief in Vienna, down to that of the lowest employee; and all pensions to retired servants, widows and orphans in this branch of the service.[70]

According to Julius Marx, the witty Berliner, Adolf Grossbrenner, got the situation right: 'He said people could hear open discussion everywhere and see forbidden books everywhere in spite of informers. Moreover, the latter, he said succeeded in worming out nothing.'[71] On the other hand, there can be little doubt both that people imagined that there were many more police spies around than there actually were, and that in certain cases – such as that of the painter Daffinger, who got three days in jail for complaining about the police in an inn[72] – the police did take 'administrative measures' to suit their own interests.

In fact, the numbers of people employed by the police were extraordinarily small as the official statistics and finances clearly demonstrate; even the number of spies employed abroad appears to have been relatively limited. Moreover, the success of police spies in infiltrating either the sects or the *Burschenschaften* seems to have been extremely modest, while international measures against them appear to have been perfunctory and often futile. Even the Federal Investigating Commission at Mainz proved hopeless from Metternich's point of view, while attempts to isolate Austria from foreigners never totally succeeded even when this was actually government policy. And as Stiles *correctly* pointed out:

> Twenty years ago, Vienna was ten or twelve days' journey from Paris, and fifteen or sixteen days' journey from London. Now the Austrian capital may be reached in three or four days from either, and for every single traveler [sic] in 1830, from France or England, there are now fifty and a hundred pouring into the Leopold Stadt and the Stephen's Platz ... Travelers [sic] propagate ideas and notions as quickly, and possibly more successfully than newspapers.[73]

Hans Stumberger in 1962 published a book in Vienna entitled *Der Weg Zum Verfassungsstaat. Die Politische Entwicklung in Oberösterreich von 1792–1861* ('The Road to the Constitutional State: Political Developments in Upper Austria, 1792–1861'). It was based on the police archives of the province and demonstrated that, for the whole of the Metternich period, the government had very little to worry about. As Turnball had pointed out in 1840, there was no need for a 'paid secret police' to oppress the people. And as Hartig had recorded, Vienna did not even have laws against riots. It would seem therefore that at least one aspect of Metternich's police state – the use of spies and secret agents – has been exaggerated both in its domestic and international roles. Yet there are several other aspects of this spectre which still have to be investigated.

Austrian Censorship in the Age of Metternich

The Austrian censorship under Metternich has been more thoroughly investigated perhaps than police practice but there is still division among the experts as to how onerous it was. Julius Marx, whose aim was to demonstrate the rationale behind the censorship,[74] concluded: 'When it is maintained that Austria was a reactionary state, surrounded by a Chinese Wall, which was intellectually separated from the rest of progressive Europe, particularly from Germany, this was simply a lie from the liberals' propaganda war (*eine Kriegslüge der Liberalen*). Surviving libraries paint quite another picture.'[75] Emerson, on the other hand, writes:

> Metternich and his Foreign Office were just as anxious and as deter-
> mined as Sedlnitzky and the Police Ministry to construct a Chinese
> Wall of censorship around the Monarchy. The two Ministers cooper-
> ated in seeking to isolate Habsburg subjects from the rest of Europe
> through censorship just as they did in the controls on movement by
> which they tried so far as they could to keep foreigners out and
> Habsburg subjects at home.[76]

To reach any considered conclusion perhaps it is best to examine some original documents. At the basis of the censorship lay the *Instructions for the Direction of the Censorship and the Behaviour of the Censors resulting from the Imperial Decision of 14 September 1810.*[77] The introduction to the twenty-two articles contained in these instructions argued that, although the Emperor 'in his unremitting efforts to promote the good of one and all' was in favour of the 'promotion of useful knowledge', 'the ennobling of minds' and 'an appropriately directed freedom to read and write', one of his 'fatherly and sovereign duties' was to provide for an 'intellectual and moral education' that would not damage the 'hearts and minds' of his subjects. Hence 'no ray of light, wherever it may come from' was to remain 'unobserved or unknown' or 'deprived of its possible useful effect'. Yet both 'the hearts and minds of minors' were to be safeguarded from the 'pernicious prod-ucts of a frightful fantasy, from the poisoned breath of self-seeking seducers, and from the chimeras of confused minds'.

The first five articles considered 'works of learning'. Article 1 stated that a clear distinction had to be drawn between works aimed at schol-ars and 'brochures, popular works, light fiction and joke-books'. Article 2 defined works of learning as follows: 'A so-called work of learning qualifies not by its bulk, but by the importance and quality of its subject matter and the manner in which the same is treated.' Article 3 divided works of learning into two categories, first those 'that distinguish themselves through new discoveries, through a convincing and illuminating representation or through the discovery of new views and so forth', and secondly 'those which insipidly and without spirit repeat what has been said a hundred times before'. According to Article 4, works of the first type were to be treated 'with the greatest indulgence' and were not to be banned, save on 'the most important grounds'. Restrictions, however, if required, were not to be made known. Works of the second type, according to Article 5, were not to be indulged at all. When it came to 'brochures, popular works, writings for the young and light fiction', the full rigour of the existing censorship laws was to be applied. According to Article 6, everything overtly or covertly critical of religion or morals, anything that undermined respect for the ruling house or the existing form of government, as well as anything 'with a tendency to arouse sensuality' was to be removed; an end was to be put to such 'unbecoming fiction'. Those 'few good novels' which enlightened the heart or mind might be allowed but not the 'endless desert' of fiction based on romance and fantasies. Article 7 placed works of poetry and humour somewhere in between serious works and works of fiction. They might be indulged but on the whole were not suited 'to promote the well-being of the individual or the whole population'.

Articles 8, 9, 10 and 11 spelled out the political principles to be incorporated in the censorship. Article 8 seemed to be reasonably open-minded:

> Works in which the state administration as a whole or in particular branches is assessed, mistakes and misconceptions discovered, improvements indicated, means and ways in which to achieve benefits shown, past events illuminated etc., shall not, without sufficient other grounds, be forbidden, even if the principles and views of the author are not those of the state administration. However, works of this kind must be composed with dignity and modesty and avoid all real and suggested personalities. Moreover, they must contain nothing against religion, morals or anything subversive to the state.

Article 9 insisted that all works had to be reviewed by the censors, while Article 10 spelled out what had to be avoided in publications at all costs:

Writings that attack the head of state and the dynasty or even foreign state administrations, whose tendencies are to spread dissatisfaction and unrest, to loosen the bond between subjects and prince, to undermine the Christian, particularly the Catholic religion, to subvert morality, to promote superstition, books that preach social- ism, deism, materialism, finally, lampoons of all kinds, are less suited to enhance the fortunes of individuals or the good of all and much more suited to destroy them fundamentally. They can therefore claim as little indulgence as assassins can claim tolerance. They are to be treated with the full rigour of the law that has existed up till now.

Article 11 applied the same principles to manuscripts. Articles 12, 13 and 14 concerned the administration of the censorship. Under Article 12, authors whose works had been refused permits could submit their manuscripts along with their grounds of complaint to the local court office of their province, which would then submit a report to the Court Police Office saying whether or not it agreed with the original judge- ment. Under Article 13, works already banned might be resubmitted to the censor if they appeared in a new edition; works that had arrived new from abroad had to be submitted for the first time. Under Article 14 the censors were instructed to expedite the return of books and manuscripts as speedily as possible and in any case more quickly than hitherto.

Article 15 laid down the four categories to be used by censors of printed works, namely *admittitur, transeat, erga schedam conced,* and *damnatur.* The first was to be awarded to writings which could be publicly sold and advertised; the second to works not suited to general circulation but not worthy of severe restriction either. They might be sold publicly and advertised in catalogues, but they were not to be advertised in newspapers. The third category was meant for works in which the improprieties outweighed the good and common usefulness and which might only be approved without danger to businessmen and academics, if sanctioned by the Court Police Office. The fourth category was the highest grade of prohibition and was to be applied only to works that undermined the state or religion. Permission to read such works could be bestowed only by the Court Police Office, which every quarter had to supply the Emperor himself with a list of persons who had been allowed to see books in the latter two categories. Article 17 then declared that 'Professors and real scholars should never be denied books which belong to their subject area or which relate to the same, save for those marked with *erga schedam* or *damnatur* which consist merely of abuse and which would in any case be worthless.' Article 17 invented a new category of *toleratur* for manuscripts which was remarkably similar to *transeat*. Article 18 dealt with republications, i.e. the publication in Austria of works that had originally been published abroad. This was a lucrative business for publishers and was not totally ruled out by the 1810 regulations. The works in question, however, had to be submitted as new ones to the censors and the Court Police Office had to give its advice. Book deals between Austrian and foreign publishers had to be approved by the respective provincial censorship authorities and a report sent to the Court Police Office, affirming that the books involved were indeed to be published in the Monarchy. They might not, however, be republished. Article 19 laid down that unless the Court Police Office made an exception, authors no longer had to submit their manuscripts in duplicate. Article 20 provided for the censorship of all adverts for books (they had to be submitted to the Court Library beforehand), Article 21 gave the Court Police Office the right to refer works to other Court Offices before publication, while Article 22, finally, stated that all earlier regulations which had not been changed or abolished by these new ones remained in force. The new regulations, therefore, were extremely succinct and not outrageously oppressive by the standards of the day. They protected the state and the Catholic Church and demonstrated a large degree of prudery, yet they also paid respect to learning while attempting to avoid controversy. Much would depend, of course, on how they were interpreted and what other instructions were received by the censors. For example, there appear to have been 'private instructions regarding the censorship of the daily press' that were 'even withheld from the censor's staff'.[78] These included instructions not to mention visits to suburban theatres by members of the imperial family; not to mention the price or monetary value of any article; rules to protect the reputation of the stage-manager of the Court Opera House, while articles on the nobility, the military 'or other outstanding professions' had to be submitted to police officials beforehand. Sedlnitzky issued a decree on 28 July 1823 obliging all books by Austrian authors published abroad to be submitted to the censorship first, although Kolowrat in 1840 got it recognised that only decrees published by the Emperor himself had the force of law.[79] Still, the real basis of the censorship was undoubtedly the 1810 regulations.

Neither Metternich nor Francis II had a high opinion of writers or professors – particularly those concerned with politics or *Staatswissenschaften* in general. Francis had notoriously told his teachers at Laibach: 'I don't need scholars, but good citizens . . . Who serves me must teach as I command. Anyone who cannot do that or who comes with new ideas can go or I will dismiss him.'[80] When asked to give Grillparzer the post of court clerk, he replied: 'Leave me in peace about your hot-headed Grillparzer: he would write verses not documents.'[81] Metternich, in 1825, after an outburst of student unrest, had hoped that 'our (i.e. Germany's) absurd university privileges together with their special legal position [would] be ended in one blow'[82] for, like Francis, he tended to think of professors as erring bureaucrats. Curiously, it was the presidents of the *Polizeihofstelle* who worried about academic standards. In fact, the 1810 regulations themselves had partly come about because the then occupant of the post, the moderate Baron Hager, had expressed his concern to Francis that the rigorous censorship was undermining the educational standards of candidates for government posts: 'the youthful generation feared that gaining a higher education would hinder their getting on in their chosen career'.[83] Sedlnitzky was condemned in his time by many as Metternich's 'poodle' (Sarau) or 'monkey' (Hormayr) or even 'the dirt on the soles of the shoes of Prince Metternich' (Hammer-Purgstall), yet Julius Marx writes:

We have proof that Sedlnitzky took a benevolent view of people who thought he was hostile to them. He had wished Hormayr and Prokesch the best of luck with their works, he had told the Emperor to buy *A True Servant*, he was for a permit for *Ottokar* at the Theater an der Wien, and had recommended Castelli's poems to the Emperor. We will not here enter into his passion for the theatre, which is known from the literature, but will stress his note to Metternich over the reproduction of *Ottokar*. In it he expressed the view that the Monarchy in part stood on a lower cultural level than several German states, yet no truly interested state administrator could wish for its subjects to lag behind others in artistic and scientific matters. Austria wanted to transmit German culture and speech to its non-German peoples, to which end only the reproduction of useful foreign writings could lead. He suggested that the Emperor should make a gift of 1,000 fl. to the rebuilding of the conservatory and concert room of the Society of the Friends of Music.[84]

Certainly, Sedlnitzky required a very high standard of censor, although liberal opponents still criticised the staff involved. The *Grenzboten*, for example, in 1846, described the censor Hasenöhrl as 'well-meaning but little educated',[85] whereas he had graduated from the University of Prague in 1823 in politics and law, and spoke fluent

Czech, German, Latin, French and Italian. When the censorship was being reorganised at the start of 1848, Sedlnitzky put down his thoughts for the Emperor as to the qualities required of the man needed to fill the post of *Zensuroberdirektor*:

> The Director must possess a complete knowledge of censorship laws and regulations, a comprehensive capacity for leadership and a precise familiarity with the offices of the institution; further, a proven dedication to Your Majesty and the royal and imperial government, the purest impartiality, decisiveness, and at the same time prudence in the strength of his character in the leadership of his office in order not to allow himself to be misled by the daily attacks of the press. Finally, he must possess a fundamental knowledge of the whole of Austrian law, some knowledge of ancient and modern literature, a comprehensive knowledge of languages (at least of Latin, Italian, and one Slav language), a higher level of intelligence and a quick and correct intellectual grasp. [He had to possess all these qualities . . .] in order to give the necessary overall direction and hence efficiency to the diverging views of the censors, to examine their submissions and to make decisions in the first instance, as well as to be able to give advice in matters of principle based on full knowledge of the subject in the interests of a truly progressive education and according to the trend of Austrian state administrative practice. Finally, in judging the suitability of the individual to be chosen in this case, it seems necessary to take into consideration the circumstance that we are here concerned with the introduction of a new institution, which requires both initiative and double the usual amount of energy, and therefore both physical and mental alertness.[86]

Sedlnitzky, in fact, was so concerned with quality in writing that he did not actually believe that people should write primarily for profit at all: 'Woeful is that human society in which merits need to be proportionately rewarded with money! Or where great men would only gain merits on account of pecuniary rewards. For in this case, merit would become synonymous with profit and the whole social order would be turned upside down.'[87] The result was that in 1822, two-thirds of the 529 authors living in Vienna were either civil servants or teachers and the other one-third were professionals (doctors, lawyers or priests). Only 22 authors of *belles lettres* claimed no other profession. The vast majority did their writing part-time.[88]

The people employed by Sedlnitzky, needless to say, were of the highest academic standards, although by the mid-1840s there were only 25 of them dealing with *c*. 10,000 titles per year.[89] There were two groups involved: regular censors on 400–500 gulden a year and assistant censors on 300–400 gulden a year. In 1844, the regular censors were for the most part renowned scholars or high-ranking civil servants who therefore also had full-time jobs to pursue.[90] They included Franz Zenner, the director of theological studies at the University of Vienna, Josef Scheiner, Professor of Old Testament Studies and Semitic Languages, Theobold Fritz, Professor of Moral Theology, Anton Ritter von Plappert, dean of the university's law school, Johann Nepomuk Ritter von Raimann, dean of the medical school and the Emperor's personal physician, Franz Cassian Hallaschka, dean of the liberal arts school, Bartholomäus Kopitar, Slavicist and head of the manuscript collection at the Austrian National Library, and others – geographers, Germanists, technologists, pedagogues – of similar academic distinction. Most assistant censors were themselves distinguished writers and civil servants such as Johann Gabriel Seidl who had supplied the words for the national anthem (*Gott erhalte*). The *Grenzboten* always referred to him ironically as 'the *gemütliche* Seidl'.[91] Schreyvogel, who was later to become director of the Burgtheater, received his appointment as assistant censor in a letter which began: 'Your well-established expertise in the field of belles lettres and associated disciplines, as well as your desire to use this for the good of this country's literature, has led me to appoint you as assistant censor in the department of Bellestrik.'[92]

Despite the fact that the censorship was operated by men of the highest intellectual calibre, they still, of course, had to stick to the regulations set out in 1810. This meant that authors were advised to avoid controversy and could not easily criticise the Austrian or other governments. Complaints and derision from the educated classes were inevitable. Helfert, for example, recorded that when one author invoked Goethe and Schiller as literary 'authorities', the censor in Prague told him: 'Authors yes, but not authorities'.[93] According to Stiles,[94] all phrases such as 'popular rights', 'popular opinion', 'public opinion' and 'nationality' were removed, while in one book which had nothing to do with Austria, the expression 'heroic champions' was replaced with 'brave soldiers' and a 'band of youthful heroes, who flocked around the glorious standard of their country' became 'a considerable number of young men who voluntarily enlisted themselves for the public service.' Koch wrote that if a historian of the reign of Leopold I wrote 'The Counter-Reformation in Hungary, promoted by the Jesuits with cruel persecution of the Protestants, has been the cause of many conspiracies', the censors would have rephrased it to read: 'The leaders of the malcontents, deluded by ambition, allowed themselves to give way to conspiracies.'[95] He related the story of how, when an essay was proposed for publication in the *Wiener Zeitung* advocating the establishment of houses of improvement for released criminals, it was turned down by the censor with the words: 'the aforementioned suggestion could be used to blame the government for the fact that no such institutions yet exist'.[96]

Clearly much of the criticism concerning the censorship was anecdotal. According to Julius Marx, most stories were based on rumour. Castelli confessed he never knew Sedlnitzky. Police and censorship got mixed up and poets feared they might end up in the Spielberg like Pellico, although the latter had committed high treason.[97] Yet the censorship existed and many authors had good reason for complaint.

The censorship was managed by the fourth (final) department of the *Polizeihofstelle*.[98] This was the one where final decisions were made and transferred to authors via the Book Revision Office, where they brought their manuscripts. There were provincial revision offices too which dealt with minor matters, although they also censored the provincial dailies and acted in a judicial capacity if the local police reported infringements of regulations. However, they could not approve the establishment of new newspapers or censor journals. Their views on local matters, on the other hand, had to be taken into account and, if an appeal were made to the Court Police Office in Vienna against a local judgement, the grounds of objection had to be accompanied by reports from the local governor's office (where the local book revision offices were situated).

The Central Book Revision Office in Vienna was directly subordinate to the Court Police Office. Here books and manuscripts entered the system and were distributed to the censors. Each one would be given to two separate censors and would be sent along with their reports to the Court Police Office. If the two censors came to widely differing conclusions, then a third would read the book or manuscript concerned or the president would decide. The latter might be asked to decide on specific difficulties, as is known from the cases of the poet Bauernfeld and the historian Schneller. The author would receive the decisions of the censors from the Book Revision Office.

Since the latter also had to deal with book deliveries from abroad, prepare the lists of those allowed and those banned and deal not merely with books and manuscripts but with newspapers, journals, music, paintings, exhibition catalogues, brochures, joke books, adverts, buttons, embroidery, pipe bowls, etc. – the Austrian censorship system was the most comprehensive in Europe – it had its work cut out. The lack of personnel always led to long delays and at one point it was taking between eight and twenty months to return works to authors. This led to many complaints and petitions from booksellers and authors, including suggestions to hire more staff and give them better conditions, and attempts were indeed made to expedite the procedure by limiting the time devoted to each item or to easing the process for more technical works. Eventually a wholesale reorganisation was planned from 1 February 1848 after the 1845 authors' petition, by absorbing the Book Revision Office in a new *Zensuroberdirektion* as an office of first instance which could give judgements in its own name. Appeals would then be allowed to a new *Oberzensurkollegium*. This was to sit under Sedlnitzky's presidency but to have two court counsellors from the Court Police Office and one each from the State Chancellery, the Court Chancellery and the Office of the Chief Justice. In the most important cases, however, the Emperor's decision would be final. Zenker,[99] however, in his analysis of the reform, which was swept aside by the 1848 revolutions of course, argued that Clause 4 of the new regulations made them self-defeating in that it laid down that no appeal could be made from the first to the second body '(a) where it is merely a matter of articles that are destined for newspapers, dailies and broadsheets, not of a purely scientific content; (b) where objections are raised to individual omissions and changes of expression; and (c) if no important consideration for the publishing of the censored matter in the press can be made.' He comments: 'In the secret *Haus-Hof und Staatskanzlei* the courage had still been found even in such critical days to ridicule and mystify the people by such a law, or – let us be kind – people still did not have the faintest idea of what must happen and what within a few days did happen.'[100]

Be that as it may, another reason for delays was that the Court Police Office in order to carry out its work had to cooperate both with the authorities in Hungary and Lombardy-Venetia and with other departments of state such as the State Chancellery. When, for example, a lithographed cartoon of Baron Haller, the Ban of Croatia, surfaced in Agram in 1846, copies were confiscated in Austria and Hungary. Metternich also had the matter investigated by the Austrian consul in Leipzig. The Hungarian authorities, via Metternich, also had him investigate the publication of a book on the clergy of Hungary published by the Leipzig publisher Wigand. With regard to Lombardy-Venetia, Sedlnitzky often took decisions on Italian publications if the authorities there were split or undecided, often as a result of a Vienna censor's report or as a result of *Staatskanzlei* intervention. On one occasion, Metternich was furious that the Turin newspaper *il mondo illustrato* had been given different verdicts by censors in Milan, Venice and Trieste – this, to his way of thinking, was exactly the kind of thing that left Austria open to ridicule. Hence Sedlnitzky took a final decision on the newspaper – which the Milanese authorities thought was too light.[101] (On another occasion Metternich was furious that while the *Österreichische Beobachter* was printing articles announcing that Turkish troops were being pulled out of the Danubian Principalities, the *Zeitungsblatt* of Lemberg was quoting an eyewitness who claimed to have seen 40,000 Turkish troops in Jassy alone.[102] Since Lemberg was close to the Principalities, liberal papers, like the Augsburg *Allgemeine Zeitung* – the most read newspaper in Austria – tended to reprint articles from the *Zeitungsblatt*. One of the great difficulties of the censorship system was that local offices would periodically come to different verdicts.)

The need to consult different court offices obviously delayed final decisions. When any manuscript came under the censors' review, Sedlnitzky had to decide whether other offices of state had to be consulted and on which grounds. Some were less than eager to be involved because of the time required. This was true both of the Chief Justice's office and of the Court Chancellery. The latter duly published decrees threatening to punish Austrians abroad who published without the approval of the censors, but in practice did nothing about it. (Several courts questioned whether this was indeed a crime.) Metternich's State Chancellery and the State Conference, on the other hand, firmly backed the censors. Indeed, the State Chancellery had a censorship department of its own, given that it was so often consulted and was so interested in censorship affairs. Its chief censor after 1814 was Franz Josef Freiherr von Bretfeld-Chlumczansky zu Cronenburg, who came recommended by Gentz, who none the less said of him: 'I don't really trust him. He looks very false when one really analyses him. He is petty in his endeavours, affected, and glib; one of those who will try to get along with everybody.'[103] According to Emerson, 'madness drove him out of the service more than twenty years later'.[104] The State Chancellery also often employed its diplomatic personnel in censorship cases – particularly the consul-general in Leipzig, the centre of the intellectual opposition abroad. The police also kept it informed of any revolts or subversion, given its belief in the European-wide organisation of the sects.

Examples of cooperation between the police and the State Chancellery included the dispute over the Russian state counsellor

Tegoborski's pamphlet on Austrian finances and the publication of a map of Galicia with statistical tables. In the first case, since the pamphlet gave rise to an attack by a critic, whose arguments were supported by Kübeck but who had not received permission to publish them abroad, Metternich was asked for his advice. Tegoborski was eventually asked to make changes when he submitted his pamphlet for publication in Austria. Both the State Chancellery and the Court War Council agreed that the general street and post map of Galicia published by the firm of Artaria was reliable. There were mistakes in the statistical tables, but these were matters, it was agreed, for critics rather than for censors. On another occasion, the Chief Justice's department was consulted by the State Chancellery concerning a manuscript on a trial then taking place in Prague. The author was suspected of having inside information. The censors were split over the case, but Sedlnitzky in the end decided to ban it.

Various bodies, including the Academy of Sciences, were subjected to self-censorship. By decrees of 16 June 1803, all directors of studies in universities were made responsible for ensuring that staff went about their business properly. Teaching books had to be censored and the Book Revision Office informed university departments of all the suitable ones available. Medical books had to be sent directly to the Police Court Office, along with reports from specialist censors within the university. If professors of theology and the police differed over theological works, the Emperor himself decided the outcome. Books by university staff had to come to the censors accompanied by reports from the head of the department (often censors themselves in any case). Theatre directors would likewise have to make the case to the censors for any new plays they wanted to put on.

The organisation of the censorship was one thing; its practice was another. Clearly from what has already been described, distinctions were drawn between the educated members of society and the masses, between worthwhile and academic literature and popular fiction. Yet fundamentally the censorship aimed at preventing anything that could undermine or damage religion, the state or good morals. It was part and parcel of a system that emphasised conservatism in politics and religion and prudery as far as morals were concerned. Thus criticisms of the monarch, his house and his governmental colleagues were not allowed. Laws that had obtained imperial sanction could not be criticised either, although later on reviews of legal decisions were allowed in law journals. Works that justified popular sovereignty or demanded a constitution were outlawed. Aristocratic and monarchical principles were always supported. Attacks on foreign states or their monarchs were not permitted either, Article 4 of the Carlsbad Decrees making this especially the case for the German states (although any mention of the Carlsbad Decrees was forbidden in Austria). Religions were also protected, especially the Catholic one. Protestant works, though, were carefully examined for false teachings and Jewish texts treated even more severely. Their importation was forbidden and each edition of domestically produced works carefully examined. The Greek Orthodox Church – not the uniate one – was protected by the Tsar and by the fact that it was of sufficient numerical strength in Hungary to merit some consideration. Erotic literature, obscene drawings and ambiguous theatre productions – not to mention adverts for plays – constituted attacks on morality. Good taste was everything. Phrases had to be modified, sharp attacks neutralised, drawings and cartoons forbidden if they produced misconceived representations. Pictures of all sorts of people – the imperial family, the Chancellor, certain murderers and criminals – were usually forbidden. And all sorts of items were perused for lapses in taste or for subversion – buttons, engravings, insignia, rings, embroidery, pipe bowls, songs, musical dedications, adverts, tombstone inscriptions and dictionaries. But the chief objects of attention, of course, were the press, books and the theatre (including musical theatre).

With regard to the press, the great complaint was of its uniformity of tone after the censors had been at work. Vienna had only three newspapers anyway (including the official *Wiener Zeitung*) and according to Salomon only allowed three or four to be imported from Germany, including Augsburg's *Allgemeine Zeitung*, which was the one most widely read. Before 1848, apparently the number of foreign newspapers allowed to be imported was diminishing.[105] However, according to contemporary sources,[106] the Graz Reading Club subscribed to 170 journals, while educated people could obtain those limited by *erga schedam*. According to Professor Rath, the Legal–Political Reading Club of Vienna had access to such newspapers as the *Leipziger Zeitung*, *Le Constitutionnel*, *Le Siècle* and even *Die Grenzboten* itself. The censors, naturally, had to make quick decisions regarding newspapers – all materials had to be with them by noon the day before and censored proof-sheets could not be shown to any private or official person without the censors' permission – something that was often a source of confusion, mistakes and chicanery – but the main pressure on the press was the threat to impose a ban or to remove the *Blatt* (the free postal delivery service). Bans were very rarely imposed and sudden ones practically never, since this created controversy; more often a paper or periodical might find that at the end of a subscription period, subscriptions could not be renewed. The *Allgemeine Korrespondent von und für Deutschland* was banned in 1817[107] after complaints in Prague that a couple of its editions had stirred up class hatred; in 1822 the Nuremberg *Korrespondent*, as well as the *Morgenblatt für gebildedte Stände* and the *Erheiterungen*, were banned; while the English magazine *Punch* was suddenly banned in 1847 after publishing offensive cartoons of the Emperor. Publishers, of course, could be kept in line in a number of ways – making them print pro-Austrian articles from time to time, blackmailing them, threatening them (Sedlnitzky for years ran a campaign against the *Allgemeine Zeitung*, threatening to ban it), refusing them permission to establish new papers, even bribing them (as for example in the case of the editor of the *Gazetta di Lugano*).[108] All these methods were used.

Metternich also used famous scholars to present the Austrian point of view for, as he told Baron Hager in 1816, the police 'must actively influence opinion, putting the actions of the government in their true light and opposing to the spread of false news the conquering power of truth'.[109] The conservative scholar Adam Müller, for example, who became Austrian consul-general in Leipzig, was only too happy to agree, 'for only in daily newspapers, blow by blow, from the standpoint of law and public decorum, can be corrected what the destroyers of the public peace bring forward daily'.[110] The *Schwindelgeist* simply had to be defeated. Yet, Gentz and Müller apart, not many famous writers were recruited.

With regard to the stage, suburban theatres were given more leeway than the world-famous Hoftheater, but all plays were carefully scrutinised. During the Hundred Days at the end of the Napoleonic Wars, for example, Caroline Pichler's play *Ferdinand II* was banned in case its theme of Habsburg victory in the Thirty Years' War would prove too contemporary and stir up political controversy. Likewise, even one of Kotzebue's plays, *The Crusader*, was banned in 1817 and 1818 since it involved the performance of full Catholic rites on stage and therefore upset religiously-minded persons – like the Emperor. Schiller's *Wilhelm Tell* had to be significantly altered before it could receive permission to be produced at the Burg.[111]

The most famous occasions for controversy regarding the theatre, however, were those regarding plays by Austria's two literary giants of the age, Grillparzer and Bauernfeld. In the case of the former,[112] his poems 'Campo Vaccino' and 'A True Servant of his Master' had earned him strong rebukes; indeed, the Emperor's own views on the latter had been made known to him. However, he threatened to leave the country when his play *König Ottokar's Glück und Ende* was refused a permit to be produced by the Hoftheater in January 1824 by the Court Police Office on the advice of the State Chancellery. In this case, however, the Emperor himself intervened, questioned Sedlnitzky for the reasons for the ban, and then had another censor, his personal physician, read the play. When the latter (and the Court Chamberlain who oversaw the theatre) pronounced in favour, Francis allowed the play to be performed, which it was a year later. Sedlnitzky subsequently raised no objection either to further performances at the Theater an der Wien or to the play's publication. Bauernfeld's play *Großjährig* also represented something extraordinary – a direct attack on Metternich on the stage of the Hoftheater largely due to the machinations of his rival Count Kolowrat.[113] The play was a comedy in which the main figure Blase was the chief administrator of the estates of Baron Hermann. The latter represented the Austrians, of course, while Blase represented Metternich. When Baron Hermann proposed to take over the adminis-tration of the estates himself, his chief administrator advised him: 'We must first wait ... wait ... Look now ... waiting – that is the main secret of good administration. When you wait ... everything happens by itself.' The play was still running in February 1848. The opposition of Austria's two greatest writers was to cost Metternich's reputation dear. Bauernfeld's satire hit the mark exactly, while Grillparzer's bitter, biting rhymes were to be forever attached to the Chancellor's name.

When it came to books and journals, the censorship differentiated between domestic and foreign works. Domestic authors had to present their work in manuscript form and to assent to changes suggested by the censors or withdraw the manuscript. Books already published could only be given a censorship category and might even be confiscated. Works that came in the form of installments were usually first given a *transeat*, but if later installments were banned, the ban was applied retrospectively to all previous installments – an excellent inducement for good practice. Works that were very expensive were usually treated leniently on the assumption that the masses could not afford them. Political writings that called for the reshaping of society were usually banned. For example the writings of Weitling or Heinzens were confis-cated. The same applied to Max Stirner's *Der Einzige und sein Eigenthum*. Academic books were generally quite mildly dealt with, as accorded with the 1810 instructions. Medical writings, however, were examined more strictly and occasionally works of linguistic research were banned – for example, Diefenbach's *Über Leben, Geschichte und Sprache*.

Constitutional law was another tricky subject; both Aretin's *Staatsrecht der Constitutionellen Monarchie* and Rotteck's *Staatslexicon* were given *erga schedam*. The Carlsbad Decrees were also relevant here with regard to the German states. Religious academic works were not treated any differently. David Friedrich Strauß's *Life of Jesus* was allowed limited publication, yet an adaptation of it was forbidden. Works on religion or religious history that attacked the Catholic faith were not permitted. Comments on contemporary religious controversies – e.g. the Reformation festival of 1817, the 300-year jubilee of the Confession of Augsburg in 1830, the Cologne Church dispute, the position of mixed marriages – caused difficulties but when the dispute over the Holy Coat of Trier gave rise to German Catholicism, this and all its works were banned from Austria. The ban on older prayer books, on the other hand, stemmed from the fact that they contained out-of-date ideas.

Historical works on great subjects were seldom forbidden so long as they were not hostile to Austria or did not pursue hidden political agendas. The world histories of Becker and Schlosser were given *erga schedam* as was Ranke's *Die römische Päpste*. Not that ancient history was always welcomed. In 1822, a reprinting of a work entitled *The History of Greece as Instruction in Translation from German to Latin* was refused permission for a reprint, despite a host of proposed alterations, on the grounds that 'it could only stamp ineradicably on the minds of students so receptive to all enthusiastic impressions, in part stimulated by recent events, the model of the democratic tendency of ancient Greece towards unlimited popular freedom'.[114] Modern Greeks, of course, were then in revolt against Austria's ally, Turkey. Works of contemporary history,[115] it has to be admitted, were difficult to get through the censor. Banned for example in 1819 was Father Aemilian Janitsch's ninth volume on the *History and Growth of the Austrian Monarchy* which covered the period from 1806 to 1817. A later work by the same author that covered the period of Joseph II was also banned on the ground that posterity could be left to judge the policies of that emperor towards the French Revolution. Janitsch's work on the Russia of Alexander I – then considered a liberal – was likewise banned. The same fate awaited Franz Carl Zoller's memoirs of Innsbruck which were viewed as a disguised political history of the Tyrol and of recent relations with Bavaria. Joseph Henniger Freiherr von Eberg's *History of the Habsburg Empire*, was also banned, although Palačky's history of Bohemia suffered only several changes suggested by the censors. The worst-treated historian was almost certainly Hormayr who, despite occupying posts such as Habsburg historiographer and keeper of the archives in the State

Chancellery, eventually left to become librarian to King Ludwig of Bavaria. The trouble started when Hormayr published an ill-received essay on Philippina Welser, wife of Archduke Ferdinand who ruled the Tyrol in the sixteenth century – their marriage was an ancient source of resentment at court – and continued for ten years until 1827 when he published an article which mentioned the illegitimate children of Ferdinand the Fair of Austria and his purported love affair with a beautiful nun. He was also to publish a critical biography of Kaunitz and later, of course, took his revenge with his study of Metternich and the Emperor Francis. Another contemporary historian who felt driven out of Vienna was Julius Franz Schneller, whose fifth volume on the *Political History of Imperial Austria* which covered the reign of Joseph II was rejected by the censors. He took up the post of professor of philosophy in Baden.

In the publication of documents, omissions were avoided, since they could have led to exposures. Popular historical writings were more harshly dealt with, although those on Joseph II, a popular hero, were more lightly treated. The Napoleonic cult, on the other hand, was suppressed and only with his death and that of his son, the Duke of Reichstadt, was the situation eased. Writings on uprisings in Greece, Poland or even on Hungarian affairs were little tolerated while, given that political heroes such as Kosciuszko, Poniatowski or Ypsilanti were often used as vehicles for political ideas, their images on rings, buttons, embroidery or pipe bowls were strictly forbidden. Genealogical works and charts were always corrected.

When it came to works of literature, those of Heine were forbidden, although others of the Young Germany school were given an *erga schedam*. They were all later banned, however, by a federal decree. Writings of classical authors and of classic German and other authors were usually allowed in editions of collected works, since these were much more expensive. Poetry was also censored: Schubert's musical arrangement of Schiller's poem *Der Kampf mit dem Drachen* passed the censors with difficulty; Goethe's *Reineke* was given only a limited permit. Austrian political poetry, such as Anastasius Grün's *Spaziergänge eines wiener Poeten*, and the later works of Rollett and Hartmann, were banned.[116] Naturally there was no tolerance of Freiligarth's *Ça ira* or Heine's *Deutschland, ein Wintermärchen*. Even if domestic poets employed patriotic material, there could be difficulties from a historical, political and monarchical viewpoint.

The greatest irony of the censorship was that, although the educated and intellectual classes complained most bitterly about it, the people who suffered most were the general public on account of the prudish attitude taken towards popular fiction. Tales of knights, robbers, ghosts and criminals were prohibited, superstitious ones were gracelessly rejected, books of dreams were unwelcome and erotic literature – even that of Boccaccio or Casanova – almost always banned. Foreign fiction was also strictly censored – French and Italian works more so than English ones, since English was less well-known as a foreign language.[117]

Finally, with regard to music, operas, song recitals and dedications were all censored; in the case of musicals all pictures in adverts were also banned. Beethoven so arranged things that his publisher Haslinger had to secure his agreement to the title pages of his works. His *Messa a quatro voci*, like a piano arrangement of Mozart's *Requiem*, received an *erga schedam*. A dedication to Chopin had to be removed from one piece; hymns to Pius IX, including one by Rossini, were not allowed. Revolutionary songs, such as the *Marseillaise* and *Noch ist Polen nicht verloren*, were banned. Julius Marx writes: 'It may be remembered that the funeral oration for Beethoven had to be given before the cemetery gates while he was on his litter, because the cemetery, as consecrated ground, might not be desecrated by profane things.'[118]

Beethoven, of course, had been a lifelong critic of the 'paralytic regime' of Vienna.[119] He had written famously in 1794: 'One must not talk too loudly or the police give you lodgings for the night.' After the Napoleonic Wars, he had characterised the Viennese as 'worthless from the Emperor downwards' and had employed the pun *Österreicher, Eselreicher* or 'Austrians, Ass-trians'. By the time of his death, his reputation in Vienna was in eclipse, although one historian has written: 'Perhaps we should be grateful to Wellington and Metternich for creating the stable anti-revolutionary era that fostered the atmosphere of artistic neglect that compelled Beethoven to turn inward and compose such towering masterpieces as the *Ninth Symphony*, the *Missa Solemnis* and the late Piano Sonatas and String Quartets.'[120]

What role then did Metternich play in the censorship system? Some authors seem to believe that the State Chancellor was the main driving force behind it. Bibl, for example in his biography of the statesman, wrote that 'here too it was the State Chancellor who prevented every more reasonable treatment.'[121] Emerson believes exactly the same.[122] Marx, on the other hand, is more reasonable and nuanced. Indeed, it is quite evident from his work that the main driving force behind the 'system' was the Emperor Francis himself who had established it well before Metternich became a dominating political influence. Thus he headed the 1798 Censorship Commission and it was only logical that in 1801 he transferred the censorship to the police. His agents spied on his own family and ministers and he was pitiless towards critics and lawbreakers, however sincerely he strove to live up to his motto *justitia regnorum fundamentum* [The foundation of monarchy is justice].[123] He described censorship to Pergen as 'this business which is so close to me' (*dieses mir so naheliegende Geschäft*), intervened regularly, read the protocols of the Court Police Office and read the lists of those who had been given access to banned and restricted works. He made difficulties for censors who believed that works that were part of collected editions could only be banned if the publishers concerned were compensated. After 1810, however, he intervened personally less often but, although he might arrange to have Grillparzer's *Ottokar* or Bauernfeld's *Großjährig* performed, his views never changed: 'Thus all censorship stories which inform us that he found the censorship stupid, that he would have preferred to see a play than ban it, that he said he was unhappy that against his will he was becoming more liberal from year to year, are pure nonsense.'[124]

Metternich for his part agreed with Francis that everything had to be done to combat the ideological legacy of the French Revolution. Yet, whereas Francis was more interested in straightforward police measures, Metternich was more interested in ideas. He would have agreed with Napoleon's definition that 'censorship is the right to prevent manifestations of ideas, which complicate the peace of the state, its interests and its good order.'[125] He therefore aimed to have newspapers that were read in Austria print only the views that the government approved. As Zenker put it:

It is not true . . . that there was no political journalism in Austria before 1848; on the contrary it was quite excellently understood how to turn newspapers into an effective political tool . . . Metternich also knew, in spite of all his contempt, how to make fertile use of 'his newspaper writers'. Only there was no organ of public opinion in Vienna before the revolution, merely an instrument for the artificial production of public opinion, in the sense of one of a single ruling party.[126]

Metternich has, as a result, been accused with reason by Julius Marx of trying 'to separate the political and the unpolitical lives of the mind',[127] since he had no desire to suppress the latter. As for controlling the police and the censors, the truth seems to be that Metternich and

Sedlnitzky simply agreed with Francis in principle that the Revolution had to be fought. The police chief was an educated aristocrat with a distinguished service record who managed to keep his position for thirty years, despite attacks by the educated classes and occasional bureaucratic skirmishes with Kolowrat. He was by no means as narrow-minded as portrayed but he did agree with Metternich on preventing revolution by censoring the press.[128] He said in 1846 after hearing Metternich state his views:

> I support the so illuminating and most important truths made in these remarks with my innermost conviction. Would that God would fill those in power everywhere at this period of time with these truths, for then those who decide fate would have control of the printing press, this most powerful lever of destruction of the *Zeitgeist*, and their task would be considerably lightened and at least a solution would be possible.[129]

Kolowrat also supported such views.[130] He was no liberal, although he occasionally undermined the system which he otherwise served faithfully by organising bureaucratic attacks on both Sedlnitzky and Metternich. However, these attacks arose from personal motives, not out of principle, and the censorship, in any case, always remained outside his authority.

Metternich – or the State Chancellery – certainly had the right to intervene in matters of censorship as the 1810 regulations made clear. Moreover, he could always rely on the Emperor's backing if and when he did. The way in which he exercised his influence varied from case to case. Marx says (in his *Die Österreichasche Zensur*) at one point: 'He not rarely saved a newspaper, which wrote in a hateful tone against Austria through his objection. Equally, his guarantee was often enough for an early permit for a journal. These then had to prove their good intentions over a long period before they were accepted into the tariff' (p. 56). At another point, however, he writes: 'All in all the State Chancellery under Metternich was more severe than the police. The police acted according to decrees, Metternich according to political principles and aims, whether with regard to religious affairs, foreign newspapers or foreign historical researchers' (p. 35). The main point to grasp is – and both Marx and Emerson give numerous examples from the documents – that each case was decided on its merits in the light of the principles already discussed. Often there were disagreements, but always over practice, never over principle.

What then were the results? To what extent did the censorship make Metternich's Austria a police state? There are a series of factors that have to be taken into account before reaching a final judgement. In the first place, clearly individuals, particularly authors and publishers – precisely the kind of people who were most likely to, and did, leave memoirs[131] – were highly vexed. One description of the respected historian Kaltenbäck in 1836 runs as follows: 'You cannot believe what trouble this journal cost him; the worries with the censors and Metternich . . . truly bordered on the incredible and the poor devil is already so mad that he has lost all enthusiasm . . . the vexations and machinations were never so difficult as now . . . it exceeds everything as yet experienced.'[132] No doubt Kaltenbäck had had a lot to put up with, but Heinrich Börstein was to write in his memoirs:

At that time many a journalist or correspondent out of favour disappeared into the cells of the Spielberg or the casemates of Munkacs for ever, for the good Emperor Francis was very jealous of his authority as Emperor, and let people who committed a crime in word or deed against the divinely established sanctity of the crown rot without pity, burdened by the heaviest chains, in the deepest cells of the Spielberg – like Silvio Pellico, Maroncelli and other Italian youths.[133]

This was pure nonsense. When in 1816, for example, the Vienna Police Directorate recommended a retraction and reprimand for an editor whose criticisms of Habsburg troops had been published abroad, Sedlnitzky ordered three days of police arrest for conducting forbidden correspondence.[134] Pellico and others had been condemned to death for high treason and had had their sentences commuted to life imprisonment. None the less, the poets and playwrights had their revenge with lasting results. Grillparzer's famous epitaph[135] on Metternich was extremely cruel:

Hier liegt, für seinen Rühm zu spät,
der Don Quichote der Legitimät,
der falsch und wahr nach seinem Sinne bog,
zuerst die andern, dann sich selbst belog,
vom Schelm zum Toren ward bei grauen Haupte,
weil er zuletzt die eigenen Lügen glaubte.

[In this dark vault, too late for his renown,
Aristocracy's Don Quixote lays him down.

Falsehood and truth he twisted to his will,
Deceived first others, then himself with skill;
Into grey-headed fool from rogue he passed,
For he believed his own fond lies at last.][136]

His lines on Metternich's 'System' were equally biting:

Ich weiß ein algewalt Wort,
auf Meilen hört's ein Tauber,
es wirkt geschäftig fort und fort,
mit unbegriffenen Zauber;
ist niergends und ist überall,
bald lästig, bald bequem,
es paßt auf ein und jeden Fall,
das Wort, es heißt: System.[137]

[I know a most powerful expression,
The deaf can hear it for miles,
It makes a steady progression,
With magic in its wiles;
Found nowhere and in every place,
Its costs we bear or miss them,
It fits in each and every case,
It calls itself the 'System'.][138]

Anastasius Grün, meanwhile, had finished his poem 'A Ball-Room Scene' with the verses:

O thou statesman, wise in counsel, since thy humour's now so good,
Since this interval of pleasure finds thee in a kindly mood,
Cast thine eyes towards the portal where a thirsty client stands,
Yearning for one sign of favour from thine all-compelling hands.

Start not, there's no cause for terror! He's as harmless as the day,
In the folds of his poor mantle, there's no dagger hidden away;
Austria's people stands there, peaceful, full of sense and loyalty,
And their prayer is simply: May we make so free as to be free?[139]

Historians also got their revenge. In 1848, Hormayr published his *Kaiser Franz und Metternich* in Leipzig where, two decades earlier, Julius Franz Schneller had published the fifth volume of his *Political History of*

Imperial Austria, together with all the censor's comments and objections plus the lengthy annotations of Gentz. German critics of the Austrian censorship were delighted, but the Austrian authorities were forced to maintain a dignified silence lest they make matters even worse. There was little hope of preventing the work from being read by Austrians if it became a *cause célèbre*.

The greatest criticism by all the intellectuals regarding censorship concerned its general effect on intellectual life in Austria. This, they all complained, had become bland, depressing and second rate. There were both specific and general complaints. As to the former, Frankl, the newspaper publisher, recorded: 'the self-assurance of those who wrote had fallen so low, that they practised self-censorship of their own and destroyed even inborn thought as Chronos did his children'.[140] Grillparzer wrote of the 'extreme distress' of playwrights who were dependent on the Vienna stage and 'the unimportant writers who could find no foreign publisher.'[141] For those who wanted information, finally, foreign newspapers were expensive and not everyone could afford the membership fees of reading clubs. On a more general level, Sealsfield found Vienna to be intellectually dead: 'No city in the world has more museums, galleries, collections or libraries than Vienna, but these treasures are unused . . . It is correct that a foreigner enjoys free access to all scientific institutions and collections, public and private, but not to the banned books . . . The art treasures and libraries are treated as showpieces and nothing more.'[142] As for Austrian writers, they were the 'most tormented creatures on earth',[143] unable to attack any named government, minister, authority, priesthood or nobility. An Austrian writer could not be progressive, humorous or philosophical – in short he could be nothing at all:

> Among forbidden things are not only satire and wit understood, he may not even express himself in something as could arouse serious thoughts. If he has anything to say at all, this must then occur to him in that most modest and respectful tone which is deemed appropriate for an Austrian subject, who dares at all, to remove the veil from such things. What would have become of Shakespeare if he had had to live and write in Austria?[144]

Koch believed much the same. If an Austrian Kant had arisen, he would have had to starve or emigrate. The middle classes were not interested in learning and the censorship had killed off good and bad literature alike for the convenience of the bureaucracy. Worse still, 'art, like writing, is levelled; everything is banned from it that could lead the spirit in a direction other than the normal or excite the capacity to feel in ways other than being sensuously charmed or flabbily content'.[145] The middle classes had no interest in it; the nobility lacked any desire to patronise it. Vienna simply liked kitsch, plays and songs. (Sealsfield, by the way, had commented that the Viennese did not like serious music – operas by Mozart and Rossini were one thing, Hayden's *Creation* quite another.)[146] The worst thing, according to Baron Andrian, was that writers eventually had to write from the most extreme oppositionist standpoint merely in order to be believed.[147]

How true, however, was this picture? Certainly, some statistics appear to back it up. According to Stiles, for example, 'A reference to the book catalogues of the Leipsic Easter fairs will present a state of facts which require no comment, that, in the year 1839, out of three thousand one hundred and twenty seven German publications, only one hundred and eighty were Austrian.'[148] According to Bachleitner, there were only 20 booksellers in Vienna in 1800, 20–30 between 1820 and 1848 and 39 in 1859. Likewise, there were only 35 printers to be found there in 1791 and only 31 in 1859. As for circulating libraries, there were two in 1790, they were banned between 1791 and 1811, while by 1850 there were only five. Clearly, therefore, the official policy of reducing the number of books and newspapers to the minimum required by learning and good taste had achieved a certain success. There was a kernel of truth in Grillparzer's jibe that in Austria geniuses were hung on crosses, not crosses hung on geniuses.[149]

However, there was a reverse side to the coin. For a start, despite all their complaints, very often neither Metternich nor Sedlnitzky could get his way. For example, Sedlnitzky's campaign to ban the Augsburger *Allgemeine Zeitung* failed;[150] Metternich was unable to hound the historian Schnabel out of academic life;[151] his plan to double the stamp tax on newspapers and journals as 'luxury articles' came to nothing;[152] Kolowrat failed to undermine Sedlnitzky;[153] while the Emperor himself allowed both Grillparzer's *Ottokar* and Bauernfeld's *Großjährig* to be performed at the Burg. In 1846, moreover, when Sedlnitzky was asked for his opinion on a Lombardo-Venetian decree of 1816 that prohibited the export of manuscripts for publication – the government may have thought of reversing the Italian position to make it the same as in the rest of the Monarchy – he replied that the ban was ineffective since anonymous authors were difficult to trace, even more difficult to have brought back and, by the time they returned, their liability to punishment was often out of date. He complained of the laxity of many of the investigating offices and the widely held viewpoint that an Austrian who did publish abroad should not be liable to punishment. Nothing, moreover, could be done at all in cases where pro-Austrian authors had attacked the government's critics. The Prague criminal court, for instance, had refused to prosecute Moritz Hartmann, whose *Kelch und Schwert* had been confiscated for incitement.[154]

There is also much evidence that banned books and journals were easily available. Booksellers who were caught dealing in these could either be fined or imprisoned for three months or, if caught more than once, could lose their licences. Yet many were prepared to take the risk and the worst offender was the prominent firm of Gerold (which still exists today). In 1843, 393 prohibited books were confiscated from it after a shop assistant who had been sacked made a report to the police. (The firm was acquitted in court – the intention to sell the books could not be proved – allowing us once again to note the independence of the legal system.) Another unlucky bookseller was fined 200 fl. for offering to sell three banned novels. The Gerold case also revealed that, when approved books were being collected from the Book Revision Office, 'a large quantity of prohibited books was [also] smuggled out.'[155]

All of this may help to explain the many reminiscences of the ease with which people could keep abreast of the latest writings in Austria. Bauernfeld recorded that the Austrian authorities 'connived at violations of the censorship and other transgressions and even helped to smuggle in published books and journals such as the *Grenzboten*.'[156] Grillparzer confirmed this of the *Vormärz*:

> In principle the censorship remained as severe as under Emperor Francis. But in practice it was infinitely milder to be sure chiefly because of the impossibility of enforcing it. The reading and circulation of foreign and prohibited writings was as general as anywhere in the world and the most dangerous ones were the most widely circulated. I myself saw a coachman reading *Oesterreichs Zukunft* on a coach box. The domestic press, of course, was supervised in every possible way. However, on the one hand, Prince Metternich from time to time took pleasure in giving proof of his liberal opinions, and men of a European-wide reputation, like Aulic Councillor Hammer, or writers who had access to the Prince's company could pretty much have published what they wanted. On the other hand, one closed his eyes all too gladly when Austrians, supposedly writers of some reputation, let their works be published abroad. They needed only, in way of an open secret, to shorten their name a syllable or assume a false one to spare themselves nearly all questioning and ward off attack.

Yes, the authorities were perhaps even secretly joyful because they believed that their necessary severity did not stand in the way of the development of the more distinguished literature. Actual political writers, of course, could count on less consideration.[157]

This state of affairs was confirmed again by both left-wing and right-wing contemporaries. A radical student who later became a university professor recorded of 1848 that the most radical of prohibited books, as well as the *Grenzboten*, were read both in the lecture halls at Vienna University and in the specially formed reading clubs which the students had deliberately established to distribute them.[158] Meanwhile, Count Hartig, Metternich's close colleague, recalled:

The strictness of the censorship more especially was only exercised against works and journals published in the country and against the public adverts of booksellers. All foreign literary productions were easily obtained in private, so that a man of any literary pretensions would have been ashamed in society to acknowledge himself unacquainted with a foreign book or journal that had excited observation; for instance, even in the presence of the highest officials and in the most public places, it was customary to speak of the worst articles in the journal *Die Grenzboten* since no one thought it his business to enquire how the speaker became acquainted with such an article. Directions were previously given to the professors, prescribing in what manner and on what subjects they were to lecture; but if they taught differently, they occurred no censure provided their teaching impugned no doctrine of Catholicity.[159]

Turnbull, for his part, wrote that booksellers could apparently import or sell whatever books they wanted, although there were various restrictions concerning how they might advertise or display works critical of the regime.[160]

In the end, it would appear that certain overall conclusions can be drawn. First, despite all the criticisms, people in this profoundly Catholic state generally supported the censorship.[161] The booksellers' and authors' petitions asked for more censors with more time to devote to their work in order to expedite the excruciating delays involved in the return of manuscripts; there was no call to abolish the censorship itself or sack the highly intelligent and respectable men employed in it. In any case, like the secret police, the censorship was a small-scale affair which was remarkably inefficient. Julius Marx concluded:

If one surveys the whole material relating to complaints, it is really rather small given 47 years of police activity. Much of it is explicable, much of it is pure rubbish. To a clear eye, malevolent, arbitrary acts appear almost totally excluded . . . The number of bans on books etc., stood, for and in itself, in no relation to the outpourings of the publishers.[162]

In practice, the educated classes could get their hands on whatever books and newspapers they wanted. The regime, perversely, may even have taken some pride in this – since it obviously differentiated between learned and popular literature. Metternich, it would seem, like Francis or Kolowrat, was prepared to work the system arbitrarily in the interests of his friends (and enemies).

Surprisingly perhaps, those who suffered most from censorship were less the intellectuals than ordinary people who had to suffer the immense prudery and tedium of the Austrian press and journals, not to mention the official prejudice against novels[163] and popular fiction of all kinds. Perhaps they did not object too much since they clearly enjoyed a wonderful musical and theatrical life. Yet, at times, they too must have wondered exactly what the point of the ineffective, arbitrary and boring system was. In the end they may well have felt embarrassed by it, just as an increasing number of the closely supervised[164] censors themselves in the 1840s apparently did, as liberal constitutionalism became ever more the fashionable political demand of the day. However, there was no general revolt against it until March 1848.

Metternich's Black Chambers

The use of post-lodges (*cabinets noirs, schwarzen Kabinetten* or 'black chambers') to intercept mail had been a fact of life in European diplomacy since around 1400.[165] The French government had had a special department for this since 1464 and had pioneered its use. Louis XIV and Napoleon had profited greatly from the system, the extraordinary success of which the latter boasted about in St Helena. Other governments, naturally, developed counter-measures – codes, false addresses, invisible inks, special scripts – to protect themselves.

The Habsburgs, for their part, entrusted their post in the old Holy Roman Empire to the house of Thurn and Taxis, although within the Austrian lands it was managed by the family of the Counts of Parr. In the eighteenth century, Michael Florence von Lilien merged the two systems and made the interception of letters a powerful instrument of state policy.

Within a short period of time, the Vienna Secret Cipher Chancellery under Ignaz von Koch was intercepting everything of importance. The despatches of the King of Prussia from his ambassador in Vienna, the reports of the Saxon ambassadors in Munich, Mannheim and Paris, even the reports of the Venetian ambassador from London, were all read by Maria Theresa (although penal codes condemned interference with the post). The Austrians specialised in codes and replacements (of seals, etc.) and made less use of special inks – save for the instructions from the central chancellery to the provincial post-lodges – and 'in the course of the eighteenth century the secret supervision of the post in Austria rose to become by common consent the best and most successful in Europe.'

The Vienna Secret Cipher Chancellery was first organised around 1716 by Count Rochus von Santa Croce, a southern Italian who worked for Charles VI, and remained almost unaltered till 1848. It was based on the French model and in the second half of the eighteenth century was commonly known as the *GeheimeKabinettsKanzlei*. Only in the nine-teenth century did it become known as the *GeheimesChiffresKabinett* or *GeheimesZiffernKabinett* which, thanks to the works of J. K. Mayr,[166] has come to be known as the *GeheimeZiffernKanzlei*. In 1780, in any case, Joseph II combined it with his own *Kabinett*, although it maintained a separate existence. (Kaunitz believed that this would protect its secrecy.) The same thing happened when in 1812 Francis I merged it with his own *KabinettsKanzlei*.

Under Joseph II, the Secret Cipher Chancellery had been used more to discipline officials than ordinary people and after his death it was found to have lost some of its technical expertise. However, the Chevalier Landriani succeeded under Francis I in developing new chem-ical writing methods and obtaining a new copying machine from England. On the other hand, the Chancellery seems to have fallen out of favour due to the Emperor's doubts regarding its legality. Its budget, for example, fell from 106,088 fl. between 1788 and 1793 to only 17,686 fl. between 1794 and 1800. However, Bonaparte's successes changed Francis's attitude, while Metternich's assumption of the lead-ership of the government represented a new stage in the history of the Austrian secret service in general and in that of the Secret Cipher Chancellery in particular: 'The Austrian manipulation of letters received a decisive boost from him and under his influence, Francis I also very quickly found his own taste for it.'[167] In future, the Emperor had to receive a 'postal packet' of intercepts and secret police reports at 7 a.m. each morning after he returned from mass (Sedlnitzky and Metternich also received these). The result was that:

in the Metternich period the supervision of the post assumed excep-
tional significance both for foreign policy and for the domestic leadership of the Monarchy – thanks to the coordinated cooperation of
the lodges, the State Chancellery and the police. Not only the
Monarchy but half of Europe was covered by a sophisticated secret
service. The intercepts included in the 'nightly and weekly reports'
were often decisive for the decisions taken by both the Emperor and
his Chancellor.[168]

There were lodges at all major post offices in the hereditary provinces
and Lombardy-Venetia, at major sea ports and border posts, as well as
at spas such as Karlsbad, Marienbad, Teplitz and Franzensbad. Indeed,
specialists from Vienna might be sent to the spas to make the Emperor's
daily postal packet more interesting. In 1807 intercepts from the Duke
of Saxe-Weimar and his friend Goethe were included in Francis's
Bäderberichte, while reports and intercepts were made after Goethe's four
visits to Marienbad. The Congress of Vienna, however, was to provide
the greatest occasion for the Secret Cipher Chancellery to display its
talents. Francis had the correspondence of his Empress, his brothers, his
generals, his leading officials (including Metternich, Gentz,
Wessenberg, Jarcke, Pilat, Hammer and Prokesch) tampered with, not to
mention that of foreign dignitaries, such as Napoleon, the Pope, the
Tsar and the Sultan. The correspondence of Metternich's father and wife
was also put under surveillance while, later, Kolowrat managed to
escape this by reaching a secret agreement with the postal authorities.[169] An indignant Gentz wrote: 'I only write through the post *comme
de raison* what anyone can or should write.'[170] It is from a letter from
Gentz to the Prince of the Wallachians that we know that Metternich's
own correspondence was not spared.[171]

   Gentz sent his own correspondence with aristocratic friends who
acted as couriers for him. (Metternich, too, refused to use the official
post for private letters.[172]) Other countries improved their own postal
services to avoid the need to rely on the Austrian one. Stiles recorded:
'to this day no foreign ambassador or minister in Vienna thinks of a
moment of committing his despatches to an Austrian post, but private
couriers take charge of and convey that correspondence'.[173] Yet they in
turn were often bribed or waylaid. Indeed, all sorts of tricks were
resorted to, with, for example, the Prussian ambassador's codebook
being purloined from the country villa of Legation Counsellor von
Piquot in Hietzing while he was entertaining dinner guests.[174] 'With
characteristic pride, Metternich believed the Hapsburg interception

service superior to that of any other government.'[175] According to the greatest authority on the subject, this was in fact true: 'in the era of the great State Chancellor the secret postal service reached its highest point',[176] although Metternich was more interested in foreign than domestic correspondence.

That is not to say however that domestic correspondence was neglected. According to Stiles:

> A correspondence . . . was carried on for the space of fourteen years, by the Chiffre Cabinet, with a person in Bohemia, whose letters had afforded grounds for suspecting his loyalty. Assuming the name and imitating the handwriting of his correspondent in Vienna, they pretended to approve his designs, encouraged him to a full disclosure of his plans, as well as accomplices, and when these were sufficiently divulged, which it seems it took fourteen years to accomplish, the whole party were immediately seized and committed for trial.[177]

The method of intercepting the mail, whether domestic or foreign, was as follows. Letters coming into Vienna would be brought to the Secret Cipher Chancellery from the post office at 7 a.m. and collected by a sub-director who would select the ones that were to be read. These were then opened, copied, closed – using a variety of instruments, waxes, candles, quicksilver, etc. – and returned by 10 a.m. If four or six officials worked on one letter, it could be opened, read or decoded, copied and resealed in a matter of minutes. Special officers were contracted to deliver these letters. Transit post could be kept until 7 p.m., although it usually had to be ready by 2 p.m., since at 11 a.m. the Chancellery received letters from all post offices concerning political prisoners, refugees and criminals. These also had to be returned by 2 p.m. From 4 p.m. the first post intended to go out from Vienna arrived. Other deliveries came in until 6 p.m., but all these had to be ready by 6.30 p.m. to catch the main post which left at 7 p.m. Once all that was dealt with, commercial transactions could be examined. The Turkish transit post, which arrived every two weeks, also had to be examined. If delays took place, letters could be sent by express post to catch up with previous deliveries. However, 'Metternich expressly made it the first duty of the Secret Cipher Chancellery not to delay the normal progress of a letter to any noticeable degree, not to disturb commercial intercourse, and not to prejudice bills of exchange.'[178] Yet clearly no mention of intercepts could be used by him in his diplomatic dealings, however useful his possession of the diplomatic correspondence of the other powers might prove to be.

The costs of the system varied. In 1811, for example, salaries and pensions for officials came to 8299 gulden for the month of December. Operating expenses varied from month to month. In 1826, for example, they varied between 352 fl. and 8762 fl. per month; in 1841, between 100 fl. and 14, 395 fl. per month.[179]

The officials of the Secret Cipher Chancellery were very small in number. In 1848 when it was dissolved (4 April) there were only 22: one director, three deputy directors, two senior officials, nine officials, four chancellery servants, one adjunct servant and two houseboys. The officials enjoyed special privileges. They were all housed in apartments in the *Stallburg*, where they lived rent- and tax-free and had access to the Emperor. Their apartments theoretically had rents of between 120 and 1000 fl. a year. Their salaries varied between 500 and 1000 fl. a year, although directors and sub-directors got about 2,500–3,000 fl. each.[180]

Clearly those involved had to have considerable skills, both linguistic and mathematical, in order to decipher the codes. Metternich boasted in 1823 that one of them, a man called Eichenfeld, had deciphered 83 codes by himself. And this was not very easy. It took four years for Wenzel Löschen to decipher the Russian cabinet code and he almost lost his mind trying to do so. The Hanoverian code also took years to decipher.[181] Officials were given awards of 500 fl. after they mastered a new language. One of them, Josef Schneid, could read and speak nineteen. Several could read coded letters fluently. As a result many retired half-blind. When they died, however, their widows continued to receive their benefits. If their widows died, their children were also provided for. Usually, given the need to preserve the secrecy of the whole operation and the need to transfer the skills involved, the service employed families of officials – Eichenfelds, Geitters, Hölzls, Kronenfelses, Langs, etc.[182] Yet, despite their privileges, according to Stiles:

> The lives of the officers and clerks of the department must have been truly deplorable. Although well remunerated, they were, indeed, but little better than state prisoners. They were so strictly watched by the police, that the minutest matters of private conduct and character were familiarly known. How they lived, what they expended, where they went, who visited them and their families; in short, all that they said or did, were matters with which the police was at all times perfectly cognizant.[183]

This was deeply ironic, of course, but the same was probably true of all members of the imperial family and of Metternich and his closest colleagues.

The secret postal service eventually came to an end in 1870. Adverse public opinion, advances in technology and the huge increase in the number of letters being sent meant that interference with the post became an anachronism. Article 10 of the constitution of 1867 prevented interference with the mail, save on the order of a judge or in times of war. On 6 April 1870, a new law protected the privacy of the post, save in wartime, at times of domestic unrest or in treason cases.

Under Metternich, of course, matters had been different. But how different? Since the archives of the Secret Cipher Chancellery were destroyed in 1805, 1809, 1848 and 1866, and since often its business was conducted orally, it is difficult to reach hard and fast conclusions about its operations. Much must depend on how many letters were intercepted each day and what proportion of the total mail they represented. Hubatschke states that at the end of the Metternich period there were about 15,000 intercepts a year (although he suggests substantially more in previous decades) and that Metternich's whole policy was framed around them.[184] Mayr gives the same figures, adding that in 1840 500 intercepts were forwarded by the Florence post-lodge alone; again, according to Mayr, the Vienna post-lodge was intercepting between 80 and 100 letters a day by the end of the Metternich period. Intercepts might be kept by Metternich for up to six months before being returned to the Secret Cipher Chancellery, which would destroy them after a couple of years. Still, despite this custom and the burning of all archives in 1848 and 1866, Mayr found that the Haus-, Hof- und Staatsarchiv none the less housed 62 fascicles of intercepts in 1935.[185]

Calculating what proportion of the post was interfered with is no easy matter. If Mayr is correct in stating that in 1817 the number of letters entering the Vienna post was 1000 a day,[186] he gives no figure for how many letters were being sent or received by 1848, by which time the practice of letter-sending must have expanded enormously. Likewise, if the Vienna post-lodge was reading 80–100 letters per day, the figure of only 15,000 intercepts at the end of the period is distinctly unreliable. Besides, neither Mayr nor Hubatschke, who presumably takes his figures from Mayr, explains this number. Still, Peter J. Katzenstein has calculated that these 15,000 intercepts represented only 0.50 per cent of Austria's foreign correspondence and 0.08 per cent of her domestic mail (compared with the corresponding figures of 25 per cent and 10 per cent during the wartime years of 1916–18.)[187] Unfortunately, he gives no basis for his calculation either.[188] However, if he is right – and the small number of officials involved suggests that the figures could not have been huge – the system could hardly have been very comprehensive. No systematic means of selecting letters had been developed[189] and in key cities it proved difficult to obtain reliable staff or sorting rooms. For example, in Tuscany, despite a Postal Convention signed in 1817, it took fifteen years to get the system properly under way. Only when a key official was sent down from Vienna did this really happen. Yet by 1838, the Florence post-lodge was being described as *comme frappé de stérilité* and in the 1840s 'in Florence Pescetti, Cassini and Matteozzi, in Livorno Mazzinghi junior and Martelli, documented their inner distaste for Austria by the narrow number and insignificance of their intercepts'.[190] As with the secret police and the censorship, therefore, it would appear that the secret postal service was a rather small-scale affair whose significance – at least for the general population as opposed to the diplomats – was much exaggerated.[191] During the Metternich period, of course, the Secret Cipher Chancellery was generally known about only through rumour and hearsay, although even this might have 'frightened subjects from undertaking action against the state'.[192] The stories that really worried the subjects of the Emperor and most tarnished his reputation abroad concerned the Monarchy's political prisoners.

Austria's Political Prisoners

Metternich was taken by surprise by the outbreak of revolution first in Naples in 1820 and then in Piedmont in 1821.[193] Austria, naturally, took steps to protect itself, and on 29 August 1820 the authorities in Milan, on the orders of the Emperor, issued a proclamation making members of the Carbonari guilty of high treason and liable to the death penalty.[194] Arrests soon followed, including that of Piero Maroncelli, a native of Forli, in the Papal States, who had come to Milan in 1815 and founded a Carbonari *vendita* there.[195] Shortly before the 1820 proclamation had been issued, he had enrolled as a member Silvio Pellico, the distinguished young poet and playwright (the author of the patriotic *Francesca di Rimini*, the first act of which has the character Paolo threaten 'the foreigner' with massacre before pledging himself to fight for Italy) and editor-in-chief of the liberal journal *Il Conciliatore*.[196] A letter of Maroncelli's, which implicated Pellico and several others, then fell into the hands of the police. Both men and several others were then tried for high treason in 1821 and sentenced to death.[197] Francis then commuted the sentence to fifteen years' imprisonment in the grim fortress of the Spielberg in Moravia, although Pellico was released in 1830.

He had been joined in the Spielberg in 1824 by Count Federico Confalonieri,[198] one of the leading figures in Milanese society, who had been concerned with public affairs since 1814 when he had gone to Paris to plead the cause of Lombard independence after Napoleon's abdication. There he had been rebuffed by Francis[199] and had joined the world of the secret societies. Later, in Milan he had contributed to *Il Conciliatore* and had produced schemes for gas illuminations, an Atheneum, a Bazaar, steam navigation of the Po, the treatment of linen by mechanical processes, and 'Lancastrian schools' in which the more intelligent pupils would help instruct the more backward ones.[200] Bored, yet excitable by nature, his former lover, the wife of the Austrian ambassador in Naples, had had cause to write to him: 'promise me to do nothing without letting me know of it; you have a taste for the extra-ordinary which frightens me.'[201] In the event, Confalonieri in 1821 became the chief Lombard negotiator with Charles Albert and the Turin conspirators over the possibility of a Lombard uprising, should the one in Piedmont succeed and the Piedmontese invade Lombardy-Venetia. A search of his house in November 1821 proved nothing but then two of his friends were arrested and during their interrogation mentioned his name. The Austrian general, Count Bubna, visited the box of his wife, the beautiful Countess Confalonieri, at the opera and suggested that she persuade her husband to flee. Yet he remained convinced that the incriminating evidence at his house was too well hidden to be discovered and was still present when after a second search it came to light. He and his friends were arrested and after a long trial he was found guilty of high treason and condemned to death. Once again, the Emperor commuted the sentence (to life imprisonment in the Spielberg) after the intervention of his Empress who had been moved to pity by the pleas of Confalonieri's beautiful, young wife.[202] Confalonieri in turn was released in 1836.

Meanwhile, he had had a second opportunity to escape imprisonment:

As he passed through Vienna on his way to prison in the fortress of the Spielberg, he received a visit from Metternich, who treated him with every courtesy and mark of regard. Would Count Confalonieri, he asked, reveal everything he knew of the Patriot movement in Lombardy or in Piedmont? Who were their leaders, and was the Prince of Carignano[203] in sympathy with them? If this information was given in strict confidence to the Emperor the count need never go to the Spielberg, but would be restored to his devoted wife and family. To the noble-hearted Confalonieri such a suggestion was an insult; he was incapable of betrayal. He would reveal nothing, and went on his way to his living tomb.[204]

The history of the prisoners of the Spielberg, however, was soon to become the stuff of legend, thanks to the overwhelming publicity given to Pellico's memoirs of his captivity, *Le Mie Prigioni* ('My Prisons').[205] Originally published in Turin in 1832, they were quickly translated into most other European languages and created a huge sensation – not on account of their politics but because Pellico's narrative, in a simple but high-minded way, simply described the prison regime of the Austrian Empire. The anonymous reviewer of the *Foreign Quarterly Review*, for example, who was no friend of Italian or any other sorts of revolutionaries, wrote:

> For our part, we will candidly say, that this little work seems to us more calculated to enlist the sympathies of mankind against Austria, to expose the cold-blooded and relentless character of its Italian administration, and to prepare the way for its downfall, than any revolutionary movements to which it is likely to be exposed, or the political invectives by which it has been assailed. It is not from secret societies and Carbonari that Austria has much to fear. Judging from the issue of the Neapolitan and Piedmontese revolutions, we should say, there was more peril in one of Pellico's pages than twenty of their swords . . . To us it seems a matter of no importance in the consideration of such a system, whether the victim was guilty of the crime which was imputed to him or not. That in any civilised country in Europe, and for any crime whatever, above all for political offences, such a system should exist in the nineteenth century, is a matter of astonishment; and if the Austrian government does not wish to place itself beyond the pale of humanity altogether, and to stand conspicuous as a monument of barbarism in the midst of surrounding civilization, it will assuredly avail itself of the disclosures which have now been given to the world in so affecting a shape, to abolish at once that disgraceful apparatus of moral and physical torture to which we have alluded.[206]

Pellico's great achievement was to take the politics out of his narrative. The end result was that his readers concerned themselves merely with the dreadful conditions of his confinement and by the end of the book were not merely overwhelmed by the almost saintly nature of Pellico's character but by the lack of humanity displayed by the

Austrian authorities (poor food, iron fetters, lack of medical attention, lack of books, solitary confinements, lack of exercise, bureaucratic vexations, damp, filthy cells, etc.). Less attention was paid to the fact that Pellico had pleaded guilty to high treason, had had his death sentence commuted to fifteen years and was released after ten by the grace of the Emperor. The upshot, none the less, was that Pellico's memoirs did more to gain sympathy for the Italian cause than the writings of anyone else other than Mazzini.

Italy's revolutionaries, however, were not immediately convinced of their effectiveness: 'those who were well aware of the politics of Italy considered Pellico's narrative gravely deficient, and expected with impatience that some of his fellow prisoners would give the world a more complete description of the atrocities perpetrated by the Austrian government upon its Italian subjects',[207] wrote one of them. This task fell to a Frenchman, who had undertaken to visit Italy on behalf of the Carbonari leader, Buonarotti, and who had been imprisoned for life in the Spielberg having been caught and tried just after Confalonieri, having also originally been condemned to death. From 1837 he published three volumes in French which also disappointed the Italian revolutionaries: 'Led away by his ardour, as also by a deep sense of his wrongs, he indulged too freely in political discussions and personal details and diffused over his pages a morbid sentimentality which is inconsistent with the dispassionate simplicity of history.'[208] The result was that the Italian nationalist Fortunato Prandi undertook to condense the three volumes in French (a very limited edition) into two in English (which still came to 900 pages of text), leaving the Italians better satisfied:

> If these memoirs, even in their present state, be considered inferior to Pellico's *Prigioni* in pathos and simplicity, they will yet, I think, be found to present a more complete picture of the mental and bodily sufferings of the state-prisoners, a greater variety of interesting episodes, and a more undisguised exposure of the trifling pretexts under which men of the highest character and rank were torn from their families and subjected to the most cruel treatment.[209]

Prandi was undoubtedly correct. Andryane's memoirs gave a similar description of prison conditions in the Habsburg Monarchy, but his account of Salvotti's interrogations and of the negotiations which took place between the Countess Confalonieri and the imperial family and of his own sister's meetings with Metternich and Francis added much greater interest to the sad history of Austria's prisoners of state. The main points which emerged from his narrative were that every detail of the arrests, interrogations and confinements were reported on an almost daily basis to the Emperor and Metternich, who clearly believed in a well organised international conspiracy to overthrow the established order. However, it was clear that the main role was played by the Emperor himself and not by Metternich, who dealt in a remarkably humane manner with the prisoners' relatives. Indeed, the Emperor himself emerges as an intensely bureaucratic but responsible head of state whose humanity clearly had to struggle with the need both to reassure his fellow sovereigns and to set an example to other, potential revolutionaries to deter them from plotting against his rule. He was also obviously a deeply religious person who took care that the prisoners should be guided by Catholic doctrine on the need to accept the powers that were. Refusal to accept religious instruction was a certain way in which to obviate imperial compassion and to defer any prospect of pardon. Even common criminals, according to Andryane, treated atheistic inmates with deep contempt, and in one passage of his memoirs he quotes the account of a priest, found guilty of treason who was ceremoniously degraded by the Church:

> One of the assistants pronounced these fatal words: 'Being accused by the Inquisitorial Commission of belonging to the Society of Carbonari, by which the most horrible plots are devised against religion, the safety of the state and private property, and thereby being convicted of the crime of high-treason against his majesty the Emperor, the priest Don Marco Fortini, chaplain of Fratta, is condemned by us, Patriarch of the metropolitan church of Venice, assisted by all the clergy, to the penalty of solemn degredation, in the forms prescribed by the canon-law.' . . . They soon led me away, to invest me with all the sacred robes, as if I had been about to ascend the alter. Then I was brought again into the presence of the Patriarch, who proceeded to strip me successively of each garment, repeating words directly contrary to those which had been pronounced by the Bishop at the time of my ordination. Nor was this all; my head was shaved, to obliterate every trace of the clerical tonsure, and the ends of my fingers were scratched with glass because they had touched the sacred utensils.[210]

This was an age of profound religious sensitivity and Austria was a deeply Catholic empire.

Yet it was the nagging suspicion that prisoners were refusing to reveal their true knowledge of the secrets of the Carbonari and other sects that worried Francis and Metternich most. Salvotti, in his interrogation of Andryane, declared: 'Everything conspires to prove you were one of the most active agents of the revolutionary party, and that you have cooperated with the criminal attempts that have that have taken place in France in these latter times. We know also that you are perfectly acquainted with all that has happened on the Spanish frontiers.'[211] On another occasion he 'dwelt with complacency on the oaths, principles, exaggerated opinions, the broad words of republic, death to tyrants, vengeance against traitors etc. which formed the thread-bare ground work of that political catechism, in which the high-sounding phrases of 1793 were set in the framework of all secret societies'.[212] Andryane replied that

> with the exception of a few bigoted and powerless old men, who viewed the republic of 1793 as the *ne plus ultra* of social organisation, I have never known any member of the secret societies of that period, who would not have thought himself insulted by the mere suspicion of believing in those wild and impracticable theories of government . . . The friends of liberal institutions, compelled to combine in order to defend them from the encroachments of despotism, joined the associations already in existence. They adopted their forms, ranks, and regulations, without wasting their time in changing the articles of a code, whose obsolete maxims were below discussion.[213]

But this was still a confession that he had been a member of the sects.

Metternich, in his interview with Confalonieri, pretended that since the revolutions of 1820–1 had clearly failed, all he wanted was some 'historical information'.[214] When Confalonieri refused, Metternich even suggested that the Emperor himself would be willing to hear his confession: ' "Perhaps you might place greater confidence in one whose rank is higher than mine. I should not be jealous", said he, smiling; "and if you authorise me, I do not doubt but the august personage will himself come to hear what you may have to say, and to change your destiny and that of your friends".'[215] But Confalonieri refused to see the Emperor. It was perhaps rather generous of the Emperor, therefore, to agree to meet both with the Countess Confalonieri and with the sister of Andryane. In any case, what clearly emerges is that both Metternich and Francis believed in the international conspiracies allegedly plotted by the sects and were reluctant to release prisoners who refused to reveal the nature of them. Still, Andryane was released in 1831, despite his death sentence, which had been commuted to life imprisonment in 1824. Francis, therefore, was hardly devoid of compassion, although he is supposed to have said: 'in forgiving and pardoning I am a bad Christian; it is too difficult for me; Metternich is much more compassionate.'[216]

The revolutions of 1830–1 in Italy brought many more political prisoners for the Austrians to deal with. One solution that was adopted was to imprison them in Hungary till the authorities could decide what to do with them. In fact, it became an abiding fear of Italian revolutionaries that they would be entombed in some fortress in Hungary which had became known as 'Austria's Siberia'. Indeed, it was a fear that was to precipitate desertions among Italian troops during the revolutions of 1848, when an official report on the 26th infantry regiment (the Archduke Ferdinand d'Este) read: 'Subverted by emissaries, they had been given to believe that the battalion was being led to Hungary to die in unhealthy fortresses etc. The soldiers believed that Judenburg was the destination appointed for them . . .'[217] Before then, as many as 560 Italian prisoners were kept in the Hungarian fortress of Szegedin, albeit under the command of an Italian general.[218]

The Hungarians, however, had become tired of their country's reputation as the Siberia of Austria and the local deputy for Szegedin, Gabriel Klauzal, had raised the issue of the prisoners in the Hungarian Diet of 1839–40, when the Lower House had unanimously supported a motion for their liberation. (A rumour that the Austrians planned to establish a prison for Hungarian subversives on an island off the Dalmatian coast helped considerably in this respect.) Still, by the time Szegedin was visited a few years later by the German traveller, J. G. Kohl, despite Hungarian rumours of the 'miserable situation' and 'ill-treatment' of the prisoners, he found a rather different situation. Perhaps, as has been argued, the publication of the memoirs of Pellico and Andryane, and the public outrage of Europe which followed, had indeed led to improvements in the conditions of prisoners held by Austria.[219]

Be that as it may, Kohl found them all in good health and animated. They were all forced to ply their trades and could buy and sell goods inside the market of the fortress. The fortress had its own priest, overseers, secretaries and physicians. The prisoners enjoyed spacious, airy rooms in the casements of the soldiers, all of them above ground. The bedsteads were clean and apparently they enjoyed good food and wine. Their relatives sent them 40,000 fl. a year between them. They had a festival every Christmas.

Their true misery, however, was that none of them knew for how long they must remain there. And:

it is dreadful to know that they are kept here by no law, but by mere exercise of arbitrary power . . . it remains certain, that in the absence of any regular trial, condemnation, or even accusation, many completely innocent persons, many, I mean who are even innocent of the remotest approximation to rebellious or unruly patriotism, are probably suffering the pains of exile and captivity at Szegedin.[220]

Kohl, rightly concluded: 'It were more creditable, therefore, to the Austrian government to find out whether it is really true, as is often stated, that many prisoners are at present confined here, who are as ignorant themselves as all the rest of the world is ignorant of any valid reason *why* they should not be at liberty.'[221] He did report, however, that eighty were about to be returned home, having 'sufficiently expiated their offences' and hoped that the rest would soon follow.

A few leading Hungarian politicians – notably Kossuth of course – were imprisoned during the Metternich period, but they were released relatively quickly and allowed to return to political life. Their fate is dealt with in the following chapter.

Conclusion

Meanwhile, it is necessary to come to some conclusion on Metternich's Austria as a police state. And the obvious one is surely this: that criticisms of Metternich in this respect have been grossly exaggerated. The police forces at his – or at the Emperor's – command were very small indeed; only a very few persons were truly oppressed by the police and usually only if they had been involved in high treason or rebellion; the censorship was boring and prudish but hardly all-encompassing and could be evaded relatively easily by the educated classes; only a small proportion of the mail was intercepted; and finally, even in cases of high treason, pardons were granted and death sentences commuted. Prisoners were not deliberately tortured and executions were extremely rare. Despite the very real fears harboured by Metternich and Francis that revolutionaries, if allowed to succeed, would again seek to murder the ruling classes and the priesthood as in 1793, and despite their belief that such revolutionaries were organised on a European scale to promote just such a revolutionary bloodbath, there was no police state in the Habsburg Monarchy.

6
Did Metternich's Austria Oppress the People and Cause the Revolutions of 1848?

Liberal historiography has always claimed that the Habsburg Empire in the age of Metternich was a backward place, full of injustices, socially and economically feudal, an empire in which nations and peoples were played off against one another by cynical, witless emperors. According to H. A. L. Fisher:

> The Government of the Austrian Empire, though sweetened by negligence and frivolity, was slow, secret, arbitrary, and confused. It was so tightly wrapped in layer upon layer of formalism, and had been so effectively screened from the spirit of improvement, that anomalies and abuses which had long been eradicated in the West here flourished in undiminished vigour. While the nobility of Austria and Hungary enjoyed every form of anti-social privilege, while they were exempt from military service, relieved of taxation, and placed beyond the reach of the common law courts, the peasantry were hard bound in the fetters of medieval subjection. Emperors came and went. Francis was succeeded in 1835 by the imbecile Ferdinand. The peasant question, which involved a radical reconstruction of the local government of the Empire, was left unsolved.[1]

Then there was the 'nationality question'. Both Metternich and Francis were convinced that sovereignty in the Empire had to reside in the monarch. The monarch alone could be a unifying force who could hold all the disparate nations together. There could be no superior body above the separate nations which would command the loyalty of the peoples of the Empire, save the monarch himself. Hence the rationality,

178

not the *egoism*, of Francis's oft-quoted remark: 'I hear he is a patriot for Austria. But the question is whether he is a patriot for me.'[2] As a common focus for loyalty, the monarch could then allow the different nations to develop separately, while coordinating foreign, defence and imperial fiscal policy. However, in the eyes of liberal historians, this willingness to allow the separate development of particular parts of the Empire was portrayed as playing them off against one another. Oscar Jászi famously quoted Francis I: 'My peoples are strange to each other and that is all right . . . I send the Hungarians into Italy and the Italians into Hungary. Every people watches its neighbour. The one does not understand the other and one hates the other . . . From their antipathy will be born order and from mutual hatred, general peace.'[3] No source was given for the quote. According to another source:

no troops were permitted to remain at home, or in those provinces where they were enlisted and belonged, but invariably transferred to another and more distant nation, where they could not speak the language, had no sympathy with the people, and where they were ready, at any moment, to shoot them down with as little compunction as they would a foreign enemy whom they had never before seen. Bohemians, for instance, were quartered upon the Hungarians; Hungarians upon the Austrians; Austrians upon the Poles; Poles upon the Italians; Italians upon the Croatians, etc.[4]

In fact, the Habsburgs could do no right in the eyes of liberal historians. For example, although the relatively feudal conditions of the peasantry in Hungary were preserved by the Hungarian nobility and gentry through the Hungarian Diet and the Hungarian constitution, any attempts by Metternich or Vienna before 1848 to undermine that constitution are always condemned by historians as illiberal.

None the less, the charges made against Metternich are difficult to sustain. No Machiavellian system of divide-and-rule existed with regard to the nations of the Empire ('nationalities' is a term developed by the Magyars to describe the lesser breeds in Hungary, those smaller nations which Marx and Engels in their true German style categorised as 'nations without a history'). R. J. W. Evans, for example, Regius Professor of Modern History at Oxford and a Habsburg specialist, has concluded:

It is frequently asserted that the Habsburgs indulged a tactic of divide and rule over the nationality frictions in Hungary before 1848 . . .

there is very little real sign of it. Metternich and his colleagues engaged in a brief flirtation with the Croats, returned a dusty answer to the Slovaks, ignored the Rumanians, alienated many local Germans, and so on.[5]

As far as the armed forces were concerned, my own research many years ago demonstrated that the largest contingent in Radetzky's army in Italy in 1848 was the Italians, constituting 39 per cent of his infantry and 33 per cent of his army as a whole; the largest contingent in Hungary at the same time comprised Hungarians, who constituted 68 per cent of the infantry and 43 per cent of the army as a whole. Some regiments (the 38th or 45th, for example) hardly ever left their home countries. It might be argued, therefore, that the real Habsburg policy was to exaggerate the proportion of troops recruited locally in any province.[6] The point to stress is that it is difficult to believe that the nations of the Empire were deliberately oppressed.

Likewise with regard to the economy, there was almost no peasant unrest, save in the very special circumstances of Upper Hungary in 1831 and Galicia in 1846, when the peasants became convinced that there were noble plots to murder them;[7] noble landlords outside Hungary paid taxes; peasants could not only sue their lords (even the Emperor himself) in court but were given public aid and lawyers free of charge to do so; their obligations to their lords were precisely written down for purposes of legal adjudication; the archives even in Hungary[8] are full of cases in which peasants did take their lords to court before impartial royal or imperial officials; the *robot* (forced labour service) might still exist but was often done very inefficiently if done at all; while the state undertook many obligations on behalf of its citizens to extend their welfare. There was, for example, a widespread system of student grants; retired public servants (officers and civil servants) were given pensions; and if and when they died their widows and children were looked after by the state. There was a huge amount of organised charity and the Empire was seen by contemporaries as economically progressive. Stiles wrote (not only of Austria but of Europe's absolutist states in general): 'They constructed roads and canals, encouraged agriculture and manufactures, and reformed the laws of trade, abolished local and subordinate oppressions, endowed seminaries of education, inculcated a reverence for religion, and patronised academies of art'.[9] He argued, cynically, that this was done to buy political peace, but Capefigue was more generous:

'Cast your eyes,' he wrote, 'over the provinces which extend from the centre of Germany into Poland, from the extremity of Gallicia [*sic*] as far as Venice and Milan, from Zara on the Adriatic to Mantua, the key to Lake Guarda and of the Tyrol, an assemblage of richer countries cannot be met with . . . Railways and industrial establishments are becoming numerous in Austria; her navy is increasing in the Adriatic, and is a means of circulating her flourishing manufactures. Metternich has caused the age of labour to succeed that of war and conquest.'[10]

In another passage he wrote:

When we look back at what Austria was after the peace of Presburg, and that we contemplate her now, greater than she had ever been, with her public credit, her ascendancy among the European states, the peace and the government of her provinces, her civil and military organisation, and then consider that all this is the work of *one* minister, who has governed the empire for the last thirty years, we may easily form an idea of some of the judgements of posterity.[11]

And why? Because, he repeated, 'Austria is in a remarkable state of prosperity . . . we may everywhere observe signs of very forward civilisation, commerce, industry, railroads . . . all are to be met with in the Austrian states; without speaking of the intellectual movement more sober, and as far advanced as in our country of little romances, novels, theatrical and literary critiques.'[12] So Capefigue's was a comprehensive seal of approval. But the British politician, world-renowned economist and crusader for free trade, John McGregor MP, who had negotiated a commercial treaty with Metternich in 1838, also wrote about this time (in fact in 1842): 'the public securities of Austria are as safe as any in the world.'[13]

Was the Habsburg Empire really so badly off then? What indeed was the quality of life there as judged by contemporary standards? Visitors to Vienna certainly agreed on one thing.[14] Its population did not seem downhearted or surly during the Metternich period. On the contrary, Goethe's friend Vernhagen von Ense could write in the early 1830s: 'The whole aspect of the city and its surroundings has something rich, pleasurable, and gay of heart about it. People here seem healthier and happier than elsewhere; the dark spirits which dog mankind, which harass us unremittingly, find it hard to breathe in this air.' Mrs Trollope endorsed his views in 1836, writing of the Viennese: 'I certainly never saw the elements of what in most other cities would have constituted a mob, so decently clothed, so generally clean and *well-to-do* in appearance, and in the midst of great gaiety and good-humour, so perfectly quiet and orderly [were the Viennese].' Finally, Lady Londonderry called the Austrians 'a very gay, junketing nation'. And with good cause. Vienna was the city of Mozart, Beethoven, Schubert and the Strauss family. Metternich's Austria was not dull, depressed, repressed and oppressed, as traditional historiography would have us believe. There may have been a nationality question, but Austria promoted the advance of national cultures; there may have been economic difficulties, but these were those associated with economic growth; in the end there was indeed an economic crisis – but this affected Europe as a whole in 1846–8 and was caused by harvest failures and bad weather, not by Metternich. In the end, too, there were revolts in Italy and Hungary in 1848. Still, no supranational empire could accept the demands of political nationalists and still remain intact. As Francis I put it bluntly: 'No, every concession is dangerous. Man with his insatiable nature always asks for something more. Give him the hand, and he wants the arm; give him the arm, and he wants the whole body; I do not wish to give them my head.'[15] Metternich was right in thinking that whatever concessions were made to nationalists, they would always simply up the ante. The Hungarians demonstrated this all too clearly in 1848 when from the very start they repudiated their agreements with Vienna and began to act like an independent state, in the expectation that the Habsburg Monarchy would soon break up.[16] Francis and Metternich were tolerant men, but they could not be expected to tolerate policies aimed at the extinction of the Habsburg Empire.

As far as the 'nationality problem' was concerned, the official dynastic line was that later articulated by the Archduke Albrecht: 'In a polyglot empire inhabited by many races and peoples, the dynasty must not allow itself to be assigned exclusively by one of these. Just as a good mother, it must show equal love for all its children and remain foreign to none. In this lies the justification for its existence.'[17] This might be seen as merely a cynical way of explaining Habsburg dynastic greed. After all, Sir Lewis Namier famously claimed that 'every piece of driftwood carried to their shore was to them a promising sprig, which might yet grow into a crown . . . Their instincts were purely proprietary; the one meaning of an Austrian state to them was that they possessed it.'[18] Napoleon after all had proclaimed to Eugene Beauharnais: 'One day you will see that nations are very much alike.' He also told him: 'The Spanish are like other nations. If any uprising takes place among the

Spanish, they will be similar to those we witnessed in Egypt.' To Murat he wrote: 'The climate in Europe is the same everywhere.'[19] Did the Habsburgs then view their lands in the same way, as all pretty much the same? Francis, as has been seen, wanted his subjects to be loyal to him personally, a claim endorsed by Metternich. *Kaisertreue*, not nationalism, was their ideal. And Metternich himself described the Empire as simply an 'agglomeration of territories'.[20] But that did not preclude argument over the pecking order of the nationalities within the Empire or the relationship, particularly of the Germans and the Italians, to German and Italian states outside it. Thus the 'nationality problem' was to be at the core of Habsburg cultural, political, diplomatic, economic and constitutional history throughout its existence.[21]

The Nationality Question in Practice

As far as Germany was concerned, Metternich and Francis had quite definitely decided that the Austrian Empire was not to act as a second Holy Roman Empire. In Metternich's eyes, Germany like Italy was 'a geographical expression' and the various rulers and subjects there had too long enjoyed their independence and local loyalties to allow for any national union: 'No Bavarian will become an Austrian, no Austrian a Prussian, no Prussian a Bavarian, no Bavarian a Würtemberger and no one in any of the German countries will become a Prussian who was not one before.'[22] As a result, the German Confederation had been established in 1815 as a very loose union of states with very little central authority. Indeed, a unanimous vote was needed to get legislation passed, with the result that its general assembly (68 instructed delegates) only met sixteen times between 1816 and 1866. Important business was therefore conducted outside its auspices – for example, the signing of the Elbe, Weser and Rhine Conventions of 1821, 1822 and 1831 or the establishment of the German Customs Union. It itself only employed 27 officials and most of its business was conducted by its Executive Committee (half a dozen people) who examined the 20–123 petitions it received each year. Its most important acts, of course, were those designed to crush revolution – the Carlsbad Decrees of 1819, the Final Act of the Vienna Congress of 1820 and the Six Acts of 1832. Given all this, plus Metternich's close cooperation with Prussia, there was some dispute at the time and has been ever since as to whether Austria was really interested in Germany. In Metternich's day, for example, only five out of seventy-one consulates in the Habsburg Empire were German while Austria had only four in the German states compared to twenty-four in the Italian ones. Austria did not join the *Zollverein*, she was slow to establish railway links with South Germany and Metternich tried to stop German and Austrian students attending each other's universities. All this has led Peter J. Katzenstein, in his brilliant little book, *Disjointed Partners: Austria and Germany since 1815*, to write of 'Austria's quest for isolation' and to argue that 'preoccupation with the consolidation of Empire at home and indifference to the amalgamation of Germany abroad went hand in hand'.[23] This seems wrong to me. Metternich was well aware of the potential dangers of the *Zollverein* – he feared it would 'create a state within a state' and 'make Austria appear a foreign country' and lead Prussia 'to weaken the influence of Austria in Germany',[24] but Austrian manufacturers were unwilling to join and face German industrial competition and there was nothing he could do. Besides, the political results of the foundation of the *Zollverein* have been hugely overestimated, as has been argued previously.[25] Finally, under the commercial treaty of 1853, Austria at last established more or less free trade with Germany.[26] It took Bismarck's wars to unify that country and to exclude Austria from Germany. During Metternich's period, on the other hand, few doubted that he was the political leader of Germany. Indeed, many non-Austrian Germans proved this by coming to Austria to work. Katzenstein's own figures prove that they represented 31 per cent of top foreign ministry posts, 35 per cent in the central administration and 35 per cent in the army in 1848.[27] Austria's leadership of Germany was as yet hardly threatened. Indeed, Metternich in 1832 could say of Prussia: she shares in the duties of the leading powers, but her geographical boundaries, combined with the lack of certain essential internal resources, force her 'back into the second rank.'[28]

Among Austrian and German intellectuals, a parallel debate went on intermittently concerning Austria's 'Germanness'. Goethe in 1792 conceded the existence of an 'Austrian nation' and later described it as 'intellectually a foreign country' (*geistiges Ausland*);[29] Friedrich Schlegel who lived in Austria before returning to Germany wrote in 1819 to his wife: 'How can you make the strange error of believing that Vienna is located in Germany or that it has the least to do with Germany? They are separated by entire continents, and one could hardly think of more polar opposites.'[30] Yet Austrian liberals of German stock who wanted a unified Germany had to take a different line. Franz Schuselka, for example, wrote: 'If Austria ceases to be German, she ceases altogether to be Austrian',[31] while Baron Viktor von Andrian-Werburg, who wrote two famous volumes on *Österreich und dessen Zukunft* ('Austria and its

Future'), denied that there were such things as Austrians at all. Austria, in his view, was 'a purely imaginary name, which signifies no self-contained people, no country, no nation, a conventional usage for a complex of sharply distinct nationalities. There are Italians, Germans, Slavs, Hungarians, who together constitute the Austrian Empire, but there is no Austria, no Austrian, no Austrian nationality, not has there ever been any save for a strip of land around Vienna.'[32] Metternich would not have radically disagreed, so long as it was conceded that all these people were subjects of the Emperor of Austria and loyal Austrians in that sense. And given the overwhelming popularity of the dynasty (republicanism was unknown in the Empire outside Lombardy-Venetia), he would have been quite right.

As has already been seen in Chapter 3, Austria accepted the kingdom of Lombardy-Venetia in order to reinforce the *cordon sanitaire* around France. If the latter ever determined to attack Germany, she could do so either through the Rhineland or through the Alps. Besides, Metternich believed that Milan was the centre of Jacobinism in Italy and only Austria would have the capability to stamp it out.[33] The new Austrian kingdom would not, of course, be allowed to run itself. Why should it? That would merely provide the rest of the Habsburg lands with an example and a grievance. Francis told his new subjects that they belonged to him by right of conquest. They would not form part of a new Kingdom of Italy (such a title would offend all other monarchs in the peninsula), and he would not himself be crowned king – although his successor would be (and was). Still, there were several advantages to Austrian rule: Napoleon's tax collectors and recruiting officers had disappeared (France had called for eighty thousand recruits to fight in Russia, most of whom never returned);[34] there would be equality before the law; the new Austrian civil law code was even more progressive than the Napoleonic one; and Italian could be used in court. The Austrians, as it turned out, also made a good job of helping the kingdom recover from the post-war economic depression.[35] And since there were to be central and provincial 'congregations' of locals to advise the Austrian administrators, and since Lombardy and Venetia were to be given separate governors and administrations under the new viceroy, the Archduke Rainer, there was at least the suggestion of some sensitivity to local traditions. Despite Napoleon's creation of a Kingdom of Italy (and the survival of the 'King of Rome', his son, who was Francis's grandson), few people actually believed in Italian unity. Italy, after all, had not been united since the Roman Empire and nobody believed that its various monarchs would suddenly agree to abolish their titles and states to make way for unification. In any case, who among them was competent to run a united Italy? Most of them were corrupt, incompetent absolutists, who oppressed their subjects. Metternich knew this, tried, as we have seen, to urge reform on them, but was not prepared to take in their subjects if and when they called for annexation by Austria. On one occasion he wrote: 'The same unquiet spirit which now led to the desire to join us would be turned against us as soon as Bologna came into our possession.'[36] Besides, Metternich believed that Italians were incapable of working together and owed loyalty only to their local town: 'In Italy province detests province, town detests town, family detests family, individual detests individual. If disorder were to burst out in Florence, the inhabitant of Pisa or Pistoia, would declare for the opposing party, because he hates Florence'.[37] This was what he called *Munizipalgeist* and it made national unity impossible. It would be better for everybody if Italy were ruled by a firm Austrian hand: this would save Italians both from anarchy at home and France abroad.

This was not to say, however, that Austrian rule was perfect in Lombardy-Venetia. Enemies were made right away. The Jacobins and revolutionaries could be taken for granted, but Austria also dismissed the civil servants and bureaucrats of Napoleon's kingdom and then gravely upset the upper classes by establishing heraldic commissions to enquire into their noble credentials.[38] As a result, whole categories of municipal and Napoleonic titles were abolished, while others were downgraded. For example, the *nobili araldici* and the *nobili diplomatici* had their titles recognised but not confirmed. The titles of the Valtelline and Sondrino were only confirmed by special grace of the Emperor as late as 1842. A *conte palatino* was in future to be a simple bourgeois. In Lombardy greater compromises proved possible than in Venetia, where the patriciate of Venice was downgraded and placed in rank behind the nobility of Mantua and Milan. (Titles bestowed by a sovereign rated higher than those bestowed by a republic.) There were also other grievances: the Italian title of *duc* was to remain untranslated north of the Alps, since it was reckoned only to be equal to the German *Graf*; holders of such titles could no longer be addressed as *altezza* or their daughters as *principessa*. The Venetian title of *conte* was also to be left untranslated, since it was reckoned only to equal the German *von*. Finally, annual incomes of a certain level were required before titles could be used and these incomes were set rather high.

The new vice-regal courts in Milan and Venice also upset the upper classes. They were run on the cheap with limited hospitality, but more to the point, individuals were summoned there rather than invited while their guests had their noble credentials checked before they were allowed to enter. The young ladies invited by several younger nobles were bluntly refused entry. By 1847, Metternich's envoy was reporting: 'to go to court and remain in the one place until your name and rank are discovered is no longer a favour it is impossible to resist.'[39] Yet these young nobles lacked the social connections to marry into the Bohemian or Hungarian high nobility. The idea of mixing the blood of the Schwarzenbergs with that of the Contarini was, as a French pamphleteer pointed out, something of a pipedream.[40] Thus the local nobles began to demand special privileges for themselves. One of them, di Capitani, even suggested to Metternich: 'The ancient families have died out . . . Grants of nobility will win over the wealthy families. The hope is spreading among the bourgeoisie understandably enough.'[41] He also pointed out that wealthy young Italians did not like hard work as a means to the top jobs:

> The possibility given to Italians of occupying only middling and lower posts which demand much more work, profound study and long practice and bring a minimum reward and very little influence cannot win the interest of the patrician families and the wealthy of the Kingdom. It is a short step, moreover, from being excluded from the service of the state and joining the opposition; yet by conceding modest rewards, it would be easy to attract Italians into ruling circles.[42]

This was a real threat. Many of the landed class in Lombardy also owned land in neighbouring Piedmont, where they could visit the court in Turin without bother and where they held Piedmontese titles. They were *sudditi misti*, subjects of both kingdoms. The Austrians began to take umbrage when Lombard nobles like the mayor of Milan, Count Casati, sent their sons to the Piedmontese military academy. But the Austrian army felt only contempt for the younger Italian nobility. In the words of General Schönhals:

> Look through the matriculations of the universities of Pavia and Padua and see if one meets with a distinguished name there. The theatres and cafes are not the places where statesmen are produced and working up the ladder of service posts is not to the taste of rich Italians. We do not blame them for this. But at the same time they cannot accuse the state of violating nationality, of partiality and of neglect.[43]

One colonel wrote: 'And for 32 years Austria has actually had her representative open his court to these people and neglect as a result the hardworking citizens and tradesmen.'[44] Nor was Metternich impressed by di Capitani's pleas for the Lombard nobility: 'this most gangrenous class of the population . . . this bastard race of a fallen aristocracy'[45] is what he called them. By 1848 then, the would-be ruling class of Northern Italy had parted ways with the actual one.

In the meantime, from 1818 onwards the new regime did not too badly. Compared with the rest of Italy, Lombardy-Venetia, in the words of one French visitor, was a 'veritable earthly paradise'[46] and the local elites were willing to cooperate for a very long time.[47] Yet nothing could disguise the fact that the kingdom was run from Vienna. All decisions of any importance had to be referred there and even the viceroy could do little more than pin on medals. Occasionally – for example in 1819 and again in 1821 – there were suggestions for minor administrative reforms (in these cases by Count Peter Goess and Count Karl Inzaghi, both governors of Venetia) but nothing ever happened.[48] Metternich, for his part, simply denied any responsibility. He told di Capitani in 1832: 'I have nothing to do with administration you understand. That's the job of the Viceroy . . . My job is more important than that.'[49] In 1845, when he met Casati, the mayor of Milan, 'Metternich was most amiable and received him with great courtesy, yet always avoided saying anything definite . . . he always embarked on generalities and what he said had no more importance than talk about . . . the weather.'[50] In fact, Metternich had managed to secure agreement from 1826 onwards that a special agent from the State Chancellery (the foreign ministry), under his direct orders, should be attached to the governor of Milan. These agents reported to him regularly on internal, external and police affairs and thus gave him a short-cut to the latest news from Italy. He knew everything that happened there. His agents included state councillor Joseph Edler von Sardegna, Count Heinrich de Bombelles, Cavaliere Peregrin de Menz and Count Alexander von Hübner. In times of emergency such as 1830 and 1847 he even sent down his presumed successors, Count Karl Clam-Martinitz and Count Karl Ludwig Ficquelmont. All were told, as was de Menz explicitly in 1833: 'You do not cease to remain directly under my orders.'[51] Until 1847, the reports received by Metternich were rather complacent. Menz in one of his stated the position of Austria as follows: 'At the time of the Romans the circus was the state secret that rendered Italians submissive to the government and modern Italians are no less difficult to please or less manageable in that regard.'[52] Mozart after all had been best able to reconcile the spirits of Austria and Italy. Yet times would change. By 1847, Verdi had replaced Mozart; his operas were regarded as nationalist musicals. Pope Pius IX – the liberal Pope that Metternich had never foreseen – had replaced the arch-reactionary Gregory XVI. The Italian circus was changing its acts. Even worse, with the harvest failures of 1846 and 1847, the bread was running out. It was now that Metternich's agent in Milan, state councillor von Philippsberg, rang the alarm. In a report of 3 April 1847, he wrote: 'In a state like Austria the variety of nationalities, if properly handled, is a source of strength; still, it does make governing difficult.'[53] He then suggested that neither the viceroy, the police chief or even the governor of Lombardy were any longer up to the task of defending Austrian interests in Italy. A 'statesman' was needed to come down to Milan to cut through the bureaucracy and give authority to the administration.[54] So Metternich sent him Count Karl Ludwig Ficquelmont, former cavalry general, former ambassador to Russia, the man who had just sorted out the Krakow annexation with a reluctant Prussia, and Metternich's own presumed successor.

Ficquelmont had little idea how Lombardy-Venetia was governed. He was under the quite false impression that the viceroy's original extended powers had somehow fallen into disuse. He therefore started to bombard Metternich with memoranda suggesting that they be restored and that Rainer be given a strengthened council of advisers to make government work. Not that he really wanted radical reform. He told Metternich: 'The question we have to solve then is as follows: How can we go on running the kingdom as a subject province, but organise and above all govern it in such a fashion that we might present it as an Italian state to the hostile movement that the other Italian states want to stir up against us.'[55] Meanwhile, he kept plugging his plan: the viceroy's original 'duty was to protect the interests of the kingdom against arrangements of the centre which often succeeded in damaging it, albeit unintentionally. He has not retained this power.'[56] To the viceroy himself, he said: 'When your position is strengthened and your effectiveness increased as a result, things will change as if touched by a magic wand. The whole country will experience a new life and will have absolute confidence in you.'[57] But there was still no approval from Vienna. Then at the end of 1847 the Central Congregations, apparently asleep for thirty years, passed a reform motion. This was followed by clashes between Austrian troops and Milanese over cigars (the tobacco riots of 3 and 4 January 1848 which started when people advocating a tobacco boycott – tobacco was an Austrian state monopoly – started knocking cigars out of the mouths of Radetzky's troops, who had been deliberately encouraged to smoke them.)[58] By now the viceroy was on the edge of a nervous breakdown and, encouraged by Ficquelmont, issued the first proclamation of his reign, indicating that he was waiting for Vienna to approve reforms. Metternich was furious. Under such conditions, reforms would be seen as extorted. So there would be none. The Emperor instead would rely on his army to deal with unrest. Ficquelmont felt duty-bound to resign.[59] Meanwhile Metternich made his own position quite clear in a series of letters to him. One read: 'Making promises is one of the surest perils of our times since by doing so the status quo is necessarily abandoned. No ruler has fallen into deeper trouble with promises than Charles Albert! The Pope is in the same position. Rulers must negotiate but never promise.'[60] Another read: 'Only by centralising the action of the various branches of authority is it possible to establish its unity and hence its force. Power distributed is no longer power,'[61] while another stressed the same point: 'Here is what is needed: that what we order on this side of the Alps should be carried out on the other; that people there should not seek to weaken our directives but to put them into effect exactly as ordered.'[62] Even if the Austrian record had been perfect, he declared to his ambassador in Rome, the challenge from the Faction would have been the same: 'I express my conviction without reserve: what we are dealing with today is not the result of our failings, but the result of different causes of trouble and death.'[63]

He may have had a point. Italian nationalists had no interest in Austria's record. Certainly all the Italian states were much worse governed, and for most of the Metternich period Lombardy-Venetia had offered positive collaboration, not resistance to Austrian rule. Indeed, Metternich had been under pressure to annex territory in the Papal States. But with the election of Pius IX in 1846, harvest failures after 1847, the appointment of an Italian archbishop in Milan in 1847, Confalonieri's funeral there that year and then the events of January 1848 – the tobacco riots in Milan and the proclamation of a constitution in Naples – peace could hardly have been bought by strengthening Rainer's vice-regal council. Metternich accepted Ficquelmont's complaints about the slowness of the central bureaucracy (he had always been its critic) but to devolve power, he believed, would have been 'dangerous' – 'the same thing would immediately be demanded by other parts of the empire'.[64] As Count Hartig, a former governor of Lombardy, who was consulted in 1847 about Ficquelmont's proposals later wrote of the Italians: 'the point in dispute was not the improvement of their condition under an Austrian government, but their actual separation from it; every concession, therefore, would have been misused to strengthen their means of opposing Austria. This was not suspected by the Austrian officials in the country.'[65] So Metternich, after several decades of preaching reform to Italian sovereigns and of presiding over a prosperous and comparatively well-administered part of Italy, prepared to allow Radetzky to crush the revolution, should it cross Austria's borders in Italy.

Galicia, the Austrian part of Poland, had been reluctantly accepted by Maria Theresa in 1772 as part of the first partition of that country. Probably she regarded it as a temporary acquisition so not a lot was done for it. But it did receive an estates-type constitution in 1775. After 1815, Galicia still remained a rather separate part of the Monarchy, situated across the Carpathians, and forming a sort of *glacis* against Russia. The Russians boasted that they ran their new kingdom of Poland much better, which perhaps they did, although the resentment of Poles against the partitions and the memory of the Napoleonic wars when they had fought with Napoleon against Russia meant that this brought little benefit to St Petersburg.

In 1817, Austria revived and reformed the 1775 Galician constitution and made Polish equal with German for use in the Diet. Educated Poles now also began to enter Austrian government service as lawyers, since knowledge of former Polish law was needed to decide cases; indeed, Poles soon dominated the Court of Appeal in Lemberg and served as councillors in the Galician Court Chancellery in Vienna, although it was not until 1849 that Count Golouchowski became the first Pole to be made governor of Galicia. Meanwhile in 1826 the Bohemian, Count Lobkowitz, was given that post. He was determined to ingratiate himself with the Polish aristocracy, learned to speak the language and promoted its academic study. In 1827, therefore, a chair of Polish language and literature was founded at the university of Lemberg (itself reopened in 1817) and the Ossilineum was opened as a centre of Polish culture and learning. Lobkowitz told Metternich in 1827 that he would like Galicians 'to have a new Galician fatherland, to which they would become devoted and through it, devoted also to their prince'.[66] He would infuriate the Russians in 1830 by opening the Galician Diet dressed in full Polish national dress.

Cultural nationalism was very much encouraged by the Austrians. Indeed, many of the German bureaucrats whose sons were sent to local schools and who from 1824 were instructed there in Polish came to think of themselves as Galicians and several even became Polonised, the brothers Krauß, one of whom became commerce minister in 1849, being the most famous. The Ossilineum was named after Count Joseph Tanczyn-Ossilinski, a graduate of Warsaw's Jesuit college, who had battled the Austrian censorship to produce Galicia's first politically progressive journal, the *Polish Patriots' Yearbook*. In 1809, Metternich had made him the prefect of the Court Library in Vienna, where he became the boss of Bartholomew Kopitar, who the previous year had published the first grammar of the Slovene language. Wishing to do the same for Polish, Ossilinski had summoned to Vienna Samuel Gottlob Linde, who since 1807 had been working on a Polish grammar in Breslau. His dictionary of the Polish language was completed in 1814. These developments along with the collection of the *Monumente* of Polish history made Vienna the centre of a new Polish cultural awakening. In 1817, however, Ossilinski returned to Lemberg with permission to found a new cultural institute and in 1827 the Ossilinium was opened.

Galicia, however, was home not just to Poles. Its population was 47 per cent Polish, 44 per cent Ruthene, 6 per cent Jewish and 3 per cent German. Moreover, Austria had no desire to play these groups off against one another. The Ruthenes (or eastern Ukrainians) therefore were also encouraged to explore their cultural roots. In Vienna, the centre for Ruthene cultural study had been the Barbareum, the former Jesuit college dedicated to St Barbara, but in 1808 this had been transferred to Lemberg, where a centre for Ruthene studies was organised at the university and a metropolitan see established for Uniate Orthodox Christians. In 1834, Josyp Levyckyi's first Ruthenian grammar was published in Przemysl, while the Ruthenian seminar at Lemberg university produced the famous troika of Ruthenian poets, Holovackyj, Vahylevyč and Saškevyč who, supported by the Slovak Šafařik, in 1827 produced both the first anthology of Ruthenian literature and the first documentary evidence of the Ruthenian literary language. This young Ukrainian movement, however, became gradually more oriented towards Kiev, so that people like Gentz, Kolowrat and Oeschsner, Austria's consul-general in Warsaw, advised Metternich to lean more towards the Poles. The latter, however, preferred political to cultural nationalism as the revolutions of 1830 and the events of 1846 were to demonstrate.[67]

The 1830 revolution in Russian Poland was sparked off by a handful of military cadets but got out of hand when the viceroy, the Grand Duke Constantine, fearful of shedding blood, astonishingly withdrew the Russian army from Warsaw. The Polish Parliament then deposed the House of Romanov and raised an army of its own to defend the country. While most Poles dreamed of restoring the Poland of 1772, however, the new government forbade any attempt to raise revolution in Galicia, preferring to treat Austria as a potential ally. Surely the Habsburgs would see a reconstituted Poland as a natural barrier against Russia?

This delusion led to all sorts of strange consequences. Just before the outbreak of revolution, for example, one of the leaders of the cadets, a Galician named Vinzenz Smaglowski, was seized by the Russian authorities in Warsaw and, as a Galician subject, transferred to Lemberg. Smaglowski had hatched a plan which saw the Duke of Reichstadt leading a Hungarian army in defence of the Polish revolution, but in Lemberg he could not under Austrian law be convicted of treason because his plot was aimed against Russia. The Grand Duke Constantine was informed of this but, having dismissed the plot as the 'aberration of a sick mind', he recommended merely that the Austrians keep him under strict observation. Smaglowski was therefore locked up in Vienna for six months as a threat to public security, but had to be released thereafter under Austrian law since he had committed no crime and in any case 'he partly recognised the error of his folly in wishing to restore a common Polish nationality . . . and there was little fear of a regression in his behaviour'.[68] Lobkowitz, meanwhile, was sending Francis reports of a conspiracy to restore Poland which had a European-wide network of supporters and wanted to know on their behalf how far Francis would support it! Metternich wrote: 'A governor ought never to listen to such words!'[69] but told Lobkowitz to find out more: 'Either a numerous conspiracy exists or it does not!'[70] But the point was that Polish revolutionaries against Russia generally assumed it would be in Austria's interest to support them. Hence the offers of the Polish crown made to the Duke of Reichstadt, Francis himself and the Archduke Charles once the Romanovs had been deposed. Czartoryski's letter to Metternich of 28 January 1831, officially proposing Austrian support for the Archduke as King of Poland, argued that France would not mind who ruled an independent Poland, that Britain would prefer an Austrian to a French candidate for the throne in the interests of the balance of power and that all the powers would be happy with such an arrangement – 'even Russia if she does not wish to keep Poland will come to terms (*trouvera son compte*)'. The means of executing such a scheme would be simple: 'The Poles will furnish the men, the money and the lives. In the name of the Archduke Charles, their zeal and devotion will double. The provinces will march en masse. An Austrian army will position itself to support their efforts and to assure them an indubitable success, which will perhaps be achieved without spilling much blood.'[71] It was all madness, of course. Metternich had no desire to go to war with Russia (he could have done that over Poland in 1814) and in any case, he loathed the Archduke Charles. But in Austria, too, there were many who took such thoughts to be rational.

Among Poland's supporters in Austria were Gentz (who after 1830 turned against Metternich, although the latter still employed him),[72] Kolowrat, Oechsner, Lorenz (Austrian consul in Krakow), Lobkowitz (who always played down revolutionary influence in Galicia and who was recalled in 1832 and put under police surveillance in Vienna), the Galician, Bohemian and Hungarian aristocracies, and many of the ordinary people, especially in Galicia and Transylvania, who feted Polish prisoners and refugees in the wake of Russia's victory against the rebels in the summer of 1831.[73] Probably some 15,000 Galician youths crossed the border to fight for Poland, while huge sums of money, arms and medical supplies were sent there from Galicia. After the revolution, some two thousand Poles simply disappeared into the Galician countryside, although most refugees and prisoners were sent home under amnesty or encouraged to move on to the German states. In Hungary, the aristocracy gave generously to the Polish cause – perhaps some 2 million gulden. Count Károly alone donated 20,000 gulden and, when reprimanded by Metternich, told him: 'Tell your emperor, my king and lord, that I, as lord of my own money, have the right to throw it in the water and logically, therefore, to give it away to whom I please, without anyone being able to stop me.'[74] But worse was to come. There were reports of Hungarian cavalry regiments deserting to aid the Poles and that sixteen northern Hungarian counties were attempting to get each county to raise 2000 men each – a potential 104,000 soldiers for Poland. Certainly, Mór Perczel began a *cause célèbre* when he got arrested for attempting to send artillery batteries there. His county then declared that only the county court could try him, which it did before releasing him. Meanwhile the vast majority of county assemblies supported the resolution of deputy Johann Nepomuk Balogh of Bars county, passed on 3 May 1831, that Hungary should aid Poland. The motion also paid tribute to the peace and order found in 'constitutionally independent' Hungary. Balogh in a speech of 25 July subsequently condemned the king's 'bad advisers' and demanded their dismissal. Metternich and the government in Vienna were described as the 'the most irreconcilable and sworn enemies of Hungary'.[75] Neograd county after the fall of Warsaw repeated the charge that ministers had failed to inform Francis of Hungarian concerns for Poland. The most famous denunciation of

Austrian policy, however, was expressed in Kossuth's speech in Zemplén county on 23 June 1831. In this Poland was made to stand for Europe and western civilisation against the barbarian hordes from the north who wanted to shackle freedom. But there were implications for Hungary:

> We are loyal subjects of our king, but we are free. However, for us as free citizens it is necessary to consider the dangers from without . . . a constitutional monarch cannot simply ignore the will of his people that is prepared for any sacrifice in this cause. Thus we beseech the king to use our readiness in a constitutional fashion. We wish the weapons of the Poles, who fight for the truth, good fortune and blessings.[76]

He, too, then counselled war. Poland, therefore, sparked off all sorts of problems. Indeed, by the end of 1831, given pro-Polish sympathies, and rumours of a Russian invasion, not to mention the fact that Upper Hungary had experienced a brutal peasant uprising in the wake of a cholera epidemic that had convinced the local peasants that their landowners were trying to murder them, Francis was warning his brother, the Palatine Joseph:

> Hungary is facing a crisis the results of which cannot be calculated in advance. If it comes to revolution, I will strike hard, for I will not voluntarily allow misfortune, and I will not surrender a hand's breadth of my rights which are the same as my duties. What then shall happen will be shown by the fact that Hungary will not be given over to any revolution. Anyone who knows me can count on that.[77]

Ironically, Austrian policy during the Polish revolution of 1830 had been one of forbearance. She had persuaded Nicholas to grant an amnesty for rebels and she had done little at first to stop students and others in Galicia and elsewhere from aiding the Poles. Francis had even been moved to tears by the offer of the Polish crown. Huge amounts of money, medical supplies and even arms had been smuggled into Poland under the eyes of the authorities, while practically the whole ruling class had demonstrated its sympathy. Ever the realist, Metternich had hoped for a quick Russian victory. There could be no question of breaking the 1815 treaties for Poland – that would have meant the end of the Metternich System and war with Russia, perhaps even a European war with Austria opposed by Russia and Prussia and supported by a revolutionary France. In short, it was unthinkable. Kossuth and Balogh – like Czartoryski – were remarkably naive in thinking otherwise, but Polish nationalism, after the success of the Greeks, had become *the* romantic cause of the day.

After the revolution, of course, Austria became the enemy of the Polish emigration which now sought to use Krakow and Galicia as a *glacis* to wage partisan war against Russian Poland.[78] This led to many treason trials and to the Münchengraetz agreement of 1833. It also led to the occupation of Krakow between 1836 and 1841. Meanwhile, the government raised the material and intellectual level of Galicia by promoting education (a Polish grammar book for elementary schools was funded), encouraging the development of trade and industry by establishing a credit bank, and gave its attention to the matter of railroads (after a long dispute, Vienna at the end of 1845 approved a private initiative to build a railway link from Bochnia to Lemberg and thence along the Russian border to Moldavia). It encouraged the spread of the local language, although opposed to Polish nationalism (and hence rejected the use of Polish alongside German and Latin in official courts of law – Polish or another local language could still, however, be used in patrimonial courts and knowledge and use of Polish was deemed necessary for entry into the local Austrian civil service). The suspicion remained in Vienna, however, that the Diet wanted to make Polish the exclusive language of administration and to exclude non-Poles from state employment. Vienna was also aware of pan-Slav societies in various parts of the Monarchy. Still it 'observed a benevolent neutrality regarding the Ruthenes, which alone served to heighten tension with the Poles. This grew as a result of the numerous high treason trials and did not fall when most of the accused avoided sentence.'[79] (Only eight out of 51 condemned to death in 1845 were actually executed.[80]) Indeed, the emigration regarded Austrian clemency as weakness.

By the 1840s, the emigration had been captured by the democrats and radicals and Czartoryski and his aristocratic followers had agreed that labour services for peasants should be ended after compensation had been paid to landlords. The Galician Diet then also began to make proposals for such schemes as well as to suggest that peasants should be allowed to work their holdings for private profit and should be given proper land-books outlining terms and conditions. The government, which in 1843 improved peasant conditions, indulged these proposals but was determined, when it agreed to establish a commission to look into them, to place the new governor, the Archduke Ferdinand d'Este, at its head along with hand-picked advisers. The commission was also to investigate voluntary agreements for the complete abolition of the robot, demarcations of peasant and noble lands and the abolition of common obligations. Vienna was still discussing its approach to all this when in 1846 a revolt broke out in Krakow and spread to Western Galicia. This proved beyond all reasonable doubt that the peasants had no faith in revolutionaries or nobles, but merely trusted the government and the Emperor.

Once the revolution broke out, Krakow was occupied by Austrian forces under General Collins, but he then withdrew far along the Weichsel, fearing the rumoured approach of 10,000 revolutionaries and leaving Galicia without military protection. The local peasants, who had been sleeping outside in freezing weather (this was February!), had been terrified by rumours that they would be killed if they failed to join the revolution. So when one noble shot a peasant who opposed his treason and a loyal local mayor was executed by the revolutionaries, nearly all of whom were members of the local nobility or their officials, the peasants hunted them down and slaughtered them in a sort of blood-lust. They then brought in their corpses to the local county officials, one of whom paid them travel expenses.[81] There were practically no troops in Western Galicia, and when Colonel Benedek arrived from Lemberg to discover what was happening, he had only 400 troops with him. Still, on his own initiative he attacked and defeated the rebel forces with aid from peasant auxiliaries, whom even he could not prevent from butchering prisoners.[82] The revolution, nevertheless, was defeated and the peasants supported their Emperor, although Austria was falsely accused by her enemies in France and Germany of having paid for the slaughter of the local nationalist Polish leadership.[83] The peasants expected to be rewarded by the abolition of the *robot* (forced labour service) but, although the Emperor thanked them publicly, all they were given were a few concessions – the right to purchase more common lands, the right to make more profits from their holdings, a few improvements in urbarial duties and a few improvements in legal and administrative arrangements. The whole issue of abolishing the *robot* and of dividing Galicia into two provinces (East and West), something promoted by Metternich, was postponed and would not be taken up again before 1848.[84]

After 1846, everything that happened in Galicia was keenly observed by Nicholas I of Russia, who had Russian troops stationed on the Galician border and who was ready in 1848, if Austria fell, to invade the province. He told Paskiewich, his commander in Poland: 'I will take neither Bohemia, nor Moravia, nor anything else under the Russian sceptre, not even if people eagerly beseech me to. For it would be against our interests. I am ready to give up half of Poland, but if the Austrian Empire breaks up, I would not allow Galicia to be ceded to anyone else.'[85] This, of course, did not prove necessary.

As with the Poles and Ruthenes, so, too, with the Czechs, Slovaks and Slovenes. The age of Metternich was an age of national revival, albeit mainly literary, historical and philological. It was also the age, however, of Austroslavism, when leading Slav intellectuals began to formulate the doctrine that the Austrian Empire, the majority of whose inhabitants were Slav, should be the political home to Europe's Slavs. Andreas Moritsch has written:

> There was a series of reasons why the Habsburg Slavs saw in the Danubian Monarchy if not the best possible state, still the one that best corresponded to their political, social and cultural situation . . . The Habsburg Monarchy was not that notorious 'prison of the peoples' (*Völkerkerker*) that nationalist historians made of it; it was much more the breeding ground (*Brutstätte*) of nations.[86]

The *Augsburger Allgemeine*, the widest read newspaper in South Germany and in the Monarchy, wrote on 12 December 1838:

> one of the most fortunate fundamental ideas of the Austrian state which has long served as a principle is complete respect for nationality, which forms an integrating force in the Monarchy. This generous and liberal outlook has solved a difficult task, that of forming the heterogeneous parts into a whole, one which other states with their system of centralisation could not accomplish. The government allows Germans to be German, Bohemians to be Bohemian, Italians to be Italian. [For Bohemian read Czech – *author*][87]

Count Lützow in his famous history of Bohemian (Czech) literature pointed out that 'from the battle of the White Mountain, Bohemian literature becomes, and continues to be for many years, an almost complete blank.'[88] Catholic, mainly Jesuit, priests took it upon themselves to burn every book in Czech: 'The famous or rather infamous destroyer of Bohemian books, the Jesuit Konias, continued his bonfires – he boasted of having burnt 60,000 Bohemian volumes – up to the year 1760 . . . In Bohemia itself, from the year 1620 to the end of the eighteenth century, no book appeared in the native language that is worthy of general notice.'[89] Indeed, apart from the peasants, the clergy and some schoolteachers, people generally gave up using Czech. In the seventeenth century the Catholic priest, Balbin, did manage to publish much censored works in Latin on Bohemian history but a national revival had to wait some time. It began in the Czech lands in the eighteenth century when members of Josef von Petrasch's Society of Learned Unknowns moved to Prague and began to collect documents on Bohemian history; from 1764, a German who identified with the Czechs, Gelasius Dobner, edited the *Monumenta Historica Bohemiae.* Then two theologians, Durich and Dobrowsky, inspired by Göttingen's biblical scholar Michaelis, devoted themselves to the study of old Slavonic Bibles and laid the foundations of the academic study of the Slav languages. Translations were made of the Bible into Czech by Durich and Prohazka. In 1775, Count Franz Josef Kinsky published a polemical pamphlet in German urging the greater use of Czech and Franz Martin Pelzel, in his *Short History of the Bohemians* of 1774 (third edition 1804), took Bohemians to be the Czechs. The following year he published Balbin's *Dissertation in Defence of the Slav Languages, Particularly the Bohemian* which had been banned when written in Latin a century before. Pelzel now, too, got into trouble with the censor, but he was protected by the fact that he had become tutor and language teacher to the four sons of Count Franz Anton Nostitz, who between 1782 and 1785 became Highest Burgrave (i.e. governor) of Bohemia. By 1774, a learned circle around Nostitz had founded a private society which in 1785 became the Royal Bohemian Society of Sciences. Nearly all the leading Bohemian aristocratic families supported it and so Pelzel was given the highest local patronage and in 1792 became the first occupant of the new chair for the study of the Czech language at the university of Prague. This allowed him to give an inaugural address 'on the use and importance of the Czech language' the following year, after which he could supervise the publication of works such as the *Principles of Czech Grammar*, which included Dobrowský's first important work on *Bohemian Prose*, which came in turn to be seen as the fundamental work on Czech poetry. The Nostitz circle was therefore the cradle of the Bohemian cultural renewal. Its members were the first to reawaken Czech culture. Yet they were still mainly Bohemian patriots, loyal to a province where two languages, Czech and German, were spoken, rather than Czech nationalists.[90]

The real founders of the nineteenth century cultural revival are usually held to have been Dobrowský, Jungmann, Kollár, Šafařik and Palacký, although attention has also to be paid to Kopitar, Bolzano and

Havlíček.[91] Dobrowský (1753–1829) was born of Czech parents in Hungary and was preparing for the priesthood when the Jesuits were abolished. He retained his orders but never held any religious office. Instead, he became a rationalist and a freemason. Enjoying the patronage of the Nostitzs and Sternbergs, he managed to pursue a career of pure research and scholarship and became the leading light of the Royal Bohemian Society and later of the Bohemian Museum Society, founded in 1818, for which he established the first Czech academic periodical, the *Časopis Musea*. Although writing mainly in German and Latin, he set stringent standards for Czech philology and his works – a detailed Czech grammar (1809), a Czech–German dictionary (1800) and a history of Czech literature (three editions, 1791, 1792 and 1818, all in German), collections of works such as *Slavin* (1806) and *Slavanka* (1814) and his *Institutiones Linguae Slavicae Veteris* (1822), which was not merely a grammar of old church Slavonic but was meant to prove that that tongue had once been common to nearly all Slavs – were of fundamental importance to the revival of Czech literature. Yet as an academic, he constantly criticised 'Bohemian zealots' and 'overexcited patriots'. He found old songs about Slav heroes ridiculous and exaggerated. He had given an address in the presence of Leopold II in Prague on 25 September 1791 'On the Devotion and Attachment of the Slavonic Peoples to the Ruling House of Austria' and his views never changed. Jungmann called him 'a Slavicising German', although he himself always considered himself a Czech and saw Czech as his native tongue. Palacký wrote of him: 'The fact that for all his love of this language he wrote so little in Czech was because he had long since abandoned the hope of a revival of the Czech national literature, and even later on was always of the opinion that it could at best be cultivated as a simple literature of the common people.'[92]

Dobrowský's most distinguished pupil by far was Bartolomeus Kopitar, who, alongside him, was to be the greatest Slavic scholar of the period. He began as a librarian and secretary in Laibach to the Slovene romantic, Freiherr Siegmund von Zois, and formed part of the second generation of the Slovene revival (before him, people like Pohlin, Zakotnik and Linhart had collected old folk songs and devised new poems; Linhart had even founded a Slovene newspaper, the *Laibach News*). But in 1808 Kopitar moved to Vienna and embarked on a brilliant career. He soon became a censor for Greek and Serb printed works but Ossilinski brought him to the court library as head of manuscripts. His regular table at the 'White Wolf' pub in Vienna thereafter became a meeting place for Slav and German literary figures from all over Europe

– including Ranke and Pertz (editor of the *Monumenta Germanicae Historica*) – and conversation took place in several languages at once. Kopitar's fame grew and eventually he became the only Austrian apart from Metternich to be awarded the *pour le mérite* from Prussia. Yet he was a political writer. His 1808 *Grammar of the Slav Language in Carniola, Carinthia and Steiermark* endorsed Herder's view of the Slavs as a pacific people. He was also a Panslavist, insofar as his work demonstrated to him the existence of a common Slav culture based on the Glagolica or old church Slavonic, although old Slovene was the nearest to it that existed. Hence Slovene, he believed, should become the basis for the entire Slav culture and the Catholic Austrian Empire should become the cultural centre for all Slavs. A central Slav academy should be founded there and 'only in Vienna, the confluence of all Slavs of all dialects, would such a centre for the most ancient communal and ecclesiastical Slav languages find its true place and be of general use.' In his *Patriotic Phantasies of a Slav*, Kopitar developed a programme for a single Slav, grammar, literature and history which opposed Austroslavism to Russian Panslavism, so that he and Dobrowský, who had become his Czech teacher, could agree on both the need for Slav unity and Austroslavism.[93] Metternich as a result would have no problems with the Slovenes.

The younger generation of Czech scholars did not follow Dobrowský's line. Their leading light was Joseph Jungmann (1773–1847), who made a name for himself by translating many great works of European and classical literature into Czech (e.g. Milton's *Paradise Lost*). More important, however, were his 1825 *History of Czech Literature* (in Czech) and his *Czech Dictionary* which covered 4,500 pages in five large volumes and was published in 1839 after decades of work often on manuscripts in uncatalogued and neglected libraries and after difficult negotiations with the censor. 'We must touch neither Eros nor politics; such are the orders and commands of the censor', he wrote.[94] Both books were exhaustive and are still indispensable to Czech literary scholarship. During the Napoleonic wars, Jungmann had been a pro-Russian Panslav who in 1815 hoped that the Tsar would liberate the Slavs of Austria. Even late in life he was sympathetic to developments in Russia. Commenting on the intellectual interest arising there after the resuscitation of the writings of a Dalmatian priest who had visited Tsar Alexis in the seventeenth century to plead for a common Slav language, he asked why should Slav cultural unity, in which he deeply believed, require political unity if German cultural unity need not involve any political unity at all? His answer was that Pangermans simply wanted to hold down the Slavs through fear of Panslavism. Jungmann's most famous follower was Wenceslas Hanka (1791–1861), who was also pro-Russian and even wanted to introduce the Cyrillic alphabet into Western Slav languages. He was an enthusiastic collector of Czech popular poems in an age when many scholars in several countries were collecting folk songs and poems and translated many poems himself. However, in an attempt to prove that Czech had as ancient a provenance as German, he and a friend 'discovered' in two abbeys of Bohemia (Königinhof and Grünberg) in 1817–18 manuscripts written in old Czech, which Hanka sent to the library of the new Bohemian Museum, which was then being founded and where he wanted the post of librarian. Dobrowský started a huge controversy by attacking the Grünberg manuscript as a forgery (he had at first been persuaded of the genuineness of that of Königinhof) but Jungmann described him as limited since the issue, he argued, was not one of truth and falsehood but national expediency. Palacký upheld the authenticity of both manuscripts as did all nationalists. Yet Dobrowský insisted: 'it is knavery which they [i.e. the discoverers] committed from hatred of the Germans and from exaggerated patriotism, for the purpose of deceiving themselves and others.'[95] One close friend and erstwhile pupil would have agreed. This was the priest and professor of religious philosophy at Prague in the second decade of the nineteenth century, Bernhard Bolzano who, as a rationalist, attempted to harmonise religion and reason, and had a profound effect on his students. The Vatican as a result expelled him from his chair in 1820 and suspended him from teaching. Bolzano wrote in German, although a Bohemian patriot, and advised:

> Away with a dividing wall! Bohemians and Germans, you must form one people; you can only be strong if you unite with each other in friendship; as brothers you must respect and embrace each other; each should learn the language of the other to be more like the other; each should share his concepts and knowledge with the other without reserve in a fraternal manner.[96]

So not all Bohemian patriots were Czech nationalists.

Certainly, Czech nationalism was appearing in Bohemia by this time, but it was still a fairly academic interest. One of its leading figures was Jan Kollár (1793–1852), a Slovak who wrote in Czech and who was the first real poet of distinction that the Czech revival produced. Like other Slovak Protestant literary leaders, he had been educated in theology in

Germany at Jena at the height of the German nationalist revival after the Napoleonic Wars and had imbibed the nationalist atmosphere. Like them, too, he used Czech as his first language. (His family was descended from Hussite refugees from Bohemia). For thirty years he was head of the Slovak Lutheran Church in Budapest, until driven to Vienna by the revolution of 1848, where from 1849 till his death in 1852 he held the chair of Slavonic archaeology at Vienna university (a reward for Slovak loyalty during the revolutions). In 1824, however, he electrified the Slav world by publishing his *Slavy Dcera* ('The Daughter of Slava'), based ironically on a German girl called Mina Schmidt, whom he later married (she was the daughter of a Lutheran pastor from near Jena and he managed to persuade himself that the family had descended from the original Slavs of Lusatia). The 1824 poem contained three cantos made up of 150 sonnets. Another two cantos were added in 1832, bringing the number of sonnets up to 622. These make up what is partly a love poem, and partly a journey through the lost lands of Slavdom from the Elbe to the Rhine, to the Moldau, to the Danube, searching for the maiden to whom the poet has dedicated his heart but from whom he has become separated. He eventually learns of her death, but the poem allows him to reflect on past glories and great memories of the Slav race. The later cantos are used to create a Slav Valhalla and Hades, where the friends and enemies of Slavdom meet their appropriate fates. Friends include Goethe, Herder and Grimm; enemies include Arpad, Henry the Lion and Charlemagne. The book-burning Jesuit, Konias, is roasted on a pile of books.

The introductory part of the poem is probably the finest and it bewails the fate of the Slavs at the hands of the Germans: 'No enemy has spilt so much blood – and ink, As did the German to destroy the Slavs.' But the introduction ends: 'The errors of centuries may yet be repaired by time.' The third canto predicts that the Slavs will dominate Europe: 'Oh! Had it but been granted to me to be born at that time when the Slavs will rule, or might I at least then rise again from my tomb!' The final words of the last canto, delivered by Mina from Heaven to the Slavs below, are: 'Hell for traitors, Heaven for faithful Slavs!' Was this then a call for war between Germans and Slavs? Certainly not.

In 1837, Kollár published a second work which was also a literary sensation, namely his *Concerning Literary Reciprocity between the Various Races and Dialects of the Slav Nation*. It was especially controversial in Hungary, where its lesson was perhaps misunderstood. And no wonder. On the one hand Kollár argued that the Slav nation was attempting to return to its original unity: 'The Slavs have come to realize after all that they are but one nation and have but one language; they have counted their numbers, and so discovered that they are the most numerous in Europe.' Indeed, he discussed proposals for a common alphabet for all Slavs and considered how the Slav languages were related. However, his main point was to encourage all Slavs to learn each other's languages – or dialects – and to become familiar with each other's customs and scripts. This policy of literary 'reciprocity', he argued, would prevent revolution and war, since there would be no need for one group of Slavs to attempt to secede from or combine with another. Everyone would already be aware of the customs and languages of the other. Indeed, it might even be better for weaker branches of Slavs to live under foreigners who would not wish to absorb them as greater branches of the Slav race might want. Indeed, these foreign rulers would have an incentive to treat their Slavs extremely well, give them proper guarantees for their languages and customs as well as for the security of their position; ideally they should encourage Slav reciprocity. Unfortunately, the Hungarians in particular did not share such an outlook. Ferenc Pulszky in his dispute with Count Leo Thun over the position of the Slovaks in Hungary argued that the English did not concede their Welsh and Scottish Celts a separate constitutional development nor did the French distinguish between French and non-French in Brittany or Alsace.[97] The Magyars, therefore, would act no differently. Rumpler has argued that Kollár's book on reciprocity became the bible of cultural Panslavs and threatened the European state system since it was so 'radically revolutionary'.[98] Not only did it offer a federal alternative to unitary or centralised states, but it appealed to Slavs to maintain links across state borders. Yet Kollár may well have intended to moderate rather than radicalise the nationality question by his proposals.

Another leading light of the Czech revival was the Slovak, Paul Joseph Šafařik (1795–1861). He, too, was from a Slovak Lutheran family and had studied at Jena university before returning to tutor a noble family at Bratislava, where he formed a youthful friendship with Palacký. In 1819, he was appointed director of the new Serb orthodox Gymnasium at Novi Sad, the centre of Serb culture in Southern Hungary near the Turkish border, and in 1826 he first attracted attention by publishing in Ofen-Pest a *History of the Slav Language and Literature in all its Dialects*, which once again started from the premise that there was a single Slav language – or at least the unity of all Slav tongues. One of these was Lusatian Sorb and Šafařik would later get in touch with Jan Smoller, the Sorb philologist, telling him in 1840 that 'Since your landowning class and nobility, as with us [Slovaks], take no heed of the nation or despise it and merge themselves with aliens, so it is your task, you schoolteachers and religious preachers, jointly to become cultivators of nationality and protectors of the language against all enemies.'[99] He bade Smoller keep in touch with Prague with the words: 'Such reciprocity, while it may be tiresome, is absolutely essential above all for our flowering.'[100] Smoller in fact set up a *Maćica Serbska* for his people on the Czech model, but the Czechs offered little help or interest in return. During the 1848 revolution, the Sorbs supported constitutional monarchy in Saxony and the king's personal bodyguard contained many Sorbs. In 1832, under pressure from the Serbs to quit his post on account of his religion, Šafařik left Novi Sad for Prague where, given his poor financial state, he wrote for various journals, even becoming a censor for a time, and helped edit the Czech journal of the museum there (see below). Full economic security came with a chair of Slavic philology at Prague university which, however, he soon abandoned to become university librarian. In 1837, he published his most famous scholarly work in Czech, the *Slav Antiquities* (a revised German edition appeared in 1842), which dealt with the history of the Slavs from the time of Herodotus to about 1000 AD and thus entirely revolutionised academic thought regarding Slav origins and early history. Šafařik's most popular work, however, published in 1842, was his *Slavic Ethnography* with its ethnical map showing the Magyars drowning in a sea of Slavs. (Herder, it should be remembered, had forecast their disappearance!) Indeed, this map, showing the true extent of the Slavs in Europe, probably did more for the revival than shelves of philological and historical research.

Hence two Protestant Slovaks who wrote in Czech and were part of the Czech renascence made an enormous difference to the development of Slavonic studies and Slav self-consciousness in Austria before 1848. There was a third, however, who, before 1848, differed in his views regarding both the Slovak language and Czechoslovak unity. He was Ludevit Štúr (1815–1856), the son of a Protestant schoolteacher who had also studied in Germany (Halle) and whose two closest colleagues, Joseph Hurban (1827–1888) and Michael Hodža (1811–1879), were Protestant pastors.[101] Slovak Protestants were often descendants of Hussite refugees from Bohemia or Moravia and thus tended to keep ties with the Czechs and to use their language. But Czech was not used by everyone. Most of the Slovak peasants, for example, would simply not have understood Kollár's poetry, even if it had been read out to them. Thus there had been attempts to revise the written language on a more local basis. In the eighteenth century these had been mainly the work of Catholics, often Jesuits, intended to separate the followers of the two religions. For example, in 1718 a Paulinian monk, Macsay, had published a collection of sermons in the western Slovak dialect. The Jesuits of Trnava had then published a number of books of devotion in a mixture of Czech and Slovak. Then in 1746, Hungary's foremost scholar, Mattew Bel, a leading pietist, wrote a preface to a 'Slavo-Bohemian' grammar expressing pride in the growing Slovak awareness of his countrymen of all classes. Yet it was the Slovak Catholic priest Anton Bernolák (1762–1813) who in 1787 published the first Slovak grammar and in 1792 founded a Slovak Literary Society at Trnava where, in the 1790s, he codified Slovak sounds by inventing new letters and discarding Czech ones (ř, ě, ů) not sounded in Slovakia. He thus made the Western Slovak dialect of the Trnava region the basis of a separate Slovak literary language, ending centuries of Slovak use of Czech. His elaborate Slovak dictionary in five languages and six volumes, however, was not published until a decade after his death. Bernolák also left behind a faithful disciple, another Catholic priest, Jan Hollý (1785–1849), who translated some of the great classics into Slovak as well as epics of his own on subjects like the lives of saints Cyril and Methodius. Hollý, however, shared the belief of others of the Czech revival that there was basically a single Slav culture.

Given the intensely Catholic nature of the *Bernolačtina*, most Protestant Slovaks remained aloof from it and remained grouped around their own literary centre at the Lutheran Gymnasium at Bratislava, where an Institute of Slavonic Language and Literature had been established in 1803. Štúr became the second occupant of the chair there and under the pressure of magyarisation in Hungary responded by developing a new variety of Slovak which, he hoped, would unite all Slovaks against the Magyars. (Czech was unknown to most Slovaks and Bernolák's system, which was only used by Catholics in the western districts, remained too close to Czech and was not comprehensible to Slovaks in the north and centre of their country.) The pressure from the Magyars on the Slovaks increased enormously in the 1840s. From 1830, the Hungarian Diet had passed laws extending the use of Magyar in public life. In 1839–40, it became the exclusive language of government and knowledge of it was made obligatory for clergy of all denominations. In 1843, it was declared the exclusive language of legislation. Meanwhile, in 1840 an open attack had been made on the Slovaks at the General Assembly of the Lutheran Church. Count Charles Zay, the inspector-general of the entire Church, i.e. its leading layman, even declared it the duty of everyone to become Magyar: 'the Magyar language is the truest guardian and protector of the liberty of our country, of Europe and of the Protestant cause';[102] Magyarisation, therefore, became the duty of every person of freedom and intelligence and its triumph would be the triumph of reason. Then came a campaign to suppress Slovak in all Lutheran churches, with Kossuth himself calling for the suppression of all Slav societies in Lutheran schools, claiming they were hotbeds of Panslavism. Since a petition of 200 Slovak clergy to the Emperor achieved nothing and since in 1842 the next inspector-general of the Lutheran Church was howled down by Magyar nationalist fanatics (primarily Kossuth himself, who came from good gentry stock from Košuty in the heart of Slovakia and who spoke Slovak, but who wrote in his newspaper that 'A Slovak nation has never existed even in a dream'[103]), Protestant Slovak leaders felt forced to respond.

Štúr himself was dismissed from his chair in Bratislava after resisting Count Zay's efforts to magyarise the Lutheran Gymnasium there. He then became editor of the *Slovak National News* with Hurban as editor of its fortnightly literary supplement. Convinced of the need to unite Slovaks politically by means of a new language, he then took the decision in favour of a central Slovak (Zvolen district) dialect. In an article in his literary supplement in 1845, he argued that the Slovaks were a separate branch of the Slav race. The controversy reached a head with the publication of his book *Slovak Dialects*, with attacks from Kollár, Šafařik and Palacký, who not merely rejected his philology but desperately wanted to retain the Slovaks as part of the Bohemian nation. Yet politically, Slovakia was part of the Kingdom of Hungary and it was the Magyars who were piling on the pressure, so that Štúr insisted that a separate Slovak solution had to be found – not that he in any way meant to stop cooperating as best he could with his fellow Slavs in Bohemia. In 1847, he was elected a deputy to the Hungarian Diet from the town of Zvolen but, as the only Slovak representative there, he could accomplish nothing. Meanwhile his new Slovak had received backing from many Protestants, students and scholars. However, in 1848 the Slovak people remained with three choices before them: the *bernolačtina*, (used by Catholics), the *štúrovčina* (used by Protestants) or Czech.

One of the voices raised against a separate Slovak language belonged to perhaps the greatest of all the figures of the Czech renascence, František Palacký (1798–1876), a Moravian Protestant, whose parents, after secretly practising the Hussite faith, took advantage of Joseph II's 1784 Edict of Toleration to send their son in 1812 to the Lutheran Gymnasium in Bratislava, where he developed a deep sympathy for the native Slovaks.[104] Intellectually, however, he seems to have been most influenced in his views on history by British authors, including Bolingbroke, Gibbon and Blair, whose now-forgotten *Lectures on Rhetoric* he admired.[105] After some years, he went to Prague with the intention of researching the history of the Hussite wars and there attracted the attention of Dobrowský, who introduced him to the Sternberg family, one of whose members made him his archivist. Through them he also got to know the group of Bohemian patriots among the nobility and in 1827 he was appointed secretary to the Bohemian Museum and editor of its Czech and German journals; in 1829, he was made historiographer of the Bohemian Estates, although the title was only confirmed by Vienna in 1838. The latter post allowed him to conduct historical research (even in foreign archives) and from 1836 he began to produce the volumes of his great *History of Bohemia*, the first of which appeared (in German) in 1836, followed by two more by 1848. The tenth and final volume would only appear in 1865, by which time he had become father of his nation. Before 1848, Palacký's work, save that on his *History*, largely revolved around his work for the Bohemian Museum which he turned into a Czech national one. He himself became the leader both of modern Czech nationalism and of Austroslavism.

The Society of the Bohemian Museum had been established in 1818 by members of the Bohemian patriotic high nobility.[106] (The Royal Bohemian Society of Sciences continued). The Highest Burgrave of Bohemia, Kolowrat, had been inspired by the foundation of the Johanneum Museum in Graz in 1811 (named after the Archduke John) and by the Franciscium, founded in Brno in 1817 and named after the Emperor. The Hungarians, of course, had founded a Magyar National Museum in 1802. The rules of the Bohemian Museum as drawn up in 1818 laid down that 'all members of the Museum must [at least] understand Czech and the secretary must [also] be able to read and write it'.[107] This testified in itself to the lack of development of Czech as a national language in 1818.

By the time of Palacký's arrival, the Museum published a monthly German journal (the *Monatschrift*) and a Czech quarterly (the *Časopis*). Palacký, not surprisingly was more interested in the latter. In fact, the German journal disappeared by 1831, partly because its more interesting articles were censored, leaving too many on cookbooks, prayer books and fairy tales, so that it was difficult to find contributors or subscribers; the second main reason was that, despite even the support of Goethe, German booksellers often refused to buy books or journals from Austria, so prejudiced were they against the regime there. So in

1831 the *Monatschrift* had to be abandoned.[108] The *Časopis*, on the other hand, did well and, given its coverage of old and new Czech literature, new poetry and prose, translations and book reviews as well as 'news' aimed at the widest readership, 'no other Czech journal has ever had such a deep and lasting influence'.[109] Nonetheless, the circulation was not very large at around 2000 copies – for example, the Catholic society, the Heritage of St Jan Nepomuk, which distributed good cheap Bibles and catechisms in Czech, could charge higher subscriptions and have a membership of 20,000. So in 1831 a Czech Literary Foundation (*Matice Česka*) was set up by the Museum to aid its work in supporting Czech literature. By 1848, it had about 2000 members, many of them students and clergy to start with but later including many small businessmen and manufacturers. Few came from southern Bohemia; most came from towns.[110] It was never very well off, even though its 50 fl. subscription was well above what an average man could afford. Some of the high nobility joined but most gave only 100 fl. Prince Kinsky gave 1000 fl., it is true, but the Archduke Franz Karl in 1840 gave a niggardly 100 fl. and the new High Burgrave, the Archduke Stefan, a mere 50 fl. in 1845. Despite two honorific volumes on Francis I and Ferdinand I published by the *Matice* in 1832 and 1835 respectively, 'not a kreuzer was donated . . . from Vienna'.[111] In 1840, its total funds amounted to only 18,794 fl. – absolutely nothing compared with the 118,000 fl. donated by Counts Széchenyi, Károlyi, Vay and Andrássy to found the Hungarian Academy in 1826 and far, far less even than the 50,000 fl. it needed to fund its favourite project of producing a Czech encyclopaedia. Still, it did what it could. It published books and journals (taking over the *Časopis* in 1831), awarding grants and prizes, raising standards of literary criticism and promoting spelling reforms. Its first decade saw it publishing both Jungmann's *Czech–German Dictionary* and Šafařik's *Slavic Antiquities*, even though these put it into debt. In 1841, therefore, there was a new appeal for members, a reshuffle of the executive council and a new publishing programme aimed at a wider readership. In the 1840s, it began to collect manuscripts and rare books and between 1841 and 1851 published 37 volumes, including histories and translations, if no encyclopaedia. Yet it still grew very slowly – an indication that support for Czech nationalism should certainly not be overestimated at this time. Clearly not so many middle-class Czechs had a good command or even any real knowledge of their language. One result was that German Bohemians simply tended to ignore them and their interests. (This was certainly true of Ignaz Kuranda's *Die Grenzboten*, of which one expert has written that of all developments in Bohemia, it 'took the least notice of those within the Czech community'.[112] Since clearly 'most German liberals and intellectuals had little interest in Bohemian history and politics before 1848',[113] they were quite unprepared for developments there after the revolutions of that year.) It might well be argued that the government in Vienna took little notice of these developments either. One scholar has written: 'Of much more significance, however, than the trifling note that Vienna did take of the *Matice* is the fact that Vienna did not seriously hound or persecute it'[114] – yet the legend has arisen that Metternich was Palacký's greatest enemy.

Palacký himself is responsible for this myth. He was to call Metternich's Austria 'a realm of darkness and slavery of every kind' and Metternich himself 'the greatest enemy of freedom, but also the most ferocious dedicated enemy of all the Slavic nationalities in Austria'. His regime was 'dedicated not to furthering but rather to hindering historical studies'.[115] Yet even Palacký's most fervent admirers have had to concede that the Austrian censorship, which gave rise to most of his complaints, 'was not the flawlessly efficient, totalitarian machine its enemies have depicted.'[116] Indeed, both Kopitar and Šafařik – the two greatest living Slavonic experts of the Metternich period apart from Dobrowský – had both been employed by it! That was the key to the censorship of course: for academics the process was very often akin to a peer review for an academic journal. Palacký's chief censor till the mid-1830s, for example, was a Father Jan Zimmermann whose edition of a fifteenth-century chronicle Palacký had earlier criticised. True, Sedlnitzky the police minister warned Palacký, whose treatment of the Hussite Wars was bound to upset Catholics and Germans, that, 'in a state where many nations are united under one sceptre and give their allegiance to a ruler of German blood, it cannot be allowed that one nationality attack, disparage or undermine the others, especially not the ruling one',[117] but when Metternich was consulted about Palacký's *History*, his view was simply that Palacký should stick to 'facts' and avoid 'pernicious arguments'.[118] He had no intention of banning the work. Indeed, the volumes printed before 1848 went through the censorship process remarkably smoothly and quickly. Vienna actually seems to have ignored the warnings sent secretly to it by a supposed friend of Palacký's, Josef Leonard Koll, professor of history at Prague and Vienna, who found the work subversive. In fact, Palacký seems to have had rather good relations with the censors, despite his occasional frustration. His diary shows that he and Zimmermann met socially and arranged to go out together, while in 1841 he visited Sedlnitzky in Vienna and apparently tried to convince him that a policy of

Austroslavism would protect Austria against both the Magyars and her foreign enemies. Sedlnitzky presented Palacký in return with his portrait in a gilded frame and pretended to be convinced. A friend of the family wrote: 'Palacký has been to see Sedlnitzky, who told him that the government is glad that the Czechs wish to remain Czechs . . . He [Sedlnitzky] conversed with him for more than a half-hour, telling him at the conclusion that whenever he was subjected to any pressure or injury he was to turn directly to him.'[119] This does not sound like oppression. Palacký, of course, was to continue to develop his ideas of Austroslavism – the conversion of the Habsburg Monarchy into a federal state in which the Slavs would be the majority, but in which the rights of all nationalities would be respected – until in 1848 he gave his most famous expression of it in his rejection of the invitation to be a member of the Frankfurt Parliament:

> I am no German but a Bohemian of the Slav race . . . Truly if the Austrian Empire had not long already existed, one would have to hurry to create it in the interest of Europe, nay of humanity itself . . . To want to dissolve Austria into a number of republics large and small . . . is to want to lay the foundations of a Russian universal monarchy.[120]

The Austrian Empire constituted a way out of being either German or Russian in Europe. Palacký therefore supported it till the day he died although, when squaring up to the possibility of an Austro–Hungarian *Ausgleich* at Slav expense, in a book written in 1865, he warned: 'We existed before Austria, we will exist also after her.'[121]

Another great Czech exponent of Austroslavism who was to appear in Prague was the journalist Karel Havlíček (1820–1856).[122] In his youth he had been full of romantic Panslav ideas. But having spent some time in Russia and Poland he returned to Prague in 1845 completely disillusioned. However, he quickly made a name for himself by a devastating review of the prize-winning Czech novel by Josef Tyl, *The Last Czech*. This he criticised for its high-blown rhetorical style and its superficial nationalism. He recommended a more simple language for Czechs and good translations of better books. The result was, on Palacký's recommendation, he was offered and accepted the editorship of the *Prague News* and its literary supplement. Educated Czechs had previously read the *Ausburger Allgemeine* and *Die Grenzboten* but soon they found they had a quality Czech paper of their own. He made the paper a 'diary of the times', covered all domestic and foreign news and added humorous and satirical columns as well as educational articles discussing contemporary social and political problems. In particular, he took up the cause of funding a Czech trades school (the seven existing ones taught only in German) and covered the industrial union's campaign to raise funds. He called for greater use of Czech and better school teachers:

> Who is the greatest enemy of our nationality? We are ourselves! The government cannot wipe us out, it cannot stamp out our language if we use it. In time it will even have to protect it. Who can keep us from learning Czech? And yet only a few hundred know it well enough so that they can use it in discussion and public writing![123]

He praised the peasants for keeping it alive. However, his article is yet more proof that the strength of the Czech revival should not be overestimated. Havliček also stressed the need for self-help. He called for more action in villages to get better education in schools, to raise funds for libraries and to negotiate voluntary schemes to buy out the *robot*. He used the contemporary history of Ireland as an example and praised Daniel O'Connell's Repeal Movement there and its lawful means of organisation. By January 1848, he began to examine different forms of government and new political concepts, but concluded that moral principles were what mattered most. By now the local police chief was getting worried but it was his support for Pius IX in Italy that seemed about to get him the sack when in March 1848 revolution broke out and freedom of the press was declared.

Havliček, however, was no revolutionary. He might provoke the Germans with passages such as: 'We do not deny that light came to us from Germany, especially the torch that set light to the stake of Hus . . . Then it was the Jesuits turn to enlighten us when they burned our books, doubtless in order that from these ashes Germanic civilisation should sprout.'[124] But basically he was a supporter of Austroslavism. He once wrote: 'Austria will be what we want her to be or she will cease to be.'[125] What he was not was a pro-Russian Panslav. After his stay in Russia and Poland, he described both peoples as wolves who fought over the Ukrainian lamb. In a famous series of articles in the *Prague News* in March 1846 entitled *The Slav and the Czech*, he said he considered himself to be a Czech but not a Slav. He almost parodied Metternich when he wrote:

> The Russian cold and other peculiarities have seemed to extinguish in me the last sparks of love for Panslavism . . . so I returned to

Prague an uncompromising Czech with even a secret dislike of the concept, Slav, which an adequate knowledge of Russia and Poland had made suspicious to me. Most of all I wanted to express the firm conviction that the Slavs, that is the Russians, the Poles, Czechs, Illyrians etc., are not one people. *The name Slav is a mere geographical and scientific term and should remain so for ever* (author's emphasis).[126]

Why then should Metternich have worried about the Czechs?

For the most part, he simply did not. Yet the Bohemian Estates became a rather tiresome problem for Vienna during the 1840s.[127] Events in Hungary, not to mention the policy of the new King of Prussia, Friedrich Wilhelm IV, of favouring a greater say for Prussian provincial diets after 1840, leading to the convocation of a United Diet in Prussia in 1847, meant that Bohemian nobles began to resent the fact that their Diet only really met to give approval of Vienna's plans for taxation, which approval had to be agreed before they even had the opportunity to express their own wishes. They therefore invented a history of Bohemia which gave them the right to scrutinise the budget and to hold ministers accountable, something which even Metternich and Kolowrat could agree was nonsense. Kolowrat, of course, came from a high noble Bohemian family himself and had been highest burgrave in Prague before being summoned to Vienna in 1826. However, he was no genuine reformer and, according to Hanns Schlitter, whose four volumes on the 1840s remain the only ones to have systematically examined the records of the State Council and the Ministerial Conference, his liberalism 'clearly was not genuine (*waschecht*)'.[128] When a delegation of the estates of Bohemia proposed to visit Vienna to explain their case on the grounds that they were *Volksvertreter* or representatives of the people, he rather embarrassedly explained to his colleagues that he did not want to debate the issue with them. They did not mean, he said, to sound democratic. Thus, although he himself distrusted 'overexcited and confused theories' which differentiated between estates and representation and saw the exclusion of the broad masses as a defect, he hoped to avoid any clash of opinions which might have 'an unpleasant importance'.[129] In fact, Metternich had to take the leader of the delegation aside on 7 May 1845 and tell him bluntly that the estates represented no one but themselves. For the most part, however, Vienna took the softest of lines with the Bohemian Estates and bent over backwards to avoid anything like confrontation. Time and time again their requests were investigated by the *Hofkanzlei* and debated in reports to the State Council and the Ministerial

Conference. Even Hartig, the greatest centraliser in the State Council, confessed that central government had made all diets feel 'worthless in public life', although he insisted that they should stick only to their legal powers as otherwise any conversion to what amounted to a demo-cratic regime – approval of taxes and partnership in government – would mean 'the fall of the Empire'.[130] The great problem was that what was conceded to one diet would be immediately demanded by all the others. Yet only the common monarch could provide imperial unity. A collection of democratically self-governing states would never hold together. Metternich himself told Kolowrat that Bohemia was amongst the most loyal of provinces; he defended its leading men and even their patriotic wish to strengthen their diet and to have the most indepen-dent administration.[131] However, the mania for novelty simply had to be contained. The influence of moderates, he argued, should never be overestimated, since it was a thankless task to want to dictate to a moral movement how far it should go. A better strategy was to do what was right but never to condescend to supposed improvements. Still, he agreed to the appointment of the ambitious young Archduke Stefan as Highest Burgrave in 1845 as a sop to local feeling and showed remark-able patience in the long negotiations with the estates between 1842 and 1848. Perhaps it was this long-drawn out process of tedious and repetitive negotiation that actually saved the situation from getting out of hand before 1848. Yet another explanation is that the Bohemian Estates merely had little to offer a wider audience, since their motives were so obviously self-serving. Neither *Die Grenzboten* nor the Czech Slavonic camp had much time for them. Despite all the fuss over their Bohemian patriotism, the *Matice* still lacked its much-needed financial backing; despite their desire to be seen as the representatives of the people, the diet turned down any democratic scheme of municipal reform (the towns, it argued, should be represented by seven local worthies) and in May 1847 it rejected Count Lamberg's proposal for a modern judicial system. The diet also opposed the government's proposals to charge the nobility with the higher costs of municipal justice and expected central government to pay, although in effect this would have meant being subsidised by other provinces; if in 1846 it took over 350,000 gulden worth of peasant dues in the wake of the events in Galicia, this was less out of concern for the peasants (who in fact it blamed for the poor state of agriculture) but a political ploy based on the assumption that the government would reimburse the nobles and thereby face bankruptcy in the province. When the government simply accepted the nobles' generosity, and still increased taxes, they then argued that the gesture had been for one year only. There was no intention to democratise Bohemia, merely to force Vienna to grant the estates the power to scrutinise the budget and to take part in determining the levels of taxation, all of this predicated on a false reading of Bohemian constitutional history.[132] Count Johann Thun, a leading supporter of Bohemian rights, declared: 'To take away the political rights of a rich and illustrious aristocracy, such as exists in the Habsburg Monarchy, would be to kill it morally and thereby to contribute an influential element to the corruption of the people as a whole.'[133] The nobles achieved very few successes: the ousting of Count Chotek in 1843 as Highest Burgrave ('A short time ago Chotek was the idol and they were his priests. Today they throw him out of the temple,' mocked Metternich)[134] hints, if only hints, that Vienna would take greater care to consult them and would appoint only nobles with estates in Bohemia to high office; and endless negotiations with Vienna over their powers. However, in the end their powers remained the same – an example to other provinces. As far as Czech nationalism was concerned, Metternich did say: 'In normal times Czechism is an inclination that leads to few aberrations, but in a time of general unrest works upon the people like a bean salad during a cholera outbreak.'[135] Yet even as late as March 1847 a worried lord mayor of Prague was informed by Vienna: 'Slavism is allowed unlimited freedom so long as it remains within the limits of the law, refrains from interfering in the jurisdiction of the governmental authorities and does not descend into political delusions.'[136] His worries were merely 'recorded'.[137] There is practically no evidence that Metternich or anyone else in Vienna was greatly interested in Czech nationalism, far less wanted to suppress it. Its political potential was simply not yet recognised.

The nation whose political activities caused real concern was the Hungarian. With the revocation of most of the reforms of Joseph II in 1790 and Hungary's recognition as a free and independent kingdom by his successor Leopold II, Magyar nationalism regained self-confidence. Many factors spurred it on, including the memory of Joseph II's attempt to introduce German, instead of Latin, as the language of administration in Hungary, the legacy of the Enlightenment, and last but not least the persistent fear that Herder's forecast that the Hungarian language would disappear, and that the Hungarians would be absorbed by their numerically greater Slav and Romanian neighbours, would prove true. Joseph II's attempt to replace Latin with German had naturally given rise to the thought that if a 'dead language' needed to be replaced (despite the fact that all the educated classes in Hungary and Croatia learned to speak it at school), there was every reason to choose Magyar rather than German. True, the Magyars were a minority of the overall population of the Kingdom of Hungary – according to the statistics for 1846 there were only 4,774,899 Magyars out of 11,895,796 inhabitants[138] – but they constituted the dominant nation and the nobility everywhere (save for part of that in Croatia) was either Magyar or had become magyarised. So in 1790 a number of delegates to the Diet demanded that Magyar should become the national language of the kingdom. However, the Croats resisted vigorously – no one understood Magyar there, they argued, whereas Latin was the traditional language of government. Besides, how could they take part in debates in the Diet if Magyar were introduced or how could their sons become members of the Hungarian civil service? This was understandable, if only up to a point. In fact, including both houses, there were only about 15 Croats eligible to be members of the joint Diet – at most maybe one fifteenth of the membership – so why should they not have been asked to learn Hungarian, if they wanted to be associated with Hungary? This, not surprisingly, was the view of most Magyars. However, the Ban of Croatia declared that no kingdom could force its laws on another (*regnum regno non praesribit leges*); the Bishop of Zagreb maintained to do so would be undignified and unjust; while several Croat counties threatened to use Croat in response to Magyar.[139] In 1791, therefore, the Diet voted to retain Latin. The language question was brought up again, however, in 1796, 1802, 1805 and 1811. Then as a result of the French revolutionary and Napoleonic wars, no diet was summoned till 1825. It was then again agreed that Latin should remain the language of administration but this time the Croats agreed that it could be made a compulsory subject in all schools in Croatia, a decision approved in turn by the Croatian Diet. In 1830, however, knowledge of Magyar was made obligatory for anyone holding public office or an advocate's diploma. In 1835, its use was extended to law courts, though still as an alternative to Latin, while it was made an optional language for all official documents and obligatory for the register in all parishes where Magyar services were held. In 1839, dietal addresses to the throne were for the first time drawn up in Magyar, while in 1840 Magyar superseded Latin as the language of government and parliament. All clergy were to learn it and all registers were to be compiled in it within three years. In 1843, therefore, Magyar was declared the exclusive language of government, parliament, administration and public instruction. (In practice, in any case, Hungarian counties were using it as the language of administration and education long before then.) Hungarian nationalists believed that citizens of Hungary should all be taught the national language and that government and administration even in areas not dominated by Magyars should be required to communicate in Magyar (although the internal administration of Croatia could continue to use Croat).

The obsession with the language question reflected both the influence of the Enlightenment in general and the influence of Herder in particular.[140] For Herder there was nothing more precious than a language:

> Does a people (*Volk*), especially a backward people, have anything more precious than the language of its forefathers? In this language lives a whole world of custom, history, religion, and principles of life, all of a people's heart and soul. To take this language away from such a people, or to degrade this language, means to take way from it its one immortal possession, that has passed from generation to generation.[141]

Other Germans thought much the same: 'Language is in fact the true Fatherland', said von Humboldt; Schlegel in Vienna in 1812 had warned that 'each significant and independent nation has the right to possess its own peculiar literature and it is the worst barbarism which oppresses the language of a people.'[142] Yet Herder, known as the *praeceptor Slavorum*, had praised the peace-loving and democratic virtues of the Slavs, while forecasting that the Magyars would disappear into the Slav sea that surrounded them. The fear this caused among Magyars should not be underestimated. Count István Széchenyi, for example, Hungary's greatest reformer of the Metternich period, wrote in his diary on 30 June 1829: 'Every day I see more [clearly] that Herder is right. Soon the Hungarian nation will cease to exist.'[143] Later, on 17 June 1832, he would complain: 'I see everything in the darkest light. The flourishing of all peoples in Hungary. I am totally depressed.' On 22 July 1830, he wrote: 'I am waking up about Hungary. She is stone dead. Drowned in German intelligence.' Finally, in a letter addressed to a friend in July 1832, he noted that in Buda and Pest there were more Germans than Hungarians.[144] Yet, as has been seen, the Magyars had been fighting back with regard to the language laws and during the decades of the Enlightenment they, too, had taken the opportunity to prune their own language of its more obsolete and ungainly expressions. Poets, playwrights and novelists had demonstrated its ability to express emotion, sensitivity of feeling and nuance, while scholars, linguists and lexicographers had provided evidence of its range of meaning and precision. But if the goal of these scholars was to prove Herder wrong, in another sense they would prove him right. Language could be used as a means of strengthening and furthering Magyar national consciousness.

By the 1790s, there were already signs of an interest in cultural renewal. Samuel Decsy in 1790 had asked whether the schools and churches might not be used for 'imperceptible Magyarisation'.[145] The press, pamphlets and county assemblies had echoed the thought, although people like Mátyás Rát, editor and publisher of the first Magyar newspaper, the *Magyar Hirmondó*, while furthering Magyar literature and scholarship, rejected linguistic intolerance. The economic reformer, Gergely Berzeviczy, who published in Latin and German, also thought in terms of a multi-ethnic Hungary and made social and economic reforms his main priority. However, most thinkers, especially those who wanted a national historical institute or a national academy, thought in terms of the use of Magyar promoting academic advance. For example, Ferenc Kazinczy, one of the founders of the first Hungarian literary periodical, the *Magyar Museum*, the 'father of Hungarian literary criticism' and 'literary dictator of Hungary', regarded literature as a 'nation-sustaining force'. This attitude predominated.[146] The brilliant young poet Csokonai used the text of a Hungarian folk-tale in his 1793 play *Tempeföi*, while striving to enrich the language with translations of works from English, French, German, Italian, Latin and Greek. (Kazinczy also wanted to 'transplant the flowers of European literature to Hungarian soil'.) Count György Festitich, after unsuccessfully petitioning for Magyar as the language of command in Hungarian army corps, retired to build the Monarchy's first agricultural institute, the Georgicon, on the shores of Lake Balaton and later organised annual cultural festivals. The first Magyar newspaper to be edited in Pest (from 1806), the *Hazai Tudósitások*, edited by István Kulcsár, concentrated on Magyar language, literature and culture and the promotion of learning. Yet, given the lack of any outlets for culture – save the often magnificent palaces of the nobles – there were few opportunities for Hungarians to partake in cultural events. There was also censorship. Fazekas's epic poem *Ludas Matyi* had to be published abroad and Katona's play *Banus Bánk* was not performed till 1848. The first dealt with social antagonisms, the second with anti-German feeling. Still, patriotism permeated the odes of the highly talented Dániel Berzsenyi and Ferenc Kölcsey (later a famous left-wing parliamentarian), even if a critical review of the former's poetry by the latter almost led Berzsenyi to stop writing. Kölcsey's *Hymnus*, one of his many political and philosophical poems, on the other hand, would become Hungary's national anthem. Then from 1821 the literary almanac *Aurora* marked a new period in Hungarian literary life. Published in Pest, it opened its pages to old and new writers and was the brainchild of Károly Kisfaludy, one of two noble brothers whose literary works now became very popular. Károly wrote romantic and patriotic dramas, comedies, poems and short stories while Sándor also wrote well-loved romantic and patriotic poetry, based on a nostalgia for the nobility and heroism of past times. *Aurora*, however, also opened the way for the romantic poet Vörösmarty, whose epic, *Zalán's Flight*, about the conquest of the country by Árpád coincided with the opening of the 1825 diet and the establishment of the country's national academy. His poem inaugurated an era of national romanticism that helped unite Magyar intellectuals; the historical novels of Barons József Eötvös and Zsigmond Kemény confirmed the trend.[147]

Still, the great debate in Hungary centred less round cultural than political and economic issues. The defeat of Joseph II's plans regarding the introduction of German and the abolition of the counties, Leopold II's reaffirmation of the country's ancient constitution and independence, and the need for Vienna to summon diets after 1825 after an interval of thirteen years all meant that Magyars were acutely aware of the need to safeguard their political inheritance. (Before 1825, when fifteen counties had refused Francis's demand for extra recruits and taxes, the king had told their representatives in person that he would never grant a constitution 'even if the entire world went crazy' and demanded one.)[148] At the same time, their defensiveness over Herder's forecasts and the Slav renascence made them fearful of the future. Some sort of vision was needed and at the centre of the ensuing debate over Hungary's future stood the young aristocrat, Count István Széchenyi, who as a captain of the Hussars in 1825 had offered a whole year's income, some 60,000 fl., towards the foundation of a national academy 'to propagate the national idiom and to raise sons worthy of a fatherland like ours'.[149] (His father, Count Ferenc, in 1802 had founded the Hungarian National Library and Museum.) He had then become the academy's first vice-president in 1830, when it began to operate. Earlier in life, the young count had been attached to Schwarzenberg's staff during the Napoleonic wars and had been a well-decorated dandy at the Congress of Vienna. Thereafter, he had read voraciously and had travelled extensively in England, western Europe and the Balkans. He became a disciple of Benjamin Franklin, imbibed west European liberalism and yet was related by birth and marriage to the greatest families in central Europe. He was always anti-revolutionary and abhorred violence and therefore in 1825 offered to mediate between Metternich and the reformers, although in 1827 he set up a National Casino (a political club on the English model) at Pest for liberal noble members of the Hungarian Diet. His first book, *On Horses*, was published in 1828 in Hungarian but was concerned with broader social and economic issues than just animal husbandry. Then came his first major work, *On Credit*, in 1830 which argued that, despite his tax exemption, fertile lands and herds of animals, the Hungarian nobleman was condemned to poverty for lack of credit. (He himself had been refused a loan by his banker in 1828!) Outdated feudal institutions and traditions meant that he needed to improve his farming methods and roads but lacked the credit to do so. The cure was to be found in not just a credit bank but in the legal protection of creditors, financiers and merchants and the abolition of noble privileges including entail. He wanted an end to tax exemption and condemned forced labour services as unfair to peasants, useless to landlords and subversive of public works (upkeep of roads, bridges, etc.) He wanted to improve domestic demand by forcing landlords to pay their way and lift the burden from the peasantry. He also wanted every-one to have civil rights. His book ended with a plea for a national debate and it certainly started one. He told his readers to forget the past and look to the future: 'Many think: Hungary *has been*. I like to believe: she *will be!*' His next polemic, *Light*, of 1831 demonstrated how backward Hungary had become and how feudal conditions prevented foreign investment in new industries and the settlement in the country of foreign craftsmen; he called either for the destruction of feudal privi-leges or their extension to everybody. Given the divide between land-lord and peasant, a Hungarian *nation*, he insisted did not exist.[150] The condition of the peasant, it should be noted, had been miserable for centuries. After several uprisings had been put down with great cruelty, the Diet of 1514 decreed that 'all peasants in the realm (except those who dwell in the Royal Free Cities, and those who remained true to their masters and to the Holy Crown) do henceforth lose their liberty of movement and are henceforth subjected to the masters in true and perpetual serfdom'. By the end of the eighteenth century, peasants were obliged to pay a 'military contribution' to the crown to provide for the army, a *cassa domestica* to the county to pay for local officials, police and the upkeep of roads and prisons; and an *imposta* to pay the county for local assessors. They were also required to feed and quarter troops, cart salt, provide horses to local officials and undertake public works free of charge. They had to pay a tithe (tenth) to the Church, a ninth

part of their wine, poultry and livestock and field produce to their landlords, as well as a house tax and rent, while they were to supply their
lords with horses and oxen and to send their women to do domestic
service. Fortunately, money played little part in the local economy; the
state tried to prevent encroachments by the landlord on urbarial land,
Maria Theresa's 1767 Urbarial Patent restricted *robot* duties to one day
per week (with animals) or two days without; and land-holdings tended
to be quite large in an under-populated country. But clearly the peasants were still at the economic and legal mercy of their landlords. How
discontented they were is hard to say but the horrific peasant uprising
of 1831 in five counties of Upper Hungary in the wake of the cholera
epidemic there (which killed quarter of a million), when nobles were
tortured and killed by 40,000 peasants who mistook the cholera cordon
and military steps to enforce it (e.g. disinfection) as part of a plot to
keep them from earning their livelihood, if not to poison them, unsettled many. It was the greatest peasant uprising since the Transylvanian
one of 1784 and had to be harshly suppressed. Little, therefore, was in
fact done for the peasant. In 1838, however, the Diet restored freedom
of movement to the agricultural labourer and he was allowed, if he
could negotiate it, to compound and settle his obligations to his land-
lord in exchange for a fixed sum of money. (Only one per cent of peasants had availed themselves of this right by 1848.) In 1843, it was also
agreed that all native non-nobles of a 'received religion' could possess
'noble' lands and might even be eligible for election to public office.[151]

In 1833, Széchenyi published *Stages* which not only set down a
timetable for his reforms but extended his criticism to guilds, monopolies and other forms of bureaucratic interference with commerce and
industry. He advocated the abolition of entail, the *robot*, the ninth, the
internal tariff between Austria and Hungary and manorial jurisdiction.
Again he exposed the drawbacks of the feudal system even for its
supposed beneficiaries although he called for the elevation of its victims
'within the bulwark of the constitution'. He believed that Hungary
would never prosper until she was economically modernised – constitutional challenges to Austria, he believed, would be unwise before
then. In any case his loyalty was to the Monarchy rather than just to
Hungary. His actions as an economic moderniser included being the
motivator behind the activities of the Danube Steamship Company
which created an efficient link between Vienna and the Lower Danube
by the 1830s. Economic modernisation also came about thanks to his
work on river regulation, since he was responsible for both regulating
the Danube in the 1830s and the Tisza in the 1840s in line with plans

drawn up by Pál Vásárhelyi. Again, he was behind the scheme to build the first permanent (chain) bridge between Buda and Pest, constructed under the direction of British engineers between 1842 and 1849. Indeed, Széchenyi was at the forefront of several banking and industrial schemes to develop Hungary economically for several decades.

One of his motives was his belief that Hungary's national existence was at stake. 'Every year the foreign population which has settled in Hungary grows. The old Hungarian stock approaches sterility.' He himself believed strictly in the unity and integrity of all the lands of the Hungarian crown and in the spreading and establishing of Magyar as the national language. But he also believed that if Hungary were modernised and reformed, the non-Magyar peoples would be ready – or much more ready – to accept magyarisation. They would see its benefits and accept the Magyar way of thinking. Magyarisation would then become spontaneous, voluntary and organic and need not involve the use of coercion. In his books such as *Hunnia* and *People of the East*, therefore, he warned against premature measures to further the spread of Magyar. If Slavs and Germans were allowed to use their own tongues as much as possible in private, they would more readily accept Magyar as the official language. There had to be mutual respect and tolerance and pursuit of the golden ethical rule to do unto others as you would be done unto you. Otherwise magyarisation would backfire.[152]

One of Széchenyi's closest friends was the left-wing radical leader of the Magyar opposition in Transylvania, Baron Miklós Wesselényi,[153] who had accompanied him on his travels in the 1820s and who had written a book, *On Prejudices*, which had promoted reforms similar to his own. However, the Transylvanian wanted the state to undertake the transformation from serfdom although he also advocated an end to absolutism and its replacement by constitutional monarchy and civil rights. He reckoned he could sell this project to the Magyar Estates by couching it in terms of a return to the ancient Magyar constitution and 'noble democracy'. As for national rights, he proposed a plan to turn the whole Monarchy into a federation of five units – the German lands, Bohemia, Galicia, Lombardy-Venetia (including the Italian-speaking parts of Dalmatia and Istria) and a fully integrated (i.e. magyarised) Kingdom of Hungary. There was no question then of federalising Hungary itself (as some of the Hungarian Jacobins of the 1790s had proposed). His aim was to give the Magyars control of Hungary and to banish their fear of Panslavism by allowing the Germans, Italians and Magyars together to dominate the Monarchy. In his 1843 publication entitled *A Word on Magyar and Slav Nationality*, he argued that out of

Hungary's 15 million inhabitants, there were just over 4.5 million Magyars. However, since the Greek Orthodox were not Slavs, this reduced the number of Slavs by 5.5 million, and of the remaining 5 million about one million Germans and Saxons could be subtracted, so that altogether there were only around 4 million Slavs and Romanians, thus fewer altogether than there were Magyars. He was absolutely convinced of the justice of magyarisation.

Another important Hungarian politician and intellectual who gave great thought to the nationality question was Baron József Eötvös,[154] who was to become education and culture minister in 1848 and 1867. Some authorities regard him as the most profound Magyar thinker on the issue and his views fell somewhere in between those of Széchenyi and Kossuth. His most important political work published before 1848 was called *Reform in Hungary* and appeared in 1846. The most decisive points as far as he was concerned were first that he was a believer in the organic development of the historic Hungarian state and rejected any claims from natural rights that might be put forward by Hungary's Slav or Romanian nations. In other words, he believed in the political unity of the Hungarian nation as the basis for the modern Hungarian state. As a liberal (he, too, had travelled widely in western Europe and idolised the British Whigs as well as French liberals such as Constant and de Tocqueville) however, he believed, secondly, in the humanity and idealism of the individual, who had to be accorded freedom, equality and nationality. But individual freedom took precedence over equality (i.e. private property above socialism), while equality meant that no national group could receive special privileges. This latter point was important, since he recognised the forces within nationalism that always strove for superiority over others. Hence he believed that nationalist leaders were egoists whose policies would lead to the break-up of the multi-national Empire. Peoples left to themselves would not feel any need for special rights and privileges. The leaders he had in mind, however, were those of Hungary's non-Magyar peoples, whose demands for corporate rights or autonomy were to be condemned. His solution, instead, was to rely on the freedom of individuals without regard to their status, nationality or religion: 'When equality of treatment of the individual is guaranteed through the constitution, the question of equal treatment of a nationality has lost its practical significance. When each has the same rights as another, no matter what nationality he belongs to, no nationality can be viewed as favoured by the state.' This was wishful thinking rather than profound thought. Eötvös recognised, finally, however, that some demands of nationalists were justified.

These should be addressed so long as no other nationalities suffered and so long as the state as the instrument of order and stability was not damaged. In practice this meant making concessions to the nationalities only on the very lowest levels of local administration. Before 1848, he was something of a centraliser, rejecting political action based on instructions from county assemblies as inferior to legislation enacted by a strong, elected and accountable central government. His most famous novel, *The Village Notary*, of 1845 had satirised county politics. Altogether, though, his constitutional views, like those of most Magyars, provided little cheer for Hungary's 'nationalities'.

There had been some writers in the earlier part of the nineteenth century who had advocated a form of Hungarian patriotism that allowed all inhabitants of Hungary to see themselves as 'Hungarians' whether they were Slovaks, Romanians or Magyars. These had mainly been progressives who had advocated reform without magyarisation and had included the economic and social thinker, Gergely Berzeviczy, many of whose ideas had anticipated Széchenyi's. But they had little chance to withstand the tide of Magyar nationalism, associated above all with the great Magyar hero Lajos Kossuth, that swept the country from the 1820s onwards.

Kossuth[155] was also a Magyar liberal who believed that the granting of full civil rights to everyone would solve the nationality question. In return for equality before the law, an elected parliament and the abolition of serfdom, everyone should be happy to belong to a modernised Magyar state (his economic reform programme was not much different from Wesselényi's) in which the only nation was the Magyar one and whose only official tongue would be Magyar. He wrote in the *Pesti Hírlap* on 19 December 1847: 'I will never ever recognise under the Holy Hungarian Crown another people or another nationality than the Magyar one.'[156] Yet, on account of his rhetorical and journalistic skills, his frequent attacks on Vienna, the Metternich System, German centralism and absolutism, he gained a greater popularity than Széchenyi who, famously, he called 'the greatest Hungarian'. His policies were based on first, the maintenance of the territorial integrity of the Hungarian state as a strong and equally respected part of the Habsburg Monarchy; copying the French conception of nationality, he insisted, secondly, on the political unity of Hungary with all subjects treated the same and without special privileges for nationalities (cf. the treatment of Bretons in France or the Scots, Irish and Welsh in the United Kingdom), even if this meant the use of force;[157] in contrast to Széchenyi, he believed, thirdly, that the constitutional position of Hungary with respect to the crown, the dynasty and other parts of the Monarchy took first priority and had to be clarified, leaving Hungary with the greatest degree of self-rule possible; only then could a reformed Hungary undertake economic and social modernisation. Clearly, therefore, the 'nationalities', in particular the Croats and Romanians, were being offered next to nothing by the Magyars before 1848. All this was clear from debates at the Diet and from the arguments that broke out between Kossuth and Széchenyi, who became jealous of his younger rival, and in books (*The People of the East* of 1841 and *Fragments of a Political Programme* of 1847), speeches (most famously his 1842 speech to the National Academy in which he declared that all Magyars took leave of their senses as soon as the language or nationality issue was discussed) and newspaper articles, he attacked Kossuth on the issue. He even got himself elected to the Lower House of the Diet in 1847 to weaken Kossuth's position there. Meanwhile, the whole country was in a ferment over the constitutional issue, especially after the treason trials of the late 1830s, and the political divisions to which they gave rise by the 1840s (see below). Curiously, however, very little was achieved in the way of reform, despite the period being known in Hungarian history as 'the reform era'. As has already been seen, little was done for the peasants, although the Jews were allowed greater freedom with regard to free choice of residence, trade and profession, and even with regard to ownership of real estate. In 1840, there were also some new laws establishing a more liberal legal framework for business and commerce. But on the major issues the liberal reformers remained divided. Nobles did not want to surrender their privileges. Even during the Diet elected in 1847, relatively progressive government proposals with respect to entail, compensation for freeing serfs and prison reform divided them again. Indeed, even on the issue of county administrators (see below) no headway could be made, so that by February 1848 the Diet was deadlocked.[158] It was the totally unexpected news from Paris that allowed that deadlock to be broken with the fall of Metternich. Until then, there was no indication that Hungary would break her usual political mould.

Given the open debate over nationality in Hungary and the political divisions there, the Croats for their part were aware of the Magyar consensus regarding the situation of the 'nationalities'. Their own relationship with Hungary had been defined by the union of the crowns of 1102, when the Croat nobility recognised the kings of Hungary as their own in return for the preservation of their rights and privileges. In 1527, after Hungary recognised the Habsburgs as its kings, the Croats followed suit, although they still reserved their privileges. In 1712, when they accepted the Pragmatic Sanction eleven years before Hungary, they still maintained: '. . . According to law we are a land affiliated with Hungary and in no way a subject people of Hungary . . . We are free and not slaves.'[159] But after the reaction to the reforms of Joseph II, the Croat Diet or *Sabor* in 1790 and 1791 agreed that the three Croatian and the three Slavonian counties would be placed under the administration of the Hungarian Council of Regency, although the country still remained legally independent. This meant that only in local matters of justice and education would the *Sabor* be decisive. In most matters the Hungarian government and the Hungarian Diet would decide. Indeed, the *Sabor*, between 1790 and 1848 would really only meet to give instructions to Croat (not Slavonian) delegates going to Pozsony and to approve their votes after their return. Croatia seemed in a poor way by 1830. The so-called 'Triune Kingdom' of Croatia, Slavonia and Dalmatia was divided up between several authorities. Dalmatia and the Croatian–Slavonian Military Border (a large border area with Turkey run by the army and populated by military colonists) were ruled from Vienna; the 'Hungarian Littoral' (Fiume with the county of Severin) was ruled jointly with Hungary from 1825; while Croatia–Slavonia was in most important matters run from Hungary. Hungarian had even been made a compulsory subject in all Croatian schools, with the approval of the *Sabor*.

After 1830, however, there was a significant cultural and political reaction in Croatia, which had been affected by all sorts of political events from the French Revolution to Napoleon's establishment of the 'Illyrian Provinces' between 1806 and 1814 (they would include most of Croatia, Slavonia, Slovenia and Dalmatia), from the Serb revolts of 1804–12 and 1815–29 against the Turks, to the Greek War of Independence and the revolutions of 1830. Herder and the German Romantics, of course, also played their part. In any case, it was clear that the agreement to teach Magyar as a compulsory subject had enraged many. One young poet, Pavel Štoos, wrote these lines: 'Other people rejoice in themselves, but I, my son, am ashamed. Even their language, the Croats want to forget; and they want to become another people.'[160] Croat students at Graz university began to think what they should do. Their leading light, Ljudevit Gaj, the son of a pharmacist, would soon lead the way.[161] He was a great admirer of Kollár and Šafařik and was determined to unite all South Slavs against the Magyars. (The Serbs, however, would never fall into line.) He was well aware of the force of the threat from Hungary. Pest he had seen as a student in 1825 as a mainly German town where Magyar was spoken only by those who had recently arrived from the countryside. By 1829, thanks to Magyar students tearing down signs written in German, however, Magyar had become the dominant tongue. Hence Gaj was determined to reform the Croat language to ensure that the 'Illyrians' or South Slavs could unite to save their heritage. He did this by reforming Croat on the basis of the most widely used *što* dialect and in 1830 published his *Brief Foundations of the Croatian–Slavic Orthography*. This made him the leader of the young South Slav patriots. Two other works were also published around this time, however, which were of equal historic significance. In May 1832, Ivan Derkos published in Zagreb his *Genius patriae super dormientibus filiis suis*. This was meant to awaken in Croats an interest in their past and in their language; it held up the Serbs as an example of a people who had fought for their freedom and also advocated a common language based on the *što* dialect, which was spoken by the Serbs and the inhabitants of the Military Frontier. Finally, Count Janko Drašković, a Croatian noble with valuable connections in Vienna and a personal friend of Kolowrat, in 1832 supplemented Derkos's cultural programme with a political one. His *Disertatia iliti Razgovar*, written in the *što* dialect and published at Karlovac, examined the ideas of liberty, equality and fraternity but also promoted the idea that all Croat delegates to the Hungarian Diet should demand the unity of the South Slavs and Slovenes in a Kingdom of Greater Illyria, presided over by a Ban with historic, extensive powers, with Illyrian as its official language (based naturally on the *što* dialect) and under Habsburg rule but closely associated with Hungary as an independent commonwealth. (He was prepared to allow Magyar to be taught in this Greater Illyria as an optional subject.) In fact political nationalism had by now taken off. In 1832, General Rukavina thanked the members of the *Sabor* for having elected him its captain (and thus in charge of military affairs); however, he did so in Croatian to thunderous applause, it being the very first time that the language had been used in that body. Thereafter Croatian delegates in the Hungarian Diet argued regularly over Croatia's *municipal rights*, as they were rather curiously called, and beat off demands regarding urbarial reform and extended rights for Protestants (their nationalism was not necessarily progressive). However, it was Gaj's permission from January 1835 to establish a new newspaper with a literary supplement that attracted most attention. It had taken three years of discussions between Vienna, Buda-Pest and Zagreb to bring this about.

Gaj's newspaper was supposed to be called *Croatian News* while the supplement was to be entitled *The Croatian, Slavonian and Dalmatian Morning Star*.[162] But very soon changes happened, changes which took place without permission. After the death of the Emperor Francis in 1835, Gaj published an article calling for the use of the *što* dialect and pleading for Illyrian unity. The same issue carried a poem entitled 'Croatian Fatherland' by Antun Mihanović, which later became the Croatian national anthem. From 18 June 1835, the *Morning Star* was being written in the new orthography with the *što* dialect, although the old orthography was occasionally used for another year. In December 1835, Gaj was writing of his 'Illyrian' brothers and of a common language for 'Greater Illyria', while from January 1836, again without permission, the titles of the newspapers changed to *Illyrian National News* and *Illyrian Morning Star*. Gaj was soon responsible for a whole series of developments. He encouraged the use of songs as a vehicle for nationalism, 'Croatia has not yet fallen', in particular. Along with Drašković, he helped found the Society for the Promotion of a National Language and Literature. This acquired reading rooms in Karlovac and Varaždin in 1836 and one in Zagreb in 1841. From the latter other societies emerged, including the Economic Society in 1841 and the Matica Ilirska in 1842, organised to fund works in Croatian literature and culture. Despite criticisms, however, the State Conference in Vienna seemed to appreciate Gaj's role in limiting magyarisation. If the local censor blamed his papers for the defeat of the pro-Hungarian faction in the elections to the Diet in 1840, the State Conference in Vienna praised them for raising the educational standards of the local clergy. But when Gaj was accused by a fiscal official and the local bishop of propagandising his views in the Military Border, Metternich, much as he deplored the activities of the Magyar fanatics, upheld the view of the new Ban and of the Palatine that the Illyrians were now seeking to create a unified South Slav state from which to attack Hungary. The Turks were also reporting their displeasure about Illyrian activities in the Balkans, as were the Russians and the Vatican. In 1843, therefore, Metternich introduced new regulations concerning Illyrianism and Magyarism. The words Illyria and Illyrian were to be banned, but Gaj's newspapers were to continue under their original titles. Croatia's municipal rights were to be protected against Hungary. The local pro-Hungarian censor was to be suspended from his post. Gaj now lost influence but Croatian and Illyrian defiance continued. In 1845, the first steps were taken to reform the *Sabor*, while in 1847 Croatian was proclaimed the official language of the country instead of Latin.

With regard to the Romanians of Transylvania, there, too, cultural change was taking place and a reaction was setting in against Magyar chauvinism. Yet the Transylvanian Romanians were in a very weak position, although they made up half of the total population and were more numerous than the Magyars, the Saxons and the Szeklers combined.[163] They possessed only an extremely small intellectual class and very few newspapers. The only newspaper, which covered political rather than merely cultural matters, was *The Transylvanian Gazette*, which was founded as late as 1838 with only 500 subscribers. It was conciliatory in its approach and not very readable. Often it was reduced to reprinting articles which had already appeared in Saxon newspapers. Its first editorial expressed real gratitude for being able to further Romanian culture through the use of the Romanian language.

The undisputed cultural leaders of the Romanians until the 1830s had been the clergy of the Uniate and Orthodox churches and the only places of higher education were the schools operated by the Uniate church at Blaj and the Orthodox seminary at Sibiu. The Romanians were not recognised as one of the official constitutional nations of Transylvania (these were the Magyars, the Saxons and the Szeklers) but their religious leaders were used by Vienna, almost as civil servants, to communicate with their followers and made responsible for their behaviour. In 1834, when the Transylvanian Diet was called into session after twenty-three years, the Uniate and Orthodox bishops, Lemenyi and Moga, submitted a petition to it, arguing that the Romanians should be recognised as a fourth nation and that neither nature or the laws prohibited the Romanians achieving full rights of citizenship. But neither this nor the subsequent petitions submitted to the Diets of 1837–8 and 1841–3 received any positive response, something that undermined the reputations of the church leaders amongst intellectuals.

The latter were enraged when on 31 January 1842 the Diet passed a language law replacing Latin with Magyar as the official language of Transylvania. With immediate effect, Magyar was to become the language of the Diet, of legislation, of official correspondence at all levels of government, in the higher courts and in the correspondence of the government with the several churches. Beginning immediately, all candidates for the Orthodox priesthood were to be trained in Magyar and as soon as practicable Magyar was to be introduced as the language of instruction in all village elementary schools. Within ten years it was to be the language of all Uniate and Orthodox schools including those in Blaj and no one could be admitted to any church office who could not read and write Magyar. The leading Transylvanian secular intellectual, the philosopher Simion Bărnuțiu, denounced the law in an article in the literary supplement of the *Transylvanian Gazette*. He declared that 'if a people should lose its language, it would at the same time lose its character and nationality. It would no longer be honoured by other peoples, but would be an object of mockery before all.' The Romanians – 'the colonists of Trajan' – 'were destined for a higher civilisation, in which they can make progress only with the aid of their mother tongue', so he concluded: 'The obedience of men is not unconditional, and neither Saxons nor Romanians will submit, nor, indeed, can submit, to a law of absorption which destroys nationality.'[164] George Barniţiu, the editor of both papers, condemned the law as a death sentence for Romanians and the Romanian nation. He predicted, however, that their large numbers, their self-consciousness, their Eastern Orthodox faith, the example set to them by their brothers in the Danubian Principalities beyond the Carpathians and the development there of a national literature, a national church and national governments would mean that it could never be carried out. As it happened, the Emperor did not sanction the language law, which was never put into effect. The status quo remained.[165]

From all this, it can be seen that Vienna allowed the development of cultural nationalism to proceed in Hungary and Croatia and prevented a drastic experiment in magyarisation from occurring in Transylvania in 1842. When political issues were at stake (the censorship, the question of monarchical versus representative government, upholding the Hungarian constitution, excesses in the country assemblies or the Diet, the deliberate stirring up of the constitutional question by Kossuth and others in the 1830s, for example), dramatic steps could be taken leading to the imprisonment of key figures (Kossuth himself, Wesseléni and Lovassy between 1835 and 1839), although the 1840 Diet demanded and secured an amnesty. Still, Wesselényi had gone blind, Lovassy had gone mad, while Kossuth had taught himself perfect English.[166] The government now took a more circumspect line. Kossuth was allowed to edit a new liberal newspaper, the *Pesti Hírlap* (*Pest News*), which received 5,000 subscribers (and therefore perhaps 50,000 readers) within a month. Its revolutionary style of journalism and its coverage of many social issues meant that in 1844 Kossuth had to be evicted from his post[167] (Metternich refused his request for the right to start a new paper, although a hint was dropped that this might be possible if he supported the government)[168] but he soon became its most prominent opponent once again by occupying the presidency of the newly created National Protectionist Association, dedicated to maintaining a tariff barrier between Austria and Hungary to protect emerging Hungarian industries, along lines suggested by the German economist Friedrich List.

(Support for it soon dwindled; Austrian goods were simply better and cheaper. Austria saw the customs line between the two countries as a means of indirectly taxing Hungary and thereby gaining compensation for the taxes Hungary refused to pay. She would have preferred, however, to abolish it, have the Hungarians pay taxes and make Hungary part of a Habsburg customs union.[169]) By now Vienna was putting its faith in two strategies to protect its political position: first, under a new Hungarian Chancellor, Count György Apponyi, it began to control the counties by replacing elected county sheriffs with nominated and well-paid administrators (Eötvös backed this and promised his support in return for reforms), while secondly, it cooperated with a new conservative party, founded in November 1846, in a mild reform programme formulated by Counts Emil Dessewffy and Anton Széchen.[170] These strategies actually seemed to work. Despite the politicisation of Hungary during the 1840s through hundreds of charity associations, reading clubs and casinos whose memberships in total must have reached 100,000, the liberals could not win an outright majority in the 1847 Diet.

With regard to nationalism, however, there is no evidence that Vienna or Metternich was ever interested in playing off the nationalities against one another. From the Czech experience, it has already been shown that the policy was to let cultural nationalism blossom, so long as it did not enter the realm of political delusion. This was true of Hungary also. The Magyars in Transylvania were not allowed to threaten unrest by their language law of 1842, while in Croatia, Illyrianism was tolerated even while it broke the letter of the law. When, however, Metternich feared that it was getting out of hand by upsetting the Turks and interfering with the Military Border – perhaps even threatening to destroy the link with Hungary amidst student demonstrations and unrest – he reined it in. The Palatine was now arguing that 'Gaj can justifiably be called the Croatian Kossuth' and was even predicting a future alliance between them in favour of ultra-liberalism.[171] The documents concerning Metternich's decision, however, are quite revealing. The Hungarian Palatine, the Archduke Joseph, was no friend of the Croats: on 28 June in the Upper House of the Hungarian Diet, he declared: *itt nincs ilyr; nincs más nemzet – mint magyar.* ('Here [meaning the Kingdom of Hungary] there are no Illyrians; there are no other nations, save the Magyar one.')[172] The Hungarian Chancellor was also anti-Croat. However, Metternich insisted that the decree banning the use of the word Illyrian had to be imposed even-handedly: 'The evil has two starting points – illyrianism and magyarism – so that it is not sufficient for His Majesty to declare against the one. He must oppose both.'[173] The nub of the decree read:

> Croatia is in great turmoil. And there will be no turmoil in any country which lies under the protective sceptre of His Majesty.
>
> I will have order in my Empire. My duty is to uphold it where it exists and to restore it where it is endangered. This can only be achieved when justice is protected. Thus there will be no contest between illyrianism and magyarism.
>
> Croatia has rights. I will know how to protect them.

The palatine was instructed that, although there were no 'Illyrians' in Hungary, the 'natural development of the various languages' there was to be 'given a free run', although care was to be taken to avoid political abuse. He was also told by the Emperor: 'I could only regard it as expedient if it were arranged in both countries by means of suitable regulations written in conciliatory tones, that a friendly relationship between the various nationalities, based on mutual respect, could once more be maintained.' Likewise, it was stressed to the Ban of Croatia that: 'no obstacles are to be placed to the encouragement of the national language so long as it takes place within the limits of the law'. The Hungarian Court Chancellery meanwhile was told to remove the causes of current events in Croatia and to 'rein in by royal authority the inexperience and disregard with which unthinking enthusiasts aim to spread the Magyar language at the cost of other nationalities'. It was about this time that Metternich wrote at the bottom of a memo from Kolowrat, to which he gave his approval: 'I hereby declare that what goes for the Magyars, is also applicable to the Slavs.'[174]

Altogether, it is difficult to avoid the conclusion that Metternich's policy with regard to nationality was simply to accept and neglect it, to tolerate its natural cultural development, but to take action only if and when it threatened to cause unrest or upset the political status quo. He had no objections to Slavs, Hungarians or Romanians or anyone else using their language or researching its history and philology or reforming its orthography. He certainly had no intention of Germanising the Monarchy although he thought of it as being German through and through and forming an integral part of the German Confederation. Yet the Monarchy was a unique creation in which subjects of many nationalities owed their allegiance to the Emperor whose personal sovereignty alone held all his various realms together. An alternative allegiance to a sovereign nation would therefore threaten the viability of the

Monarchy, although love of one's native language in itself would not. Before 1848, therefore, Metternich could concentrate his activities on combating Italian and German nationalists who were actively seeking to create Italian and German sovereign nation-states. For most of the time, therefore, he had little to worry about.

The Economy

What about the economy? How did it perform in the Metternich period and to what extent did economic and social problems threaten to undermine the regime?[175] As has been seen, most foreign visitors to Vienna found it a merry, cosy place with the inhabitants enjoying its musical and theatrical life. Today the consensus is that sustained economic growth took off in Austria during the Metternich period with the beginning of industrialisation and the building of railroads and factories, although this did lead to the usual economic problems – the closing of uncompetitive small workshops and the employment of large numbers of women and children in bad conditions in factories. On the other hand until the late 1840s, when harvest failures occurred in the Monarchy as in the rest of Europe, the standard of living appears to have risen. The bourgeoisie began to buy up houses in the smart suburbs, while the level of taxation by European standards did not seem high. True, the Austrian economy seemed to produce for the upper and lower ranges customers in terms of quality of goods (relative backwardness meant that Austrian industrialists were opposed to membership of the German Customs Union or *Zollverein*) and credit was scarce (private banks being used as the National Bank would not lend to entrepreneurs). In fact, much of the investment in industry came from landowners (with coal on their lands or rivers which could be made into canals) or foreigners. Yet Austrian protectionism did not help – cheaper goods were kept out and competition was diminished – while the attempt to create a smoothly functioning internal market kept receiving setbacks, such as Kossuth's National Protectionist Association in Hungary. On the other hand, there were few problems. Until the agricultural depression spread to industry in the late 1840s, there seemed little to complain about: there were more railways, steam-driven locomotives, steamships and steam engines. Trieste and Venice were in competition for foreign trade, Bohemia and Lower Austria were centres of industrialisation, in Vienna there was an obsession with the fashion industry, the iron industry was flourishing in Styria, the glass and silk industries were flourishing in Lombardy-Venetia. The Austrian Lloyd became the leading freight line using the Mediterranean. Between 1816 and 1846, there were thirty years of uninterrupted prosperity. The middle classes were well looked after by the government, which employed them as doctors, lawyers, teachers, academics, civil servants, indeed, even as journalists and censors. One key factor was what I have elsewhere described as the 'Habsburg welfare state', the student grants, the retirement pensions for state servants – navy and army veterans and civil servants – and for the widows and children of these people should anything happen to their husbands or parents. According to Austria's leading authority, Professor Waltraud Heindl, there were about 140,000 civil servants in the Monarchy in the 1840s out of an empire of 56 million people.[176] The contemporary English traveller Peter Evan Turnbull, whose investigations of the Monarchy were published in 1840, estimated that there were 120,000 civil servants. Both writers stress the dependence of these people on the state.[177] Another contemporary witness, William H. Stiles, the American *chargé d'affaires* at Vienna in the Metternich period, wrote that the middle classes were 'possessed of a mania for entering the bureaus'. But his calculation of those dependent on the government in some way amounted to no less than 3,154,000 people, including nobles, clergy, civil servants, industrialists and merchants, pensioners, soldiers and the proprietors of houses in cities. Fewer than half that number, he calculated (once he excluded women, children and imbecile old men), were independent of it, out of Austria's 38 million inhabitants. (Presumably he excluded Hungary and Transylvania.)[178] (Heindl, however, has shown that during the Metternich period, the percentage both of high nobles (24 per cent) and bourgeoisie (47 per cent) in the bureaucracy rose at the expense of the small nobility (30 per cent).)[179] Apart from its bureaucracy, Austria's citizens also had access to a large charity network in almost all towns and villages, with churches forced to work with the state to relieve local poverty. (The imperial family was very active in charity work.) Medical services in Vienna and some other towns were also good and in most of German Austria almost all children went to school, although in places like Galicia and the Adriatic coast, relatively few (14–18 per cent) did. Jews were still officially discriminated against (they needed permits to settle in towns and were excluded from government and academic employment, although they could join the army) and were disliked by Catholic Austrians (who rioted against them in 1848), but unofficially they were making good progress. They were protected in Hungary by magnates who used them as their agents in the grain trade and allowed them to establish themselves in villages and suburbs, whereas they found that if they bribed Viennese officials or invented businesses elsewhere in Austria or Turkey, they could even acquire permission to reside in Vienna. The Monarchy was also a *Rechtsstaat*, a country run according to the rule of law, with an enlightened civil legal code. Indeed, peasants could take their landlords (including the Emperor himself!) to court and be given state legal aid to prosecute their claims. Noble landowners could not take part in judging cases in which they were themselves personally involved. As for the peasants, it is difficult to state how disaffected they were, if at all. They could certainly react with great cruelty and viciousness against their landlords in the more backward parts of the Monarchy – Upper Hungary in 1831[180] and Galicia in 1846 – when they felt that their landlords were plotting to murder them. These jacqueries involved the torture and murder of local landlords, their families and their agents and had to be put down by government troops. But since the peasants concerned showed no hostility to the Emperor – indeed, in the latter case (Galicia) claimed to be acting in his defence against the Polish revolutionaries – this gave the government an unfounded confidence that the masses would always back it against its critics. In normal times, the peasants had to pay a whole series of taxes and dues, but according to the latest research their burden was not unbearable. By 1848, they had the right to buy out their landlords by paying them off in a final settlement that would end forced labour. The fact that practically nobody did so may well have been due to an expectation that the government would soon abolish the *robot* anyway or to the fact that in many places the work involved was done without enthusiasm or efficiency. Certainly many landlords would have preferred a final financial settlement, although others would have resented the loss of status involved in competing with former peasants as farmers.

During the recession of 1846–8, both workers and peasants suffered enormously. Huge numbers of deaths were reported in Galicia after the harvest failures.[181] Lack of produce then forced up prices in the towns and even factory workers (the highest paid) discovered that their wages bought very little food. Many children died as a result of malnutrition and the cold. (The price of firewood rose enormously.) As more and more workers were laid off (the agricultural depression meant no money to buy goods), there was simmering discontent, but this was manifested against factory owners in Vienna (as in Bohemia in 1844) and against Jews (who were often traders, innkeepers, peddlers and factory owners.) Significantly, when revolution broke out in Vienna in 1848, imperial buildings were spared.

Kolowrat and his friends blamed the Monarchy's financial difficulties in 1848 on Metternich. Thanks to the need to increase both troop numbers and the salaries of troops by putting them on a war footing and sending them to Italy, there was no money to spare for other emergencies. Indeed, it had been the need to use force to intervene in Italy in 1820 and 1830, according to Kolowrat and his circle, that had unbalanced the budget and forced the government to resort to loans, the interest on which after many years took up between a quarter and a third of the budget. But this was simplistic. Any great European power had to reckon on having to use its armed forces from time to time and Metternich, in fact, used Austrian forces very sparingly. Moreover, both officers and men were poorly paid and at least one-third of the army was usually on leave. Money certainly was not squandered on that arm of the state. No, the real problem underlying the financial difficulties of the Monarchy was Kolowrat himself, who had been in charge of domestic finances since 1826, but who had never been able to expand the narrow base of government tax revenue. Kübeck as far back as 1816 had complained: 'The sources of direct income have been withdrawn almost totally from the influence of the state administration. Their calculation has been entrusted, particularly with respect to the land tax, to those persons and authorities who partly have no interest in collecting them and partly have an interest in putting all possible obstacles[182] and difficulties in the way.'[183] Yet thanks to Kolowrat's dilatory administrative methods and lack of imagination, the Monarchy could neither afford to keep a proper army nor finance a peasant buy-out of *robot* by organising state payments to landlords which peasants could later redeem. A strong financial base – if only Kolowrat had been able to create it – would have totally transformed the Empire's political prospects.

As it was, apart from customs dues, most of the government's revenue depended on the land tax, the house tax, various sales taxes and the government monopolies of salt and tobacco. Yet, to keep the land tax and house tax revenues up to date and expand them, a new land survey was needed to show the net profits being made from various land uses and rents and to do away with the differences between the provinces. This 'gave the prospect of increased revenues that could have put an end to the deficit at a stroke', according to Rumpler,[184] but alas the work of the survey was opposed by court officials and by 1834 only Upper and Lower Austria, Lombardy-Venetia, Dalmatia, Carinthia, Styria and Carniola had been measured and assessed. The reform of taxes on consumer goods only took place in 1829 when they were united in one sales tax but again this manoeuvre was botched; milk and potatoes were indeed taxed – to the horror of the poor – but Tyrol, Galicia, Lombardy-Venetia were freed from levying the tax on liquors, while Hungary refused to tax any goods. As for the tobacco and salt monopolies, which could also have made a difference, Bohemia, Moravia and Silesia reserved the right to sell salt to their landowners, while the cost of salt in Hungary was so low that the monopoly brought in next to nothing. The tobacco monopoly only brought in a profit after a new retail system was introduced in 1834–5. Fortunately, customs revenues did increase from 988 million gulden in 1825 to 1937 million gulden in 1847. But Austria still had a small budget deficit as well as a balance of payments deficit. Her state debt, however, was still huge. Bankers were becoming reluctant to lend her more, no interest, for example, having been paid into the sinking fund at the National Bank since 1838. None the less, Kolowrat, when asked his opinion on affairs in Hungary in the *Staatskonferenz* on 17 August 1843, could give the following reply: 'Let the Diet be dissolved . . . We don't need taxes. We have more than two years' tax arrears to collect.'[185] It was a damning admission.

Another relevant factor was that although railways were being built by 1848, there had been a slow start. Yet if Austria was to survive as an internal market outside the *Zollverein*, an extended domestic transport network was required. In the late eighteenth century, an imperial network of canals had been planned to link the rivers Elbe, Danube, Moldau, Save and Drau. By 1803, only a Danube–Theiss canal, the Bega Ship canal in the Banat and the Wiener Neustadt Canal had been built, the latter as part of a system to link Vienna via Hungary with Trieste. Then came the age of the railway. The first plan was to lay down a stretch of railroad between Linz and Budweis to take salt to Bohemia. Eventually in 1836, this was achieved and the railroad extended to Gmunden. It meanwhile had to be rescued by the Rothschild Bank, which also now undertook to participate in a scheme to construct a railway network for the Empire as a whole. Rothschild was to finance the Northern line running from Vienna to Bochnia in Galicia; another banker, Sina, the stretch from Vienna to the Adriatic, while the bankers Arnstein and Eskales were to finance the railway between Milan and Venice. The Southern line, however, ran into difficulties as it was designed to avoid Hungary and go through Graz and over the Semmering to Trieste. It reached Graz in 1844 but Sina now supposedly ran out of funds, leaving the state to take over in 1847, albeit with money loaned by Sina and Arnstein. The Austrian military was desperate for the link, as was the Austrian Lloyd shipping company based at

Trieste, but it was not completed till 1857. No railway had encountered such terrain before. Meanwhile, the Northern line was more successful and by 1846 had linked Vienna to Brunn, Prague and Krakow. By 1848, freight could be sent from Vienna to Hamburg within 44 hours. Hungary was brought into the network between 1846 and 1849. The parallel development of steamship traffic on the Elbe and Danube also increased trade and prosperity. Hamburg lowered its tolls on Austrian goods; the first Danube steamship company was established in 1829, the trip between Vienna and Budapest taking three days. In 1834, the first trip was made to the mouth of the Danube itself. All sorts of materials were soon being transported by ship and rail to Hungary, whose industrialisation was furthered by such developments. Meanwhile, the link to northern Italy was incomplete. This was a great misfortune. So, too, was the fact that the bankers by 1847 had got out of railway financing – the rate of return was only 1.2–1.48 per cent – so that the state had to take over not only the financing of the southern link but also the Lombardy-Venetian and Hungarian lines, for which it had to pay a more profitable rate of interest on loans. Still, Rumpler's assertion that the failure to complete the southern link between Bohemia and Vienna and Trieste before the link with North Germany amounted to a 'first-rate failure of state policy and economic policy' seems rather harsh.[186] It may have been unfortunate that technical difficulties and Sina's banking priorities delayed matters, but what exactly was Metternich or Kolowrat supposed to have done? The state did take over the building of the railways after all. And railway building had commenced immediately after the death of Francis I, the man who had so much distrusted railways and had delayed their introduction in the first place.

The imperial family, including the mentally retarded Emperor Ferdinand himself, was very popular.[187] People from all over the Habsburg lands had grown used to meeting the Emperor in Francis's day. They could go to the palace once a week and tell him their troubles or often he would go around the countryside meeting them and allowing them to do the same there. He rarely needed a bodyguard, even when accompanied by the Empress. He talked to them in their local Viennese dialect in the capital and elsewhere would speak the prevailing language. Even Ferdinand could open the Hungarian Diet in Magyar. (The Palatine, the Archduke Joseph until 1847, was probably Europe's last statesman to use fluent Latin in conducting business there until the mid-forties.) The Habsburgs' subjects had hosts of stories about their emperors – Ferdinand was known as 'Ferdinand the Good' as well as 'Ferdinand the Loony'. The family's love of the theatre and of music (several past emperors had themselves been composers) was well known and made them true Viennese.

The imperial family was also identified with the Catholic Church and on great ceremonial occasions – for example the Corpus Christi festival – would demonstrate this. The Church, however, was kept under political control, especially since the days of Joseph II. Rome relied much more on Vienna than vice versa. Metternich, after his marriage to the devout Princess Melanie Zichy – like Francis I after his fourth marriage, came under pressure from his wife to grant greater freedom to Rome, but although there were investigations by the government into the possibility of a Concordat or some alliance of throne and altar that would give greater freedom to the Church, the question of mixed marriages, not to mention the continued strength of Josephinism inside the bureaucracy, always precluded a successful outcome. (Metternich's policy on mixed marriages, on which he even got the Hungarian Diet to agree in 1844, he described as one of 'tolerance'.)[188] None the less, Austria considered herself to be the leading Catholic monarchy and her mainly Catholic subjects appreciated this.[189]

Inevitably, it was the Emperor's advisers – especially given Ferdinand's well-known mental health problems – who took the blame for anything that went wrong. But right up till the late 1840s there was very little to worry about. Europe had weathered the revolutions of 1820 and 1830; the war scare of 1840, like the Eastern Question, had come and gone. Metternich, who had defeated Napoleon, was still in charge. And whereas there was diplomatic rivalry between Britain and France over all sorts of issues, Nicholas I of Russia was cooperating with Austria over Poland – he even forced Austria to annex Krakow in 1846 – and had kept his promise of 1833 to keep a benevolent eye on Ferdinand. He had no designs on Habsburg territory and, when Gaj in 1840 secretly offered to support him in Panslav schemes, he not only ignored him, but had him thrown out of Russia when he visited the country (and was silly enough to raise the subject with Russian ministers).[190] Friedrich Wilhelm IV of Prussia, on the other hand, was a nuisance. He had vague notions of German unity and made promises of greater powers to Prussia's provincial diets and even conceded the summoning of a united diet in 1847. Metternich feared that this would influence affairs in Austria, but in fact, as has been seen, the challenge from the Bohemian Diet, which was not of great significance, was met with tedious negotiations but no fundamental concessions over powers or finance. The Hungarian Diet proved a greater problem, largely on account of Hungary's unique constitutional position, but even there, the opposition could not control the Diet, which by February 1848 was deadlocked. Curiously, there was no attempt before 1848 by opposition politicians in Hungary to work with critics in other parts of the Monarchy. Instead, it was Count Leo Thun, a Bohemian patriot, who took the lead in criticising the Magyar treatment of the Slovaks in northern Hungary.[191]

In Austria itself, there were some stirrings of discontent, but not many. In Upper Austria, for example, where the local Diet met once a year for a three-hour morning session to approve government plans and taxes, there was, according to local police reports, some interest in events in the Bavarian Parliament, sympathy after 1831 for the Poles, concern over the Archbishop of Linz's policy regarding Protestants after 1837, when he re-introduced the Jesuits, but little political interest.[192] In Lower Austria, where the Diet met in Vienna, there was much greater political awareness.[193] Among its members were leading liberal writers who published in the German press – people like Baron von Doblhoff, Count Albert Montecuccoli and Cavalier Anton von Schmerling – who expressed real political criticism for the first time and passed motions calling for the abolition of peasant dues and services, the reduction of taxes, the establishment of a credit bank, municipal reform, the introduction of income tax and the extension of elementary education. Early in 1848, the Diet even called for the abolition of conscription, while on various occasions it asked for the non-privileged classes to be represented and for the budget to be made public. It demanded to be consulted whenever necessary. This activity reflected a series of books by Austrian critics published in the 1840s, mainly in Leipzig or Hamburg. The process had started with the founding of *Die Grenzboten* in Brussels in 1841 by the Czech exile, Ignaz Kuranda, as a rallying point for oppositionist groups, through Baron Victor von Andrian-Werburg's *Austria and its Future* of 1842, Franz Schuselka's many pamphlets of the decade (*German Words of an Austrian*, *Austria Rules Supreme if She Only Wills It*, *Austria's Forward and Backward Steps*, etc.), through the most important works of 1847, Count Schnirding's *Austria's Internal Politics with Reference to the Constitutional Question* and Karl Beidtel's *The Financial Affairs of Austria*, to Karl Moering's work of January 1848, *The Sibylline Books from Austria*. The general trend of these got more radical as the decade wore on. Von Andrian's book had been primarily an attack on the central bureaucracy, a call to strengthen the provincial diets by allowing them to vote provincial taxes, choose their own officials and allow the middle classes and peasants to be represented. They should also be allowed to petition the monarch. As for central government, he suggested an imperial diet formed of representatives from the provincial estates. A second volume published in 1847 repeated this programme and added the need for a free press, greater academic freedom and the abolition of feudal dues. Schuselka, however, had no faith in the aristocracy and wanted a king to rule in alliance with the people. Schnirding wanted rights to be given to the peasants and middle classes and called for more industrialisation and the abolition of feudal dues, while Beidtel frightened the life out of those with savings by stressing that there was not enough gold and silver in the reserves to cover the amount of banknotes in circulation and pointing to the unbalanced budget. A national assembly was needed to supervise a partial bankruptcy and reform of the currency. This immediately recalled the events of 1811. The curious thing about all these activities and all this literature, however, was, as the leading historian of the Viennese revolution of 1848 has pointed out, that the main demand was for a more representative but still consultative assembly to recommend mild reforms and approve the budget and at most with a veto over taxation. 'There were no demands, however, for a ministry responsible to a modern parliament, which should rule while the monarch reigned.'[194] Even the petitions which poured into the Hofburg after March 1848 were very mild in their demands: 'The hesitant appeals for provincial assemblies and a united diet, with members chosen by traditional Austrian, not democratic methods and with the limited prerogatives of approving taxes and the budget and sharing in the legislation, are certainly a far cry from the demands of modern liberals.'[195] So, even in Vienna, there was no real pressure for anything but mild reform, although the leaders of the Lower Austrian estates were put under police surveillance.[196] Little else was done regarding the estates, whose ambitions were seen, none the less, as potentially subversive. Eventually, after turning down another suggestion from Metternich in 1847 that an executive ministerial council was needed to speed government action, as well as a linked proposal from Count Hartig that such a council could shape business agendas with dietal leaders before provincial diets met, Kolowrat managed to persuade the State Conference to water down these proposals to the appointment of a single state councillor – Count Prokop Lazansky, as it turned out – to deal exclusively with the estates. This solved nothing since the civil service put everything on hold till Lazansky could establish his plans.

By 1848, however, problems were piling up. After the Galician horrors of February 1846, Metternich had let it be known in unambiguous terms that the local aristocracies in Lombardy-Venetia and Hungary might expect similar fates if they pushed their luck too far, nor did they disbelieve him.[197] Yet the election of a liberal and reforming Pope in 1846 had set Italy ablaze. Then came the crisis over Ferrara in 1847 and the news of the tobacco riots at the start of 1848. In Hungary there was the tension leading up to the elections for the 1847 Diet. Along with the harvest failures and the rising unemployment throughout the Monarchy, all these factors contributed to the air of pessimism in Vienna and, given Metternich's long tenure of office, the feeling of a need for change. He could hardly be blamed, of course, for the harvest failures – a liberal and parliamentary regime in contemporary Britain did not prevent the Irish Potato Famine of 1846 – but interest payments on the state debt were taking up 28 per cent of the budget, which was slightly in deficit overall and the balance of payments was in the red. This was hardly disastrous, but the need for extra troops to keep law and order in Lombardy-Venetia now also put a strain on the Treasury. Beidtel's book made this seem all the more sinister and it was harder to negotiate a loan from the Rothschilds to tide things over. Indeed, the combination of Beidtel's book and the fear that war would break out over Italy caused a run on the banks. Yet, as in 1914, it was foreign policy that was to tip matters over the edge. The news from Paris that Louis Philippe had been overthrown by revolution brought with it the fear of an all-out European war. Metternich was not the only one who foresaw a return to 1793. Investors thought that state finances would collapse if this happened. So to forestall this they clamoured for his resignation, as did the students of the city, and after a street riot which revealed that Vienna had few resources to contain a mainly student mob, which should and could have been dispersed by a few militiamen, the imperial family lost its nerve, made promises that would all too soon be repudiated, and allowed Metternich to resign: 'I see myself forced to take a step, whose cause I view as an obligation of conscience and to lay before Your Majesty all my burdens of office (*Beichte*.)'[198] According to his wife, Princess Melanie, he was then forced to steal away, unprotected like a criminal: 'The imperial family never liked him, never appreciated him. These imbeciles never knew what he was . . . If on the 13 March his head had been demanded on the scaffold, they would have signed his death warrant.'[199] In short, he had received the traditional 'thanks of the House of Habsburg'. Archduchess Sophie, wife of Franz Karl and mother of the future Emperor Franz Joseph, had once told Princess Melanie that individuals made no difference in history. One man could always be found to replace another.[200]

There was no revolution. Metternich's colleagues continued in government, but events spun out of control in Italy and Hungary (and almost in Germany), before the 'system' triumphed, Hungary and Lombardy-Venetia were again brought under control, and Metternich himself could return to Vienna. He was no longer personally in control, of course, and had to witness the failures of Schwarzenberg, Buol and Rechberg before he died in 1859. They had been too impressed by military success in Italy and Hungary and were ready as a result to confront first Prussia, then Russia and then (unknowingly) France. Metternich, as always, urged cooperation with both Prussia and Russia, but was ignored. Lesser men were now in charge of the Monarchy, although it would survive every challenge, save the First World War.

7
Conclusion

Metternich by 1848 had had an exceptionally good run for his money and, during his years in office, the Habsburg Monarchy had helped overthrow Napoleon, managed to contain revolution and had enjoyed peace and prosperity. There had been very little opposition, the various peoples of the Monarchy had been allowed to develop their national cultures, the censorship had been mild, if irritating, and even in Italy Austrian rule had been the best in the peninsula. Metternich could never see where he had gone wrong, and by his own principles he simply had not. He continued to maintain the same thing in exile and was not surprised to be able to return home. His unwavering insistence that he was right and had always been right enraged his critics then and has always done so since.

Modern historians and liberals insist that he was the great enemy of democracy. And he was. He simply equated it with Jacobinism – and in an era when only 1–3 per cent of the population in England, Belgium, France or Hungary for that matter were allowed to vote, clearly he was not the only one. He was also supposedly the enemy of accountable government. That was also true: accountability to mob orators held no attraction for him. He preferred responsible government in the sense that trained statesmen should work for the good of their country, to the best of their abilities and in the light of conscience. He was a man of the Enlightenment, a rationalist, who believed in debating issues and analysing them in the light of the facts. He also believed in the force of tradition. He was no fanatic; he did not want to execute or imprison anyone; he did not wish to keep people in ignorance. He simply wanted states and classes to cooperate to avoid revolution and to maintain an orderly civilised society in which rational progress could be made. He did not believe in utopias but had seen the results of the work of those who did. He admired Napoleon for conquering the Revolution. But

244

Napoleon had wanted to conquer the world as well. Metternich after conquering Napoleon wished to conquer the Revolution also. But the world that had emerged from the Congress of Vienna he wanted to retain as it was. And thanks mainly to his efforts it remained more or less like that for forty-five years – not a bad record when all is said and done. Bismarck, once he had changed Europe, had a similar problem – containing France and preserving the status quo. Perhaps Metternich made a better job of this for longer. He certainly spared Europe the triumph of German nationalism – or at least delayed it. For that at least we should be thankful. Did the eventual unification of Germany or Italy really contribute to European progress? Today, in an age of European nationalism, perhaps we all should ponder that question. The future is not always better.

Metternich, for his part, preferred a rationally, organically evolving status quo. In 1847 he wrote to his ambassador in Rome:

> if people would only view our Empire impartially: everything there is progressing; everything that is good and useful is advancing . . . all the reasonable demands preached by progressives have been fulfilled by us. Our Empire acknowledges the perfect equality of citizens before the law; we have no tax privileges or feudal burdens; in our Empire is found equality of taxation and the independence of justice. All parts of the Empire have assemblies of estates and a municipal system much more liberal than that which exists in countries ruled by the representative system. In no other empire are the nationalities more respected than ours; respect for the nationalities is indeed a necessary condition of our existence; nowhere is there less absolutist government than in our Empire, nor could there be any.[1]

There is more truth in that statement than historians have traditionally allowed, although clearly there is also much exaggeration and self-delusion. Kolowrat's reactions to Metternichian optimism of this kind is well known. He condemned the 'intolerable vanity' of one 'who in all his life has never been wrong, has foreseen everything and still foresees everything that happened and didn't happen. In a word I can't get on with him'.[2] Yet the curious fact is that when one examines the record, despite all the mutual insults, both these men (along with others such as Hartig and Kübeck) did thrash out the issues of domestic high politics in the State Conference for almost a decade and a half, went over affairs in detail for years, and still managed to work together without one dominating the other. My own conclusion, therefore, is that

Metternich played the larger part in running the Monarchy, since Kolowrat took no part in directing foreign affairs, and that in domestic affairs both worked together reasonably well despite personal animosities. Schlitter's four well-researched volumes on Austria in the 1840s proves this despite the fact that he condemns Kolowrat and praises Metternich. It is not therefore a very fruitful exercise to try to determine if Kolowrat was really 'prime minister' or not. Similarly, it is not very useful to attempt to determine whether Metternich 'really' wanted to spare Napoleon or not and whether he had a 'secret plan' to do so. The diplomacy of the anti-Napoleonic coalition was so multilateral and open, and Napoleon so determined to master his own fate, that that issue, too, is a pointless one to pursue. So if these red herrings are put aside, the main points of this evaluation must simply be that Metternich was the most important and successful diplomat of his time and that while he was in office after 1815 the Habsburg Monarchy experienced three decades of peace, prosperity, stability, cultural renewal and economic transformation. The years 1846–8 brought many challenges, not merely to Austria but to the whole of Europe. A panic reaction to a street riot in Vienna then brought Metternich's resignation,[3] which in turn caused revolutions, but the radicals behind them were soon defeated and Metternich returned. If he could not see where he had gone wrong, it is difficult to show, without resorting to ideology or anachronism, where indeed he had.

Notes

Notes to Chapter 1: Introduction

1. Eric Hobsbawm calls it 'the greatest jacquerie since the days of the French Revolution of 1789', although he does not mention that the peasants supported the Austrians. See E. J. Hobsbawm, *The Age of Revolution* (London, 1977), p. 155.

2. 'Censorship, though irksome, was less oppressive than in most Italian states and the bureaucracy ... was neither marred by corruption nor unsympathetic to the conditions of the local population; the judicial system was characterised by remarkable even-handedness. Indeed the "black legend" of oppressive Austrian rule was the invention of patriotic propagandists who paid scant attention to reality' (David Laven, 'The Age of Restoration', in John A. Davis (ed.), *Italy in the Nineteenth Century* (Oxford, 2000), pp. 51–73, 58–9). Cf. similar statements by Denis Mack Smith, *Victor Emanuel, Cavour, and the Risorgimento* (Oxford, 1971), pp. 7–9.

3. After a revolt in 1845 in the Papal States, for example, the American consul in Turin reported home: 'The Legations are reduced to such dreadful extremities that they would gladly seek refuge from priestly extortion in the more orderly and better regulated despotism of an Austrian Prince.' See Howard A. Marraro, 'An American Diplomat Views the Dawn of Liberalism in Piedmont, 1834–48', *Journal of Central European Affairs*, vol. 6 (1946–7), pp. 75–6.

4. For a *revisionist* account of Hungarian affairs with respect to Austria and Croatia, see Alan Sked, 'Mirror Images: Kossuth and Jelačić in 1848–49', in L. Péter, M. Rady and P. Sherwood (eds), *Lajos Kossuth Sent Word ...* (London, 2003), pp. 135–82.

5. For the historiography on Metternich the best source is still Paul W. Schroeder, 'Metternich Studies since 1925', *Journal of Modern History*, vol. XXXIII, no. 3 (1961), pp. 237–200. The only substantial attempt to interpret his whole career since then has been G. de Berthier de Sauvigny, *Metternich* (Paris, 1986), although it mainly concentrates on the period up to 1815 and eschews footnotes. It should be supplemented by his indispensable collection of document extracts, *Metternich and His Times* (London, 1962). See also Alan Sked, *The Decline and Fall of the Habsburg Empire, 1815–1918*, 2nd edition (London and New York, 2001). There have been a couple of popular biographies but they are not serious additions to the historiography. The definitive and enduring biography is Heinrich Ritter von Srbik's monumental *Metternich: der Staatsman und der Mensch*, 2 vols (Munich, 1925) along with its posthumously published historiographical third volume,

Quellenveröffentlichungen und Literatur; eine Auswahlübersicht von 1925–1952 (Munich, 1954).

6. *Tablettes Autrichiennes, contenant les faits, des anecdotes et des observations sur les moeurs, les usages des autrichiens et la Chronique Secrete des cours d'Allemagne, par un temoin secret* (Brussels, 1830), p. 191.

7. Viktor Bibl, *Metternich. Der Dämon Österreichs*, 4th enlarged edition (Leipzig and Vienna, 1936). The introduction blames Metternich for Solferino, Königgraetz, the First World War and the dissolution of the Monarchy.

8. 'As in Greek tragedy, the success of Clemens von Metternich made inevitable the ultimate collapse of the state he had fought so long to preserve.' This 'rococo figure' was 'all surface . . . but without depth' . . . 'a truly successful policy may have been impossible for Austria in a century of nationalism. Tragedy can be the fate of nations, no less than of individuals, and its meaning may well reside in living in a world with which one is no longer familiar. In this sense Austria was the Don Quixote of the nineteenth century. Perhaps Metternich's policy should be measured, not by its ultimate failure, but by the length of time it staved off inevitable disaster.' 'Even Austria's most successful policies amounted to no more than a reprieve, a desperate grasping to commit allies, not a work of construction, but to deflect part of the inevitable holocaust . . . (the skill of Metternich's virtuoso performance) testified to its ultimate futility . . .' 'But had all the revolutions of 1819–20 occurred simultaneously, there is no doubt that the Austrian Empire would have collapsed a century before its ultimate demise.' Henry Kissinger, *A World Restored: Metternich, Castlereagh and the Problems of Peace, 1812–1822* (London, 2000), p. 8, p. 9, p. 174, p. 281 and p. 283. And yet Kissinger is always quoted as an unabashed admirer of Metternich!

9. Quoted in Helmut Rumpler, *Österreichische Geschichte 1804–1914: Eine Chance für Mitteleuropa. Bürgerliche Emanzipation und Staatsverfall in der Habsburgermonarchie*, p. 35.

10. *Parliamentary History*, vol. xxix, p. 826.

11. Quoted by Constantia Maxwell in her essay, 'Chateaubriand and the French Romantics' in F. C. Hearnshaw (ed.), *The Social and Political Ideas of Some Representative Thinkers of the Age of Reaction and Reconstruction 1815–1865. A Series of Lectures Delivered at King's College London During the Session 1930–31* (London, 1932), pp. 29–51, p. 31.

12. *Parliamentary History*, vol. xxx, p. 278 (1 February 1793).

13. Ibid., vol. xxxiv, p. 1051 (7 June, 1799).

14. For a good, brief discussion of this debate, see Hugh Gough, *The Terror in the French Revolution* (Basingstoke, 1998), pp. 1–9.

15. Alfred Cobban, *In Search of Humanity: The Role of the Enlightenment in Modern History* (London, 1960), p. 188.

16. The title of a brilliant book by J. L. Talmon (London, 1952). But see Cobban's critical discussion of it in *In Search of Humanity*, pp. 182–5. See,

too, Norman Hampson, 'The Heavenly City of the French Revolutionaries' in Colin Lucas (ed.), *Rewriting the French Revolution* (Oxford, 1991), pp. 46–68.

17. Quoted by A. Cobban, *In Search of Humanity*, p. 189.
18. Quoted in Norman Hampson, *St Just* (London, 1981), pp. 132–3.
19. See the discussion in Gough, op. cit., pp. 55–7.
20. In Francis's own words to Count Clary, Head of the Supreme Judiciary: 'They are to be tried as speedily as possible, but in accordance with the formalities prescribed by the law.' Quoted in Henry E. Strakosch, *State Absolutism and the Rule of Law: The Struggle for Codification of the Civil Law in Austria, 1753–1811* (Sydney, 1967), p. 184.
21. J. Belin, *La Logique d'une idée-force* (Paris, 1939), p. 400.
22. *Parliamentary History*, vol. xxx, pp. 901–2 (6–7 May 1793).
23. Quoted by Norman Hampson in 'From Regeneration to Terror: The Ideology of the French Revolution' in N. O' Sullivan (ed.), *Terrorism, Ideology and Revolution* (Brighton, 1986), p. 58.
24. Quoted in J. M. Burney, 'The Fear of the Executive and the Threat of Conspiracy: Billaud-Varenne's Terrorist Rhetoric in the French Revolution', *French History*, vol. 5 (1991), p. 162.
25. Metternich's account of his role during the French revolutionary and Napoleonic wars is included in the first two volumes of his memoirs. Very recently an English translation of the autobiographical parts of these two volumes was published with an anonymous introduction and no mention of a translator. The translation appears to have been lifted from the 1880 translation of the first five volumes of the memoirs by Mrs Alexander Napier. Still, students will now have an accessible version of Metternich's own account. For the quote in the text see, therefore, *Metternich: The Autobiography. 1773–1815* (Welwyn Garden City, UK, 2004), p. 14.
26. For an excellent modern survey, see Gough, op. cit.
27. Quoted by Morris Slavin in 'Terror and Revolution: France and Russia' in *The Left and the French Revolution* (Atlantic Highlands, New Jersey, 1995), pp. 119–20.
28. Ibid., p. 120.
29. For a discussion of the figures see, Gough, op. cit., pp. 77–8, and Slavin, op. cit., pp. 118–19. Note also Slavin's comparison of the French and American revolutions with regard to the percentages of émigrés and property confiscations, namely: 'From this point of view, our own brand of "terror" was more drastic and thorough than that of the French Revolution.'
30. Even Thiers the French statesman who wrote a multi-volume history of the Napoleonic period and who later arranged for Napoleon's remains to be returned to Paris agreed that Napoleon had caused the deaths of more men than any of the greatest Asiatic conquerors. See Sudhir Hazareesingh, *The Legend of Napoleon* (London, 2005), p. 176. Thiers, however, still wanted a war in Europe in 1840. See below.

31.   Quoted in Michael Scott Christofferson, 'An Antitotalitarian History of the French Revolution: François Furet's *Penser la Révolution française* in the Intellectual Politics of the Late 1970s', *French Historical Studies*, vol. 22, no. 4 (Fall 1999), pp. 557–611, p. 608. This article is probably the best account of Furet's career. But see, too, the first chapter of Furet's *The Passing of An Illusion: The Idea of Communism in the Twentieth Century* (Chicago, 1999). That is not to say, however, that the Jacobin regime does not still have its defenders. Jean-Pierre Gross, for example in *Fair Shares for All: Jacobin Egalitarianism in Practice* (Cambridge, 1997), examines the Jacobin policy of social justice that apparently aimed at complementing one of upholding human rights. He concludes (pp. 203–4):

> Although during the eventful months of the Terror they [the Jacobins] were brought face to face with the risks of arbitrary power, they rarely if ever sought expediency at the expense of legality . . . The real problem lies elsewhere: in the manner in which equality is promoted, in the extent to which some are prepared to use coercive force to impose it, but also in the stubborn refusal of hardened self-seekers to entertain the demands of social justice, or in the reluctant acquiescence of those who have something to lose and may be prepared to call out the Riot Act to defend their interests.

In short, it was the victims who were to blame for the Terror! This sort of reasoning is discussed by Slavin, op. cit. in his essay 'Terror and Revolution: France and Russia', where he points to Trotsky's assertion that there would have been no violence in Russia if the opposition had just given in.
32.   Quoted in Lloyd S. Kramer, 'The French Revolution and the Creation of American Political Culture', in Joseph Klaits and Michael H. Hatzel (eds), *The Global Ramifications of the French Revolution* (New York, 1994), pp. 26–54, p. 31.
33.   Ibid., p. 46.
34.   Ibid., p. 46.
35.   Ibid., p. 43.
36.   Patrice Higgonet in his *Sister Republics: The Origins of French and American Republicanism* (Cambridge, Mass., 1988), p. 4, agrees: '. . . the two revolutions . . . developed as mirror opposites; the centrality of individualism that triumphed in the one (the USA) was badly shaken in the other (France).'
37.   Quoted in Joseph E. Ellis, *Founding Brothers: The Revolutionary Generation* (London, 2002), p. 237.
38.   Quoted in Hazareesingh, *The Legend of Napoleon*, p. 65.
39.   Ibid.
40.   Roger Bullen, 'France and Europe, 1815–1848: the Problems of Defeat and Recovery', in Alan Sked (ed.), *Europe's Balance of Power, 1815–1848* (London, 1979), pp. 122–44, p. 123.

41. The episode is related in Hazareesingh, *The Legend of Napoleon*, pp. 151–3.
42. Nassau William Senior, *Conversations with M. Thiers, M. Guizot and Other Distinguished Persons during the Second Empire, edited by his Daughter, M. C. M. Simpson*, 2 vols (London 1878), vol. I, p. 131.
43. *Joseph Mazzini. A Memoir by E.A.V. with Two Essays by Mazzini: Thoughts on Democracy and The Duties of Man* (London, 1877), p. 172 and p. 174.
44. Cf. Hobsbawm's *Age of Revolution*, p. 140. '[The revolutionary wave of 1830] marks the definitive defeat of the aristocratic by bourgeois power in Western Europe. The ruling class of the next fifty years was to be the "grande bourgeoisie" of bankers, big industrialists, and sometimes top civil servants, accepted by an aristocracy which effaced itself or agreed to promote primarily bourgeois policies.' Or Jacques Droz, *Europe Between the Revolutions, 1815–1848* (London, 1967), pp. 37–9:

> The period 1815–1848 was characterized, in all countries of Europe by the steady rise of the bourgeoisie . . . In every state of Europe the pattern of development was the same: everywhere money assigned a place to the individual inside the bourgeoisie and in relation to it . . . It was in France that the rise of the bourgeoisie was most spectacular. It was there that it distinguished itself most clearly from the aristocracy from which it had seized power in the 1830 Revolution, and to the 'common people' from which it felt separated by its wealth and its occupations. The July Monarchy can be regarded as the most typical example of a regime in which money became the basic factor of social discrimination.

And after a discussion of Metternich, Droz asks (p. 17): 'Did the governing classes attain their objects?' And answers No –

> it was precisely the fact of economic growth which was to send the whole restoration system sprawling . . . The development of heavy industry, spreading from England to the Continent, would break the social structure of the Ancien Regime and make the middle class the chief element of political life . . . The props supporting the restoration were to be knocked away by the moral forces that sprang from the Industrial Revolution.

(p. 18), however, begins with the sentence: 'Profound as was the economic transformation of Europe in the first half of the nineteenth century, the Continent remained essentially as it had been under the Ancien Regime.' Gosh! Finally, Mack Walker in his introduction to a very useful collection of documents *Metternich's Europe, 1813–1848* (New York, 1968), argues: 'Metternich's Europe knew revolution was made in cities, and cities were made by the accumulation of population and by industrialization . . . To anyone who had a vision of the new economy and society that was coming inexorably into being – whether he liked it or not – what had been done at Vienna seemed a fossil remnant of another age.' Thus the diplomatic settlement of 1815 is again linked to the challenge of rising capitalism and its doom foretold. In short, Metternich was a political and diplomatic relic whom the rise of industrial capitalism would sweep away. I regard all this as simplistic nonsense.

45.   The whole debate about the role of the bourgeoisie in the French revolution was begun by Cobban, whose views anticipated those of Furet by decades. For an account of the early international ramifications, see Eberhard Schmitt, *Einführung in die Geschichte der Französischen Revolution* (Munich, 1976). For Furet's contribution see his *Interpreting the French Revolution* (Cambridge, 1991). Also the article cited above by Christofferson. Hobsbawm in a more recent discussion of the 'bourgeois revolution' in which he takes its defence less from Marx than the Restoration historians – Tocqueville, Mignet, Guizot and Blanc – has now conceded

> that many of the 'revisionist' criticisms of the orthodox interpretation are both factually and conceptually legitimate. There was not in 1789, a self-conscious bourgeoisie class representing the new realities of economic power, ready to take into its own hands the destinies of the state, eliminating the declining feudal aristocracy; and insofar as there was such a class in the 1780s, a social revolution was not its object, but rather a reform of the institutions of the kingdom; and in any case its conscious objective was not the construction of a capitalist economy. Nor was this the result of the Revolution, which almost certainly had a negative effect on the French economy.

See Eric Hobsbawm, 'The Making of a "Bourgeois Revolution"' in Ferenc Fehér (ed.), *The French Revolution and the Making of Modernity* (Berkeley, 1990), pp. 30–48, p. 38. The main defender of the 'bourgeois revolution' now seems to be Colin Lucas. (See, for example his essay 'Bourgeois Revolution Revivified' in Colin Lucas (ed.), *Rewriting the French Revolution* (Oxford, 1991), pp. 69–118.)

46.   A. Cobban, 'The Middle Class in France, 1815–48' in A. Cobban (ed.), *France Since the Revolution* (London, 1970), pp. 7–21.

47.   D. H. Pinkney, 'The Myth of the Revolution of 1830' in D. H. Pinkney and D. Ropp (eds), *A Festschrift for Frederick B. Artz* (Durham, N. Carolina, 1964).

48.   Cobban, 'The Middle Class in France', p. 14.

49.   The best discussion of all this remains Albert Goodwin, 'The Landed Aristocracy as a Governing Class in XIX Century Britain' in H. Mikoletzky (ed.), *Rapports du Comité International des Sciences Historiques* (XII Congrès International des Sciences Historiques, Vienne, 29 août–5 septembre 1965) vol. 1, Grands Thèmes (Horn/Vienna, 1965), pp. 386–74.

50. Ibid.
51. John Snell, *The Democratic Movement in Germany, 1789–1914* (Chapel Hill, 1976), p. 25.
52. P. Ginsborg, *Daniele Manin and the Venetian Revolution of 1848–9* (Cambridge, 1979). But see criticisms of his views as also expressed in an earlier article in Alan Sked, *The Survival of the Habsburg Empire, Radetzky, the Imperial Army and the Class War, 1848* (London and New York, 1979), pp. 279–80.
53. Kent Roberts Greenfield, *Economics and Liberalism in the Risorgimento: A Study of Nationalism in Lombardy, 1818–48*, revised edn (Baltimore, 1965), pp. xvii and xii.
54. Alan Sked, *The Survival of the Habsburg Empire* brings this out very clearly, especially in Part Three.
55. E. Pamlény (ed.), *A History of Hungary* (London, 1975), p. 239.
56. Louis Chevalier, *Working Classes and Dangerous Classes in Paris during the First Part of the Nineteenth Century* (New York, 1971). See the debate involved in George Rudé, *Debate on Europe, 1815–1850* (New York, 1972), pp. 78–87.
57. David H. Pinkney, 'A New Look at the French Revolution of 1830', *Review of Politics*, XXIII (1961), pp. 490–501.
58. For a good discussion of Tilley's work, see Rudé, *Debate on Europe*, pp. 78–87.
59. For Milan, see Piero Pecchiarni, 'Caduti e fereti nelle Cinque Giornate di Milano: ceti e professioni cui appartanaro' in *Atte e Memorie del XXVII Congresso Nazionale* (Milan, 19–21 March 1948), pp. 533–7. For Berlin, see R. Hoppe and J. Kuczynski, 'Eine Berufsbzw – auch Klassen – und Schichten – analyse Märzgefallen 1848 in Berlin' in *Jahrbuch für Wirtschaftsgeschichte* (1964), Part IV, pp. 204–7. The 1848 documentary collection at the Weidner Library, Harvard, contains some lists of those who fell in Vienna.
60. Quoted from Rudé, *Debate on Europe*, p. 197.
61. On the German student movement in general before 1848, see Karl Griewank, *Deutsche Studenten und Universitäten in der Revolution von 1848* (Jena, 1949), pp. 8–18. For Metternich's views on students and professors as well as those of the students on the Germany of his day, see the documents contained in Mack Walker (ed.), *Metternich's Europe, 1813–1848*, pp. 44–8 and 63–7.
62. See M. S. Anderson, *The Ascendancy of Europe: Aspects of Europe in the Nineteenth Century 1815–1914* (London, 1972), p. 86. For Metternich's problem with the Bund, see Chapter 3 below.
63. As stressed by Pierre Renouvin, *Histoire des Relations Internationales. Le XIX Siécle. Première Partie. De 1815 à 1871*, pp. 19–20.
64. Ibid.
65. Ibid.

66. Theodor Schieder, 'Das Italienbild der deutschen Einheitsbewegung' in *Studien zür Deutsch–Italienischen Geistesgeschichte* (Cologne and Graz, 1959), pp. 141–62, p. 145.
67. Quoted in Anderson, *Ascendancy of Europe*, p. 87.
68. Ibid.
69. See a review of the press coverage in 'Die Gute Presse Ostreichs und ihr Verhalten bei den galizischen Ereignissen' in *Unser Gegenwart und Zukunft*, vol. 3 (Leipzig, 1846), pp. 67–107.
70. Raymond Williams, 'The Press and Popular Culture: An Historical Perspective', in G. Boyce et al. (eds), *Newspaper History from the 17th Century to the Present Day* (London, 1978), pp. 46–7.
71. Ivon Asquith, 'The Structure Ownership and Control of the Press, 1780–1855' in Boyce et al., *Newspaper History*, p. 99.
72. Anderson, *The Ascendancy of Europe*, pp. 89–90.
73. Ibid.
74. Ibid.
75. François Fejtö (ed.), *The Opening of an Era: 1848* (London, 1948), p. 25.
76. According to the figures tabulated by Robert Justin Goldstein in his *Political Repression in 19th Century Europe* (Beckenham, 1983), pp. 4–5, the percentage of the total population entitled to vote in Hungary in 1845 was 1%; the relevant figures for France, Britain, Belgium and the Netherlands given are 0.7%, 3.6%, 1.1% and 3.4%. Norway scored 8%.
77. See the discussion in William L. Langer, 'The Pattern of Urban Revolution, 1848' in E. M. Ancomb and M. L. Brown (eds), *French Society and Culture since the Old Regime* (New York, 1966), pp. 90–108.
78. The next two paragraphs are based on the excellent discussion of the weakness of socialism in Europe at this time contained in Rudé, *Debate on Europe*, pp. 114–20.
79. Ibid., p. 119.
80. Ibid., pp. 115–16.
81. Hans Hautmann and Rudolf Kropf, *Die österreichische Arbeiterbewegung vom Vormärz bis 1945* (Vienna, 1974), pp. 113–20.
82. E. A. V., *Joseph Mazzini*, p. 246.
83. The document was presumably stolen from the Austrian archives during the 1848 revolution in Milan or Venice and then published in Count F. A. Gualterio's *Gli Ultimi Rivolgimenti Italiani, Memorie Storiche con Documenti Inediti*, 4 vols (Florence, 1852), vol. 2, pp. 286–7.
84. J. R. Rath, 'The Carbonari: their Origins, Initiations, Rites and Aims' in *American Historical Review*, LXIX (1963–4).
85. P. Savigear, 'Carbonarism in the French Army 1815–1824' *History*, vol. LIV (1969).
86. Quoted in Edgar Holt, *Risorgimento: The Making of Italy, 1815–1860* (London, 1970), p. 83.
87. Roland Sarti, 'Guiseppe Mazzini and his Opponents' in Davis (ed.), op. cit., pp. 74–107, p. 83.

88. For Mazzini's revolutionary activities described above, see the accounts in both Holt, pp. 74–106 and Sarti, pp. 82–92.
89. Quoted in Sarti, op. cit., p. 86.
90. From 'Thoughts upon Democracy in Europe' in E. A. V., *Joseph Mazzini*, p. 173.
91. Fenner von Fenneberg, *Oesterreich und seine Armee* (Leipzig, 1847), pp. 131–2.
92. L. Thürheim, *Mein Leben* (Munich, 1914), vol. 3, pp. 232–4. For the views of Archduke John that any revolution would be 'grizzly' (*gräulichen*), see B. Sutter, 'Erzherzog Johanns Kritik an Österreich', *Mitteilungen des österreichen Staatsarchiv* (1963), p. 184.
93. I am hoping to publish my own account of 1846 soon, but in the meantime see the brief overview in Alan Sked, *The Survival of the Habsburg Empire*, pp. 165–6. Key documents from the civil-military government of Galicia, which have traditionally been overlooked, can still be found in the Austrian archives.
94. Vienna, *Haus-Hof und -Staatsarchiv* (Provinzen Lombardei-Venezien, 1848), Karton 23, Metternich to Ficquelmont (Vienna, 1 March 1848).

Notes to Chapter 2: What Part Did Metternich Play in the Downfall of Napoleon?

1. M. Capefigue, *The Diplomatists of Europe* (London, 1845), p. 1.
2. Ibid., p. 3.
3. Ibid., p. 56.
4. New York, 2 vols, 1852.
5. Ibid., vol. 1, pp. 56–7.
6. Ibid., vol. 1, p. 62.
7. Ibid., vol. 1, p. 62.
8. Ibid., vol. 1, p. 65.
9. Letter of Daniel Webster to Chevalier Hülsemann (21 December, 1850), quoted in ibid., vol. 1, p. 1.
10. Ibid., vol. 1, p. 60.
11. Ibid., vol. 1, pp. 61–2.
12. Ibid., vol. 1, p. 62, footnote.
13. Quoted in Gunther E. Rothenberg, 'The Origins, Causes and Extension of the Wars of the French Revolution and Napoleon', *Journal of Interdisciplinary History*, vol. 18, no. 4, 'The Origin and Prevention of Major Wars' (Spring, 1988), pp. 771–93, p. 789.
14. Helmut Rumpler, *Österreichische Geschichte, 1804–1914: Eine Chance für Mitteleuropa. Bürgerliche Emanzipation und Staatsverfall in der Habsburgermonarchie* (Vienna, 1997), p. 125.
15. Felix Markham, *Napoleon* (New York, 1966), p. 201.
16. Felix Markham, *Napoleon and the Awakening of Europe* (London, 1958), p. 133.

17. Paul W. Schroeder, *The Transformation of European Politics, 1763–1848* (Oxford, 1994), p. 405.

18. For example, Josephine Bunch Stearns, *The Role of Metternich in Undermining Napoleon* (Urbana, 1948), Peter Richard Rohden, *Die Klassische Diplomatie von Kaunitz bis Metternich* (Leipzig, 1939), and Albert Sorel, *L'Europe et la revolution française*, 8 vols (Paris, 1885–1904), vol. 8.

19. Among others, Hellmuth Rössler, *Österreichs Kampf um Deutschlands Befreiung: Die deutsche Politik der nationaler Führer Österreichs, 1805–1815*, 2 vols (Hamburg 1940), Emil Lauber, *Metternichs Kampf um die Europäische Mitte: Struktur seiner Politik von 1809 bis 1815* (Vienna and Leipzig, 1939) and Enno E. Kraehe, *Metternich's German Policy*, vol. 1, *The Contest with Napoleon, 1799–1814* (Princeton, 1963).

20. See, for example, Henry A. Kissinger, *A World Restored: Metternich, Castlereagh and the Problems of Peace, 1812–1822* (London, 1957). Also Heinrich Ritter von Srbik, *Metternich: der Staatsman und der Mensch*, 3 vols (Munich, 1925–1957).

21. Srbik in the above-cited and other works thought that Metternich's refusal to restore the old German Empire was a mistake. Viktor Bibl, on the other hand, in his *Metternich: Der Dämon Österreichs* (Leipzig and Vienna, 1936), and other works, thought that Metternich's opposition to German nationalism eventually destroyed the Monarchy.

22. Schroeder, *The Transformation*, p. 460.

23. Ibid.

24. For the surprising economic background, see Rumpler, *Österreichische Geschichte, 1804–1914*, pp. 116–24.

25. As arrogantly vouchsafed by Napoleon himself to Metternich at Dresden in June 1813. See Prince Richard Metternich (ed.), *Memoirs of Prince Metternich*, 5 vols (London, 1880), vol. I, p. 188.

26. Robert M. Epstein, 'Patterns of Change and Continuity in Nineteenth-Century Warfare', *The Journal of Military History*, vol. 56, no. 3 (July 1992), pp. 375–88, p. 375. The statistics and argument taken in this paragraph are from Epstein.

27. Quoted in Markham, *Napoleon* (1966), p. 206.

28. Stadion for example. His biographer – Rössler – whose views on Metternich have already been noted in footnote 19, echoes Stadion's views in calling Metternich 'practically the Secretary for Austrian Affairs of His French Majesty'! See Hellmuth Rössler, *Graf Johann Philipp Stadion, Napoleon's deutscher Gegenspieler*, 2 vols (Vienna, 1966), vol. 2, p. 69.

29. One way of dealing with Stadion, whose martial spirit had seen him appointed Austrian representative to the Russians and Prussians, was simply to explain to him that Metternich was much more enthusiastic about challenging the French militarily in 1813 than Francis. For example, Metternich wrote to Stadion from Gitschin on 13 June 1813: 'As for

me, I would have struck long since, but the *Emperor* is more unwilling than ever. My position is not cheerful any more than yours, but what is to be done?' Quoted in Edward de Wertheimer, *The Duke of Reichstadt (Napoleon II): A Biography Composed From New Sources of Information* (London and New York, 1906), p. 61.

30. This is what Metternich stated in his *Memoirs of Prince Metternich*, vol. I, p. 64, and what most historians have asserted since but, according to the outstanding work on Metternich as ambassador to France, this was not the case. Napoleon had only asked for a member of the Kaunitz family and Metternich's name was never mentioned. Talleyrand thought of Kaunitz's nephew, Prince Aloys Wenzel Kaunitz, formerly Austrian ambassador to Naples, while Napoleon probably had Prince Johann Lichtenstein in mind. See Manfred Botzenhart, *Metternichs Pariser Botschafterzeit* (Münster, 1967), pp. 7–9.

31. Metternich wrote to Stadion on 25 July 1813 that Napoleon 'struggled against negotiations like a devil in a vessel of holy water'. Francis told Marie Louise (and it was true, given Metternich's correspondence with Stadion): 'That Fate which rules the world has frustrated all my endeavours for peace. I have done what I could to being the matter to a sound conclusion, but all my attempts have been in vain.' De Wertheimer, *The Duke of Reichstadt*, pp. 63–4.

32. Quoted in Rumpler, *Österreichische Geschichte etc.*, p. 131.

33. Heinrich Ritter von Srbik, *Metternich* (his published essay-length biography) (Munich, 1956), p. 20.

34. The account here follows that given by Enno E. Kraehe, *Metternich's German Policy*, vol. I: *The Contest with Napoleon, 1799–1814* (Princeton, 1963), Chapter 1, since Kraehe is sensitive to the issue of where the Metternichs stood in the German aristocratic hierarchy and how they fitted into imperial society.

35. Entitled *On the Necessity of a General Arming of the People on the Frontiers of France by a Friend of Universal Peace*, reprinted in the *Memoirs of Prince Metternich*, vol. I, pp. 340–7.

36. *Memoirs of Prince Metternich*, vol. I, pp. 18–19. Page 17 records Metternich's 'profound disapproval' of the conduct of the Prince of Wales in supporting the opposition. When he reminded him of this thirty years later, George IV told him 'You were very right then!'

37. E. E. Kraehe, *Metternich's German Policy*, vol. I, p. 22.

38. Ibid., p. 33. N.b. Since the title was attached to the estate and not to the family, Clemens remained a count. He only became a hereditary prince after the battle of Leipzig.

39. *Memoirs of Prince Metternich*, 18 Oct. 1819, vol. III, p. 337.

40. Ibid., 26 July 1819, vol. III, p. 249.

41. See Heinrich Ritter von Srbik, *Metternich: Der Staatsmann und der Mensch*, 3 vols, Munich, 1926–54, vol. I, pp. 345ff.

42. 'Metternich's Sketch of a Political Scheme, January, 1806' in *Memoirs of Prince Metternich*, vol. II, pp. 121ff. For differing interpretations about how serious Metternich was see M. Botzenhart, *Metternichs Pariser Botschafterzeit*, pp. 4–5 and E. H. Kraehe, *Metternich's German Policy*, vol. I, pp. 44–5.

43. See *Memoirs of Prince Metternich*, vol. II, p. 176, where in a report from Paris of 18 January 1808, Metternich quotes Talleyrand as saying that Napoleon wants both to partition Turkey and to lead an expedition to India, and that Austria should participate in both. He added: 'French and Russian soldiers should not appear without Austrian soldiers at the same time.' This was meant to feed Metternich's fear of Austrian isolation. Yet Talleyrand was also echoing his master, since in a recent conversation with Napoleon (*Memoirs of Prince Metternich*, vol. II, pp. 185–93), the latter had told Metternich: 'I see what ought really to unite us very closely is the partition of Turkey' – although he claimed that he was not planning it just yet.

44. This is the main point of Botzenhart's book.

45. M. Botzenhart, *Metternichs Pariser Botschafterzeit*, p. 69.

46. Ibid., p. 89.

47. Ibid., p. 92.

48. Constantin de Grunwald, 'Les Débuts diplomatiques de Metternich à Paris. Documents inédits' in *Revue de Paris*, vol. 43, 1936, pp. 492–537, p. 503.

49. Duc de Broglie (ed.), *Memoirs of the Prince de Talleyrand*, 5 vols (London, 1891–2), vol. 1, p. 221.

50. *Memoirs of Prince Metternich*, vol. 2, p. 169, from a report of 12 Nov., 1807.

51. M. Bozenhart, *Metternichs Pariser Botschafterzeit*, p. 124.

52. *Memoirs of Prince Metternich*, vol. 2, p. 169, from a report of 12 Nov., 1807.

53. Ibid., vol. 2, p. 145, from a report to Stadion of 26 July 1807. Metternich ended: 'It is in truth curious that Napoleon, continually troubling and changing the relations of the whole of Europe, has never taken one single step tending to insure the existence of his successors.' Talleyrand also saw this weakness. Napoleon, however, simply believed in his destiny.

54. M. Bozenhart, *Metternichs Pariser Botshafterzeit*, p. 163, quoting from a report of 16 October 1807.

55. *Memoirs of Prince Metternich*, vol. 2, p. 210, from a report to Stadion of 23 June 1808.

56. M. Bozenhart, *Metternichs Pariser Botschafterzeit*, p. 110.

57. Émile Dard, *Napoleon and Talleyrand* (London, 1937), p. 102.

58. *Memoirs of the Prince de Talleyrand*, vol. I, p. 228. 'Those conditions were harsh indeed, and the treaty made with Count von Haugwitz made it impossible for me to mitigate them in any other clauses than those relative to the indemnity paid to France.'

59. *Memoirs of the Prince de Talleyrand*, vol. I, p. 308, pp. 328–9, p. 340.

60. *Memoirs of Prince Metternich*, vol. 2, p. 298, ft. from his memorandum on the eventuality of war with France, dated Vienna, 4 Dec. 1808. The translation in Dard, *Napoleon and Talleyrand*, p. 184 is slightly different: 'The Rhine, the Alps, the Pyrenees are the conquests of the French people and the Emperor is responsible for the remainder. France does not want them.'
61. See M. Botzenhart, *Metternichs Pariser Botschafterzeit*, pp. 160–75.
62. Ibid., p. 206, ft. 206. 'The feeble remains of Prussia itself are destined to be eliminated from the list of powers.'
63. Ibid., p. 186.
64. *Memoirs of Prince Metternich*, vol. II, pp. 181–2, from a report to Stadion, dated 18 January 1808.
65. For Vienna's wariness, see Manfred Botzenhart, *Metternichs Pariser Botschafterzeit*, p. 223 and pp. 55–257.
66. Ibid., pp. 212–14.
67. Ibid., p. 214.
68. 'Your reports are . . . like gold and are here received as gold. For the first time I have some hope that people know what they must know and that they want what they must want.' Stadion to Metternich, 11 April, 1808. Ibid., p. 218.
69. *Memoirs of Prince Metternich*, vol. 2, p. 221, report to Stadion of 1 July 1808.
70. M. Bozenhart, *Metternichs Pariser Botschafterzeit*, p. 218.
71. Ibid., p. 237.
72. *Memoirs of Prince Metternich*, vol. II, pp. 228–34, reports to Stadion of 26 July and both of 2 August 1808.
73. M. Botzenhart, *Metternichs Pariser Botschafterzeit*, p. 243.
74. Ibid., pp. 246–7 and p. 254.
75. Ibid., p. 249.
76. Paul W. Schroeder, *The Transformation of European Politics, 1783–1848* (Oxford, 1994), p. 354 and p. 355.
77. For a review of the historiography, see M. Bozenhart, *Metternichs Pariser Botschafterzeit*, pp. 263–4. Metternich's support of the war of 1809, for example, was one of the few things on which Srbik and Bibl ever agreed.
78. E. E. Kraehe suggests that Metternich acted like all the other German princes who had lost lands through the establishment of the Confederation of the Rhine (Ochsenhausen had been incorporated into Württemberg). Relying on the evidence of the Archduke Charles, he states (*Metternich's German Policy*, vol. 1, p. 78) that 'All in all, it would be fair to conclude that, as often before, Metternich, though perhaps less doctrinaire and sentimental than other German refugees, was nonetheless still one of them, full of a *Reichsgraf*'s fervor for freeing Germany.' On p. 65 and again on p. 321, Kraehe states that, like Stadion, Stein, Kleist and Arndt, 'he threw himself into' a 'people's war' – 'a war replete with a mass army, national appeals, and incendiary propaganda' (p. 321). Metternich had concluded from the Spanish example that 'Public opinion is the most

powerful of all means; like religion it penetrates *the* most hidden recesses where administrative measures have no influence' (p. 65). This a quote from *The Memoirs of Prince Metternich*, vol. II, p. 226. Kraehe fails to mention, however, that Metternich is complaining about how the press feeds false rumours to the public and that the quote is from a memo to Stadion of 23 June 1808 on *The Necessity of a Censorship of the Press!*

79. Manfred Bozenhart, *Metternichs Pariser Botschafterzeit*, p. 283. He concludes that Metternich found the war party so strong that he could no longer oppose it. So he assumed the case for war rather than originate it in any way.

80. Included in the *Memoirs of Prince Metternich*, vol. II, pp. 289–300. It included the passage (p. 299): 'We have, therefore, arrived at a period when allies seem to offer themselves to us even in the interior of this Empire. These allies are not vile and low *intriguants*; the men who may represent the nation claim our support; this support is our cause itself, our cause wholly and that of posterity.' He then went on to defend Talleyrand and his associates. But although Metternich, as ambassador to Napoleon, always overestimated the amount of domestic opposition to his rule, he did not use this memorandum to positively advocate war – indeed he warned that 'one false step on our part might stultify at one stroke, the good intentions of some of the heads of administration in France, one tergiversation would take away all their confidence' (p. 300).

81. The second memorandum is not printed in Metternich's memoirs. But in it he advised that Russia would probably remain neutral. However, he did stress the advice of Alexander's recent envoy to Paris, Count Romanzov, namely: 'Undertake nothing – you would place Russia in the gravest difficulty.' That was the basic tone of all Romanzov's statements on Austro–Russian relations. See Manfred Bozenhart, *Metternichs Pariser Botschafterzeit*, pp. 279–80.

82. Included in the *Memoirs of Prince Metternich*, vol. II, pp. 301–8. This was based on the assumption that given his Spanish commitments, Napoleon would only have 206,000 troops to use against Austria and that almost half would be raw recruits from Germany. So Austria at first had a fighting chance. But he also stressed (p. 306) that: 'Calculations on military operations are so little in my line that I make them only with great reserve.'

83. *Memoirs of Prince Metternich*, vol. II, p. 283. Talleyrand was 'pre-eminently a politician and as a politician, a man of systems'. The same report to Stadion of 24 September 1808, however, included the warning: 'Men like M. de Talleyrand are like sharp-edged instruments, with which it is dangerous to play; but for great wounds great remedies are necessary; and he who has to treat them ought not to be afraid to use the instrument that cuts best.'

84. Manfred Botzenhart, *Metternichs Pariser Botschafterzeit*, p. 279.

85. Ibid., p. 289, ft. 87.

86. Ibid., p. 290. E. Dard, *Napoleon and Talleyrand*, pp. 203–8, provided the same evidence in 1937, although Botzenhart does not say so.

87. Ibid., ft. 91, again with no reference to Dard, who only gets a passing one on p. 291 quoting his view that 'From 1809 on, Talleyrand only acted according to his understanding with Metternich'.

88. E. Dard, *Napoleon and Talleyrand*, p. 208.

89. Ibid., pp. 230–1.

90. Ibid., pp. 231–2.

91. Ibid., p. 232 and p. 323 ft.

92. Ibid., p. 209.

93. *Memoirs of Prince Metternich*, vol. I, p. 136. Napoleon said: '. . . you must either unite with France or you must side with Russia, and in the latter case you would remain neutral. The course last named would lead you to nothing . . . you will get small thanks . . . and small profit from such a course.'

94. Ibid.

95. Ibid., pp. 140–2. See also vol. II, pp. 474–519.

96. *Memoirs of Prince Metternich*, vol. I, p. 150.

97. Ibid., p. 154.

98. For an excellent account of the diplomacy leading up to and including the Congress of Vienna, see Douglas Dakin, 'The Congress of Vienna, 1814–1815, and Its Antecedents', in Alan Sked (ed.), *Europe's Balance of Power, 1815–1848* (London, 1979), pp. 14–33.

99. *Memoirs of Prince Metternich*, vol. I, p. 186.

100. Ibid.

101. Ibid., p. 192.

102. Ibid., vol. II, p. 546.

103. Ibid.

104. Capefigue, *The Diplomatists of Europe*, p. 25.

105. Ibid.

106. J. Holland Rose, 'Austria and the Downfall of Napoleon', in *Napoleonic Studies*, pp. 243–73, p. 245, ft. 1.

107. Ibid., p. 270.

108. Dard, *Napoleon and Talleyrand*, p. 301.

109. The problem was Napoleon. If he had been killed there might well have been a regency under Marie Louise. And according to Coulaincourt, Napoleon did try to commit suicide. However, with him alive there could be little question of a regency. In the end he made sure that there was not one by ordering Joseph, his brother, to keep Marie Louise and the King of Rome out of the hands of Talleyrand when the allies were about to enter Paris. Talleyrand wrote to the Duchess of Courland on 17 March 1814: 'if the Emperor were killed . . . the King of Rome would come to the throne and his mother would be regent.' On 18 March, Metternich wrote to

Coulaincourt: 'Austria is in favour of a dynasty so closely related to her own.' But so long as Napoleon was alive, such schemes were doomed. Napoleon would always be around to cause trouble for his son. 'Why a regency?', he asked Fleury de Chamboulon at Elba, 'Am I dead?' See Dard, *Napoleon and Talleyrand*, pp. 299–313.

110. *Memoirs of Prince Metternich*, vol. I, pp. 227–30.

111. It should not be thought that Talleyrand now took control of the conference as some historians believe. See *inter alia* Harold C. Nicolson, *The Congress of Vienna* (New York, 1946), Duff Cooper, *Talleyrand* (New York, 1932), Crane Brinton, *The Lives of Talleyrand* (New York, 1936), and Guglielmo Ferrero, *The Reconstruction of Europe* (New York, 1941). Henry Kissinger in his interesting article on 'The Congress of Vienna: A Reappraisal' in *World Politics*, vol. 8, no. 2, January 1956, pp. 264–80, p. 267 talks of the 'myth about Talleyrand's role at the Congress of Vienna, of the diabolical wit who appeared on the scene and broke up a coalition of hostile powers, who then regrouped them into a pattern to his liking by invoking the magic word "legitimacy" and from outcast emerged as the arbiter of Europe.' In a footnote on the same page, he then says:

> It is a legend spread by those who confuse results and causes and by professional diplomats wont to ascribe to mere negotiating skill what is possible only through the exploitation of more deep-seated factors. It has gained currency because Talleyrand, whose monarch had not come to Vienna, was obliged to write voluminous reports, and in order to cement his shaky domestic position, the former Foreign Minister of Napoleon tended to emphasise his indispensability.

All of this is absolutely true. Talleyrand for a start had been instructed to back the claims of the King of Saxony in the cause of legitimacy since the start of the conference; he could hardly now back Prussia. Besides if war broke out, revolution would break out also and the Bourbons would be expelled (exactly what happened during the Hundred Days). Castlereagh's problem was that if war broke out while the allied armies were still in France, some sort of agreement was needed with the French concerning the movements of troops. Besides, given Talleyrand's record, he could simply be blackmailed if necessary.

112. D. Dakin, 'The Congress of Vienna', p. 31.

113. A. Sked, *Europe's Balance of Power*, p. 4.

114. D. Dakin, 'The Congress of Vienna', p. 32.

115. Arthur Hassall, *Viscount Caltlereagh* (London, 1908), p. 184.

116. See his memoir on the Congress of Vienna, reprinted in *Memoirs of Prince Metternich*, vol. II, pp. 553–86.

117. Jacques Droz, *Europe between Revolutions, 1815–1848* (London and Glasgow, 1967), p. 216.

118. P. Schroeder, *The Transformation of European Politics*. For the general argument regarding Schroeder, see below.

119. Paul Schroeder, *The Transformation of European Politics*. 'Did the Vienna System rest on a Balance of Power?', *American Historical Review* (June 1992), pp. 683–706; 'Balance of Power and Political Equilibrium: A Response', *The International History Review*, XVI, 4 (November 1994), pp. 661–880. (A full list of Schroeder's works is to be found on pp. 755–7); 'The 19th-Century International System: Changes in the Structure', *World Politics*, vol. XXXIX (Oct. 1986), pp. 1–26.

120. Author's emphasis. Schroeder's point is that the European state system was fundamentally changed by the Congress of Vienna.

121. Schroeder, *Did the Vienna System etc.*, p. 684. Cf. p. 691, footnote 24.

122. Schroeder, 'Did the Vienna System?', p. 687.

123. Ibid., p. 692.

124. Ibid., p. 695.

125. Ibid.

126. Ibid.

127. Ibid., p. 698.

128. Ibid., p. 696.

129. Ibid., p. 701.

130. Schroeder, *The 19th-Century International System*, p. 2. Author's emphasis. Cf. note 121 above.

131. Schroeder, *The 19th-Century International System*, p. 17.

132. Schroeder, 'Did the Vienna System?', p. 695.

133. Ibid., p. 693.

134. H. M. Scott, 'Paul W. Schroeder's International System: The View from Vienna', *The International History Review*, 4, XVI (Nov. 1994), pp. 661–80.

135. Charles Ingrao, 'Paul W. Schroeder's Balance of Power: Stability or Anarchy?', *The International History Review*, XVI, 4 (Nov. 1994), pp. 681–700.

136. Ibid., p. 698.

137. Enno E. Kraehe, 'A Bipolar Balance of Power', *American History Review* (June 1992), pp. 707–15.

138. Schroeder, 'Did the Vienna Settlement?', pp. 699–700.

139. Quoted in Roger Bullen, *Palmerston, Guizot, and the Collapse of the Entente Cordiale* (London, 1974), p. 53.

140. Bullen, op. cit., p. 36, ft. 51.

141. Bullen, op. cit., p. 36.

142. Bullen, op. cit., p. 40.

143. Quoted in Alan Sked, *Europe's Balance of Power*, p. 6.

144. (London, 1989). Schroeder seems to start to go wrong regarding sub-hegemonies when in *The Transformation of European Politics*, he discusses the Treaty of Ried between Austria and Bavaria. On p. 482 he insists that this 'did not and could not' rest on a balance of power since 'balance-of power

considerations would have led Bavaria, as it always had, to seek allies *against* Austria . . .'. Yet on p. 480 he has just related how Bavaria had to be 'dragged into the treaty' because both Napoleon and Alexander had rejected the King of Bavaria's pleas for military aid! Evidence on one page doesn't seem to count on the next.

145. Schroeder, 'Balance of Power and Political Equilibrium: A Response', p. 748.
146. M. S. Anderson, *The Rise of Modern Diplomacy 1450–1919* (London, 1993), p. 183.
147. For all his talk of Russian hegemonic status in the nineteenth century, there is a revealing passage on p. 553 of Schroeder's *Transformation of European Politics*, where he writes of Russian military intervention against Napoleon in 1815: 'Russia's slow mobilization and financial weakness (the minister of finance warned Nesselrode that without British subsidies on a scale far greater than 1814 the war would bankrupt Russia) and Alexander's fear of another European alliance against Russia enabled the British to ignore his rashness and presumption and turn his ideals to good purpose.'
148. For the best discussion of the balance of power in theory and practice, see Anderson, *The Rise of Modern Diplomacy*, Chapter 4.
149. Quoted in Jeremy Black, *The Rise of the European Powers, 1679–1793* (London, 1990), p. 162.
150. Ibid., p. 152.
151. Kissinger, Diplomacy, p. 119.
152. Keith Wilson (ed.), *British Foreign Secretaries and Foreign Policy From Crimean War to First World War* (London, 1987), p. 18.
153. Wilson, Ibid., p. 11.
154. Wilson, Ibid., p. 14.
155. Ibid.
156. Ibid.
157. Ibid.
158. Ibid., p. 5.
159. Quoted in Alan Sked, 'Great Britain and the German Question', in A. M. Birke and M.-L. Recker (eds), *Das gestorte Gleichgewicht: Deutschland als Problem britischer Sicherheit im neunzehnsten und zwanzigsten Jahrhundert* (Munich, 1990), p. 54.

Notes to Chapter 3: Was Metternich Europe's Leading Statesman in the Period 1815–1848?

1. F. R. Bridge, *The Habsburg Monarchy Among the Great Powers, 1815–1918* (Oxford, 1990), pp. 26–41.
2. See Enno E. Kraehe, *Metternich's German Policy*, vol. II: *The Congress of Vienna, 1814–1815* (Princeton, 1983), pp. 6–7, for Austria's rejection of a

regency for Francis's grandson. On doubts about Austria's gains at Vienna generally, see Helmut Rumpler, *Österreichische Geschichte, 1804–1914, Eine Chance für Mitteleuropa, Bürgerliche Emanzipation und Staatsverfall in der Habsburgermonarchie* (Vienna, 1997), p. 137.

3. Quoted by R. F. Bridge, *The Great Powers and the European State System 1814–1914* (Harlow, 2005), p. 29.

4. As underlined by Field Marshal Radetzky in January 1828. See his *Militärische Betrachtung der Lage Oesterreichs* (Military Observations on the Position of Austria) in his *Denkschriften militärisch-politischen Inhalts aus dem handschriftlichen Nachlaß des k. k. Österreichischen Feldmarschalls Grafen Radetzky* (Stuttgart and Augsburg), 1858, pp. 423–51. Radetzky, however, thought that Prussia was in an even weaker position regarding Russia and therefore 'inevitably' needed Austrian support. The essay is most famous, however, for its consideration of 'the wise and great principle' of granting constitutions, which he foresaw as happening everywhere in Europe within thirty years. However, according to Radetzky, if Prussia became a constitutional state, then the danger to Austria would increase. Russia, on the other hand, despite her great potential dangers to Austria if she became a foe, would never, even in a hundred years, be in a position to grant a constitution to her backward subjects. Radetzky ended by considering the advantages of a citizens' army over a standing one. The former would be needed under a constitutional regime, since constitutional governments would be reluctant to spend money on defence. In his 1829 report from Buda, *Ueber den Werth der österreichischen Kavallerie und einige Mitteln ihn zu heben* (On the Value of Austria's Cavalry and Some Means to Increase It), pp. 452–79, p. 453, Radetzky stated: 'This state is making no progress in the development and perfection of its armed forces; little attention is paid to improvements in other states; and so it remains behind them in all respects.' Radetzky was always critical of Austria's military establishment and after 1830 was given the task of reforming the army in Italy, where he triumphed in 1848–9. See Alan Sked, *The Survival of the Habsburg Empire. Radetzky, the Imperial Army and the Class War, 1848–49* (London and New York, 1979).

5. Quoted in W. E. Mosse, *The European Powers and the German Question, 1848–71* (New York, 1979), p. 14.

6. Most of these points will be dealt with in detail below. For this one, see J. Angelow, *Von Wien nach Königgrätz: Die Sicherheitspolitik des Deutschen Bundes im europäischen Gleichgewicht (1815–1866)* (Munich 1996), pp. 130–1 and pp. 335–44. The latter pages reproduce the rather bitter report of 1831 of Major-General von Roeder on his 1831 trip to Vienna to consult on military cooperation between Austria, Prussia and other members of the German Confederation.

7. Quoted in Constantin de Grunwald, *Trois Siècles de Diplomatie Russe* (Paris, 1945), p. 191, ft. 1.

8.   Quoted in Jacques Droz, *Europe Between Revolutions, 1815–1848* (London and Glasgow, 1967), p. 223.

9.   Quoted in Herbert C. F. Bell, *Lord Palmerston*, 3 vols (London, 1936), vol. 1, p. 398.

10. For France during this period, see Roger Bullen, 'France and Europe, 1815–48. The Problems of Defeat and Recovery' in Alan Sked (ed.), *Europe's Balance of Power, 1815–1848* (London and Basingstoke, 1979), pp. 122–44.

11. For these and other statistics, see M. S. Anderson, *The Ascendancy of Europe, Aspects of European History, 1815–1914* (London, 1972), p. 12.

12. Quoted in W. Bruce Lincoln, *Nicholas I: Emperor and Autocrat of All The Russias* (London, 1978), p. 215.

13. Metternich to Hügel, 22 Oct. 1833, *Memoirs of Prince Metternich*, 5 vols (London, 1879–82), vol. 5. pp. 370–1.

14. H. Contamine, *Diplomatie et Diplomates sous la Restauration 1814–1830* (Paris, 1970), p. 83.

15. K. Hammer, *Die französische Diplomatie der Restauration und Deutschland* (Stuttgart, 1963), pp. 147–8.

16. See V. J. Puryear, *France and the Levant* (Hamdon Connecticut, 1968), pp. 76–9. Roger Bullen, *France and Europe, 1815–48*, p. 136, comments: 'It was certainly Polignac's intention to remove the losses of defeat at one stroke. He thought that if the Russians were prepared to accept his plan the two powers could impose it on the rest of Europe, if necessary by force. War was the logical outcome of his plan. In fact the Russians regarded the proposals as entirely unrealistic and did not give them the slightest encouragement. Consequently they came to nothing.'

17. Philip Mansel, *Paris between the Empires* (London, 2001), p. 383.

18. Philip Mansel, 'Paris, Court City of the Nineteenth Century', *The Court Historian*, vol. 11, no. 1 (July, 2006), 'Courts and Capitals, 1815–1914', pp. 15–28, p. 27.

19. R. Marquant, *Thiers et le Baron de Cotta* (Paris, 1959), p. 501.

20. J. P. B. Bury and R. P. Tombs, *Thiers, 1797–1877: A Political Life* (London, 1986), p. 71.

21. Ibid.

22. Mack Walker (ed.), *Metternich's Europe* (New York, 1968), p. 80.

23. As reported by Princess Lieven to General Benkendorf in October 1829. See L. G. Robinson (ed.), *Letters to Dorothea, Princess Lieven, during Her Residence in London, 1812–1834* (London, 1902), p. 199.

24. A. H. Everett, *Europe: or a General Survey of the Present Situation of the Principal Powers* (London, 1822), p. 360. On p. 350 he wrote that the proceedings of the congresses of Troppau and Laibach in 1820–21 amounted to a claim by Russia to 'universal supremacy'.

25. Lincoln, *Nicholas I*, p. 135.

26. The phrase comes from the *Eclectic Review*, new series, vol. 4, 1815, p. 375. According to Anderson, *The Ascendancy of Europe*, p. 6, who quotes it, the

fear of Russia after 1815 was due to her general underestimation during the French revolutionary wars. See M. S. Anderson, *Britain's Discovery of Russia, 1553–1815* (London, 1958), pp. 207ff.

27. For statistics, see Anderson, *The Ascendancy of Europe*, p. 7.

28. For the following quotes see, E. L. Woodward, *War and Peace in Europe 1815–1870 and other essays* (London, 1963), p. 11.

29. For the causes of this famous regimental mutiny, see Joseph L. Wieczynski, 'The Mutiny of the Semenovsky Regiment in 1820', in *Russian Review*, vol. 29, no. 2 (April 1970), pp. 167–80.

30. Woodward, *War and Peace*, p. 11, ft. 1.

31. Lincoln, *Nicholas I*, p. 116.

32. Ibid.

33. Count Zichy to Metternich, 24 April, 1848 in *Memoirs of Prince Metternich*, vol. IV, p. 439.

34. See Matthew Anderson, 'Russia and the Eastern Question, 1821–1841', in Sked, E*urope's Balance of Power*, pp. 79–97, p. 81.

35. Lincoln, *Nicholas I*, p. 126.

36. Constantin de Grunwald, *Tsar Nicholas I* (London, 1954), p. 91.

37. For Krasinsky's report, Russian military statistics and arrangements with Austria, the fear of an Austrian war, and Russia's disillusionment with her position in Poland, see Gernot Seide, *Regierungspolitik und öffentliche Meinung im Kaisertum Österreich anläßlich der polnischen Novemberrevolution (1830–1831)* (Wiesbaden, 1971), p. 26, p. 37, p. 38, pp. 41–42, p. 60 and p. 63.

38. Metternich to Apponyi, 25 January 1832, *Memoirs of Prince Metternich*, vol. V, p. 180.

39. Metternich to Apponyi, 14 May 1832, *Memoirs of Prince Metternich*, vol. V, p. 189.

40. Sir Charles Webster, 'Palmerston, Metternich and the Eastern Question, 1830–1841', in Sir Charles Webster, *The Art and Practice of Diplomacy* (London, 1961), pp. 152–80.

41. Aberdeen was even more explicit. Writing to Metternich on 6 May 1849, he declared: 'We must hope that since the entrance of a Russian force was indispensable, that it will act with vigour and that we shall see a campaign in Hungary made and finished *à la Radetzky*.' British Library, Add MS 43128, Aberdeen Papers, pp. 280–300.

42. For Palmerston's speech of 21 July 1848 in the House of Commons, see *Hansard*, 3rd series, CVII, 808–15.

43. For the text, see Michael Hurst (ed.), *Key Treaties of the Great Powers, 1814–1914*, vol. I (1814–1870) (London, 1972), pp. 121–4.

44. G. de Bertier de Sauvigny, *Metternich et la France après Le Congrès de Vienne*, 3 vols (Paris, 1968–71), vol. 2:, *L'époque des Grands Congrès* (Paris, 1970), pp. 194–5.

45. *Memoirs of Prince Metternich*, vol. 3. p. 144.

46. Ibid., vol. 3, pp. 251–2.
47. Ibid., vol. 3, p. 324 (Kissinger's translation is used here).
48. Henry Kissinger, *A World Restored. Metternich, Castlereagh and the Problem of Peace 1812–1822* (London, 2000), p. 243.
49. For most of the text, see Kenneth Bourne, *The Foreign Policy of Victorian England, 1830–1902* (Oxford, 1970), pp. 198–207.
50. Bertier de Sauvigny, *Metternich et La France*, vol. 2, p. 322.
51. Capodistrias was opposed to revolution and deplored the fact that, as he put it to Richelieu, 'the pernicious influence of these enemies of society has penetrated everywhere and everywhere propagates itself with fatal activity.' But the solution to the problem, he believed, lay with constitutions. 'The Emperor of Austria has always professed the principles of absolute monarchy. Russia, on the other hand, has looked to the proper mixture of liberty and constitutional rights, that affords a more enlarged and better basis of government.' Lebzeltern, the Austrian ambassador to Russia, reported to Metternich his 'fear of the pleasure that Capodistrias finds in working on constitutions'. See Patricia Kennedy Grimsted, 'Capodistrias and a "New Order" for Restoration Europe: The "Liberal Ideas" of a Russian Foreign Minister, 1814–1822' in *The Journal of Modern History*, vol. 40. no. 2 (June, 1968), pp. 166–92, p. 180 and p. 183.
52. Bertier de Sauvigny, *Metternich et La France*, vol. 2, p. 380.
53. Ibid., p. 389.
54. For the text, see Walker, *Metternich' s Europe*, pp. 127–9.
55. Bertier de Sauvigny, *Metternich et la France*, vol. 2, pp. 437–9. The French were very upset at Metternich's unwillingness to treat them as equals or to allow their Charter any role. On 21 August 1820, Metternich had written to Richelieu:

> The treaties of 1814 and 1815 are the immutable basis of the policy of the five great courts. They are united in upholding them, they have decided to alter them in no respect, and they will not allow others to do so. They will tell the world in clear and simple terms that such is their decision and their unchanging desire. They will announce this to console the good, sustain the feeble and challenge the wicked.

Yet during the congress at Laibach, Richelieu was writing to Caraman, one of the two French observers there:

> Do people think, without danger to Europe, that France can remain in a secondary and passive state, in a condition that would humiliate her and from which she would attempt to extract herself either by agreement or by force? The allies stated in 1815 that it was necessary for France to be strong, powerful and respected (*considerée*). Are the means

really being employed to do this when they want to annul all French influence? I hope that in spite of them and for their own good, they shall not succeed in this endeavour.

See G. de Bertier de Sauvigny, *France and the European Alliance, 1816–1821: The Private Correspondence between Metternich and Richelieu* (Notre Dame, 1958), p. 105 and p. 114.

56. Quoted in Sir Charles Petrie, *Diplomatic History, 1713–1933* (London, 1948), p. 132.
57. Contamine, *Diplomatie et diplomates*, p. 82.
58. See his *Metternich's Diplomacy at its Zenith: Austria at the Congresses of Troppau, Laibach and Verona* (Austin, 1962).
59. See Sir Charles Webster, *The Foreign Policy of Palmerston. Britain, the Liberal Movement and the Eastern Question*, 2 vols (London, 1969), vol. 1, p. 224.
60. Roy F. Bridge, 'Allied Diplomacy in Peacetime: the Failure of the "Congress System", 1818–23' in Alan Sked, *Europe's Balance of Power*, pp. 34–53 and 45–6.
61. On the Congress System, the best account remains R. F. Bridge, *Allied Diplomacy in Peacetime etc* But see, too, Schroeder's *Metternich's Diplomacy at its Zenith* and Irby C. Nichols, *The European Pentarchy and the Congress of Verona* (The Hague, 1971).
62. See Hansard, for 12 December 1826, new series, XVI, 367–98.
63. Metternich to Neumann, Vienna, 14 June 1824,Vienna, Haus-Hof- und-Staatsarchiv (HHSA), *Weisungen nach England*, 224.
64. Metternich to Vincent, Vienna, 18 March 1824, HHSA, *Weisungen nach Frankreich*, 360.
65. Ibid.
66. Metternich to Vincent, Vienna, 12 May, 1824, HHSA, *Weisungen nach Frankreich*, 360.
67. For a very full discussion of Metternich's policy towards the Spanish colonies and Brazil, see William Spence Robertson, 'Metternich's Attitudes Towards Revolutions in Latin America', *The Hispanic American Historical Review*, vol. 21, no. 4, November, 1941, pp. 538–58.
68. Canning to Bagot, no. 20, 24 April 1824, in Sir Charles Webster (ed.), 'Britain and the Independence of Latin America, 1812–1830', *A Selection of Documents from the Foreign Office Archives*, 2 vols (London, 1938), vol. 2, p. 300.
69. The significance of Canning's letter, quoted in footnote 68, for his place in British foreign policy and Canning's position between Liverpool, on the one hand, and Wellington on the other has been clarified in exemplary fashion by the outstanding young Japanese scholar, Norihito Yamada. See his unpublished London University doctoral dissertation of 2004, entitled *George Canning and the Concert of Europe, September, 1822–July, 1824*.

70. The best account is Roger Bullen, 'The Great Powers and the Iberian Peninsula, 1815–1848' in Alan Sked (ed.), *Europe's Balance of Power etc.*, pp. 54–78. But see his other articles, which are footnoted there.

71. Bullen, The Great Powers and the Iberian Peninsula, p. 77 and p. 78.

72. See F. R. Bridge, *The Habsburg Monarchy*, Chapter 2, part one, 'The Metternich Era, 1815–1848'.

73. Viktor Bibl, *Metternich: Der Dämon Österreichs* (Leipzig and Vienna, 1936), p. 208.

74. British Archives, PRO. Foreign Office, FO 78/110, Strangford to Canning, no. 162, 26 November 1822. Quoted in Yamada, *George Canning and the Concert*, p. 255.

75. Ibid.

76. Liverpool to Hastings, 11 April, 1824, Liverpool Papers, British Library, Add MSS38298, quoted by Yamada, *George Canning and the Concert etc.*, p. 300.

77. G. de Bertier de Sauvigny, *Metternich and His Times* (London, 1962), p. 251.

78. Ibid., p. 251.

79. Ibid.

80. Matthew Anderson, *Russia and the Eastern Question*, p. 82.

81. *Memoirs of Prince Metternich*, vol. IV, Zichy to Metternich, 12 April 1828, p. 479. Many authorities seem to believe that the phrase was Metternich's own. See, for example, G. de Bertier de Sauvigny in his *Metternich* (Paris, 1986), p. 407, seems to imply this.

82. K. Bourne, *The Foreign Policy of Victorian England*, p. 23.

83. Matthew Anderson, *Russia and the Eastern Question*, p. 85.

84. Hansard, new series, XXII, p. 142.

85. Ibid.

86. Ibid., p. 147.

87. Matthew Anderson, *Russia and the Eastern Question*, p. 86.

88. Ibid., pp. 86–7. But see also H. W. V. Temperley, *England and the Near East: The Crimea* (London, 1964), pp. 57–8. On p. 57 he quotes Nesselrode, who sat on the committee:

> Is the preservation of the Ottoman government hurtful or useful to Russia? . . . The idea of hunting the Turks out of Europe and re-establishing the worship of the true God in St Sophia is certainly very fine and, if realised, would make us all live in history. But what will Russia gain by it? Glory undoubtedly, but at the same time she would lose all the real advantages offered by being a neighbour to a state weakened by a series of wars, and [she would have] inevitable struggles with the chief powers of Europe.

Hence the recommendation in favour of the status quo.

89. Matthew Anderson, *Russia and the Eastern Question*, p. 89.

90. Bertier de Suvigny, *Metternich*, p. 409.
91. Friedrich Engel-Janosi, 'Österreich und die Anfänge des Königreichs Griechenland', in *Geschichte auf dem Ballhausplatz: Essays zur österreichischen Außenpolitik 1830–1945* (Graz, 1963), pp. 29–64, p. 35.
92. Ibid., pp. 32, 44 and 33.
93. Ibid., pp. 44–5.
94. Lincoln, *Nicholas I*, p. 131.
95. See Angelow, *Von Wien nach Königgrätz*, pp. 87–109.
96. The 'blemish on his life' was what Metternich called it according to Srbik. See his *Metternich*, p. 47.
97. For a very useful overview of events in Germany during the Metternich period, although one that is perhaps too generous to liberal influences there and too hard on Metternich, see Brendan Simms, *The Struggle for Mastery in Germany, 1779–1850* (Basingstoke, 1998).
98. See Alan Sked, *The Decline and Fall of the Habsburg Empire, 1815–1918*, 2nd enlarged edition (London and New York, 2001), pp. 160–1.
99. F. Engel-Janosi, *Geschichte auf dem Ballhausplatz*, pp. 66–7.
100. F. R. Bridge, *The Great Powers*, p. 91.
101. For Metternich's efforts to introduce reform into the Papal States, see the works of Alan J. Reinerman. These include *Austria and the Papacy in the Age of Metternich*. vol. 1: *Between Conflict and Cooperation, 1809–1830* (Washington, DC) 1979 and vol. 2, *Revolution and Reaction, 1830–1838* (Washington, DC, 1989), as well as several articles. Volume 2 of *Austria and the Papacy* includes an account of how Metternich recommended 'a modern, efficient administration responsive to popular needs, humane and equitable laws, a sound financial system, a paternalistic welfare policy for the poor, and government encouragement of economic development' (p. 36). Metternich, for example, first tried to reform the Papacy after 1831 by using the conference of ambassadors installed there and the reforms drawn up by the (protestant!) Prussian one. When these were rebuffed by the Cardinals and the Roman ruling class, he sent an experienced administrator from Lombardy-Venetia, Giuseppi Mari Sebregondi, to advise the Pope. Sebregondi very nearly succeeded, while there, but left no cadre of reformers behind him when he left in 1833. In the end, to reform the Papal States was 'to make dead men walk' as Reinerman heads Chapter 4 of his book. For Metternich's plans for an Italian League, see Karl Großmann, 'Metternichs Plan eines italienishen Bundes', *Historische Blätter*, vol. 4 (1931) pp. 37–76.
102. See 82 above.
103. G. Seide, *Regierungspolitik etc.*, p. 63. For Polish attempts to win over Austria, see pp. 45–57.
104. *Memoirs of Prince Metternich*, vol. V, pp. 107–8.
105. Ibid., pp. 17–19.
106. G. Seide, *Regierungspolitik*, p. 63.

107.   Ibid. Most probably Nicholas was jealous of Metternich, although perhaps he knew that Metternich had allowed the Turks secretly to import weapons from Austria during the 1828–9 war or that in 1830 he had allowed Galicians to cross over to Russian Poland to support Polish independence rather than cause trouble in Galicia. See p. 41 and p. 35.

108.   This was exactly what Clam-Martinitz was told by Metternich to tell the Polish envoy, namely that 'Austria did not fear Russia since the Turkish war had proved that the Russian colossus was not so dangerous as it appeared.' G. Seide, *Regierungspolitik*, p. 47.

109.   H. W. V. Temperley, *England and the Near East*, p. 64, obviously does not believe this. However, he cannot give any alternative explanation.

110.   For cabinet divisions in London and Palmerston's confession regarding Metternich, see Sir Charles Webster, *The Foreign Policy of Palmerston,* vol. 1, pp. 281–4.

111.   H. W. V. Temperley, *England and the Near East*, p. 68.

112.   Quoted in Philip E. Mosely, *Russian Diplomacy and the Opening of the Eastern Question in 1838 and 1839* (Harvard, 1934), p. 20.

113.   Ibid., p. 26.

114.   Princess Melanie's Diary, 10 Sept., 1833, *Memoirs of Prince Metternich*, vol. 5, p. 307.

115.   Matthew Anderson, *Russia and the Eastern Question*, p. 92.

116.   Lincoln, *Nicholas I*, pp. 209–10.

117.   For one such lurid assurance by Metternich, see Comte de Ste. Aulaire, *Souvenirs* (Paris, 1926), p. 60. Metternich told the French ambassador in Vienna: 'It would be better for the Empire of Austria to face the risk of a war of extermination rather than to see Russia aggrandised by a single village at the expense of the Turkish Empire.' The ambassador thought Austria more likely to allow Russia to do whatever she wanted to 'up to and including the occupation of Constantinople'. Ibid., p. 63.

118.   See Sir Henry Lytton Bulwer, *The Life of Henry John Temple, Viscount Palmerston with Selections from his Diaries and Correspondence*, 3 vols (London, 1878–1880), vol. 2, pp. 270–1.

119.   Quoted in Mosely, *Russian Diplomacy*, p. 76.

120.   For Austria's part in the capture of Acre and the campaign in 1840, see Lawrence Sondhaus, *The Habsburg Empire and the Sea, Austrian Naval Policy, 1797–1866* (West Lafayette, 1989), pp. 102–5.

121.   Mosely, *Russian Diplomacy*, p. 85.

122.   For Palmerston's reactions during the crisis, see Sir Henry Lytton Bulwer, *Palmerston*, vol. 2, pp. 324–9.

123.   J. P. T. Bury and R. P. Tombs, *Thiers*, p. 73.

124.   Ibid., p. 76.

125.   M. C. M. Simpson (ed.), *Conversations with M. Thiers and M. Guizot and other Distinguished Persons of the Second Empire by the late Nassau William Senior, Edited by his Daughter*, 2 vols (London, 1878), vol. I, pp. 130–3.

126. Ibid., pp. 131–2.
127. British Library, Add MSS 43,211 (1), Aberdeen Papers, Sir Robert Gordon to Lord Aberdeen, Vienna, 13 December 1842.
128. Ibid.
129. Ibid.
130. Ibid.
131. See note 118 above.
132. J. P. T. Bury and R. P. Tombs, *Thiers*, p. 34.
133. See note 117.
134. See note 117.
135. For its history and details of its breakdown in the 1840s, see Lucille Iremonger, *Lord Aberdeen* (London, 1978), Chapter 12.
136. For a view from the French side, see Guizot's *The Last Days of the Reign of Louis Phillipe* (London, 1867). For a more balanced one, see Roger Bullen, *Palmerston, Guizot and the Collapse of the Entente Cordiale* (London, 1974).
137. Kenneth Bourne, *The Foreign Policy of Victorian England*, p. 62.
138. For differing views as to whether Palmerston deliberately delayed, see Ann G. Imlah, *Britain and Switzerland, 1845–60* (London, 1966) and Roger Bullen, 'Guizot and the Sonderbund Crisis' in the *English Historical Review*, vol. LXXXVI (July 1971), pp. 497–526.
139. See note 9.
140. See Roger Bullen, 'The Great Powers and the Iberian Peninsula', pp. 54–9.
141. Philip E. Mosely, *Russian Diplomacy*, p. 59.
142. Roger Bullen, 'The Great Powers and the Iberian Peninsula', p. 59.
143. Ibid., p. 58.
144. Ibid., p. 57.
145. Mabell, Countess of Airlie, *Lady Palmerston and Her Times*, 2 vols (London, 1922), vol. 1, p. 173.
146. Palmerston on 2 August, 1832, quoted in H. G. V. Temperley, *England and the Near East*, p. 60.
147. Ibid.
148. For the full text, see Lloyd C. Sanders (ed.), *Lord Melbourne's Papers* (London, 1890), pp. 337–40.
149. British Library, Add MSS 51599, Holland House MSS, Palmerston to Lord Holland, 9 April, 1831.
150. Sir Henry Lytton Bulwer, *Palmerston*, vol. 3, p. 195f.
151. Ibid.
152. Evelyn Ashley, *The Life of Henry John Temple, Lord Palmerston: 1846–1865*, 3 vols (London, 1877), vol. I, p. 81.
153. C. F. Bell, *Lord Palmerston*, vol. I, p. 424.
154. Arthur Hassal, *Viscount Castlereagh* (London, 1908), p. 220.
155. J. P. T. Bury and R. P. Tombs, *Thiers*, p. 9.
156. Gavin Burns Henderson, 'The Foreign Policy of Lord Palmerston', in *Crimean War Diplomacy and Other Essays* (Glasgow, 1947), pp. 190–206, p. 191.

157. Ibid., p. 193.
158. Hassal, *Viscount Castlereagh*, pp. 202–3.
159. Ibid., p. 203.
160. See J. P. T. Bury and R. P. Tombs, *Thiers,* p. 42 and p. 88.

Notes to Chapter 4: Did Metternich Plan to Federalise the Empire?

1. Peter Viereck, 'New Views on Metternich', *Review of Politics*, vol. XIII (1951), pp. 211–28, p. 225.

2. Wiesbaden, 1963. Cf. the comments of Enno E. Kraehe in Kraehe (ed.), 'The Metternich Controversy' (New York, 1971), p. 110.

3. A. G. Haas, 'Kaiser Franz, Metternich und die Stellung Illyriens', *Mitteilungen des Österreichischen Staatsarchivs*, XI (1958) 373–98, and 'Metternich und die Slaven', *Gedenkschrift Martin Göhring* (Wiesbaden, 1968), pp. 146–61.

4. Haas, 'Kaiser Franz', p. 397.

5. Professor John Rath, curiously enough, in his book *The Provisional Austrian Régime in Lombardy-Venetia, 1814–1815* (Austin, 1969), has nothing to say about Haas's work, even in passing.

6. In *Revue d'Histoire*, vol. 12 (1965) 72.

7. (Vienna and Munich, 1964); see p. 113.

8. Vol. 36 (1964), 341–2.

9. Alan Sked, 'Metternich and the Federalist Myth', in A. Sked and C. Cook (eds), *Crisis and Controversy: Essays in Honour of A. J. P. Taylor* (London and Basingstoke), 1976, pp. 1–22.

10. For example, Konrad Clewing, 'Staatlichkeit und nationale Identitätsbildung. Dalmatien in Vormärz und Revolution', *Südosteuropäische Arbeiten*, vol. 109 (Munich, 2001), pp. 24–5; and David Laven, *Venice and Venetia under the Habsburgs, 1815–1835* (Oxford, 2002), pp. 60–1.

11. *Memoirs of Prince Metternich*, vol. 2, pp. 519–28.

12. See Chapter 2.

13. *Memoirs of Prince Metternich*, vol. 1, p. 147.

14. Ibid., p. 148.

15. Ibid., pp. 151–2.

16. On Francis, see Walter Consuelo Langsam, 'Emperor Francis II and the Austrian "Jacobins", 1792–1796', *The American Historical Review*, vol. 50, no. 3 (April, 1945), pp. 471–90. See also his *Francis The Good. The Education of an Emperor, 1768–1792* (New York, 1949).

17. Friedrich Walter, *Österreichische Verfassungs-und Verwaltungsgeschichte von 1500–1955: Aus dem Nachlass heraugegeben von Adam Wandruschka* (Vienna, 1972), p. 128.

18. Walter, *Österreichische Verfassungsi-und Verwaltungsgeschichte*, p. 129.

19. Quoted in E. Radvany, *Metternich's Projects for Reform in Austria* (The Hague, 1971), p. 15.
20. Viktor Bibl, *Metternich. Der Dämon Österreichs*, 4th expanded edition (Leipzig and Vienna, 1936), p. 8.
21. Bibl, *Metternich*, p. 356.
22. Radvany, *Metternich's Projects.*, p. 15.
23. Radvany, *Metternich's projects*, p. 136 and p. 14.
24. On Kolowrat, see Elizabeth Herzog's unpublished 1965 doctoral thesis for the University of Vienna, *Graf Franz Anton Kolowrat-Liebsteinsky: Seine politische Tätigkeit in Wien, 1826–1848*.
25. Walter, *Österreichische Verfassungs-und Verwaltungsgeschichte*, p. 137.
26. Herzog, *Graf Franz Anton Kolowrat-Liebsteinsky*, pp. 62–3.
27. Quoted by Hans Leo Mikoletzky in 'Bild und Gegenbild Kaiser Ferdinands I von Österreich. Ein Versuch' in *Bausteine zur Geschichte Österreichs: Archiv für österreichische Geschichte*, vol. 125 (1966), pp. 173–95, p. 178.
28. For the two documents and the version of the crisis over them which is given here see Walter, *Verfassungs-und Verwaltungsgeschichte*, pp. 137–8.
29. For a complete description of the 1836 crisis, see Hanns Schlitter, *Aus Österreichs Vormärz*, 4 vols (Zurich, 1920), vol. IV, *Niederösterreich*, pp. 37–46 and the extremely well-documented and very full footnotes.
30. Radvany, *Metternich's Projects*, p. 110. Walter more or less agreed (see fotnote77).
31. Ibid.
32. For the one desciption of the rivalry, see the important article by Ronald E. Coons, 'Reflections of a Josephinist: Two Addenda to Count Franz Hartig's "Genesis der Revolution in Oesterreich im Jahre 1848"', *Mitteilungen des österreichischen Staatsarchivs*, vol. 86, (1983), pp. 204–36.
33. Ibid. But very important for the position of Francis Charles and his wife are the memoirs of his confessor, which can be found in E. Kovács (ed.), 'Geheime Notizen des Joseph Columbus 1843–1848', *Wiener Beiträge zur Theologie*, 39 (Vienna, 1971). Princess Melanie clearly thought the court was behind it – she wondered why Count Louis Széchenyi had told Princess Felicie Esterházy before 13 March that the Metternichs would be leaving that day. The former, she noted, 'spent all his life at court'. See H. Schlitter, *Niederösterreich*, p. 37.
34. Antonio Schmidt-Brentano, *Die Armee in Österreich: Militär, Staat und Gesellschaft, 1848–1867* (Boppard am Rhein, 1975), p. 106. The figures on military expenditure quoted in the text are also found here.
35. Quoted in Alan Sked, 'Living on One's Wits: J. A. Blackwell's vain attempts to become British Consul in Hungary' in L. Péter and M. Rady (eds), *British-Hungarian Relations since 1848*, SEESS Occasional Papers No. (University College London, 2004), pp. 13–31, p. 19.
36. C. A. Haillot, *Statistique militaire et récherches sur l'orginisation des armées étrangères*, 2 vols (Paris, 1846), vol. 1, p. 12.

37. Viktor Bibl, *Metternich der Dämon Österreichs* (Leipzig and Vienna, 1936), p. 208.
38. Ibid.
39. Bibl., *Metternich*, p. 230.
40. See Alan Sked, *The Survival of the Habsburg Empire: Radetzky, the Imperial Army and the Class War 1848* (London and New York, 1979), Part One.
41. Johann Springer, *Statistik des österreichischen Kaiserstaates*, 3 vols (Vienna, 1840), vol. 2, p. 254.
42. J. H. Blumenthal, 'Vom Wiener Kongress zum Ersten Weltkrieg' in *Unser Heer 300 Jahre österreichisches Soldatentum im Krieg und Frieden* (Vienna, Munich and Zurich, 1963), p. 216.
43. Vienna, *Kriegsarchiv, K. A. CK (Präs.) 1848, no. 475*, Emperor to Hardegg, 27 February 1848.
44. Ibid.

Notes to Chapter 5: Was Metternich's Austria a Police State?

1. Norbert Bachleitner, 'The Politics of the Book Trade in Nineteenth Century', *Austrian History Yearbook*, XXVIII, (1997) pp. 95–111, p. 95.
2. Berthold Sutter, 'Die politische und rechtliche Stellung der Deutschen in Österreich, 1848 bis 1918' in A. Wandruszka und P. Urbanisch (eds), *Die Habsburgermonarchie 1848–1918, Vol. III/I, Die Völker des Reiches* (Vienna, 1980), pp. 154–339, p. 164 and p. 158.
3. Viktor Bibl, *Die Wiener Polizei. Eine kulturhistorische Studie* (Leipzig, Vienna and New York, 1927), p. 274 and p. 276.
4. Georg Franz, *Liberalismus: Die deutschliberale Bewegung in der habsburgischen Monarchie* (Munich, 1955), p. 18.
5. Quoted in J.G. Legge, *Rhyme and Revolution in Germany: A Study in German History, Life, Literature and Character, 1815–1850* (London, 1918), p. 164.
6. Julius Marx, *Die österreichische Zensur im Vormärz* (Vienna, 1959), p. 6. See also his two articles, 'Metternich als Zensor', *Jahrbuch des Vereins für Geschichte der Stadt Wien*, XI (1954) and 'Die Zensur der Kanzlei Metternichs', *Österreichische Zeitschrift für öffentlicher Recht* IV (1951).
7. See Donald E. Emerson, *Metternich and the Political Police: Security and Subversion in the Habsburg Monarchy (1815–1830)* (The Hague, 1968).
8. For example, the historian Matthias Koch's pseudonymous *Oesterreichs innere Politik mit Beziehung auf die Verfassungsfrage* (Stuttgart, 1847) in its discussion of the censorship in Metternich's Austria recalls Joseph II's decree of 1781, which included the words 'criticisms, so long as they are not libels, be they made either by princes or the lowest subject, are not to be forbidden, particularly if the author has his name printed beside them and thereby gives a guarantee for the truth of the matter.'
9. See Friedrich Walter, 'Die Organisierung der staatlichen Polizei unter Josef II', *Mitteilungen des Vereins für Geschichte der Stadt Wien*, vol. VII (1927),

pp. 22–55; also H. Gnau, *Die Zensur unter Joseph II* (Strasbourg and Leipzig, 1911). Emerson, op. cit., Chapter 1, gives a good account of Pergen, whose statue still graces the Minoritenplatz in Vienna.

10. Walter, op. cit., p. 46–50; Emerson, op. cit., pp. 12–13.

11. Ibid.

12. Ernst Wangermann, *From Joseph II to the Jacobin Trials: Government Policy and Public Opinion in the Habsburg Dominions in the Period of the French Revolution* (London, 1959), pp. 92–3.

13. Ibid.

14. Ibid., op. cit., pp. 128–32; Emerson, op. cit., p. 23.

15. Wangermann,, op. cit., p. 182; Emerson, op. cit., pp. 25–6.

16. Pergen to Francis II, 21 March 1802, quoted in August Fournier, *Die Geheimpolizei auf dem Wienerkongress, Eine Auswahl Ihren Papieren* (Vienna and Leipzig, 1913), pp. 6–7. Cf. Emerson, op. cit., p. 29.

17. Freiherr Kübeck von Kübau, *Tagebücher*, 2 vols (Vienna, 1909), vol. 1, p. 622.

18. Donald E. Emerson, *Metternich and the Political Police: Security and Subversion in the Hapsburg Monarchy (1815–1830)*, p. 37.

19. William L. Langer, 'The pattern of urban revolution in 1848', in E. M. Ancomb and M. L. Brown (eds), *French Society and Culture since the Old Regime* (New York, 1966), pp. 90–108.

20. Count Hartig, 'Genesis or Details of the Late Austrian Revolution by an Officer of State' translated as vol. 4 or *Continuation* of Archdeacon Coxe's *History of the House of Austria* (London, 1853), p. 39.

21. R. John Rath, *The Viennese Revolution of 1848* (Austin, 1957), p. 11.

22. Marx, *Die österreichische Zensur*, p. 8.

23. Ibid., p. 25.

24. Quoted in Emerson, op. cit., p. 38.

25. Karl Mendelssohn-Bartholdy (ed.), *Briefe von Gentz an Pilat, Ein Beitrag zur Geschichte Deutschland im XIX Jahrhundert* (Leipzig, 1868), p. 422. Cf. Emerson, op. cit., p. 36.

26. Emerson, op. cit., p. 48.

27. Ibid., op. cit., p. 47.

28. Ibid., op. cit., p. 48.

29. Ibid.

30. Quoted in Alan Sked, 'Austria and Germany: the Growth of an Inferiority Complex?' in F. Parkinson (ed.) *Conquering the Past, Austrian Nazism Yesterday and Today* (Detroit, 1989), pp. 11–33, p. 24.

31. Emerson, op. cit., p. 49 and ft. 60, p. 49.

32. Ibid., pp. 94–5.

33. For further information, see the series *Quellen und Darstellungen zur Geschichte der Burschenschaft und des deutschen Einheitsbewegung*, particularly the article by Max Doblinger, *Der burschenschaftliche Gedanke auf Österreichs Hochschulen vor 1859* in vol. VIII (1925), pp. 31–150.

34. Gentz–Pilat correspondence, p. 285.
35. Emerson, op. cit., p. 116.
36. Ibid., op. cit., p. 109.
37. Prince Wittgenstein. Emerson, op. cit., pp. 118–19. Walter M. Simon, *The Failure of the Prussian Reform Movement* (Ithaca, 1955), p. 138 ft., refers to 'the obvious fact that Wittgenstein was in Metternich's service'.
38. Minister Campz, Emerson, op. cit., p. 128.
39. Emerson, op. cit., pp. 122–4, quote on p. 123.
40. Doblinger, op. cit., pp. 53–72. Cf. Emerson, op. cit., p. 121.
41. Emerson, op. cit., pp. 124–5.
42. Ibid., pp. 131–4.
43. Count F. A. Gualtario, *Gli Ultimi Rivolgimenti Italiani. Memorie Storiche con Documenti Inediti*, 4 vols (Florence, 1852), vol. 2, pp. 286–7.
44. Emerson, op. cit., pp. 68–70, and pp. 92–3.
45. Ibid., pp. 52–5.
46. Ibid., p. 54.
47. Ibid.,. p. 61.
48. Ibid., p. 77.
49. Ibid., p. 79.
50. Ibid.
51. Ibid., p. 77.
52. Ibid., p. 75.
53. Ibid., p. 78.
54. Ibid., p. 76.
55. Ibid., p. 92.
56. Ibid., p. 96.
57. Reproduced in Fenner von Fenneberg, *Oesterreich und seine Armee* (Leipzig, 1847), pp. 131–2.
58. Emerson, op. cit., p. 130.
59. Hsi-Huey Liang, *The Rise of Modern Police and the European State System from Metternich to the Second World War* (New York, 1992), p. 20.
60. Ibid.
61. Ibid.
62. Ibid.
63. Liang, op. cit., p. 21. (Both assessments were made during the Commission's third sitting on 15 November 1819.)
64. Ibid., pp. 21–3.
65. Ibid., p. 23.
66. Ibid.
67. Charles Sealsfield (Karl Postl), *Österreich Wie Es Ist* (Vienna, 1919), p. 190. (The original in English, *Austria As It Is*, was published in English in London in 1828.)
68. William H. Stiles, *Austria in 1848–49, Being a History of the Late Political Movements in Vienna, Milan, Venice and Prague; with Details of the Campaigns of*

Lombardy and Novara; a Full Account of the Revolution in Hungary; and Historical Sketches of the Austrian Government and the Provinces of the Empire, 2 vols (New York, 1852), vol. 1, pp. 86–8. Stiles's work is rather curious. In places he plagiarises directly from Sealsfield (and presumably others); elsewhere he quotes his sources; while in places he has something highly original to say.

69. (London and Canberra, 1983), pp. 69–70.
70. 2 vols (London, 1840), vol. 2, pp. 255–63, p. 253.
71. Marx, *Die österreichische Zensur*, p. 8.
72. Bibl, op. cit., p. 279.
73. Stiles, op. cit., p. 95.
74. Marx, *Die österreichische Zensur*, p. 10.
75. Ibid., p. 67.
76. Emerson, op. cit., p. 150.
77. These became known to the Austrian public in 1847 – thus heightening criticism of the Metternich system – through publication in *Die Grenzboten* (1 Quartal, 1847, pp. 376–81), and through Dr A. Wiesner's book of the same year, *Denkwürdigkeiten der österreichischen Zensur vom Zeitalter der Reformazion bis auf die Gegenwart* (Stuttgart, 1847), pp. 211–19, criticisms, pp. 220–40. For the modern reader, the most accessible source is the appendix in Marx, *Die osterreichische Zensur etc.*, pp. 73–6.
78. Legge, op. cit., p. 175. His examples are culled from Wiesner.
79. Marx, *Die österreichische Zensur*, p. 14.
80. Heinrich, Ritter von Srbik, *Metternich, Der Staatsmann und der Mensch*, 2 vols (Munich, 1925), vol. 1, p. 513.
81. Sealsfield, op. cit., p. 197.
82. Emerson, op. cit., p. 130.
83. Hager to Francis II, 14 March 1810, quoted in Emerson, op. cit., p. 29.
84. Marx, *Die österreichische Zensur*, pp. 40–41.
85. *Die Grenzboten*, Heft 47, 1846, p. 338f.
86. Marx, *Die österreichische Zensur*, pp. 48–49.
87. Bachleitner, op. cit., p. 101.
88. Ibid.
89. Bachleitner, op. cit., p. 103.
90. Ibid.
91. Marx, *Die österreichische Zensur*, p. 46.
92. Ibid., p. 45.
93. Legge, op. cit., p. 176, quoting from Joseph Alexander Freiherr von Helfert, *Die Wiener Journalistik im Jahr 1848* (Vienna, 1887).
94. Stiles, op. cit., vol. 1, p. 85.
95. Koch, op. cit., p. 186.
96. Ibid., p. 206.
97. Marx, *Die österreichische Zensur etc.*, p. 6 and p. 8.
98. The description of official censorship procedure in this book unless otherwise stated is taken from Marx, *Die österreichische Zensur etc.*

99.   E. V. Zenker, *Geschichte der Wiener Journalistik während des Jahres 1848* (Vienna and Leipzig, 1893), p. 9.
100. Zenker, op. cit., p. 10.
101. For Austrian censorship in Lombardy-Venetia see the unpublished university of Vienna dissertation of 1955 by F. Leonardelli, *Der Kampf gegen die presse-politischen Maßnahmen der österreichischen Regierung in Lombardo-Venetien, 1815–1848.*
102. Emerson, op. cit., pp. 144–5.
103. Ibid., p. 167, ft. 91.
104. Ibid., p. 196.
105. L. Salomon, *Geschichte des deutschen Zeitungswesens*. 3 vols (Oldenburg and Leipzig, 1906), vol. 3, pp. 467ff.
106. Marx, *Die österreichische Zensur*, p. 56, quotes a 'J. G. Kohl'. See also John R. Rath, *The Viennese Revolution of 1848* (Austin, TX, 1957), p. 31, n. 53.
107. Emerson, op. cit., p. 145.
108. Ibid.
109. Emerson, op. cit., p. 138.
111. Emerson, op. cit., p. 141.
112. For these examples, see Emerson, op. cit., pp. 151–2.
112. For Grillparzer, see Julius Marx, *Die österreichische Zensur etc.*, pp. 28–9. (Francis also intervened in other cases.)
113. For this episode see Bibl, op. cit., p. 322.
114. Emerson, op. cit., p. 159.
115. For the following discussion on contemporary historians, see Emerson, op. cit., pp. 158–65. During the Hormayr controversy, Sealsfield wrote of him in 1823 as: (op. cit., p. 198):

> a nobleman of significant talent who most dutifully researched among the old castles and dusty parchments of the Austrian nobility. He fell into disgrace, because he composed one of the most harmless works, which, however, did not quite agree with the government's views. All his efforts during the Tyrolese uprisings could not soften the imperial mistrust. He bore the mark of a freethinker, the worst crime in Austria, although he has published a number of historical works and an Austrian Plutarch, wherein he proves that all Austrian rulers, even Albrecht I and Ferdinand II are examples of heroism and virtue. Who would dare under such and similar circumstances to draw upon himself the displeasure of a monarch, who believes and maintains that philosophy, poetry and history-writing are dangerous things that only turn the heads of young people and fill them with harmful nonsense.

Part of the problem according to Koch in 1847 (op. cit., p. 214) lay in 'the remarkable fact that the nobility of today does not know its own history and despite all pride in its ancestors does not research the deeds and opinions of its forefathers'.

116. For Austrian political poetry, see Antal Mádl, *Politische Dichtung in Österreich, 1830–1848* (Budapest, 1969).
117. For a list of 1,250 titles of English and French novels prohibited between 1815 and 1848, see Norbert Bachleitner, *Quellen zur Rezeption des englischen und französischen Romans in Deutschland und Österreich im 19 Jahrhundert* (Tübingen, 1990), pp. 60–93.
118. Marx, *Die österreichische Zensur*, p. 64.
119. For what follows on Beethoven, see John J. Haag, 'Beethoven, the Revolution in Music and the French Revolution: Music and Politics in Austria, 1790–1815', in Kinley Brauer and William E. Wright (eds), *Austria in the Age of the French Revolution* (Minneapolis, 1990), pp. 107–23. Cf. Frieder Reininghaus, *Schubert und das Wirthaus: Musik unter Metternich* (Berlin, 1979).
120. Haag, op. cit., p. 122. Ironically, Beethoven's greatest financial and popular success was constituted by his *Wellington's Victory or the Battle of Vittoria, Op. 91* (Haag, pp. 120–1). Haag also makes the point (p. 112):

> Unlike Haydn and Mozart, Beethoven in no way played the servant's role; he considered himself socially to be his noble patrons' equal and spiritually, by virtue of his gift of musical genius, to be their superior. Both Haydn and Mozart had achieved fame and some degree of financial success (although Mozart mismanaged his income), but both men were in truth little more than well-treated servants. Beethoven revolutionized this relationship, accelerating the social emancipation of European musicians.

This may seem rather hard on Mozart who wrote to his father in 1791: 'It is the heart [alone] that confers the patent of nobility on man – although I am no count, I surely have more honour within me than many a count.' See Doris P. Tishkoff, 'The Call to Revolution in the Boudoir: A New Look at Mozart's Susanna in The Marriage of Figaro' in Brauer and Wright (eds), op. cit., pp. 91–106, p. 106. Mozart, however, was no revolutionary. His *Clemenza di Tito*, for example, which played at Prague's National Theatre at the height of the French Revolution, celebrated the enlightened monarchy of Leopold II: 'If in the finale to Act I Mozart evoked the horror and the tragedy of revolution, in the finale to Act II he evoked, with equal power, the grandeur, stability and strength of enlightened depotism.' See John A. Rice, 'Political Theater in the Age of Revolution: Mozart's La Clemenza di Tito', in Brauer and Wright (eds), op. cit. pp. 125–49, p. 146.
121. Viktor Bibl, *Metternich. Der Dämon Österreichs* (Leipzig and Vienna, 1936), p. 318.
122. See footnote lxxiv. However, this is the whole tenor of Emerson's book.
123. For a discussion of Francis's attitude towards the rule of law, see Alan Sked, *The Decline and Fall of the Habsburg Empire, 1815–1918*, 2nd enlarged edition (Harlow and New York, 2001), pp. 288–94.

124. For Francis and the censorship, see Marx, *Die österreichische Zensur*, pp. 25–30. For this quote see p. 30.

125. Quoted by Srbik, op. cit., vol. I, p. 348 from H. Welschinger, *La Censure sous le Premier Empire* (Paris, 1882), p. 29.

126. Zenker, op. cit., p. 3.

127. For Metternich and the censorship, see Marx, *Die österreichische Zensur*, pp. 30–6. For this quote see p. 32.

128. For Sedlnitzky and the censorship, see Marx, *Die österreichische Zensur* , pp. 36–43. Emerson, op. cit., pp. 34–5 gives a good account of his previous career.

129. Marx, *Die österreichische Zensur*, p. 43.

130. For Kolowrat and the censorship see Marx, *Die österreichische Zensur*, pp. 49–54. Marx's conclusion, p. 53, is: 'If one surveys Kolowrat's activity, one must say that he contributed greatly to undermining the Vormärz system of government and did so purely out of a yearning for power although vanity and hatred also contributed much.'

131. For example, Eduard Bauernfeld, *Errinerungen aus Alt-Wien*, edited by Josef Bindtner (Vienna, 1923); Ludwig August Frankl, *Errinerungen*, edited by Stefan Hoch (Prague, 1910); for Franz Grillparzer, see *Grillparzer's sämtliche Werke*, edited with an introduction by August Sauer, 20 vols, Stuttgart, n.d., especially vol. 20, pp. 185–202 (*Errinerungen aus dem Jahre 1848*) and vol. 14, pp. 51–188 (*Historische und politische Studien*); C. L. Costenoble, *Aus dem Burgtheater, 1818–1837*, 2 vols (Vienna, 1889); Josef Freiherr von Hammer-Purgstall, *Errinerungen aus meinem Leben, 1774–1852, Fontes rerum austriacarum, Diplomataria et Acta* (Vienna and Leipzig, 1940).

132. Bibl, *Metternich*, p. 318.

133. H. Börstein, *Fünfundsiebzig Jahre in den alten und neuen Welt, Memoiren eines Unbedeutenden*, 2 vols (Leipzig, 1884), vol. 1, p. 142. Cf. Emerson, op. cit., pp. 174–5.

134. Emerson, op. cit., p. 175.

135. Quoted in Franz, op. cit., p. 27.

136. Translation in Legge, op. cit., p. 264.

137. Quoted by Legge, op. cit., p. 26.

138. Translation by Alan Sked.

139. Translation in Legge, op. cit., p. 134.

140. Quoted in Rath, op. cit., p. 10.

141. Rath, op. cit., p. 11.

142. Sealsfield, op. cit., p.p. 201–2.

143. Sealsfield, op. cit., p. 197.

144. Ibid.

145. Koch, op. cit., pp. 212–16, p. 213.

146. Sealsfield, op. cit., p. 151.

147. Marx, *Die österreichische Zensur*, p. 59.

148. Stiles, op. cit., vol. 1., p. 83.

149. Quoted in Franz, op. cit., p. 27.

150. Emerson, op. cit., pp. 146–8.

151. Ibid., pp. 168–9.

152. Ibid., p. 149: 'Since newspapers and journals are mere luxury articles, in my opinion a doubling of the previous stamp tax . . . is neither an unjust nor oppressive measure.'

153. Marx, *Die österreichische Zensur*, pp. 50–2.

154. Ibid., p. 39.

155. For the above information on Gerold and the other bookdealer, see Bachleitner, op. cit., pp. 104–5.

156. Bauernfeld, op. cit., p. 221.

157. Quoted in Rath, op. cit., pp. 10–11.

158. Rath, op. cit., pp. 45–6.

159. Hartig, op. cit., pp. 38–9.

160. Turnbull, op. cit., vol. 2, pp. 255–61.

161. Marx, *Die österreichische Zensur*, p. 56.

162. Ibid., p. 66.

163. Ibid., p. 27. Francis would have liked to ban all novels, but the book trade dissuaded him from taking such a step.

164. The idea that individual censors were laws to themselves, an idea that regularly appears in the contemporary and secondary literature, is wrong. Marx, *Die österreichische Zensur*, p. 49, writes: 'The activities of the censors were strictly supervised – we know of many rebukes as well as of sackings – as well as restricted by the criticisms of the public.'

165. Unless otherwise stated, the history of the secret postal service described here follows Harald Hubatschke, 'Die amtliche Organisation der geheimen Briefüberwachung und des diplomatischen Chiffrendienstes in Österreich. (Von den Anfängen bis etwa 1870)', *Mitteilungen des Instituts für Österreichische Geschichtsforschung*, vol. LXXXIII (1975), pp. 352–413. Hubatschke successfully submitted a six-volume dissertation on the subject to the University of Vienna in 1975. His fifth volume covering the Metternich period is over a thousand pages in length.

166. Josef Karl Mayr, *Inventare Österreichischer Staatlicher Archive, V, Inventare des Wiener Haus-Hof Und Staatsarchivs 2*, 'Geschichte der Österreichischen Staatskanzlei im Zeitalter des Fürsten Metternich' (Vienna, 1935) and 3, 'Metternichs geheimer Briefdienst Postlogen und Postkurse' (Vienna, 1935).

167. Hubatschke, op. cit., p. 371.

168. Ibid., p. 372.

169. Mayr, *Metternichs Geheimer Briefdienst*, p. 25.

170. Fournier, op. cit., p. 11, ft. 2.

171. Ibid., p. 227f.

172. Mayr, *Metternichs Geheimer Briefdienst*, p. 21.

173. Stiles, op. cit., vol. 1, p. 92.

174. Hubatschke, op. cit., p. 374.
175. Emerson, op. cit., p. 46.
176. Hubatschke, op. cit., p. 374.
177. Stiles, op. cit., vol. 1, p. 91.
178. Hubatschke, op. cit., p. 378.
179. Ibid., p. 385.
180. Ibid., p. 388.
181. Ibid., pp. 382–3.
182. Ibid., p. 386.
183. Stiles, op. cit., vol. 1, p. 90. He adds: 'many of their principal adepts lost their minds'.
184. Hubatschke, op. cit., p. 384.
185. Mayr, *Metternichs Geheimer Briefdienst*, pp. 20–1.
186. Ibid., p. 15.
187. Peter J. Katzenstein, *Disjointed Partners, Austria and Germany since 1815* (Berkeley, 1976), pp. 61–2.
188. He quotes Mayr in footnote 46, p. 61, although Mayr gives no indication whatsoever of the total number of letters distributed through the Austrian post. Later on, however, in a discussion of the Austrian post, he refers (p. 63, footnote 51) to the relevant tables of the Austrian *Statistische Zentralkomission* for the years 1831 and 1845–1846.
189. Mayr, *Metternichs Geheimer Briefdienst*, p. 4.
190. For these quotes and on Tuscany in general, see ibid., pp. 16–18.
191. For the significance of the surveillance of diplomatic correspondence, on the other hand, see the chapter on Metternich's diplomacy.
192. Emerson, op. cit., p. 46.
193. 'From Naples on 7 May 1819, travelling with the Emperor about a year before the revolution there, Metternich assured Gentz that Italy was completely quiet and that no movement of any sort was likely without some great political event in Europe. Certainly the recent assassination of Kotzebue, soon to be used for new repressive measures in Germany, was no such event. Metternich believed that the Neapolitans in particular were largely satisfied with their government and with Austria. And he urged Sedlnitzky to have the Habsburg local police conduct their careful surveillance with moderation and wisdom.' Emerson, op. cit., p. 84.
194. For the text, see Alessandro Luzio, *Il Processo Pellico-Maroncelli, Secondo Gli Atti Ufficiali Segreti* (Milan, 1903), pp. 554–6.
195. He was born in 1795, imprisoned with Pellico in the Spielberg, released in 1830, and died in 1846. After his arrest on 6 October 1820, he made up the incredible defence that he, Pellico and others were in contact with the Piedmontese liberals in order to effect the fusion of Piedmont and Lombardy under *Austrian* rule. Thanks to his statements and those of others, Pellico eventually confessed to having participated in a Carbonari conspiracy.

196. For *Il Conciliatore*, see Kent Roberts Greenfield, *Economics and Liberalism in the Risorgimento: A Study of Nationalism in Lombardy*, revised edition (Baltimore, 1965), pp. 152–6.

197. Luzio, op. cit. See also his *Antonio Salvotti e I Processi del Ventuno (Biblioteca Storica del Risorgimento Italiano, Serie III, Nos. 1–2* (Rome, 1901). Salvotti was the Austrian prosecutor.

198. A. D'Ancona, *Federico Confalonieri* (Milan, 1897). For a short but good account of his progressive activities in Lombardy before his arrest and trial, see Greenfield, op. cit., pp. 199–203.

199. Francis told him: 'It is essential that the Lombards should forget that they are Italians. Obedience to my wishes will be the link which will bind the Italian provinces to the rest of the empire.' See Carlo Tivaroni, *L'Italia durante il dominio austriaco*, 3 vols (Turin and Rome, 1892–4), vol. 1, p. 326.

200. Greenfield, op. cit., pp. 199–203.

201. G. Gallavresi, *Il Carteggio del Conte Federico Confalonieri*, 2 vols (Milan, 1911–1913), vol. I, p. 294. Further correspondence can be found in *Memorie e lettere di Federico Confalonieri pubblicate per cura di Gabrio Casati*, 2 vols (Milan, 1889).

202. For Confalonieri's trial, see A. Luzio, *Antonio Salotti*, and Alessandro Luzio, *Nuovi documenti sul processo Confalonieri (Biblioteca Storica del Risorgimento, serie V, no. 5.)*

203. The title of Charles Albert, King of Sardinia Piedmont, 1831–1849, who had hesitated about joining the 1821 rebellion, before finally condemning the rebels who had foolishly placed their hopes in him. However, in a circular to all his ambassadors in Europe, Metternich wrote: 'There is no material proof against the Prince of Carignano positive enough to make it possible to judge and condemn him legally.' See Tivaroni, op. cit., vol. 2, p. 103. The Italians were to call Charles Albert *'Il Re Tentenna'* or 'The Waverer King'.

204. Mary Clive Bayley, *The Making of Modern Italy* (London, New York, Toronto and Melbourne, 1919), p. 18.

205. For a useful modern paperback edition, see Silvio Pellico, *Le Mie Progioni con le Addizioni di Piero Maroncelli*, Biblioteca Universale, Rizzole, Milan, originally published in 1953 with an introduction by Silvia Spellanzon.

206. *Foreign Quarterly Review*, vol. XI, 1833, pp. 473–502, pp. 474–5.

207. *Memoirs of a Prisoner of State in the Fortress of Spielberg; by Alexander Andryane, Fellow-Captive of Count Confalonieri; with an Appendix by Maroncelli, The Companion of Silvio Pellico. Translated by Fortunato Prandi.* 2 vols (London, 1840), Preface by Prandi, vol. I, pp. iii–ix, p. iii.

208. Ibid., preface by Prandi, pp. iv–v.

209. Ibid., preface by Prandi, p. vii.

210. Ibid., vol. 2, pp. 64–6.

211. Ibid., vol. 1, p. 97.

212. Ibid., vol. 1, pp. 103–4.
213. Ibid., pp. 104–5.
214. Ibid., vol. 2, p. 55.
215. Ibid., vol. 2, p. 55.
216. Stiles, op. cit., vol. 1, p. 62, footnote.
217. Vienna, *Kriegsarchiv*, Regimental Command to General Command, 5 June 1848, KA.MK (1848) No. 2306.
218. All the information on the Italian prisoners in Szegedin comes from J. G. Kohl, *Austria, Vienna, Prague, Hungary, Bohemia, and the Danube; Galicia, Styria, Moravia, Bukovina and the Military Frontier* (London, 1844), pp. 336–9.
219. Cf. the introduction by Silvia Spellanzon (p. 10) to the edition of Pellico's *Le Mie Prigioni*, cited in note 205 above.
220. Kohl, op. cit., p. 338.
221. Ibid.

Notes to Chapter 6: Did Metternich's Austria Oppress the People and Cause the Revolutions of 1848?

1. H. A. L. Fisher, *A History of Europe*, vol. II, *From the Early 18th Century to 1935* (London and Glasgow, 1970), p. 1007.
2. Quoted in Oscar Jászi, *The Dissolution of the Habsburg Monarchy* (Chicago and London, 1966), p. 83.
3. Ibid., p. 82.
4. William H. Stiles, *Austria in 1848–49*, 2 vols (New York, 1852), vol. I, p. 94.
5. R. J. W. Evans, 'The Hapsburgs and the Hungarian Problem, 1790–1848', in *Transactions of the Royal Historical Society*, Fifth Series, vol. 39 (London, 1989), pp. 41–62, pp. 59–60.
6. Alan Sked, *The Survival of the Habsburg Empire: Radetzky, the Imperial Army and the Class War, 1848* (London and New York, 1979), p. 49.
7. For the lack of peasant unrest in Hungary and the generally good relations between peasants and lords, see the forthcoming paper by Robert Gray of University College, London to be published in the proceedings of the UCL School of East European and Slavonic Studies' conference on *Resistance, Rebellion and Revolution in Central Europe: Commemorating 1956*, held on 21–22 September 2006, and entitled '*Revolutionary Forces in a "Traditional Society": the Place of the Peasantry in 1848*'.
8. In the archives of the Lieutenancy Council. Information received with thanks from Orsolya Szakály of the Institute of History, Budapest.
9. W. Stiles, *Austria in 1848–49*, vol. I, p. 47.
10. M. Capefigue, *The Diplomatists of Europe* (London, 1845), p. 1.
11. Ibid., pp. 54–5.
12. Ibid., pp. 56–7.
13. John McGregor, *Commercial Statistics*, 5 vols (London, 1843–50), vol. I, p. 15.

14. The following quotes are taken from Alan Sked, 'Franz Joseph and the Creation of the Ringstrasse' in *The Court Historian*, vol. 11, no. 1 (July 2006), *Courts and Capitals, 1815–1914*, pp. 29–41, p. 29.
15. Francis to Judge Antonio Salvotti. See Alesandrio Luzio, *Antonio Salvotti e i processi del ventuno* (Rome, 1901), p. 129.
16. For this interpretation of Hungary in 1848, see Alan Sked, 'Mirror Images: Kossuth and Jelačić in 1848–49' in L. Péter, M. Rady and P. Sherwood (eds), *Lajos Kossuth Sent Word . . . Papers Delivered on the Bicentenary of Kossuth's Birth* (London, 2003), pp. 135–82, especially pp. 166–71.
17. Brigitte Hamann, 'Die Habsburger und die deutsche Frage im 19. Jahrhundert' in H. Lutz and H. Rumpler (eds), *Österreich und die deutsche Frage im 19. und 20. Jahrhundert. Probleme der politisch-staatlichen und soziokulturellen Differenzierung im deutschen Mitteleuropa* (Munich, 1982), pp. 212–30, p. 222.
18. Lewis Namier, *Vanished Supremacies* (Harmondsworth, 1962), pp. 139–40.
19. For all these quotes, see E. Dard, *Napoleon and Talleyrand* (London, 1937), pp. 145–6.
20. Berthold Sutter, 'Die politische und rechtliche Stellung der Deutschen in Österreich, 1848 bis 1918' in A. Wandruschka and P. Urbanitsch (eds), *Die Habsburgermonarchie, 1848–1918*, vol. III, *Die Völker des Reiches* (Vienna, 1980), pp. 154–339, p. 164.
21. For enlightenment on this topic, see some of my other works, particularly, Alan Sked, *The Decline and Fall of the Habsburg Empire, 1815–1918* (London and New York, 2nd expanded edition, 2001); Alan Sked, 'Explaining the Habsburg Empire, 1830–1890', in Bruce Waller (ed.), *Themes in European History, 1830–1890*, pp. 123–58; and Alan Sked, 'Austria and Germany: The Growth of an Inferiority Complex?' in F. Parkinson (ed.), *Conquering the Past. Austrian Nazism Yesterday and Today* (Detroit, 1989), pp. 17–33.
22. O. Jászi, *The Dissolution*, p. 82.
23. (Berkeley, Los Angeles and London, 1977), pp. 42–9.
24. Richard Metternich (ed.), *Mémoires de Prince Metternich*, 8 vols (Paris, 1880–4), vol. V, pp. 517–36. By 1841, Metternich's fears had grown worse, since he thought that relative to Germany Austria's industrial position had deteriorated, although she still lacked a truly Austrian commercial policy. See ibid., vol. VI, pp. 561–9.
25. See Chapter 3, p. 87.
26. Thomas Francis Huertas, *Economic Growth and Economic Policy in a Multinational Setting: The Habsburg Monarchy, 1841–1865* (Chicago, 1977), pp. 30–5.
27. P. J. Katzenstein, *Disjointed Partners*, p. 49.
28. *Memoirs of Prince Metternich*, vol. 5, p. 368.
29. B. Sutter, 'Die politische and rechtliche Stellung', p. 158 and P. J. Katzenstein, *Disjointed Partners*, p. 52.

30.   P. J. Katzenstein, *Disjointed Partners*, p. 59.
31.   Adam Wandruschka, 'Grossdeutsche und Kleindeutsche Ideologie, 1840–1871', in Robert A. Kann and Friedrich Prinz (eds), *Deutschland und Österreich; ein bilaterales Geschichtsbuch* (Vienna and Munich, 1980), pp. 110–42, p. 113.
32.   B. Sutter, 'Die politische und rechtliche Stellung', p. 164.
33.   Heinrich Ritter von Srbik, *Metternich: Der Staatsman und der Mensch*, 3 vols (Munich, 1927–56), vol. I, p. 120.
34.   E. L. Woodward, *Three Studies in European Conservatism: Metternich, Guizot and the Catholic Church in the Nineteenth Century* (London and Edinburgh, 1963), p. 92.
35.   R. John Rath, 'The Habsburgs and the Great Depression in Lombardy-Venetia, 1814–18' in the *Journal of Modern History*, vol. 13, no. 3 (Sept. 1941), pp. 305–20.
36.   *Memoirs of Prince Metternich*, vol. III, p. 93.
37.   Ibid., pp. 279–80. My translation is slightly different.
38.   For the following data on the nobles of Lombardy-Venetia, see Berthold Waldstrum-Wartenberg, 'Österreichische Adelsrecht, 1804–1918', *Mitteilungen des Österreichischen Staatsarchivs*, vols 17–18 (1964–5), pp. 117–24 and 140–2.
39.   Vienna, *Haus-Hof und Staatsarchiv, Provinzen, Lombardei-Venezien* (HHSA, PLV) Karton 23, Ficquelmont to Metternich (Milan, 3 December 1847).
40.   The pamphlet was the anonymous *L'Autriche et ses Provinces Italiennes* (Paris, 1859).
41.   Franco Arese, 'La Lombardia e la politica d'Austriaca: un colloquio inedito del Metternich nel 1832', in *Archivo Storico Lombardo*, LXXVII (1950), pp. 5–57, p. 24.
42.   Joseph Alexander Freiherr von Helfert, 'Zur Geschichte des Lombardo-venezianischen Königreichs' in *Archiv für Österreichische Geschichte*, vol. 98 (1908), pp. 18–19.
43.   For the whole issue of *sudditi misti* and the army's view of them, see General K. von Schönhals (Radetzky's adjutant), *Erinnerungen eines österreichischen Veteranen aus dem italienischen Krieg der Jahre 1848 und 1849* (Stuttgart, 1853). See pp. 23–4 for quote.
44.   Joseph Alexander Freiherr von Helfert, 'Casati und Pillersdorf und die Anfänge der italienischen Einheitsbewegung', *Archiv für Österreichische Geschichte*, vol. 91 (1902), pp. 500–2.
45.   Vienna, HHSA, PLV, Karton 23, Metternich to Ficquelmont (Vienna, 8 January, 1848).
46.   Quoted in E. L. Woodward, *Three Studies*, p. 104, ft. 1.
47.   On the latest research regarding this cooperation, see David Laven, *Venice and Venetia under the Habsburgs, 1815–1835* (Oxford, 2002); Marco Meriggio, *Amministrazione e classi sociali nel Lombardo-Veneto (1815–1848)* (Bologna, 1983), and Eugenio Tonetti, *Governo autriaco e notabili sudditi: Congregazioni e municipi nel Veneto del Restaurazione (1815–1848)*.

48. For a detailed account of Metternich's position with regard to Lombardy-Venetia, see Alan Sked, 'Metternich and the Ficquelmont Mission of 1847–48: the Decision against Reform in Lombardy-Venetia' in *Central Europe*, vol. 2, no. 1 (May 2004), pp. 15–46.

49. F. Arese, 'La Lombardia', p. 10.

50. Carlo Casati, *Nuove Rivelazione su i fatti di Milano nel 1847–48*, 2 vols (Milan, 1885), vol. 1, p. 47.

51. Count F. A. Gualterio, *Gli uiltimi Rivolgimenti italiani: Memorie storiche con documenti inediti*, 4 vols (Florence, 1852), vol. II, p. 284.

52. Ibid., p. 314.

53. Vienna, HHSA, PLV, Karton 40, Von Philippsberg to Metternich (3 April, 1847).

54. Ibid.

55. Ibid., Karton 23, Ficquelmont to Metternich (Milan, 27 December, 1847).

56. Ibid., Karton 23, Ficquelmont to Metternich (Milan, 3 December 1847).

57. Ibid., Karton 23, Ficquelmont to Rainer (Milan, 15 December 1847).

58. For the tobacco riots, see A. Sked, *The Survival of the Habsburg Empire*, Chapter 6.

59. See A. Sked, 'Metternich and the the Ficquelmont Mission', pp. 38–40.

60. Vienna, HHSA, PLV, Karton 5, Metternich to Rainer (Vienna, 9 January, 1848).

61. Ibid., Karton 23, Metternich to Ficquelmont (Vienna, 23 January 1848).

62. Ibid., Karton 23, Metternich to Ficquelmont (Vienna, 17 February, 1848).

63. *Memoirs of Prince Metternich* (Fch version), vol. VII, pp. 242–5, Metternich to Lützow (10 October, 1847).

64. Vienna, HHSA, PLV, Karton 23, Metternich to Ficquelmont, Vienna (23 January, 1848).

65. Count Franz Hartig, *Genesis of the Revolution in Austria*, appended to Archdeacon William Coxe's *History of the House of Austria* (London, 1853), p. 68.

66. Gernot Seide, *Regierungspolitik und öffentliche Meinung im Kaisertum Österreich anläßlich der polnischen Novemberrevolution (1830–1831)* (Wiesbaden, 1971), p. 92.

67. For these cultural developments, see Helmut Rumpler, *Eine Chance für Mitteleuropa: Bürgerliche Emanzipation und Staatsverfall in der Habsburgermonarchie* (Vienna, 1997), pp. 155–9.

68. For the Smaglowski case, see Seide, op cit., pp. 17–18.

69. Ibid., p. 19, ft. 53.

70. Ibid., p. 19.

71. The text of Czartoryski's letter is given in ibid., Appendix 1, p. 159.

72. *Memoirs of Prince Metternich*, vol. 5, Princess Melanie's Diary. Also Prokesch-Osten, *Tagebücher*, p. 108.

73. G. Seide's *Regierungspolitik* details all of this.

74. Ibid., p. 114.

75. Ibid., p. 116 for Perczel; pp. 122–9 for Bors county and consequences.

76. Ibid., p. 126 for Kossuth; p. 137 for Neograd county.
77. Ibid., pp. 119–120.
78. The following section on Galicia is based on Hanns Schlitter, *Aus Österreichs Vormärz*, vol. I, *Galizien und Krakau* (Zurich, Leipzig and Vienna, 1920). Schlitter's four-volume work is the only one that uses the records of the Staatskonferenz and gives generous quotes from them.
79. Ibid., p. 11.
80. Ibid., ft. 39, p. 76.
81. For the revolution of 1846, see Arnon Gill, *Die Polnische Revolution, 1846: Zwischen nationalen Befreiungskampf des Landadels und antifeudaler Bauernerhebung* (Munich and Vienna, 1974). Gill, unfortunately does not use Austrian sources, but I hope to make up for this in a couple of articles I intend to publish soon.
82. For part of Benedek's account, see the relevant sections of Heinrich Friedjung (ed.), *Aus Benedeks Nachgelassenen Papiere* (Leipzig, 1901).
83. For example, the anonymous French work, *La Vérété sur les Événemens de la Galicie* (Paris, 1847).
84. For the debate in Vienna concerning appropriate responses in the aftermath of 1846, see Schlitter, *Aus Österreichs Vormärz*, pp. 38–71.
85. Olga V. Pavlenko, 'Rußland und die Donauslaven (1848 bis 1871)', in Andreas Moritsch (ed.), *Der Austroslavismus: Ein Verfrütes Konzept zur politischen Neugestaltung Mitteleuropas* (Vienna, Cologne and Weimar, 1996), pp. 156–77, p. 166.
86. Andreas Moritsch (ed.), *Der Austroslavismus*, p. 8.
87. Ibid., p. 14.
88. Count Lützow, *A History of Bohemian Literature* (London, 1907), p. 354.
89. Ibid., pp. 354–5.
90. For a good overview of the cultural revival, see Rumpler, *Eine Chance*, pp. 178–92.
91. The best accounts in English of their roles are to be found in Lützow's *A History of Bohemian Literature*, Chapter VII and R. W. Seton-Watson's *A History of the Czechs and Slovaks* (London, 1943), Chapters XI and XIV. Also indispensable is Peter Brock and H. Gordon Skilling (eds), *The Czech Renascence of the Nineteenth Century: Essays presented to Otakar Odložilík in Honour of his Seventieth Birthday* (Toronto, 1970). A. Moritsch (ed.), *Austroslavismus* should also be consulted.
92. On these views of Dobrowský, see Robert Auty, 'Changing Views on the Role of Dobrowsky in the Czech National Revival', in P. Brock and H. G. Skilling (eds), *The Czech Renascence*, pp. 14–15, p. 17.
93. For Kopitar, see Rumpler, *Eine Chance*, pp. 190–2.
94. R. W. Seton-Watson, *A History of the Czechs*, p. 172.
95. Count Lützow, *A History of Bohemian Literature*, p. 362.
96. H. Rumpler, *Eine Chance*, p. 180.
97. R. W. Seton-Watson, *A History of the Czechs*, p. 182.

98.   H. Rumpler, *Eine Chance*, p. 184.

99.   Peter Brock, 'Jan Ernst Smoller and the Czech and Slovak Awakeners. A Study in Slav Reciprocity' in P. Brock and H. G. Skilling (eds), *The Czech Renascence*, pp. 74–94, p. 81.

100. Ibid.

101. For the following discussion on Slovak developments, see Thomas G. Pešek, 'The Czechoslovak Question on the Eve of the 1848 Revolution', in P. Brock and H. G. Skilling (eds), *The Czech Renascence*, pp. 131–45 and R. W. Seton-Watson, *A History of the Czechs*, pp. 258–62. Also relevant is Alexander Maxwell, 'Why the Slovak Language has Three Dialects: A Case Study in Historical Perceptual Dialectology', *Austrian History Yearbook*, vol. XXXVII (2006), pp. 141–62.

102. R. W. Seton-Watson, *A History of the Czechs*, p. 260.

103. Ibid., pp. 260–1.

104. On Palacký see the introductory essay by Moritsch in A. Moritsch (ed.), *Der Austroslavismus*.

105. R. W. Seton-Watson, *A History of the Czechs*, pp. 156–7.

106. For the institutional and cultural history of the Museum and its offspring, the *Matice Česka*, see Stanley B. Kimball, 'The Matice Česka, 1831–1861: The First Thirty Years of a Literary Foundation', in P. Brock and H. G. Skilling (eds), *The Czech Renascence*, pp. 53–73.

107. Ibid., p. 54.

108. Josef P. Zacek, 'Metternichs Censors: The case of Palacký', in P. Brock and H. G. Skilling (eds), *The Czech Renascence*, pp. 95–112, pp. 98–9.

109. S. B. Kimball, *The Matice Česka*, p. 61.

110. Miroslaw Hroch, 'The Social Composition of the Czech Patriots in Bohemia, 1827–1848', in P. Brock and H. G. Skilling (eds), *The Czech Renascence*, pp. 32–52.

111. S. B. Kimball, *The Matice Česka*, p. 65.

112. Frances G. Loewenheim, 'German Liberalism and the Czech Renascence: Ignaz Kuranda, *Die Grenzboten* and Developments in Bohemia, 1845–49', in P. Brock and G. H. Skilling (eds), *The Czech Renascence*, pp. 147–75, p. 155.

113. Ibid., ft. 24.

114. S. H. Kimball, *The Matice Česka*, p. 65. This should be compared with his remark on p. 60 that those active in the foundation 'realised the necessity in the police state in which they lived of disguising their national and political efforts as literary activities'. Kimbell, however, could not find any archival evidence of any interest on the part of Vienna in the Matice.

115. J. P. Zacek, 'Metternich's Censors', p. 97.

116. Ibid., pp. 111–12.

117. Ibid., p. 107.

118. Ibid., p. 108.

119. Ibid., p. 101, ft. 22. This footnote is the best part of the article.

120. See the cover of A. Moritsch (ed.), *Der Austroslavismus*.
121. Ibid., p. 21.
122. Barbara Kohák Kimmel, 'Karel Havlíček and the Czech Press before 1848', in P. Brock and G. H. Skilling (eds), *The Czech Renascence*, pp. 113–30.
123. Ibid., p. 70.
124. R. W. Seton-Watson, *A History of the Czechs*, p. 184.
125. Ibid.
126. A. Moritsch (ed.), *Der Austroslavismus*, p. 15.
127. Absolutely fundamental for this aspect of the story is Hanns Schlitter, *Aus Österreichs Vormärz*, 4 vols (Zurich, Leipzig and Vienna, 1920), vol. 2, *Böhmen*.
128. Ibid., p. 34.
129. Ibid. Indeed, Schlitter blames Kolowrat for the problems of the monarchy. The publisher's advert for his four volumes reads: 'Not Prince Metternich, whose advice was mainly overlooked, but Count Kolowrat was responsible for the sins of omission of the Vienna government during the Vormärz.'
130. Ibid., p. 55.
131. Ibid., p. 11.
132. Ibid., pp. 45–52.
133. Ibid., p. 69.
134. Ibid., p. 7. Chotek's sins were minor in the extreme, but some faults were found in the accounts of the local government and in any case he was a rival of Kolowrat's in Bohemia.
135. Ibid., p. 76.
136. Ibid., p. 80.
137. Ibid.
138. Alexius Fényes, *Ungarn im Vormärz* (Leipzig, 1851), p. 37, quoted by Elinor Murray Despalatović, *Ljudevit Gaj and the Illyrian Movement* (New York and London, 1975), p. 16. But according to László Kontler's, *A History of Hungary* (London, 2002), p. 242, the 'famous statistician Elek Fényes' calculated Hungary's Magyar population in 1842 at 4.8 million out of a total population of nearly 13 million (i.e. only 38 per cent).
139. Wayne S. Vucinich, 'Croatian Illyrism: Its Background and Genesis', in Stanley B. Winters and Joseph Held (eds), *Intellectual and Social Developments in the Habsburg Empire from Maria Theresa to World War I: Essays Dedicated to Robert A. Kann* (New York and London, 1975), pp. 55–113, p. 70.
140. Johann Gottfried Herder, *Sämmtliche Werke*, B. Suphan (ed.) (Berlin, 1909), vol. XIV, *Ideen zur Philosophie der Geschichte der Menschheit*. See pp. 227–80 for the Slavs, pp. 268–9 for the Magyars.
141. Ibid., vol. VII, *Briefe zur Beförderung der Humanität*, p. 58.
142. W. S. Vucinich, *Croatian Illyrism*, p. 66.
143. Gyula Viszota (ed.), *Gróf Széchenyi István Naplói*, 6 vols (Budapest, 1925–1939), vol. 3, p. 320 and vol. 4, p. 281 and p. 301.

144. Horst Hazelsteiner, *Ungarische Nationalkonzepte, die Slaven und der 'Austroslavismus'*, in A. Moritsch (ed.), *Der Austroslavismus*, pp. 86–101, p. 93, ft. 19.

145. George Barany, 'The Age of Royal Absolutism, 1790–1848,' in P. Sugar et al. (eds), *A History of Hungary* (London, 1990), pp. 174–208, p. 180.

146. For the above views, ibid., pp. 181–2.

147. For this cultural background, ibid., pp. 183–7.

148. Ibid., p. 188.

149. Ibid., p. 190.

150. On Széchenyi, see George Barany, *Stephen Széchenyi and the Awakening of Hungarian Nationalism, 1791–1841* (Princeton, 1968). Also Hazelsteiner, *Ungarische Nationalkonzepte*, pp. 93–5.

151. Details on peasants from C. A. Macartney, *Hungary* (London, 1934), pp. 227–8.

152. See ft. 150. Also L. Kontler, *A History of Hungary*, p. 232.

153. On Wesselényi, see Hazelsteiner, *Ungarische Nationalkonzepte*, pp. 89–91, Samu Kardos, *Báró Wesselényi Miklós élete és munkái* (Budapest, 1905), and Zsolt Tróchányi, *Wesselényi Miklós* (Budapest, 1965).

154. On Eötvös, see Hazelsteiner, *Ungarische Nationalkonzepte*, pp. 95–7. Curiously, Hazelsteiner believes that Eötvös was Hungary's 'most profound/informed *(fundierteste)* theorist' on the nationality question. On the man himself, see Johann Weber, *Eötvös und die ungarische Nationalitätenfrage* (Munich, 1966) and Paul Bödy, *Joseph Eötvös and the Modernization of Hungary, 1840–1870* (Philadelphia, 1972).

155. On Kossuth, see Istvan Deak, *The Lawful Revolution: Louis Kossuth and the Hungarians, 1848–1849* (New York, 1979), but in particular, L. Péter, M. Rady and P. Sherwood (eds), *Lajos Kossuth Sent Word . . . Papers delivered on the Occasion of the Bicentenary of Kossuth's Birth*, SSEES Occasional Papers, No. 56, School of Slavonic and East European Studies (London, 2003). Also Domokos Kosáry, *Kossuth Lajos a reformkorban* (Budapest, 1946).

156. H. Hazelsteiner, *Ungarische Nationalkonzepte*, pp. 98–9, p. 98, ft. 34.

157. It should be noted, however, that in 1842 he had persuaded the Pest county assembly to pass a resolution allowing Croatia to split off from Hungary entirely if it so wished. See Gy. Szabad, 'Hungary's recognition of Croatia's self-determination in 1848 and its immediate antecedents' in Béla Király (ed.), *East European Society and War in the Era of Revolutions, 1775–1856* (New York, 1984), pp. 599–609.

158. L. Kontler, *A History of Hungary*, pp. 245–7.

159. E. M. Despalatović, *Ljudevit Gaj*, p. 11.

160. W. S. Vucinich, *Croatian Illyrism*, p. 73.

161. For Gaj and Illyrianism, see the works already cited by Despalatović and Vucinich.

162. For an extremely good account of the newspapers between 1835 and 1843, see Arnold Suppan, *Der Illyrismus zwischen Wien und Ofen-Pest: Die*

illyrischen Zeitungen im Spannungsfeld der Zensurpolitik (1835 bis 1843), in A. Moritsch (ed.), *Der Austroslavismus*, pp. 102–24.

163. For a good overview, see Keith Hitchins, *The Rumanian National Movement in Transylvania, 1780–1849* (Harvard, 1969).

164. Ibid., pp. 170–1.

165. Ibid., pp. 172–3.

166. For a good account of Metternich's campaign against subversive Hungarian liberalism, see É. Andics, *Metternich und die Frage Ungarns* (Budapest, 1973). Cf. Metternich as quoted on p. 81: 'The Opposition today is a subversive one which exploits moderate constitutionalism to overthrow the government and the constitution. The Hungarian polity is a monarchical-aristocratic one. It cannot be accommodated to democratic institutions. Such institutions are in contradiction with the existing order.'

167. According to one authority, Kossuth's mistake was his more radical tone from 1843, when he convinced himself that the nobility alone could not regenerate Hungary and that the reformers had to appeal to a wider section of the population. See Gábor Pajkossy, 'Kossuth and the Emancipation of the Serfs' in Péter, Rady and Sherwood (eds), *Lajos Kossuth Sent Word*, pp. 71–80, p. 76.

168. See Hanns Schlitter, *Aus Österreichs Vormärz*, 4 vols (Zurich, Leipzig and Vienna, 1920), vol. IV, *Ungarn*.

169. See both Rudolph Sieghart, *Zolltrennung und Zolleinheit: Die geschichte der österreichisch-ungarischen Zwischenzoll-Linie* (Vienna, 1915) and Alan Sked, 'Living on One's Wits: J. A. Blackwell's vain attempts to become British Consul in Hungary', in L. Péter and M. Rady (eds), *British–Hungarian Relations since 1848* (London, 2004), pp. 13–31. Blackwell was Britain's representative in Hungary whose job was to further free trade there. His views on Kossuith's Protectionist Association are therefore rather interesting. Basically he saw it as a front to enable Kossuth to have well-paid agents in every part of the country to carry on his liberal agitation within the limits of the law. See pp. 20–1.

170. A secret committee composed of Apponyi's predecessor, Count Anton Mailáth, Hartig and Kübeck, was set up which worked out this plan. It was also to include a reform of the Palatine's Council and the Hungarian Chancellery in Vienna. Kübeck was willing to authorise an extra 300,000 gulden to further the cause. (He would authorise another 200,000 for the 1847 elections.) However, Mailáth proved unfit for the job of carrying out the reforms and the new Palatine in 1847, the Archduke Stefan Viktor, saw himself as an independent presence between the government and the Magyars. Hence the government was stymied. See H. Schlitter, *Ungarn*, pp. 22–8 and p. 77.

171. Gyula Miskolcsy (ed.), *A horvát kérdés története és irományai a rendi állam korában*, 2 vols (Budapest, 1927–8), vol. II, p. 22. Archduke Joseph to Archduke Ludwig, Buda, 1 December 1842.

172. A. Suppan, *Der Illyrismus*, p. 118, ft. 78.
173. All the documents subsequently quoted on this issue can be found in Gyula Miskolcsy (ed.), *A horvát kérdés története*, vol. II, pp. 21–31. There is a long and very useful historical essay as an introduction to vol. I.
174. H. Schlitter, *Ungarn*, p. 10.
175. The following discussion of the economy is taken from the survey in Alan Sked, *The Decline and Fall of the Habsburg Empire, 1815–1918*, 2nd and expanded edition (London and New York, 2001), pp. 68–82, and pp. 294–9 and H. Rumpler, *Eine Chance*, pp. 215–59.
176. For Heindl's work, see W. Heindl, *Gerhorsame Rebellen: Bürokratie und Beamte in Österreich 1780 bis 1848* (Vienna, 1991) and 'Bureaucracy, Officials, and the State in the Austrian Monarchy: Stages of Change since the Eighteenth Century', *Austrian History Yearbook*, XXXVII (2006), pp. 35–57.
177. For a discussion of Turnbull's views on the bureaucracy, see my own article commenting on Heindl's, namely, Alan Sked, 'Power and Professionalism', in the same edition of the *Austrian History Yearbook*, pp. 62–7. Turnbull, for example wrote: 'The ministers Metternich and Kolowrat are well aware of their existence [i.e. abuses] and abundantly anxious for their removal . . .' For an overview of the state of the Austrian bureaucracy in the period 1815–1914, see the whole of my article.
178. W. H. Stiles, *Austria*, vol. I, p. 78, second footnote.
179. W. Heindl, *Gehorsame Rebellen*, pp. 142–59.
180. On Upper Hungary, see G. Seide, *Regierungspolitik etc.*, pp. 133–4 and L. Tilkovszky, *Az 1831. évi parasztfelkelés* (Budapest, 1955). For 1846 in Galicia, see ft. 81.
181. Roman Rodolsky, *Die Bauernabgeordneten im konstituierende österreichischen Reichstag 1848–1849* (Vienna, 1976), pp. 1–2.
182. For the miserable conditions of officers and men, see Alan Sked, *The Survival of the Habsburg Empire: Radetzky, the Imperial Army and the Class War, 1848* (London and New York, 1979), Part One. For the state's inability to find the money to redeem *robot* payments, see Hanns Schlitter, *Aus Österreichs Vormärz*, 4 vols (Vienna, 1920), vol. IV: *Niederösterreich*, p. 20.
183. H. Rumpler, *Eine Chance*, p. 248.
184. Ibid.
185. H. Schlitter, *Ungarn*, p. 10.
186. H. Rumpler, *Eine Chance*, p. 254.
187. See A. Sked, *The Decline and Fall*, 2nd edn, pp. 288–94.
188. H. Schlitter, *Ungarn*, p. 83.
189. On Austria and the Catholic Church in the Metternich period, see A. Sked, *The Decline and Fall*, 2nd edn, pp. 282–8.
190. See W. C. Vucinich, *Croatian Illyrism*, pp. 92–3, for this episode.
191. Graf Leo von Thun und Hohenstein, *Die Stellung der Slovaken in Ungarn* (Prague, 1843). On Thun himself, see C. Thienen-Adlerflycht, *Graf Leo Thun im Vomärz* (Graz, 1967).

192.   On Upper Austria, see Hans Sturmberger, *Der Weg zum Verfassungsstaat: Die politische Entwicklung in Oberösterreich von 1792–1861* (Vienna, 1962).
193.   H. Schlitter, *Niederösterreich* and Viktor Bibl, *Die niederösterreichischen Stände im Vormärz: Ein Beitrag zur Vorgeschichte der Revolution des Jahres 1848* (Vienna, 1911).
194.   R. John Rath, *The Viennese Revolution of 1848* (Austin, 1957), p. 27: 'In all the opposition literature not once was the demand made for revolution.'
195.   Ibid., p. 35.
196.   H. Schlitter, *Niederösterreich*, pp. 29–30.
197.   See, for example, Vienna, Haus-Hof-und Staatsarchiv, Staatskanzleiakten, Provinzen, Lombardei-Venezien, Metternich to Radetzky, Vienna, 16 March 1846 (Karton 38) and Metternich to the Archduke Rainer (Vienna, 5 March 1846) (Karton 5).
198.   H. Schlitter, *Niederösterreich*, p. 49.
199.   Ibid., p. 118.
200.   Ibid.

Notes to Chapter 7: Conclusion

1.   Metternich to Count Lützow, 10 October, 1847, *Mémoires*, vol. 7, pp. 424–5.
2.   R. W. Seton-Watson, *A History*, pp. 180–1.
3.   To see how poorly defended Vienna was from mob rule in 1848 compared to Paris or London, where revolution, unlike in Vienna, was actually expected, see William L. Langer, 'The Pattern of Urban Revolution, 1848', in E. M. Ancomb and M. L. Brown (eds), *French Society and Culture since the Old Regime* (New York, 1966), pp. 90–108.

Annotated Bibliography

Scholars seeking detailed bibliographical aid on Metternich should consult both the third volume of Heinrich Ritter von Srbik's *Metternich: Der Staatsmann und der Mensch. Quellenveröffentlichungen und Literatur: Eine Auswahlübersicht von 1925–1952* (Munich, 1954) and Paul Schroeder's 'Metternich Studies since 1925' in the *Journal of Modern History*, vol. xxxiii (1962). Unfortunately, there have been rather few relevant studies in English since then and I fear I am rather critical of most. It goes without saying that the first two volumes of Srbik's *Metternich: Der Staatsmann und der Mensch*, 2 vols (Darmstadt, 1957), remain the best biography, although Viktor Bibl's *Metternich, Der Dämon Österreichs* (Vienna and Leipzig, 1934) should be consulted for an exceptionally critical viewpoint. Most English-language popular biographies simply follow Srbik. The latest are by Alan Palmer, *Metternich* (London, 1972) and Desmond Seward, *Metternich: The First European* (New York, 1991). A good starting point, however, is still Enno E. Kraehe, *The Metternich Controversy* (New York, 1971), while much of the flavour of Metternich can be gained from G. de Bertier de Sauvigny, *Metternich and his Times* (London, 1962). A good selection of documents illustrating these times can be found in Mack Walker (ed.), *Metternich's Europe, 1813–1848* (New York, 1968).

The indispensable basis for all work on Metternich is his memoirs. Unfortunately only the first five volumes were translated into English, namely Richard von Metternich (ed.), *Memoirs of Prince Metternich*, 5 vols (London and New York, 1880–2). These were translated by Mrs Alexander Napier. Most of the first volume was published recently as *Metternich: The Autobiography, 1773–1815* (Welwyn Garden City, 2004). The full eight volumes are Prince Richard Metternich (ed.), *Aus Metternichs nachgelassenen Papieren*, 8 vols (Vienna, 1880–4). A full French edition, *Mémoires de Prince Metternich*, 8 vols, edited by Prince Richard, was published in Paris at the same time.

For the diplomatic background, see Paul Schroeder's *The Transformation of European Politics, 1763–1848* (Oxford, 1994), despite its flawed thesis; Henry Kissinger's still excellent *A World Restored: Metternich, Castlereagh and the Problems of Peace, 1812–1822* (London, 1957); and Enno E. Kraehe's two volumes on *Metternich and the German Question*, vol. I: *The Contest with Napoleon, 1799–1814* (Princeton, 1963) and vol. II: *The Congress of Vienna, 1814–1815* (Princeton, 1983). Two little-known works that deserve much greater fame are E. Dard, *Napoleon and Talleyrand* (London, 1937) and M. Capefigue, *The Diplomatists of Europe* (London, 1845). Among the few monographs in English on Metternich's diplomacy after 1815 are Paul Schroeder, *Metternich's Diplomacy at its Zenith: Austria at the Congresses of Troppau, Laibach and Verona* (Austin, 1962), Alan J. Reineman's two volumes on *Metternich and the Papacy in the Age of Metternich*, vol. I: *Between Conflict and Cooperation, 1809–1830* (Washington, DC, 1979) and vol.

II: *Revolution and Reaction* (Washington, DC, 1989), and Robert D. Billinger Jr, *Metternich and the German Question: States Rights and Federal Duties, 1820–1834* (Cranbury, NJ, 1991). F. R. Bridge's *The Habsburg Monarchy among the Great Powers, 1815–1918* (Leamington Spa, 1990) is the only good account of the Habsburg Monarchy's foreign policy for the whole nineteenth century. Bridge also contributes to the clearest coverage of the period 1815–1848, namely Alan Sked (ed.), *Europe's Balance of Power, 1815–1848* (London, 1979). More detailed and foreign language studies can be found in the footnotes, but indispensable to any assessment of Metternich's foreign policy are Manfred Botzenhart's *Metternichs Pariser Botschafterzeit* (Münster, 1967) and Gernot Seide's *Regierungspolitik und öffentliche Meinung im Kaisertum Österreichs anläßlich der polnischen Novemberrevolution, 1830–1831* (Wiesbaden, 1971).

With regard to Austria's domestic policy during the Metternich era, the best coverage is to be found in the second and expanded edition of Alan Sked, *The Decline and Fall of the Habsburg Empire, 1815–1918* (London and New York, 2001), the last chapter of which takes a second look at the Metternich period. Other surveys include A. J. P. Taylor, *The Habsburg Monarchy, 1809–1918: A History of the Austrian Empire and Austria–Hungary* (London, 1948) and subsequent editions; C. A. Macartney, *The Habsburg Empire, 1790–1918* (London, 1968); and Robin Okey, *The Habsburg Monarchy, c. 1765–1918: from Enlightenment to Eclipse* (Basingstoke, 2000). For detailed studies of Metternich and domestic policy there are Arthur G. Haas, *Metternich, Reorganisation and Nationality, 1813–1818: A Story of Foresight and Frustration in the Rebuilding of the Austrian Empire* (Knoxville, 1964) and Egon Radvany, *Metternich's Projects for Reform in Austria* (The Hague, 1971). But see Alan Sked, 'Metternich and the Federalist Myth', in Alan Sked and Chris Cook (eds), *Crisis and Controversy: Essays in Honour of A. J. P. Taylor* (London, 1976). Also on domestic policy, there is Donald E. Emerson, *Metternich and the Political Police: Security and Subversion in the Hapsburg Monarchy, 1815–1830* (The Hague, 1968). For the economic background, see the relevant chapters in my *Decline and Fall*, and on the army see Part One of Alan Sked, *The Survival of the Habsburg Empire: Radetzky, the Imperial Army and the Class War, 1848* (London and New York, 1979) and, more generally, Gunther E. Rothenberg, *The Army of Francis Joseph* (West Lafayette, 1976). On the nationality question, key works include R. W. Seton-Watson, *A History of the Czechs and Slovaks* (London, 1943); P. Brock and H. G. Skilling (eds), *The Czech Renascence of the Nineteenth Century* (Toronto, 1970); Keith Hitchins, *The Rumanian National Movement in Transylvania, 1780–1849* (Harvard, 1969); Elinor Murray Despolatović, *Ljudevit Gaj and the Illyrian Movement* (New York and London, 1975); Wayne S. Vucunich, 'Croation Illyrism: Its Background and Genesis', in S. B. Winters and J. Held (eds), *Intellectual and Social Developments in the Habsburg Empire from Maria Theresa to World War I: Essays Dedicated to Robert A. Kann* (New York and London, 1975), pp. 55–113; David Laven, *Venice and Venetia under the Habsburgs, 1815–1835* (Oxford, 2002); Alan Sked, 'Metternich and the Ficquelmont Mission of 1847–48: the Decision Against Reform in

Lombardy-Venetia', *Central Europe*, vol. 2, no. 1 (May 2004) pp. 15–46; I. Deak, *The Lawful Revolution: Louis Kossuth and the Hungarians, 1848–1849* (New York, 1979); L. Peter, M. Rady and P. Sherwood (eds), *Lajos Kossuth Sent Word: Papers Delivered on the Occasion of the Bicentenary of Kossuth's Birth*, Occasional Papers No. 56, School of Slavonic and East European Studies (London, 2003); and R. J. W. Evans, 'The Hapsburgs and the Hungarian Problem, 1790–1848', in the *Transactions of the Royal Historical Society*, 5th series, vol. 39 (London, 1989), pp. 41–62. Two key works in German are E. Andics, *Metternich und die Frage Ungarns* (Budapest, 1973) and Andreas Moritsch (ed.), *Der Austroslavismus: Ein verfrütes Konzept zur politischen Neugestaltung Mitteleuropas* (Vienna, Cologne and Weimar, 1996). Absolutely fundamental to the study of Habsburg domestic policy after 1835 remain Hanns Schlitter's four volumes entitled *Aus Österreichs Vormärz* (Zurich, Leipzig and Vienna, 1920), which use the records of both the State Council and the Ministerial Conference. References to other books and articles can be found in the footnotes.

Index